CHOICES *for the* POOR

Lessons from national poverty strategies

Edited by Alejandro Grinspun

with Mercedes González de la Rocha ■ Jaroslaw Górniak

■ Alf Morten Jerve ■ Julian May ■ S.R. Osmani ■ Pierre Hassan Sanon ■

and Julia Harrington ■ Catherine Porter ■ Sanjay Reddy

The views expressed in this publication are those of the authors and do not necessarily represent those of the member countries of the UNDP Executive Board or of the institutions of the United Nations system that are mentioned herein. The designations and terminology employed and the presentation of material do not imply any expression of opinion whatsoever on the part of the United Nations concerning the legal status of any country, territory, city or area, or of its authorities, or of its frontiers or boundaries.

■   ■   ■

Copyright © 2001
by United Nations Development Programme
One UN Plaza, New York NY 10017, USA

ISBN Number: 92-1-126138-4
UN Sales Number: E.01.III.B.6

Book design: Kayley LeFaiver

Foreword

At the dawn of the 21st century almost a quarter of the population of the developing world — over one billion people — still live in extreme poverty, a number little changed from over a decade ago. Tackling this problem is now rightly a global priority, enshrined in the commitment by world leaders at the United Nations Millennium Summit to 'spare no effort to free our fellow men, women and children from the abject and dehumanising conditions of extreme poverty'.

But if we are to meet the global target of halving the proportion of people living in extreme poverty by 2015, we must first learn better the many lessons of past successes and failures. That is the aim of *Choices for the Poor*. It is a comprehensive external evaluation of the strengths and weaknesses of the Poverty Strategies Initiative that was launched in 1996 by the United Nations Development Programme, together with the Government of Norway and other bilateral donors. Designed to respond to the challenges outlined at the 1995 World Social Summit, it has since funded a wide range of programmes and activities to try to leverage pro-poor changes in national policy across the developing world.

Overall, the book testifies to the broad success of the Initiative to date, but it also bears witness to the technical and political complexity of developing comprehensive anti-poverty policies. The preparation, implementation and assessment of such strategies are frequently hampered by the lack of sufficient capacity. And while the book confirms that strategic external support can help this critical process, it cautions that it can also hurt when overly technocratic and when disengaged from local institutions.

Perhaps the most valuable lesson is that successful anti-poverty strategies must be based on a consensus building among key national actors and combined with proper coordination between donors and national partners. Strategies conceived outside political processes are simply not sustainable. Above all, there is a critical need for overall policy coherence, particularly for national macroeconomic frameworks to be fully aligned with poverty reduction targets.

We hope that these and other issues discussed in *Choices for the Poor* will prove useful to all our development partners in the global effort to achieve the targets set out in the UN Millennium Declaration.

Anne Kristin Sydnes
Minister of International Development
Royal Ministry of Foreign Affairs
Oslo, Norway

Mark Malloch Brown
Administrator
United Nations Development
Programme

Preface: Choices for the Poor

Not since the early 1970s, when concern with basic needs was a rallying point for development agencies, has the international development agenda coalesced around the issue of poverty reduction with such unanimity.

The story may be said to have begun with the resolutions taken during the 1995 World Summit for Social Development. In 1996, the United Nations Development Programme (UNDP), with financial support from the governments of Denmark, Finland, Netherlands and Norway, decided to launch a global initiative aimed at assisting countries in the development of national and local strategies for poverty reduction. The initiative was implemented through country projects in more than one hundred countries, under the label of the Poverty Strategies Initiative (PSI). Funding was open to all of the 134 countries with UNDP offices, although preference was given to sub-Saharan Africa and Asia, where the huge majority of the world's poor are concentrated.

Each of the country projects was intended to play a catalytic role in moving the poverty agenda forward. In some countries, poverty had not yet been defined. In many more, there were huge gaps in poverty data. In all countries, the challenge was to establish poverty firmly on the policy agenda and establish the basis of a global campaign to eradicate poverty. The PSI became UNDP's main vehicle for supporting the implementation of the commitments to poverty eradication made by governments at the 1995 World Summit for Social Development.

Since the inception of the PSI, two sets of developments have given yet more relevance, as well as urgency, to the challenge of developing national poverty reduction strategies.

In the first place, the international community has agreed to a set of international development targets leading to a halving of extreme poverty by 2015. Commitment to poverty targets has now been reaffirmed by the UN Millennium Summit of September 2000, the largest high-level development constituency ever.

Secondly, the World Bank and the IMF decided in 1999 to require countries to prepare a Poverty Reduction Strategy Paper (PRSP) as a condition for qualifying for concessional assistance and debt relief under the Heavily Indebted Poor Country Initiative (HIPC).

The work initiated by the PSI in many countries has become increasingly relevant as a result of these developments. Poverty targets are being explicitly built into longer-term national poverty strategies. And the preparation of PRSPs, which have a shorter (initially three-year) time-span, has built upon PSI work in many instances.

The growing relevance of the PSI work has given new importance to the programme evaluation that this report embodies. It is for this reason that UNDP has decided to publish the report in full. The external evaluation was commissioned in late 1999 and conducted during 2000. While geographically representative, the choice of 18 countries to be evaluated was not wholly random. It was important to concentrate on a sample of countries from which a range of lessons could be drawn. Some other countries where there had been successful interventions were excluded, and so were countries where the PSI had a limited impact. The result, however, has been positive for UNDP and its partners for two reasons. First, the evaluation has identified many valuable lessons from experience — as many don'ts as do's — that can help guide the nature and orientation of development cooperation in this critical area in the future. The emphasis of aid agencies has shifted noticeably toward providing policy advice and institutional support for the design of national policies and strategies for poverty reduction, as well as their implementation, monitoring and evaluation.

Secondly, the evaluation has helped to illuminate the special role that UNDP can play in supporting the development of poverty reduction strategies. This role falls naturally within its human development mandate, which UNDP defined as the 'widening of choices'. Poverty eradication is fundamentally about extending those choices to the poor. But doing so often requires delicate political decisions, as this book makes abundantly clear. Poverty eradication is a primary responsibility for governments, but entails consultation and cooperation with civil society at large, and the poor in particular. Through the PSI programme, UNDP has been able to capitalise on its special status as a close but objective partner of governments as well as civil society organisations, academics and entrepreneurs, maintaining a seat at the table from Laos to Lebanon and Lesotho, Uruguay to Uganda. Sometimes, UNDP sits almost alone there.

Because of the importance of the lessons of the evaluation, it was decided with the Government of Norway to hold a conference at the Christian Michelsen Institute at Bergen in March 2001 to discuss the role of development cooperation in poverty reduction. This book is the main documentation for that conference.

Stephen Browne
Principal Poverty Adviser
Bureau for Development Policy, UNDP

Acknowledgements

No evaluation with a scope such as the one presented in *Choices for the Poor* — spanning several months and covering some fifty countries, eighteen of which were visited for in-depth analysis — would have been possible without the extraordinary commitment and support of a large number of individuals scattered around the globe.

Choices for the Poor is a product of the Bureau for Development Policy of UNDP, under the direction of Eimi Watanabe. It has been edited and assembled by a team led by Alejandro Grinspun and comprising Elizabeth Satow and Rasheda Selim, each of whom has made invaluable contributions to the evaluation exercise and the book itself. The team wishes to thank Stephen Browne, Principal Poverty Advisor, for his guidance during the preparation of the book, as well as Thierry Lemaresquier, former Director of the Social Development Division, for his leadership during the lifespan of the Poverty Strategies Initiative.

Many other individuals contributed in various ways to the publication. We would especially like to acknowledge Shawna Tropp for her editorial work, as well as Patrick Tiefenbacher and Piyadasa da Silva from the UN Office of Project Services. Radhika Lal, Richard Ponzio, Jim Lang, Pratibha Mehta, Melaia Vatucawaqa, Dasa Silovic, Mumtaz Keklik, Samir Wanmali, Maureen Lynch, Liz Scott-Andrews and Rachel Sambour-Moïse from UNDP all helped at various stages along the process.

Away from New York, the professionalism, support and cooperation of UNDP staff in the field were critical to the success of this enterprise. We cannot mention all of them here, but would like to express our special gratitude to the UNDP Resident Representatives in the 18 countries visited by the evaluators, as well as to the following individuals: Alexander Aboagye and Joao Freire (Angola); Ana Atanassova (Bulgaria); Reyna de Contreras (Guatemala); Elena Borsatti and R. Sudarshan (India); Adarsha Tuladhar (Lao PDR); Dace Dzenovska (Latvia); Randa Aboul-Hosn (Lebanon); Mathasi Kurubally (Lesotho); Shaheem Razee and Phylippe Zisset (Maldives); Alissabatou Goune, Renata Lok-Dessalien and Rosine Sori-Coulibaly (Mali); Dempa Diop (Mauritania); Saraswathi Menon (Nepal); Sufian Mshasha (Palestine); Maite Mendizábal (São Tomé e Principe); Sascha Graumann (Tajikistan); Joseph Opio-Odongo (Uganda); Pablo Martínez. (Uruguay); and Delia Yerokan (Zambia). We are thankful to every one of them for their assistance in the planning and successful conclusion of the country missions as well as for their comments to previous drafts of the chapters.

The information for *Choices for the Poor* did not come simply from documents and publications, but also from interviews with government officials, non-governmental organisations, academics and other people in the countries visited. Although they are not mentioned by name, the book owes much to their predisposition to give their time and opinions to the members of the evaluation team.

Finally, we would like to express our thanks to the governments of Norway, the Netherlands, Denmark and Finland for their financial contribution to the Poverty Strategies Initiative. Because the book is the result of an external evaluation of that programme, the views expressed in it are exclusively those of the authors and should not be construed as representing the official position or policy of any of the governments mentioned above, or UNDP, or the institutions with which individual authors are affiliated.

Table of Contents

PART 1
Policy Issues

PART 2
Country Cases

List of Acronyms

BSS . . . . Basic Social Services
CCA . . . . U.N. Common Country Assessment
HDI . . . . Human Development Index
HDR . . . . Human Development Report
HIPC . . . . Heavily Indebted Poor Country Initiative
HPI . . . . Human Poverty Index
HVI . . . . Human Vulnerability Index (Maldives)
ILO . . . . International Labour Organization
IMF . . . . International Monetary Fund
LDC . . . . Least Developed Country
LSMS . . . . Living Standards Measurement Survey
MLC . . . . Mapping of Living Conditions (Lebanon)
MTEF . . . . Medium-Term Expenditure Framework
NGO . . . . Non-Governmental Organisation
NHDR . . . . National Human Development Report
NORAD . . . . Norwegian Agency for Development Cooperation
NPRAP . . . . National Poverty Reduction Action Plan (Zambia)
NPRSF . . . . National Poverty Reduction Strategic Framework (Zambia)
PEAP . . . . Poverty Eradication Action Plan (Uganda)
PGI . . . . Poverty Gap Index
PL . . . . Poverty Line
PNLCP . . . . Programme National de Lutte contre la Pauvreté (Mauritania)
PRGF . . . . Poverty Reduction and Growth Facility
PRSP . . . . Poverty Reduction Strategy Paper
PSI . . . . Poverty Strategies Initiative
RTM . . . . Round Table Meeting
SHDR . . . . State Human Development Report
SIDA . . . . Swedish International Development Agency
SISAP . . . . Système d'Information pour le Suivi et l'Analyse de la Pauvreté (Mali)
SNLP . . . . Stratégie Nationale de Lutte contre la Pauvreté (Mali)
TLSS . . . . Tajikistan Living Standards Survey
UBN . . . . Unsatisfied Basic Needs
UNDP . . . . United Nations Development Programme
UNFPA . . . . United Nations Fund for Population Activities
UPA . . . . Urban Poverty Assessment (Lesotho)
UPPAP . . . . Uganda Participatory Poverty Assessment Project
VPA . . . . Maldives Vulnerability and Poverty Assessment
WHO . . . . World Health Organisation
WSSD . . . . World Summit for Social Development

CHOICES *for the* POOR

CHAPTER 1

Introduction:
Stimulating policy change

Alejandro Grinspun

At the dawn of a new millennium, all significant actors in the development process have converged their agendas upon this — the importance of poverty reduction as the cornerstone of all development efforts. The renewed attention to issues of poverty and distribution constitutes a welcome departure from the themes that dominated much of the development discourse during the last quarter century, when concern with macroeconomic stabilisation and adjustment was at the centre of the policy agenda.

Despite expectations that countries undergoing adjustment would be able to resume economic growth after a few years and thus presumably reduce poverty, growth has eluded a large number of developing countries — and poverty rates today remain largely what they were a decade ago. The persistence of massive poverty is morally unconscionable, since the world has the resources and know-how to vanquish it. It is also a major challenge to governance, a contagion increasingly unchecked by national frontiers as the pace and density of global exchange increases. Poverty inevitably spills over from one country to another in various guises — disease, conflict, child trafficking and exploitation, as well as the unrelenting surges of refugees and other migrants seeking livelihoods.

The publication of the first *Human Development Report* (HDR) by the United Nations Development Programme (UNDP) in 1990 played a critical role in refocusing attention on poverty and its distribution. By demonstrating that development involves much more than economics alone, the HDRs have helped shift the development debate back to what matters most — people and their choices. In 1995, the first World Summit for Social Development (WSSD) sponsored by the United Nations in Copenhagen, Denmark, gave leaders from over 180 countries an opportunity to commit themselves to the fight against poverty as an 'ethical, social, political and economic imperative'. Actions taken at both the national and international levels during the latter part of the 1990s further reinforced the impetus created by the 1995 Summit, culminating in the United Nations Millennium Declaration of September 2000, through which the international community unambiguously endorsed the goal of halving extreme poverty by the year 2015.

Poverty reduction has now returned to its proper place — at the centre of the development agenda. There is now a clear understanding that success in meeting this challenge requires mobilising all national actors behind common policy goals embodied in a national strategy or plan against poverty. As the lead development agency of the United Nations system, UNDP has a major responsibility to assist countries in fulfilling this task. This requires close cooperation among all donors but, above all, the creation of space for a truly nationally driven process of change. Only through national debate and consensus can solid foundations be laid for a sustained attack on poverty.

A catalyst for poverty reduction strategies

To fulfil this mission, UNDP launched its Poverty Strategies Initiative (PSI) in 1996 — a global programme that supported country efforts to diagnose poverty, improve their capacity for policy analysis and implementation, and develop national and local strategies for reducing poverty.[1] Offered in more than 100 countries, the programme had two key objectives: the establishment of the technical, institutional and political foundations for policy action, and the mobilisation of local constituencies so as to expand public discourse on poverty. The PSI not only responded to the appeal made at the World Summit for Social Development; it became a precursor of subsequent initiatives, most recently one adopted by the World Bank and the International Monetary Fund (IMF) in 1999 that requires the preparation of a Poverty Reduction Strategy Paper (PRSP) as a condition for country eligibility to concessional assistance or debt relief.[2]

When the PSI was launched five years ago, the 100 countries it addressed found themselves in very different stages of preparing poverty strategies. At one end of this spectrum, some had already incorporated poverty *per se* into their development planning frameworks. At the other were countries in which virtually no public debate about poverty had taken place. In some of these, the phenomenon had not even been explicitly recognised. Wide variation therefore existed in the nature of PSI activities, making every country initiative unique. This, of course, reflects the fact that the programme was a fully country-driven exercise. For purposes of analysis, however, PSI activities may be grouped under the following headings:

Qualitative poverty assessments

Many countries — from Grenada and Latvia to Papua New Guinea and Uganda — have undertaken qualitative assessments and profiles of poverty and of specific vulnerable groups — indigenous communities, unemployed youth, persons infected with HIV/AIDS, women, and street children. What makes these activities distinctive is their use of a range of non-traditional approaches — among these, participatory techniques drawn from anthropological and rural development research — that set them apart from studies based on the conventional quantitative survey methodology. Qualitative assessments generally aim at examining poverty from the perspective of the dispossessed, at discovering the causes and effects of poverty within the local context and the many ways in which poor people cope with uncertainty. Many of the assessments have shed light on crucial dimensions hitherto neglected — such as social isolation as both an outcome of poverty and a cause of further impoverishment, or the economic contribution of women's activities in household subsistence, as well as in the informal sector.

Household surveys and poverty maps

Measuring and monitoring poverty have been central to many projects, from Angola to Indonesia and Turkmenistan. Household surveys were designed — and sometimes conducted — with funding from the PSI, using a combination of income, consumption and welfare indicators. Surveys were needed for different reasons. Where poverty had not been a specific focus of past policies, basic data on its breadth and depth were often missing. Even where surveys had been conducted, conflicting data or unclear definitions of poverty often hampered the formulation of policies and programmes. New indicators were constructed in many countries to reflect the impact of such complex phenomena as rights on poverty or to capture the changing dynamics of poverty and vulnerability more accurately. Apart from improving the countries' databases on poverty, many projects created poverty maps to highlight disparities within national borders so as to better identify specially disadvantaged groups or regions.

Poverty reduction strategies and programmes

In countries from Kyrgyzstan to Mali, where the necessary policy conditions appeared to be present, PSI funds directly supported the development of national poverty reduction strategies. This took the form of technical assistance for the selection of appropriate poverty indicators and targets, as well as for defining policy priorities and institutional mechanisms for implementing these strategies. Since national ownership was a key premise of the programme, these countries emphasised involving a variety of local actors in processes of public debate and consultation at all stages of planning and formulation. What UNDP brought to the process was its ability to work with different parties and to act as an honest broker in debates on politically sensitive issues.

Analyses of social spending and aid flows to basic services

PSI also earmarked funding for the preparation of social sector expenditure reviews in almost 30 countries, particularly in sub-Saharan Africa and Latin America. These reviews aimed at examining the volume of public and aid resources spent on providing basic social services, the equity and efficiency of such spending, and the flexibility for devoting more resources to the social services, as well as improving their effectiveness and impact. These studies have encouraged debate on social policy goals and the financing of priorities by providing options and recommendations for mobilising additional funding to expand the coverage and improve the quality of services. The studies also provide baseline information on budget expenditures and social outcomes that may be used in future for tracking a country's performance in meeting the basic human rights of its citizens.

National Human Development Reports

As a contribution to the national debate on development priorities, the PSI programme sponsored many Human Development Reports at the national and even provincial levels in countries ranging from Botswana to India. While the process of preparing these reports has varied from one country to another, they have often brought into focus issues around which new constituencies could mobilise politically for the first time. These range from the rights of minorities and indigenous groups to gender disparities through failures of governance. National HDRs have proved particularly useful in environments where poverty and related issues are politically charged; they have often provided vehicles for airing questions that appear less controversial to those involved, thereby permitting indirect discussion of poverty.

Capacity development for planning and coordination

PSI aimed explicitly at using local institutions and expertise. Local participation in preparing assessments and strategies was viewed not only as a vehicle for enhancing local capacities for poverty analysis and planning, but also a means of nurturing the commitment of local actors to the outcomes of the exercise. Government planners, district authorities and community leaders in countries as varied as Romania and Zimbabwe were sensitised and trained in poverty analysis and monitoring, gender statistics, budgeting, participatory evaluation and other areas of policy and programming to ensure the sustainability of anti-poverty actions. With the same goal, national machineries were created or strengthened to coordinate policy among the various governmental and non-governmental actors involved in poverty reduction.

Evaluating the past

To assess the results and impact achieved by PSI, UNDP commissioned an independent evaluation in 1999-2000. Its purpose was twofold: first, to gauge progress in bringing the poverty agenda forward, particularly from the point of view of the national partners; second, to draw lessons from PSI-funded work in policy and analysis so as to inform future UNDP advice and support, as well as that of other donors.

Eighteen countries were selected for in-depth evaluation and visited in early 2000:
- India, Laos, Maldives and Nepal from Asia;

- Lebanon and Palestine from the Middle East;
- Angola, Mali, Mauritania, Lesotho, São Tomé e Principe, Uganda and Zambia from sub-Saharan Africa;
- Guatemala and Uruguay from Latin America;
- Bulgaria, Latvia and Tajikistan from Europe and Central Asia.

Broadly, these countries represent the full range activities summarised above. In addition to the country visits, the evaluation team undertook an extensive literature review of poverty surveys, Human Development Reports and a large number of policy and strategy documents sponsored by the PSI in another 32 countries. In short, the evaluation exercise covered a total of 50 countries — a sample large enough to permit a distillation of many lessons relevant to both poverty analysis and the formulation of anti-poverty policy.

Choices for the Poor presents the results of the evaluation. It is divided into two parts. Drawing on the findings from the literature review to investigate a number of issues that affect policy formulation, Part I attempts to distil lessons that may inform the development of anti-poverty policy. By contrast, Part II represents the findings of the evaluation team in their visits to the 18 countries listed earlier. Part II therefore focusses on the results and impacts of PSI activities in those countries, so as to clarify the roles that development organisations can play in supporting countries' own efforts to stem poverty.

Part I opens by exploring the concepts, analytical approaches and methods used in developing countries to define and measure poverty and vulnerability. In Chapter 2, Julian May questions the notion of a broad-based consensus among experts on these issues. Researchers from developing countries have deepened conventional definitions by revealing the inadequacies of measures based on income or consumption. These new investigators point to other dimensions of poverty, both measurable and elusive, above all its context-specific nature. They look at poverty as a phenomenon of many layers, determined by cultural norms and practices and by relations of power and dependency within social groupings that range from the household unit to the nation. They also show how seasonal changes and short-term shocks affect people's movements into and out of poverty. Analyses draw our attention to the importance of such intangibles as trust and solidarity and thereby illuminate the concepts of exclusion, stigma and powerlessness and the ways in which these shape both people's lives and development outcomes. Not surprisingly, researchers from developing countries also highlight phenomena that no longer dominate daily life in most of the industrialised world, such as war and civil strife and physical infection, including the HIV/AIDS pandemic. Because exposure to violence in particular affects a large proportion of the world's poor, we must look more closely at the social and political milieux that engender poverty.

All these insights have led to a great deal of experimentation with various approaches to poverty measurement. Among the innovations are the widespread use of composite indices, as well as of relative poverty lines, notions of poverty dominance and qualitative research methods, applied either alone or combined with quantitative survey techniques. While these recognitions of complexity have already enriched the understanding of local realities, May also points to areas in which further enquiry is needed — intra-household distribution of resources and income flows, macro- and microeconomic consequences of HIV/AIDS, or exposure to violence as a determinant of poverty.

Mercedes González de la Rocha and Alejandro Grinspun concentrate on some of these issues in Chapter 3, which examines how poverty is experienced at the household level. The authors demonstrate how economic hardship forces poor people to deploy a number of strategies to protect their level of consumption from deteriorating. Paramount among these is the mobilisation of household labour, which expands the pool of income earners — often to include children — lengthens working hours and diversifies income sources. Other domestic responses supplement these strategies — changing consumption habits, going into debt and, eventually, liquidating property and savings when increased labour fails to offset the shrinking of household resources. Much of the literature on household responses has emphasised the *agency* of the poor, their capacity to adapt to worsening conditions by foregoing consumption and escalating effort. But González de la Rocha and Grinspun remind us that coping usually involves a delicate balance between short-term survival and long-term social reproduction. A coping strategy that relies on intensifying the use of household resources cannot be sustained permanently. It may even undermine a household's ability to move out of poverty. As the authors stress, the resilience of the poor has definite limits. They deploy their livelihood strategies in an environment of increasing constraints that can become crushing. Household restructuring takes a particularly heavy toll on women, who typically assume a disproportionate share of the burden of adjustment without improving their subordinate position within the household. And because women normally constitute the major links of the informal networks of reciprocity based on solidarity and mutual help, their absorption in the survival of their own households weakens these vital support systems of the poor, spreading, deepening and perpetuating poverty itself.

Chapter 4 supplements this analysis by addressing an issue often neglected in the poverty literature: the multiple interdependencies between rural and urban spheres. Alf Morten Jerve contends that most poverty research treats the rural and urban spheres as distinct sectors, even though developing countries typically manifest a spatial continuum from remote hamlets to large urban centres that precludes any sharp demarcation between the two. Static poverty measures fail to capture cyclical movements of people and the transfers of resources that bind rural and urban areas together. Because war or economic hardships often divide families, many adopt a mix of rural-*cum*-urban livelihood strategies that include migration and intra-family transfers. Remittances from the urban economy frequently constitute a vital income source for rural households. At the same time, relatives in the countryside often provide a safety valve for urban residents, especially when labour markets become slack. Neglecting these issues reduces our understanding of poverty and impairs the design of policies to promote broad-based economic growth.

But no consensus exists on how to address the problems associated with escalating urbanisation and rural-urban disparities. Given the dependence of rural families on remittances and wage work, stemming the tide of rural poverty cannot rely solely on developing rural-based alternatives for income generation. The answer, says Jerve, lies in strengthening the ties between the rural and urban economy, and stimulating economic growth in secondary towns so as to create employment for the rural poor. Support to the urban informal sector may create ripple effects in the rural economy, provided urban-rural transfers can be harnessed for reinvestment in agriculture. Women entrepreneurs, who already play a major role in rural-urban trade in many African countries, could emerge as a natural link between the two spheres in that part of the world. There and elsewhere, small town development and peri-urban smallholder farming could also foster new forms of centre-periphery relations, thereby contributing to better-balanced regional development.

Fostering better relations between centre and periphery also calls for a good measure of decentralisation, an issue that S. R. Osmani takes up in Chapter 5. The author demonstrates that local governance can yield benefits in terms of efficiency as well as equity. It gives people a sense of ownership, utilising their skills and knowledge about local conditions and giving them the opportunity to allocate resources according to their perceived needs. All too often, however, the slogan of 'decentralisation' covers various types of administrative reorganisation that do not in fact empower people at the local level. At least in part in many countries, fiscal constraints have driven decentralisation. Politicians at the national level have sought grassroots participation as a means of ensuring the implementation of preconceived plans without changing earlier relations between the centre and local communities.

Apart from the reluctance of the centre to transfer power downwards, elite domination of local government has also obstructed effective decentralisation. Some countries have tried to circumvent this problem of traditional power structures by either bypassing or co-opting the local elite. Others have introduced popularly elected structures at the community level, sometimes fortified by statutory reservations of seats for women and other under-represented groups. Nonetheless, truly participatory governance requires organising people at the grassroots level so that they can not only raise their voices, but make critical decisions about community affairs. Osmani proposes a two-fold empowerment strategy based on social mobilisation and livelihood security. Group formation enables the poor to overcome their fragmentation and convert their numerical strength into genuine bargaining power. However, as long as they have to cope with extreme deprivations on a day-to-day basis, organising for the long term will not rank high among their priorities. NGOs can act as change agents, helping the poor achieve immediate economic gains while simultaneously transcending the immediate tasks around which they initially happen to organise. Creating a civil society where none exists, or strengthening it where it does, is therefore a vital ingredient of participatory local governance.

The next two chapters move beyond poverty analysis into the realm of policy design and implementation. In Chapter 6, Jaroslaw Górniak provides a detailed assessment of the poverty debate in former socialist countries, where a dramatic deterioration of incomes and widening social disparities have accompanied the transition to market economies. To alleviate poverty, these countries have grappled with defining a threshold for social assistance. But because all such thresholds — indeed, all poverty measures — are arbitrary in one way or another, they invite controversy. Choosing a poverty yardstick must meet several criteria: the yardstick must be theoretically sound so as to depict poverty rates accurately; it must also be realistic from a fiscal point of view; and, most importantly, it needs broad public acceptance if society is to agree that certain groups, rather than others, deserve public support.

Moreover, in a context of rapid economic change, poverty affects people in numerous ways, and its multiple dimensions correlate weakly with one another. For this reason, countries have resorted to a combination of poverty lines to depict the multi-faceted character of poverty and to identify potential target groups for public policy. The design of such policy has itself been mired in controversy. While these countries cannot maintain the system of universal benefits inherited from the Soviet era, adopting a targeted policy entails many risks. A system based on strict targeting carries high administrative costs and is open to abuse. Groups entitled to benefits may not apply if the system is too complex, while others may question its legitimacy if they feel that they are being punished for not meeting official criteria for eligibility. Means testing, in particular, seems impractical in countries in which the extent of the 'grey economy' equals or exceeds that of the formal sector. It also carries the risk of stigmatising potential recipients who, for that very reason, may not claim their benefits. Given this situation, Górniak concludes, a policy of broad targeting seems a more attractive option, provided that fiscal revenues allow for it.

Chapter 7 explores fiscal policy issues further by examining the share of public resources that poor countries devote to the financing of basic health and education. Julia Harrington, Catherine Porter and Sanjay Reddy show that the absolute level of funding for basic services falls far short of people's needs in many poor countries, even though their governments spend a substantial proportion of their budgets on social sector investments. However, the limited size of their economies, their small revenue bases and their debt service obligations severely limit the resources available for social expenditures. Without dramatic economic growth or increased revenue generation, these countries have little or no scope for increasing their activities in health and education. The fiscal austerity programmes they have negotiated with the international financial institutions prevent them from expanding total public spending. And, as indicated earlier, their heavy debt burdens siphon off resources that could most effectively be spent on basic service provision. Indeed, some of the poorest countries spend more on servicing their debt than their people — a strong argument for debt forgiveness. Defence, too, absorbs resources for basic services and is therefore another promising target for government budget cuts.

Even within existing social appropriations, spending is not well targeted. Much that now goes to housing, hospital and school construction might be better spent in basic service delivery, which tends to result in higher human development outcomes more rapidly. Donors, too, need to increase their ODA for basic services, especially in countries whose development budget is almost entirely externally financed — as is the case in much of sub-Saharan Africa, where the spread of HIV/AIDS is stretching government resources to their outer limits. Improving the financing of basic services calls for common definitions and standardisation of national budgets and aid reporting. It also requires broad-based public support, which may sometimes call for broader over narrowly targeted approaches to provision.

Chapters 8 to 10 review the experience of seven sub-Saharan African countries, three each from West and Southern Africa, and the last from the continent's east. Five of the countries are eligible for debt relief under the enhanced HIPC Initiative, and all seven are engaged in formulating Poverty Reduction Strategy Papers. Chapter 10 also focuses on Maldives, an Indian Ocean country that provides an interesting counterpoint to the continental African cases.

The experience of Angola is examined in Chapter 8. Despite a history of protracted civil conflict and failure to sustain the implementation of development plans, Angola had a small cadre of highly qualified professionals who could have played a crucial bridging role between policy analysis and design. Acting strategically, UNDP undertook to support these experts through a series of studies that encouraged a fledgling debate on the root causes of poverty and gender discrimination in Angolan society. The chapter shows that donor support may be critical to the development of indigenous technical capacity for poverty analysis, although donor-funding cycles often undercut the process of learning-by-doing that is required. The institutional fragility typical of many countries constitutes an overwhelming constraint to their accumulation of the knowledge and competencies necessary for policy development. As González de la Rocha argues, the establishment of broad partnerships may somehow compensate for the prevailing institutional weakness that undermines policy formation. Unfortunately, in Angola, efforts in this direction failed.

Chapter 9 focusses on West Africa, specifically Mali, Mauritania and São Tomé e Principe, three of the world's poorest countries. Pierre Sanon begins by showing how their existing debt burden obstructs their development efforts. Driven in part by the international agenda and in part by domestic considerations, each of these countries had embarked upon the elaboration of national anti-poverty policies prior to the launch of the HIPC Initiative. Particularly in Mali and Mauritania, this work prepared their governments for subsequent negotiations with the Bretton Woods institutions, paving the way for the approval of their interim PRSPs and their qualification for debt relief under HIPC terms. Each has begun evolving a home-grown poverty reduction drive by establishing an institutional framework that steers and coordinates the process of policy formation. The most notable example is Mali, whose *Stratégie Nationale de Lutte contre la Pauvreté* (SNLP) took almost two years to develop through a countrywide process of consultation and validation. Support from external agencies facilitated and strengthened this national process rather than substituting for it. Nonetheless, as this chapter soberly reminds us, the success of Mali and countries like it depends not only on substantial external support for the implementation and monitoring of anti-poverty policy, but the dovetailing of those contributions. Competing donor agendas may derail the emergence of local responses to poverty.

In Chapter 10, Julian May examines Lesotho, Uganda and Zambia, supplementing these cases with that of Maldives, where UNDP supported a comprehensive assessment of vulnerability as well as poverty for all the islands and atolls that compose this physically fragmented country. May provides a rich comparative analysis of the determinants of success or failure in all four initiatives, identifying four such factors: local ownership through consensus-building, the development of local capacities, the formation of strategic alliances with local actors, and the ability to engage with local processes of policy design.

Most of these elements were present in Uganda, and in varying degrees in Maldives and Zambia as well. Their absence in Lesotho thwarted the prospects for translating the results of a study of urban poverty into concrete policies to improve urban planning and arrest the rise of poverty in the major towns of the country. Like Mali and Mauritania, Uganda and Zambia had developed their respective national poverty reduction plans before the IMF and World Bank announced the terms of the enhanced HIPC, linking debt relief to the elaboration of anti-poverty policy documents. Both countries initiated intense domestic consultation processes to prepare their strategies. However, in Uganda, a strong coordinating ministry led the exercise, while in Zambia, the mandate for coordinating anti-poverty work remained uncertain for a long time, weakening the commitment of many key actors within the government and outside it. This highlights the need to understand the impact of intra-government dynamics on policy change.

Competition between government agencies often reduces the prospects for shared ownership, thereby undermining the process of policy formation. Learning to hone the 'tactics of coordination' becomes essential for preventing policy stalemates that may arise from competing interests within government. To support this process, donor organisations must be willing to learn from and with national actors rather than merely acting as external providers of technical assistance. Ultimately, this is what 'shared learning' means.

The next two chapters discuss three cases from Asia: India, Nepal and Laos. In Chapter 11, S. R. Osmani demonstrates the impact of the elaboration of Human Development Reports on public discourse, strategic thinking and policy formation in both India and Nepal. India's decision to produce these reports at the State level proved particularly interesting because it brought the debate closer to the public at large. In examining the cases of Karnataka, Madhya Pradesh and Rajasthan, the author demonstrates how policy-makers and citizens learned that 'development is more than building roads and dams.' The HDRs drove home the need to redress huge disparities among regions, castes and sexes, and to empower disadvantaged groups through social mobilisation and livelihood security. In explaining the success of the HDRs, Osmani points to two important factors: the process through which policy outputs are generated, and the perception that those outputs are not hostage to narrow political interests or driven by particularistic agendas. The most successful HDRs involved the participation of a range of local actors from government, the political class, civil society, academia and the press. This inclusiveness enhanced ownership and capacities whose value may well outlive the reports themselves. In addition, the absence of political interference contributed to a perception that the HDRs transcended politics because they were guided instead by a genuine spirit of enquiry. This perception gave them credibility and respect, facilitating their acceptance by groups and individuals of different persuasions. Under such conditions, ownership may easily extend beyond government to encompass groups in civil society who can use the reports to advance their own social causes.

The case of Laos, reviewed in Chapter 12, contrasts markedly with India or Nepal. Public debate on poverty *per se*, which affects a large proportion of the country's 236 ethnic minorities, barely exists. The Laotian government has adopted an ideology of modernisation and nation-building, which has engendered a dominant strategy of rural development based on settled agriculture and village consolidation. It has also given rise over the years to mutual suspicion and mistrust between the government and major donors who contend that the official rural development strategy could lead to forced relocation and assimilation of non-ethnic Lao minorities. Further complicating the picture, a number of institutional problems concerning the management and monitoring of rural policy — notably the apparent competition between state and Party organs — has damaged policy coherence and the coordination of development planning. By encouraging reformers in government, UNDP has tried to bring ethnic minority issues to the fore. Nonetheless, its efforts to broker agreements between Laos and its donors by shedding the most controversial aspects of the rural development strategy have met with little success. As Alf Jerve points out, Laos illustrates the difficulty of promoting policy change in a context of limited institutional capacity and ownership. Raising the issue of poverty is particularly sensitive for donors, as it implies engaging in basic conflicts over rights and entitlements.

This issue receives further support in Chapter 13, in which Mercedes González de la Rocha explores the cases of Uruguay and Guatemala. Despite very dissimilar trajectories, these two Latin American countries face the challenge of addressing social inequities and poverty as a major governance concern. Indeed, the author argues, developments in the polity and in society are inextricably linked; democratic governance rests upon social equity. In Guatemala, the historic subjugation of the indigenous majority eventually erupted into open violence that, after four decades of armed hostilities, the country finally seems eager to resolve. Restoring peace and building a framework for harmonious coexistence cannot be dissociated from the larger challenge of rectifying the plight of the indigenous poor. By contrast, Uruguay's enduring democracy has been predicated upon a highly integrated and mobile society — yet one that now shows fissures as distinctions among social strata emerge and harden. UNDP illuminated issues each country needs to confront so as to address these larger governance challenges: overcoming both ethnic discrimination in Guatemala and rising vulnerability in Uruguay. The effort in Guatemala was particularly notable because it involved the mobilisation of Mayan organisations through self-awareness. This impetus, it was felt, would spur the landless peasantry to take an active part in the political process — itself a precondition for consolidating the peace process.

The chapter points to a second issue that links poverty reduction to the governance agenda: the impact of the political cycle on public discourse and policy formation. Presidential elections in late 1999 halted progress in addressing poverty in both countries. Because reducing poverty is intrinsically a long process, stretching well beyond the mandate of any particular government, candidates were wary of investing their political capital in a task whose fruits they could not hope to reap during their four or five-year terms. Ultimately, González de la Rocha stresses, political change does not conform to carefully constructed scenarios; it requires accommodation, along with a willingness to forgo expectations of clear dénouements and resolutions.

In Chapter 14, Alf Jerve vividly depicts the difficulties of developing a national discourse and policy on poverty in two conflict-ridden societies: Lebanon and Palestine. In Lebanon, public discussion of poverty raises the spectre of divisiveness, as the fragile post-war governance structure rests on the preservation of popular images that sanction a power-sharing arrangement among the various religious factions. In Palestine, discussions of poverty are not only tied to the lingering question of formalising citizen's rights in the emerging state, but threaten the prevailing view that attributes poverty to the constraints on nationhood, thereby absolving domestic political actors of responsibility. Because of the issue's volatility, only agencies perceived as neutral and trustworthy partners can act as catalysts of policy change. A flexible funding mechanism such as PSI seems particularly well-suited to this purpose, although work on poverty may have to be conducted under different banners. In Lebanon, for instance, UNDP focussed on living conditions, avoiding direct reference to poverty.

In assessing the conditions that facilitate policy reform, Jerve replays a number of themes from previous chapters: the importance of brokering partnerships among key local actors, of a strong policy-making body with the mandate and capacity to lead policy reform, and of institutionalising the reform process. This last thrust is exemplified by Palestine's creation of a National Poverty Commission. Governments, the author reminds us, cannot be considered monolithic entities; the push to reform often arises from opposing forces within governments as well as societies. Both Lebanon and Palestine show how closely poverty is bound up with questions of governance.

Jaroslaw Górniak reviews the experience of three former socialist countries in Chapter 15: Bulgaria, Latvia and Tajikistan. Despite massive impoverishment, awareness of poverty remained low during the early years of the transition, partly because of a Soviet legacy that ascribed it to individual failings rather than those of the social system. Raising awareness and improving the measurement of poverty were therefore necessary first steps for the development of policy. Support from UNDP and the World Bank has led to remarkable results. 'Poverty' has finally entered the political vocabulary of policy-makers; poverty-monitoring capacities have improved; high-level coordinating mechanisms have been set up; and government strategies and actions plans are being prepared in the three countries. Górniak analyses the conditions that facilitated these outcomes, notably different models of interaction between foreign and local experts and institutions. He concludes that developing local capacities depends on exploiting opportunities for a bilateral transfer of skills and knowledge through training and 'learning by doing' under the supervision of experienced foreign consultants. Such training and transfer of know-how enhanced policy research capacity in Tajikistan, along with the ability of government personnel to absorb research results and apply them to the design of public policy. Nonetheless, capacities for policy design and implementation remain weak in all three countries, making support from foreign institutions essential for sustaining current progress in anti-poverty policy. As the case of Bulgaria shows, donors need to be aware that technical solutions cannot work unless they are politically acceptable. The implementation of poverty reduction efforts requires wide public approval.

Looking ahead

Many of the lessons in this book are specific to particular countries. Nonetheless, a number of general precepts emerge that may be of great value to development organisations and practitioners. These can be grouped under four headings: politics, institutions, capacities, and external support.

Politics

During the last few years, development agencies have tried to move away from low-impact projects into the provision of policy advice for the design, implementation and monitoring of national anti-poverty strategies. Moving decisively into the policy arena poses a host of new challenges. First and foremost is the difficulty of framing a workable solution to a problem that often seems intractable because it has become a way of life over the course of centuries.

In most societies, poverty stems from disparities in the distribution of power, wealth and opportunities. Changing these disparities always risks pitting certain groups against others. Those who benefit from existing arrangements and values are likely to resist efforts to reduce poverty, as they may see their position threatened by any change in the *status quo*. A feeling of deprivation may exist among groups who may be better off only in relative terms. Given the limitations of public and other resources, attempts to address the plight of certain groups may be viewed as unfair by others who feel equally entitled to public support, but are denied such advantages because of their marginally better position.

Poverty reduction is not simply a technical problem. If it were, solving it would simply require identifying its causes and prescribing effective, cost-efficient remedies. But fighting poverty is highly political. It entails a number of assumptions and perceptions that unconsciously condition mind-sets at every level of governance, from the household to the state. By doing so, poverty develops a web of relationships that become self-perpetuating well beyond the ambit of the poor themselves. For this reason, poverty reduction cannot be dissociated from governance; they are two sides of the same coin.

Institutions

Politics, though, is only one aspect of the problem. Another concerns institutions, especially as one moves from initiating policy change to the greater challenge of sustaining it. Institutions can play a decisive role in translating policy-relevant knowledge, to which donors often contribute by funding poverty surveys and analyses, into actual policy.

This poses a major challenge to local actors as well as development agencies, given the prevailing institutional weakness and fluidity found in many countries. This weakness manifests itself in multiple ways: high turnover among key personnel, a change of direction in a critical agency, or general fragmentation and lack of coordination among entities responsible for policy implementation. The regular business of politics causes a particular type of institutional problem. Presidential or congressional elections may temporarily push the poverty debate to the background as candidates seek to build the broadest coalitions possible to carry them to power. But campaigning and electioneering may also provide an opportunity for projecting certain sensitive issues into the public arena.

Whatever the cause, any of these factors tends to disrupt the policy formation process. Institutions take time to develop and mature. As the donor community seeks to promote the twin goals of poverty reduction and democratic governance, it will have to devote greater attention to the challenge of strengthening institutions as well as to the impact of the political cycle on policy-making. This will not only require long-term commitment, but also tight coordination among development agencies to ensure that investments in institutional development support rather than undercut one another.

Capacities

Development agencies, therefore, need to emphasise a capacity development agenda as a means of overcoming the institutional gaps present in many countries. Success in policy reform depends, in large measure, on building long-term capacity of key local actors to analyse a problem correctly and design the best solutions for it. But capacity development goes far beyond local actors — governmental or non-governmental — using information and analyses funded by a donor in formulating policy. It calls for strengthening their ability to *identify* problems that need action, to *commission* work as required, to *interpret* its results and, finally, to *use* them for policy purposes.

It is important, for instance, to distinguish between funding a poverty assessment and undertaking a systemic effort to build long-term technical capacities for monitoring poverty. In the first case, even if new information is produced, there is no guarantee that local actors are empowered to carry out a future assessment. The second type of capacity development agenda typically requires intensive training of local actors to enable them to perform their tasks effectively after the withdrawal of external support. Sharing of learning between local and international experts and developing tools for further learning are necessary. A conscious effort to transfer skills and know-how must inform donor actions.

Relying on national as opposed to international experts is thus less important than the manner in which both engage with one another. For similar reasons, the involvement of individuals is not as significant as that of institutions like think tanks, research centres and universities, endowed with the technical expertise required for high-quality results to assist policy formation.

Donors

The ability of donors to leverage policy reform does not depend only on the overall relevance and soundness of the policy analysis and advice provided. Knowledge can create change only to a limited extent. Institutionalising and embedding it in policy-making is critical. Along with high-quality policy inputs, therefore, inclusive consultation processes are needed to ensure policy impact and ownership.

Because poverty reduction is embedded in local power and governance structures, donor organisations may inevitably be drawn into the murky waters of politics. Many may lack an intimate knowledge of the local political setting, which makes them unfit to navigate its currents. Fears of external interference can also make donors suspect in some countries, especially when such qualms are freighted by perceptions that they may be trying to impose conditionalities or, worse, pursue agendas irrelevant or contrary to national aspirations. Whether or not these perceptions are justified does not particularly matter. Their very existence means they must be reckoned with.

To the extent that poverty reduction is politically charged, multilateral organisations — especially those of the United Nations — may be better placed than bilateral donors or development banks to act as trusted, impartial advisers of governments and of civil society in convening national debates on the topic. But such trust cannot be taken for granted. Nor should it preclude seeking a broader engagement of the donor community at large in a constructive manner — and in accordance with countries' development priorities.

Lessons for the future

Still, donor contributions, however small, can nurture pro-poor policy change if used strategically. The first critical factor is choosing some local *actor*, either within or outside the government, who has sufficient stature to command credibility and thereby become the standard-bearer of policy reform — at least within its own constituency. This actor need not be a single entity. Consultative bodies with broad multi-party representation like National Poverty Commissions or Working Groups, as well as Social and Economic Councils or Legislative Committees have been responsible for steering, overseeing or at least validating work on poverty in many countries around the world. Strengthening existing high-level planning and coordinating mechanisms is vital for enhancing national ownership of the policy process.

Choosing a weak counterpart can doom the prospects of any policy-oriented project. In the absence of such coordinating bodies, therefore, the best choice appears to be a 'strong' ministry within government — or an umbrella organisation from civil society. Putting a 'strong' ministry like finance or planning in a lead role can certainly enhance the prospects for policy change. Nonetheless, poverty concerns may be slighted if the lead ministry or body is preoccupied with enforcing macroeconomic or fiscal prudence at the expense of other considerations, such as popular participation or increasing the range of social service delivery.

Equally important is the ability to broker *processes* that can ensure the sustainability of policy reforms beyond the short term. An emphasis on policy processes implies looking beyond the designated institutional counterparts for a particular project to the key societal actors and the dynamics of policy change throughout a country. These will vary significantly from one situation to another — whether recovery from conflict, imminent elections, shifts from planned to market economies or from centralised to decentralised governance structures. In these circumstances and others, facilitating change calls for the presence of the development organisations on the ground.

Third, it is crucial to contribute to some form of *institutionalisation* to the policy reform process. Without this factor, policy actions will not survive the political vicissitudes of the moment. What kind of institutional set-up is most conducive to sustaining political will varies from one country to another. What matters, though, is that institutionalising reform initiatives implies making the issue of poverty a truly national concern — one that transcends narrow sectoral, sectarian, regional or ethnic agendas to become a matter of countrywide debate and decision-making. It means transforming poverty reduction into a non-partisan issue, well beyond the concern of an incumbent government — or, for that matter, of particular donors and their funding modalities.

Donor agencies, above all, need to respect the character of each country and its specific dynamics of policy change. They must learn to recognise the constraints they will encounter, along with the opportunities they can seize. Given the complexities of policy reform and its numerous institutional and political challenges in each country, one cannot judge all donor interventions in the same terms. Each case is unique. The yardstick for evaluating donor interventions designed to nurture pro-poor policy reform remains nonetheless the same — the questioning of poverty as an intrinsic human condition, the recognition of the poor as change agents, and the shaping of viable reform processes that are rooted in sustainable, effective institutions. ■

Notes

Alejandro Grinspun is Social Policy Advisor at the Bureau for Development Policy, UNDP. Mr. Grinspun coordinated the Poverty Strategies Initiative since its launch in 1996, as well as the external evaluation of the programme that was conducted during 1999-2000. He would like to acknowledge Shawna Tropp for editing the chapter, as well as Liz Satow and Alejandra Meglioli for comments.

[1] The specific objectives of the Initiative were defined as follows: (i) To assist UNDP programme countries in the formulation of national plans and implementation strategies, with specific time-bound goals and targets, for the substantial reduction of overall poverty and the eradication of absolute poverty; and (ii) To assist UNDP programme countries in the elaboration of definitions, assessments, measurements, criteria and indicators for determining the nature, extent and distribution of absolute poverty at the country level, including its gender structure and composition.

[2] The World Bank and IMF launched the HIPC Initiative in 1996 in an attempt to reduce the unsustainable debt burden of poor countries. Growing frustration with the pace of progress in implementing debt relief motivated a review of the Initiative in 1999, which was endorsed by the Boards of the Bank and Fund at their annual joint meeting. Among other amendments designed to reduce debt burdens more rapidly, the enhanced HIPC created direct links between debt relief and poverty reduction. The primary mechanism for this connection is the Poverty Reduction Strategy Paper (PRSP) that countries must produce in order to reach the 'decision point' for qualifying for a debt relief package. In response to the enhanced HIPC, IMF replaced its Enhanced Structural Adjustment Facility (ESAF) with the Poverty Reduction Growth Facility (PRGF). PRSPs are not only a condition for debt relief, but also for future concessional assistance from both institutions.

PART 1 Policy Issues

2 CHAPTER
An Elusive Consensus:
Definitions, measurement and analysis of poverty

Julian May

The analytical work funded by United Nations Development Programme (UNDP) under its Poverty Strategies Initiative (PSI) offers an insight into the views and methodologies of researchers and policy analysts from countries in which poverty is the dominant concern. Researchers have frequently had to adapt conventional approaches to suit the data available and the policy questions that are being addressed. By looking at how poverty is defined, which type of information is gathered and how it is analysed, we shall be in a position to gauge the contributions made by the PSI to applied poverty analysis in countries characterised by substantial capacity shortfalls. This may be especially helpful at a time when the governments of poor countries are responding to renewed international attention to the issue of poverty reduction.

This chapter, which reviews 24 studies sponsored by UNDP in 11 countries, shows that there is great variation in the manner in which poverty is being defined and measured in developing countries. We first examine some alternative conceptualisations of poverty used in the countries covered in the chapter. We then look at indicators and measures, contrasting the poverty line approach with composite indicators of social wellbeing and basic need satisfaction. Measurement instruments are discussed next, including the possibility of combining quantitative and qualitative methodologies of poverty analysis. A major concern throughout the paper is to highlight the innovations and adaptations made by researchers in these countries. Our contention is that from the perspective of national policy development, it is better to conceptualise poverty as being dynamic and related to the specific life situations of a country's population. Moreover, while the wide variation of measurement practices across countries may make international comparisons impossible, what matters most to individual countries is that the tools used to measure and analyse poverty correspond to their particular information needs and capacities.

Definitions and conceptualisation

In a special edition of the *World Development* journal, published in 1997, one of the world's leading experts on poverty, Michael Lipton, argues that there is an emerging consensus on the analysis of poverty and the ways in which it can be reduced (Lipton 1997). In terms of its definition and measurement, Lipton suggests that the principal components of this consensus are based on a growing recognition that:

- Poverty may adequately be defined as private consumption that falls below some absolute poverty line, which he terms 'absolute private consumption poverty' (PCP);
- PCP is best measured by calculating the proportion of the population who fall below a poverty line (the headcount) and the extent of this shortfall (the depth or severity of poverty). This poverty line is usually based on an esti-mated minimum dietary energy intake, or an amount required for purchasing a minimum consumption bundle;
- Low levels of capabilities (such as literacy and life expectancy) are major components of poverty, but are best measured separately rather than amalga-mated with consumption measures;
- Lack of consumption is more readily measured than lack of income, due to the ability of poor households to smooth their consumption over time in the face of income fluctuations arising from seasonality or shocks.

Lipton recognises that important areas of contention remain, principally around issues of redistribution, population dynamics, government regulation and exclusionary forces. However, this chapter argues that the consensus mentioned by Lipton remains elusive, especially from the perspective of researchers and pol-icy-makers in developing countries. Poverty definitions in these countries regu-larly incorporate notions of exclusion, powerlessness and stigma. Poverty is also frequently understood as being relational rather than absolute. The methodolo-gies followed in the calculation of poverty lines vary enormously. Consumption data are rarely gathered; proxy indicators of income tend to be used instead. The headcount ratio is the most common measure of poverty, but estimates of its sever-ity are seldom available. Finally, composite measures that combine income data with other measures of human capability are often computed. These measures normally expand well beyond the formula of the Human Development Index developed by UNDP.

We begin by looking at commonly accepted definitions of poverty used by inter-national agencies, which provide a backdrop for examining the approaches adopt-ed in the studies covered in this chapter. Moving from simpler to more complex and multidimensional concepts, we will look at the innovations introduced in these countries as they struggled to adapt conventional definitions to their own context. It is easy to see there is a great emphasis on a 'political economy' of pover-ty that is far more concerned with the social milieu within which deprivation and exclusion exist. Emphasis is also placed on the temporal nature of poverty and on the differences and linkages between chronic and transitory poverty.

A minimum acceptable standard

A classic definition of poverty sees it as 'the inability to attain a minimal standard of living' measured in terms of basic *consumption* needs or the *income* required for satisfying them (World Bank 1990). Poverty is thus characterised by the failure of individuals, households or entire communities to command sufficient resources to satisfy their basic needs. Consumption-based poverty lines are primarily concerned with *physical* measures of wellbeing. The inability to attain minimal standards of consumption to meet basic physiological criteria is often termed *absolute* poverty or deprivation. It is most directly expressed as not having enough to eat or as hunger or malnutrition.

Many of the studies reviewed here take this definition as their starting point. Even when the shortcomings of an absolute concept of poverty are acknowledged, this remains a basic building block for further analysis. As an example, the *Palestine Poverty Report* (PPR), prepared by the National Commission for Poverty Alleviation of the Palestinian National Authority, criticises the World Bank definition on many accounts. According to the report, this definition begs the question of how basic needs are defined and by whom, what is an 'accepted' minimal standard of living, and who determines what is acceptable. Nevertheless, while recognising that 'poverty is a multidimensional phenomenon consisting of material, mental, political, communal and other aspects', the authors state unambiguously that 'the material dimensions of poverty expressed in monetary values is too important an aspect of poverty to be neglected'. Given the fact that there is 'a lack of consensus regarding the measurement of other forms of deprivation', the approach followed in the PPR is ultimately grounded on the notion of some minimum threshold below which the poor are categorised (Palestine 1998).

Similarly, both the *Vulnerability and Poverty Assessment* (VPA) conducted in the Maldives and the *Mapping of Living Conditions* (MLC) in Lebanon tacitly accept the notion of a minimum acceptable standard of wellbeing. In Lebanon, deprivation refers to a situation in which certain social groups, households or individuals are below some threshold deemed necessary to meet a socially accepted standard of living (Lebanon 1998). The VPA recognises that poverty can be relative, but this issue is not explored in detail. Consequently, both poverty and vulnerability appear to occur when a set of minimum needs is not met, although the distinction between the two concepts is largely blurred (Maldives 1998).

Despite their acceptance of the idea of a minimum absolute standard of living, these and other studies sponsored by UNDP try to go beyond this conceptualisation, which they regard as deficient. In order to do this, they have supplemented their analysis of poverty by adopting a wide variety of approaches, focussing, for instance, on the ability of a household to satisfy their basic needs or to withstand various forms of hardship, such as ill health or social and physical isolation. The understanding of poverty has been enriched by this search for additional meaning, even though a consensus on an alternative conceptualisation of the phenomenon is still to emerge.

Relational notions of poverty

Poverty is best understood as having both an absolute and a relative dimension. In the absolute sense, the poor are materially deprived to the extent that their survival is at stake. In relative terms, they are also deprived in relation to other social groups whose situation is less constraining. The latter notion of poverty has been explored in a number of studies, and appears to convey more accurately the manner in which poor people experience their own predicament.

Participatory research methodologies provide a rich source of information for understanding the dual nature of poverty. In Uganda, where people's own perceptions were surveyed as part of the Uganda Participatory Poverty Assessment Project (UPPAP), poverty was defined in both material and non-material terms, and viewed as a 'complex, multidimensional, cyclical, seasonal and context-specific problem'. Not only did respondents place a great emphasis on stigma, exclusion and a lack of social networks as defining features of poverty, but they also stressed the importance of their natural environment, gender relations, and cultural norms

Box 1. Experiencing poverty: Voices from Uganda

According to the participatory assessments carried out in the Kampala, Kapchorwa and Kumi districts of Uganda, poverty is perceived differently at different levels of experience. At the individual level, poverty is said to involve:

- Lack of or insecure incomes;
- Lack of or poor quality basic necessities like food, clothing, etc.;
- Lack of household assets;
- Lack of productive assets, such as utensils or land;
- Inability to maintain good health and wellbeing;
- Dependency and helplessness;
- Anti-social behaviour.

In addition to some of the above features, poverty at the household level is perceived as comprising:

- Inability to provide for the children and the family;
- Lack of support networks;
- Excessive dependence on outsiders.

Finally, at the community level, poverty also comprised:

- Lack of infrastructure and remoteness;
- Instability and disunity.

and practices as central to their livelihoods (Uganda 1999a).

Findings from participatory assessments also reveal that poverty is a layered and relational phenomenon. Differences can be discerned in the manner in which people experience poverty, depending on whether one is concerned with individuals, households or communities. At the individual level, it is perceived primarily as a lack of basic necessities and power. At the household level, perceptions tend to differ according to gender. Men generally define poverty as a lack of assets, while women see it in terms of consumption and the ability to provide for the family. In turn, what is emphasised at the community level is the lack of services, assets and social cohesion as constitutive elements of poverty (Uganda 1999b).

In a qualitative assessment sponsored by UNDP in Latvia, poverty is again treated as a relative rather an absolute notion. People's judgements concerning their present situation are formed by comparing themselves with those around them or with their own situation in the past. Many appear to take comfort in the fact that everyone, not only themselves, has become poorer in recent years, and that they are not as bad as they could be. There is, nonetheless, a lingering fear that conditions could continue to deteriorate to a point at which they would be as worse off as those with whom they compare themselves (Trapenciere et al. 2000).

These perceptions differ significantly from the attitude that prevailed under socialism, when poverty was largely attributed to individual failure. They reflect the shared experience of widespread and sudden impoverishment of a large swath of the population following the demise of the Soviet Union. In forming these perceptions, Latvians tend to rely on stereotypes of others considered to be poor. Those who live in the countryside feel that urban residents are worse off, as they cannot grow their own food. Urban residents view rural areas as desolate, isolated and subject to unemployment and alcoholism. Pensioners consider large families and unemployed people as worse off, while parents with many children feel that pensioners living alone are the poorest of the poor.

A similar depiction of poverty as relational and context-specific is present in other studies. The *Palestine Poverty Report*, for instance, devotes great attention to the relationship between the poor and the non-poor, between poverty and wealth, as well as between the powerless and the powerful. The potential for conflict over resources and rights is thus given a far greater prominence than is the case with the minimum standards approach discussed earlier (Palestine 1998).

Despite the importance attached to relational notions of poverty, none of the studies reviewed here suggests new directions for measuring it. Nonetheless, the stress placed on this conceptualisation, along with its relevance to unequal societies or those in conflict, conveys that the social and political dynamics underpinning the relationship between the poor and the non-poor is a more significant aspect for policy-makers and researchers than the conventional approaches to poverty analysis would suggest. The development of appropriate indicators to capture the relational nature of poverty thus seems an important challenge for the international community.

Social exclusion, dependence and isolation

The concept of 'social exclusion' builds on relational notions of poverty and has a long tradition of research in industrialised countries. Exclusion is seen to incorporate the lack of social ties to the family, community and, more generally, to the society to which an individual belongs (Bhalla and Lapeyre 1997). The concept has both economic and social dimensions. Being excluded implies that someone's opportunities to earn an income, participate in the labour market or have access to assets are substantially curtailed. People can also be excluded from public services, community and family support, and even participation in shaping the decisions that affect their own lives. Social exclusion denotes not only the weakening of social ties that bind individuals to their families and communities, but also exclusion from some of the most basic rights of citizenship (Barry 1998).

The Ugandan participatory studies illustrate the usefulness of this conceptualisation by highlighting the importance people attach to social networks for their own understanding of poverty. The absence of social support, for instance, is seen as a determining factor of downward mobility. The central importance of social isolation as indicating or contributing to poverty is also stressed in the *Urban Poverty Assessment* conducted in Lesotho (Lesotho 1997). In the Gambia, people stated that constant vulnerability leads to feelings of helplessness, dependence on others and a loss of dignity. The poor were said to be unable to do anything by themselves without the consent of third parties on whom they rely for assistance in implementing decisions. Often this dependence extends even to such private matters as decisions concerning marriage, naming, initiations and other crucial events in a family's life cycle. The poor are equally unable to decide on social and civic matters, and invariably respond to community patronage (Kayateh 1997b).

Increasing isolation may just as often contribute to poverty as result from it. As a result of the deep economic crisis engulfing their country, many Latvians have been forced to reduce their socialising, as they can neither afford the customary gifts to take on visits to friends and relatives nor can they afford to entertain guests at home. As people curtail their socialising, their networks of support tend to become confined to the household and the immediate family. Cut off from vital sources of information and support, people's worlds become more insular. This often results in severe depression and loneliness (Trapenciere et al. 2000). Conversely, social status and connections occupy a central place in people's perceptions of what being better off implies. Holding a job which gives influence outside the workplace, having the ability to obtain services or rationed items, and knowing people who could provide assistance in times of need were specifically mentioned as defining the characteristics of someone who is better off (Gassman and de Neubourg 1999).

These themes are repeated in a number of other studies. In Mozambique, where war and resulting displacement of people have had a negative impact on social values, the most vulnerable groups are identified as being physically and mentally isolated from their communities and families (Thompson 1998). In both the Gambia and Lebanon, weak political participation is explicitly singled out as a key dimension of poverty. This is echoed in Grenada, where the poor complained about being ignored by politicians. There is an important gender component to exclusion that was mentioned in Grenada. Men's inability to provide for their families is seen as undermining their manhood, which leaves them with an intense feeling of insecurity, shame and frustration (Kairi 1998). Ethnicity also seems to be another major source of discrimination and social exclusion, although only one country in our sample deals directly with it (Aasland 2000).

The concept of social exclusion offers one way in which an analysis of the relational aspects of poverty can be incorporated in a rigorous manner. The concepts and methods of measuring the phenomenon are, however, still rudimentary. If appropriate analytical and measurement tools are developed, this type of analysis may provide a fruitful platform for further investigation.

Capabilities and poverty

Poverty is not a static condition. While some individuals or households are permanently poor, many others constantly move into and out of poverty. In development literature, the concept of 'vulnerability' makes reference to the negative outcomes of processes of change. The factors underpinning the dynamics of poverty may be economic, social, environmental or political, and may take the form of long-term trends as well as short-term shocks and cyclical processes determined, for example, by seasonal changes (Glewwe and Hall 1998; Grooteart and Kanbur 1995; Rakodi 1995).

In order to understand the dynamics of poverty, one can draw on the notions of 'capabilities' and 'entitlements' that have received a good deal of attention since they were introduced by the economist and Nobel Prize laureate Amartya Sen. Sen's work belies the idea that income shortfalls are the main attribute of poverty. He emphasises the importance of the bundle of assets or endowments held by the poor, as well as the nature of the claims attached to them, as critical for analysing poverty and vulnerability. Unemployment, missing markets, and production and price shocks may conspire to increase the vulnerability of particular individuals, depending on their asset bundle and their capacity to mobilise the resources at their disposal to withstand crises and shocks. A livelihood system may fail to provide access to an adequate bundle of commodities, creating what Sen has called 'entitlement failure' (Sen 1981).

Box 2. The Human Poverty Index (HPI)

If human development is about enlarging choices, poverty means that opportunities and choices most basic to human development are denied. For policy-makers, the poverty of choices and opportunities is often more relevant than the poverty of income, for it focuses on the causes of poverty and leads directly to strategies of empowerment and other actions to enhance opportunities for everyone. Recognising the poverty of choices and opportunities implies that poverty must be addressed in all its dimensions, not income alone.

For this reason, the *Human Development Report 1997* introduced a Human Poverty Index (HPI) in an attempt to bring together different features of deprivation in the quality of life to arrive at an aggregate judgement on the extent of poverty in a community. Rather than measure poverty by income alone, the HPI uses indicators of the most basic dimensions of deprivation: a short life, lack of basic education and lack of access to public and private resources.

The first deprivation relates to survival: the vulnerability to death at a relatively early age, as represented by the percentage of people expected to die before age 40. The second dimension relates to knowledge: being excluded from the world of reading and communication, measured by the percentage of adults who are illiterate. The third aspect relates to a decent standard of living, in particular, overall economic provisioning. This is represented by a composite of three variables: the percentage of people with access to health services and to safe water, and the percentage of malnourished children under five.

The Human Poverty Index can be used as an advocacy, a planning and a research tool. It can provide a measure of the incidence of human poverty in a country or region, reflecting the proportion of the population that is affected by the various forms of deficiency included in the measure. It can also serve a useful function as a planning tool for identifying areas of concentrated poverty within a country. It may be used, for instance, to rank districts as a guide to identifying those most severely disadvantaged in terms of human development. Although ranking by only one index would be possible, the HPI makes possible a ranking in relation to a combination of basic deprivations, not one alone. In this way, the HPI can provide a composite measure of development, in the same manner as the Human Development Index does.

An interesting insight into the nature of poverty as an entitlement failure is provided in the Lesotho study on urban poverty (Lesotho 1997). The study argues that urban dwellers face a number of specific problems that puts them in a particularly vulnerable position. These include:

- Dependence on money and commercial exchange for sustenance;
- High living costs in urban areas;
- Vulnerability to market forces;
- Erosion of support mechanisms and atomisation;
- Crime and insecurity, which affect the poor in disproportionate numbers.

Similar themes are discussed in the *Poverty Assessment Report* conducted in

Grenada, where poor respondents see the absence of marketable skills as a reason for their plight (Kairi 1998).

The qualitative information gathered in the Ugandan participatory studies sheds light on the temporal nature of poverty. People are shown to move in and out of poverty as well as between different levels of poverty. Timelines where events such as cattle raiding and the insurgencies and civil strife that characterised Uganda during the 1970s reveal the dynamic processes leading whole communities down the path to poverty. This is also well illustrated in the participatory assessment carried out in the Ugandan district of Kapchorwa, in which ill health or the loss of a family breadwinner is shown to enhance the vulnerability of every member of a household. These dynamics also extend across generations, in cases in which parents pass on limited assets, or indeed accumulated debt, to their children on their deaths (Uganda 1999b).

Participatory research also provides insights into the seasonality of poverty. Findings from Uganda show that disease becomes most prevalent at certain times of the year (between April and August), a period that coincides with the rainy season and is characterised by increased exposure to natural hazards. Food shortages, on the other hand, are more likely from March to July (Uganda 1999c). In the Gambia, too, poverty is most severe from March to May, after the harvest and trade season, and again from July to September, when food is short. This period corresponds to the time when people are intensively involved in planting and have no money to spare. Some 60 to 70 per cent of Gambian villagers are estimated to be poor around March, and the proportion climbs even further to as many as 90 per cent by September every year (Kayateh 1997b).

The time dimension of poverty is supported by findings from Lebanon's *Mapping of Living Conditions*, which used census and survey information rather than ethnographic data to examine the extent of deprivation in the country (Lebanon 1998). The report argues that protracted war and economic turmoil, including rampant inflation, have had such disruptive effects on people's lives as to imperil their capacity to generate sufficient incomes for a decent livelihood. This may explain the high levels of income poverty observed in Lebanon compared with other indicators of basic needs or unfulfilled capability, which appear to be less susceptible to political and economic influences, at least over the short term. It is probable, however, that both sets of indicators would tend to converge over the long run if negative conditions persist for a sufficient period of time. This is illustrated, for instance, by the worsening trend in educational indicators observed in Ethiopia (Ethiopia 1998).

The Maldives VPA (1998) uses self-reported change in household income to collect quantitative information on the dynamics of poverty by asking one household member (usually the person identified as head) to indicate whether their income has risen or dropped over a given time period. But this approach seems questionable, as the perceptions of the respondent might not reflect the views of other members of the household, which could result in confusion between household and per capita income.

The notions of assets and capabilities enrich the understanding of poverty as a relational phenomenon. Here the relationship is not only between different social actors, but also between the poor and the institutions with which they must engage in order to survive. Poverty in this framework is not simply about falling below some income threshold, but also about not having the abilities and assets from which poor people can derive a livelihood in the future.

Measuring poverty

The country surveys and assessments reviewed for this chapter experiment with a number of approaches to measuring poverty and vulnerability. In many cases, the analyses adopt an eclectic approach that combines different methods and indicators, often without assessing the respective advantages and shortcomings of each. As with the conceptualisation of poverty, the multiplicity of measurement tools that have been employed belies the idea of a shared consensus amongst experts on how poverty ought to be measured.

Money metric measures

Conventionally, the money metric approach to measurement requires setting a poverty line of some type. Poverty lines are used to separate the 'poor' from the 'non-poor'. They are based on some threshold expenditure deemed necessary to buy a minimum or socially acceptable standard of nutrition and other necessities (World Bank 1993). This expenditure varies between countries and is affected by local tastes and cultural norms. For this reason, country-specific poverty lines are normally used.

Critics of money metric measures argue that money provides only an indirect means for translating inputs into human development outcomes. Hence, measures that are focussed explicitly on outcomes should be used instead. While this is partly true, it is also the case that some of the direct means to wellbeing, such as food, clothing and shelter, are purchased with money. Besides, money metric measures are often preferred because they are useful for poverty comparisons (Ravallion 1993). By contrast, other methods and indicators, including the Human Development Index (HDI) developed by UNDP, are not as well suited to comparisons between individuals or households. Analyses that require quantification thus typically rely on a money metric approach, which explains why the latter has remained a useful, albeit imperfect, tool for poverty analysis.

The VPA (1998) prepared in the Maldives follows the conventional money metric approach to measurement using household consumption as a proxy for household income. The choice of consumption over income as the welfare indicator avoids problems of over-declared income from self-employment (where turnover is reported instead of profit), seasonal variation and under-reporting of income. Information is collected on a long list of consumer items and reported at the household level. This approach, which has been followed in many of the country studies sponsored by UNDP, implies the questionable assumption that households distribute their welfare equally between all members. In most cases, analysts recognise that this assumption is problematic and probably would be proven wrong if a detailed examination of intra-household distribution was carried out. But this is seldom possible, given the information required for such analysis and the limited research and data-gathering capacity in most of the countries reviewed.

In discussing how to set a poverty line, many studies recognised that local prices may vary by region. To overcome this problem, a regional purchasing power parities (PPP) approach was investigated for the Maldives. In the end, however, the approach was found to be impractical because many of the items in the typical consumption basket are not available in all parts of the country and, when they are, the quantity and quality of many of the items consumed vary widely from one island or atoll to the next. This lack of homogeneity precludes comparison on a countrywide basis. Only three items met the necessary criteria for calculating regional PPPs, but all three were imported from abroad with prices determined by the government (Maldives 1998).

Imputations for own production are another important methodological consideration for constructing a poverty line. Typically the local prices of purchased substitutes are used for this purpose. It is also necessary to impute the value of housing, especially where some communities obtain shelter through a housing market while others use natural resources to build their homes. However, in the absence of a developed housing market in most countries, especially in the areas where the poor reside (untitled land, squatter settlements, etc.), imputing the value of housing is virtually impossible (Deaton 1997). An innovative solution to this problem was found in the Maldives. Instead of imputing the cost of housing for non-urban households, rent payments were deducted from the expenditure of urban households in order to make them comparable with those areas in which no housing market exists. In the same vein, tax and insurance payments were excluded from the calculation of household expenditures in the household budget survey undertaken in Grenada, in view of the problems associated with the collection of such data (Kairi 1998).

Many countries set an upper and a lower poverty line in order to distinguish between the poor and the 'ultra-poor'. This approach was followed in both Lesotho and Palestine. In the case of the *Palestine Poverty Report* (1998), both lines were based on a basic basket of necessary goods, which were determined according to the value of spending on the basket relative to a certain percentile of the population. The first line (the 'deep' poverty line) was calculated to reflect a budget for food, clothing and housing. It was initially developed for a reference household comprising two adults and four children, which according to the data, represents the most typical Palestinian household. Actual spending patterns revealed by the household survey were used to determine the location of the poverty line, which was then adjusted to reflect the different conditions and consumption needs of households with a different composition. Adjusting for household size and composition was deemed necessary in order to account for the impact of scale economies in consumption. It was also intended to reflect more accurately the relative needs of children, which are argued to be more sensitive to the items included in the 'deep' poverty basket. The upper threshold was determined by adding necessities like health and personal care, education, transportation and housekeeping materials. Thus, while the first line is based on the consumption of items needed for survival, the second one includes consumption items that are thought to be required for a minimally adequate standard of living (Palestine 1998).

Two poverty thresholds were used in Grenada as well. An 'indigence line' was first constructed, using a basic consumption basket consisting of low-cost food items that are consistent with the dietary habits of the country's population. The prices of the items in the selected food basket were calculated using the consumer price index (CPI) of Grenada's Statistical Department. The market cost of the food basket per adult was then multiplied by the household adult equivalent value in order to set the indigence line. The upper poverty threshold was calculated by adding a non-food cost component to the lower line. Non-food expenditures include spending on clothing, medical expenses, transportation, rent and utilities, recreation and consumer durables. They were derived from calculating the food to non-food ratio of the two poorest quintiles of the income distribution scale. Finally, this figure was divided by the number of adult equivalents in the household and added to the threshold represented by the indigence line (Kairi 1998).

In some countries where income or expenditure data were not available, other variables believed to be associated with income were used instead. For instance, the MLC in Lebanon used the number of cars owned by a household and the number of working household members as proxies for income. A scoring system was developed to account for the occupations of each working member in the household.[1] Two other variables, ownership of property and school enrolment, were considered, but then excluded. It was felt that the first one only applied to a limited segment of the population, while the second was not representative due to the peculiar nature of the education system in Lebanon.

Deciding on a poverty threshold is only one step in poverty measurement. The next step involves the selection of the measures that are judged to convey most accurately the scale of the problem. Absolute measures have been used in most countries, whether as a money metric consumption line or some threshold level of services below which deprivation is believed to occur. The most frequently used measure is the headcount ratio, which reflects the proportion of people below the line in relation to the total population in a country. Only a few studies seem to be aware of the many problems associated with the headcount index, the most prominent of which derives from its failure to account for the extent of deprivation of those who are below the line.

Recognising the largely arbitrary nature of poverty measures based upon some specified poverty line, the Maldives VPA (1998) resorts to the notion of poverty dominance developed by Atkinson (1987), Foster and Shorrock (1988), and Jenkins and Lambert (1997). This analytical framework assesses whether the results of differing poverty lines are robust in the sense that the poor are consistently identified and ranked irrespective of the poverty line used.[2] In the case of Maldives, the poverty dominance approach is not applied exclusively to a money metric consumption line. Instead, the methodology is extended to include a composite index of poverty and vulnerability that was developed especially to suit the peculiar conditions of this environmentally fragile archipelago, as well as each of the twelve indicators that make up the index. The report further recognises the limitations of a simple headcount measure, and thus also provides estimates of the poverty gap index (PGI), which reflects the depth as well as the incidence of poverty.[3] Using this approach, the VPA is able to identify the poorest islands and atolls in the country and rank them according to various measures of wellbeing.

Likewise, the PPR carried out in Palestine (1999) also recognises implicitly the limitations of the headcount index, which it supplements with other measures to account both for the incidence, depth and severity of poverty. A number of interesting adaptations have been made in other counties as well. This was done, for instance, in Mozambique by decomposing the headcount ratio in much the same manner that is often done with the Gini coefficient. As a result of this decomposition, estimates of the proportion of women, children and elderly people living in poor homes are reported (Mozambique 1997).

Unfortunately, with the exception of Grenada, few countries have tried to measure inequality. This seems an important omission, especially given the fact that most studies devote great attention to the relational context of poverty. Latvia is one of the countries that explored an alternative approach to measurement. This was partly dictated by the fact that Latvia has no official poverty line. Three different lines were thus proposed in an attempt to solve this problem:

- A relative line set at 50 per cent of mean total monthly expenditure per capita, which is the lowest threshold and can been seen as an ultra-poverty line;
- A line set at the level of the official minimum wage of 1996, which is used as the threshold below which people are considered very poor;
- A line set at the crisis subsistence minimum as calculated by the Ministry of Welfare, which is the highest threshold (Gassman 1998).

The higher lines represent a form of rights-based measurement of poverty. They are based on official standards for social assistance or intervention. This certainly appears to be an area in which international research could assist in finding measures that can be readily applied to the context of data scarcity that prevails in most developing countries.

Measuring human capability

The earlier discussion suggests that poverty analysis should go beyond money metric measures of income or consumption. Dissatisfaction with money metric methods emanates from many sources. Firstly, people are normally reluctant to divulge information concerning their spending or income patterns. Of greater concern is the fact that many aspects of wellbeing are not acquired through market transactions, especially in developing countries. This applies, for instance, to a range of needs obtained from common property resources as well as to gifts and charity, which are an important ingredient in people's survival. Consequently, deprivation in these aspects may not be adequately accounted for. Finally, consumption-based measures reflect inputs to wellbeing rather than outcomes and therefore do not necessarily reveal an improvement or a deterioration in quality of life or capabilities (Lipton and Ravallion 1997).

This has led to a search for alternative forms of measurement in many countries. Emphasis is placed on measuring development outcomes directly by focussing on unfulfilled needs or capability shortfalls.[4] Many countries provide estimates of health status and educational achievement, both of which have a fundamental bearing on people's ability to lead a meaningful and productive life. Frequently used health indicators include the ratio of health facilities, hospital beds and health care workers to population, the infant mortality rate, and public expenditure on health as a proportion of GDP. Measures of educational status that are regularly reported include the number and type of school facilities, class size (number of students per classroom), student to teacher ratios, repetition and drop-out rates, and public expenditure on education as a share of GDP.

The *Human Development Report* prepared in Ethiopia reports on the high incidence of malaria and acute respiratory infections (tuberculosis, bronchopneumonia), and sends a warning to policy-makers by calling attention to the rising AIDS prevalence in the country (Ethiopia 1998). Access to health insurance schemes was reported in Lebanon and other countries, which also examined the coverage of publicly provided safety nets, especially in the area of health. Estimates of infant mortality rates (IMR), an important component for the calculation of life expectancy, are fraught with problems in many developing countries. This arises from the lack of reliability of their Vital Registration Systems, which tend to under-report the number of births and deaths of infants.

Box 3. Measuring development outcomes

Dissatisfied with the limitations of money metric methods of poverty measurement, many countries have sought to develop indicators for gauging deprivation and disparities in development outcomes directly. On the basis of the 1998 Mapping of Living Conditions conducted in Lebanon, the methodology can be said to involve the following steps:

■ Specification of the social outcomes where a lack of satisfaction is considered to be an indicator of deprivation;

■ Choice of indicators for measuring the extent of deprivation or satisfaction;

■ Definition of a threshold or benchmark against which the indicator can be compared to determine the presence and extent of deprivation;*

■ Specification of a measurement scale for each indicator in order to assign a score of relative deprivation to each unit of analysis (household, region, cluster);

■ Construction of an index for measuring deprivation of the composite group of social indicators;

■ Definition of a classification that divides the unit of analysis into categories according to the overall index score;

■ Examination of the distribution of the index across geographic location and social group.

The thresholds determined for social indicators may be more directly affected by social traditions, cultural norms and habits than is the case for money metric measures.

To overcome this problem, the Maldives VPA (1998) provided an alternative estimate of the country's IMR, collecting the information directly from respondents. The discrepancies between the official figures and the VPA (1998) results became a matter of concern for the health authorities, who realised the need to improve their data-gathering methods in order to obtain more accurate information for policy-making. This suggests that a direct method of estimating the IMR could be an acceptable option in other countries as well.

Another important innovation introduced in the Maldives is a system of weighted penalty points to account for the level of access of the population to various services, facilities and infrastructure, as well as their quality. A ranking was first established to reflect how adequate access to various services was. This was then weighted for each atoll by the proportion of households who report that they fall into this category of deprivation.[5] The indicators were then combined into composite indices for each of the twelve main human development dimensions that comprise the Human Vulnerability Index (HVI), the report's main innovation, which will be discussed later.

Only a few studies attempted to measure food security or nutritional status, although many provide data from secondary sources. The Maldives VPA used a self-declared approach to assess food insecurity, asking respondents whether they had experienced a food crisis in the previous year and, if they had, the duration of the crisis. Nutritional status was assessed directly through the use of conventional anthropometric measures of children between the ages of one and five.[6] Technical and vocational training was also rarely mentioned in most studies, despite its importance for development. The Ethiopia HDR discusses the problems of the teacher training system and examines the availability of training facilities and the qualifications of the teaching staff. In Lebanon, the ratio of students enrolled in vocation training compared to total enrolment is seen as indicating important shortcomings in the national education system. In both countries, there is a strong correlation between school enrolment and household earnings, as is the case in other countries.

Access to housing, credit and consumer durables is discussed in a handful of countries. The inclusion of credit is justified in light of the findings of numerous studies that have confirmed the relevance of micro-credit for small non-farm and farm enterprises. Lebanon's MLC uses the respective shares of total credit obtained by the largest and smallest borrowers as an indicator of the limited access of the poor to formal credit markets. Access to consumer durables is deemed to reflect overall levels of wellbeing in the Maldives, especially when the goods in question reduce drudgery or offer productive opportunities for their owners. Finally, access to housing is extremely valuable for many reasons. Apart from providing shelter and protection against the elements to its occupants, a house performs an important productive function for many low-income families, who typically engage in home-based income-generating activities. A house, furthermore, is an asset that can be mobilised in times of need, thereby providing a cushion against vulnerability. Conventional measures of access to housing are based on the amount of living space per person, but may also include access to outside private space such as a 'compound' (Maldives) or a terrace (Lebanon).

The participatory assessments conducted in Uganda highlight the importance of material as well as non-material factors in people's own perceptions of their situation. People value not only the material possession of physical assets, but also such intangibles as trust, solidarity and respect. It is therefore not surprising that the presence of stigma and the erosion of social support networks are seen as prime indicators of distress (Uganda 1999b). Another non-material dimension of wellbeing is recreation, which the Maldives VPA (1998) incorporates into the analysis on the grounds that the lack of recreation space is linked to overcrowding and limited privacy, factors that may inhibit the development of children and contribute to social problems. It is useful to note that these issues occupy a central place in the current formulations on the role of social capital in development.

Composite measures of poverty and vulnerability

Social indicators such as those discussed above may be combined to form a composite indicator of wellbeing. Many of these composite indicators are based on the Human Development Index (HDI) introduced by UNDP (1990). The HDI measures three basic dimensions of wellbeing: longevity, education attainment and standard of living. Conventionally, these are measured by life expectancy at birth, the weighted average of adult literacy (0.66) and gross enrolment ratios (0.33) and the Purchasing Power Parity of income equivalent in US dollars.

In most countries, the data for the construction of national HDIs are readily available. Sufficient information often also exists for estimating regional or state level HDIs.[7] Despite various criticisms of composite indices, they provide nonetheless a tool for setting priority goals for policy. In Ethiopia, a desired HDI has been projected as a benchmark for deriving the policy outcomes for health and education that would be required to achieve the projected level of development (Ethiopia 1998). In Nepal, district level HDIs are used as a basis for ranking all the districts of the country according to need. These rankings are then used as a means of targeting interventions and prioritising investments in the poorest localities (Nepal 1998).

It is commonly acknowledged, however, that broad composite indices such as the HDI or similar measures may be too general for a detailed analysis of policy issues in a country or region. For this reason, the Maldives developed a Human Vulnerability Index (HVI) to capture the country's peculiarities and inform policy makers accordingly. The HVI is a composite index consisting of twelve discrete components, some of which have more than one measurable indicator, which yields a total of 40 indicators of deprivation. These components are further grouped into various categories that relate to physical and social infrastructure, housing and the environment[8] (Maldives 1998).

In Lebanon, a Living Conditions Index was developed explicitly as a measure of unsatisfied material basic needs (Lebanon 1998). The index has four components that, in many ways, are similar to the vulnerability index of the Maldives. The four components are:

- Housing indicators, which include the principal means of heating the homestead;
- Water and sewerage indicators;
- Education indicators;
- Income indicators, including a number of proxy measures such as ownership of cars.

The household level information collected in Lebanon was processed in such a manner as to obtain both the mean scores and the standard deviations for each of the four components of the Living Conditions Index. This is very useful because it makes it possible to assess the distribution of satisfaction for every living standard dimension. Analysis of the data shows, for instance, that education has the highest degree of dispersion in Lebanon. This is linked to the escalating costs of education as a result of the diminishing role of public provision. Another possible enhancement to the basic need measures, which was applied in the Maldives, is to calculate the depth of deprivation for specific dimensions as the difference between the specified threshold level and the score obtained by individual households.

Household size is a central issue in basic need measurement and poverty analysis. Larger households in Lebanon tend to be concentrated in the lower categories of the Living Conditions Index. This finding is similar to results obtained using money metric measures, despite common reservations among specialists concerning the use of households as the main unit of analysis in poverty studies. At the same time, small households comprised of elderly people living alone also scored low in the Living Conditions Index. The occupational category of the head of household is another defining feature. A higher proportion of household heads engaged in agriculture, domestic service and unskilled labour are in the households with the lowest scores (Lebanon 1998).

The notion of household headship as collected in most surveys has been under question for some time (Hedman 1996; Rosenhouse 1989). Typically, the head is defined as the person regarded as such by members of the family. In reality, however, it is quite possible that this person may not be the principal decision-maker in the family. Traditions, customs and family relationships often play an important role in determining who is nominated. This may conceal many cases in which women exercise the role of main providers and heads, even if they are not regarded as such.

It is not easy to overcome this problem with standard survey techniques, but the one conducted in Maldives for the VPA (1998) deliberately tried to explore the issue of female-headed households by probing for the reasons why women were nominated as heads. Furthermore, marriage and divorce have a prominent place under Sharia law, which permits polygamy, but may stigmatise women who are divorced. For this reason, the VPA places a greater emphasis on conjugality than might be the case where the legal marital status of women is less important. Nevertheless, a similar situation may arise in other societies as well, in which men continue to influence the ability of women to work, acquire land or control their own fertility.

In order to investigate whether there are any differences in perceived needs according to gender, the Maldives VPA ranked priority needs separately for women and men along five dimensions. These are: (1) education and literacy; (2) marriage and divorce; (3) health and nutrition; (4) employment; and (5) women's priorities. Interestingly, there were only marginal differences in the ranking of needs, indicating that female respondents did not differ much in their views from their male counterparts.

The previous points underscore the significance of taking into account social and cultural factors when assessing wellbeing and deprivation. This was done in Lesotho, where an effort was made to gather information on non-material needs.

Respondents were asked about their perceptions of the strength of community and family ties, and their level of understanding of the local political context. The first was taken as an indication of social isolation, while the second one was intended to reflect political isolation and powerlessness. Interestingly, although most respondents were knowledgeable about their basic rights and legal services available to them, they knew little about the responsibilities of the government or the public services from which they could benefit. Political isolation was indeed related to wealth disparities, as demonstrated by the fact that those earning an above average income were much more aware of the government system than the poor and ultra-poor (Lesotho 1997).

Composite indicators result from the combination of various discrete components. An important methodological problem, therefore, arises from the need to apply a weighting system to the individual components when combining them to form the index. Conventionally, equal weighting has been used, as in the case of the HDI (UNDP 1990). Alternatively, arbitrary values can be assigned to each component, so as to reflect their relative relevance based on some underlying theory. In Lebanon's MLC (1998), indicators are first converted to a standardised score. Then, the scores of the various indicators are aggregated in order to obtain the arithmetic mean value for each of the four components of the Living Conditions Index. Finally, the index is derived from its four components, as the arithmetic mean of their respective scores. This means that although a household may have extremely unsatisfactory access to one or more component of the index (e.g. water or sanitation), it may still obtain a high aggregate score if it ranks highly in the other components (e.g. income or education).[9]

An interesting alternative was followed in the Maldives VPA (1998), which used the perceived priorities of respondents as the weighting factor for the construction of the Human Vulnerability Index. The weighting process was used to rank the relative importance of the different components of the index. This process was carried out in a gender-disaggregated manner, showing the priority rankings of men and women separately and then combining both on the basis of the proportion of the total population made up by each sex. Thus, the rankings are not only reported separately for men and women, but also as a combined score (Maldives 1998).

Employment, unemployment and underemployment

Productive employment, or lack of it, is a crucial determinant of vulnerability and poverty. Countries normally track the evolution of various indicators, of which the most common are labour force participation rates, unemployment rates, women's share of the labour force, and sectoral breakdowns of employment.

The VPA (1998) estimates labour force participation as a percentage of all persons above 12 years of age, compared to the standard of 15 to 64 years of age used in conventional definitions of the labour force (e.g. in the 1998 Ethiopia HDR). The VPA also draws attention to the fact that many poor people have more than one job and often 'commute' between different sectors. The main activity of those who are employed is therefore used as the basis for estimating sectoral shares. The type of employment can also be used as an indicator of deprivation, if certain activities are deemed to be associated with hardship. In essence, this implies a segmented labour market approach in which some occupations are deemed to be less well paid, secure or skilled than others. This approach was followed in Lebanon (1998).

It is worth mentioning that, in order to arrive at estimates of unemployment, the VPA survey adopted a different methodology from the one used for the national census. The conventional definition of unemployment specifies a time period during which respondents must have looked for a job before being categorised as unemployed. Where labour markets are not well organised, however, this definition is bound not to reflect adequately the size of the unemployment problem or its characteristics. Lebanon's MLC, for instance, reports that many job-seekers give up an active search for employment in despair of finding work. For this reason, many of the studies reviewed here were reluctant to follow conventional usage, and searched instead for alternative ways of measuring unemployment.

The situation in the Maldives provides a poignant example of the inadequacy of the standard definition, due to the significant costs of job search from isolated areas. Thus, the survey dropped the reference period, and instead probed for the reasons why a person did not work. People were classified as unemployed if they indicated that they were not working at present or would be available for work if they could get a job, but were unable to find a suitable one (Maldives 1998). Definitions of unemployment have also been refined to indicate long-term unemployment (more than one year) as well as job-seekers who had never before worked (for example, Lebanon 1998, and Mozambique 1997).

In a number of instances, attempts were made to record the prevalence of underemployment as well. Underemployment indicates the availability of additional productive capacity among the working population, and can be an important factor affecting the vulnerability of household livelihoods. It is conventionally expressed in terms of time (e.g. working less than a predetermined number of hours) or productivity (e.g. the existence of productivity rates below a predetermined benchmark). The Maldives VPA (1998) defined as underemployed a person who works less than 35 hours per week or 11 months per year. This, nonetheless, must be qualified, since not all those who work less than 35 hours weekly would want to increase their working hours, and therefore could be regarded as part-time workers instead.

The share of wages in gross domestic product may also be taken as indicative of increased vulnerability, arising from growing unemployment, falling wages and the informalisation of employment. The share of wages in Lebanon has experienced a considerable decline over a 20-year period. This secular decline is interpreted as being a major contributor to poverty in the country (Lebanon 1998).

Conflict, disabilities and poverty

Another complex issue brought out in several studies relates to the hardship that results from disability due to war. In Mozambique, for example, it is estimated that there are one million physically handicapped people, many of whom were directly injured during the war or by land mines (Mozambique 1997). Besides the direct impact upon the victims, these injuries have increased the vulnerability of the households in which the victims reside by reducing the labour that is available to the household, while simultaneously increasing the care required by dependent members. Disabilities also arise from the health problems associated with poverty (such as tuberculosis), from malnutrition (rickets) and from the hazardous work that the poor often perform.

A related issue, also raised in Mozambique, is the vulnerability of children, especially those who resort to living on the street in response to conflict, including domestic conflict in the home. Amongst other issues, the risk of AIDS transmission rises when these children resort to prostitution in order to survive, as is the risk of drug and substance abuse.

Instruments for measuring poverty

In this section we look at the instruments and tools used to collect information on various aspects of poverty. Countries have resorted to both conventional household surveys and participatory forms of poverty analysis. We are particularly interested in cases in which data from different sources have been combined in order to yield new insights and perspectives into the analysis.

Official statistics

Census data provide a valuable source of information for the computation of various measures of wellbeing and access to services. Data from the national censuses were used extensively in Ethiopia, Lebanon, Maldives and Mozambique. In Lebanon, information from the health and demographic census was utilised to weight the indicators and components of the Living Conditions Index, while in Maldives official statistics were used to rank the islands as well as to calculate deprivation ratios. Although none of the studies mentions the many shortcomings frequently encountered in the collection of census data, problems with vital registration statistics were a subject of controversy in Maldives. The VPA team, in fact, found much higher levels of infant mortality compared to the official statistics collected by the Department of Health. This in itself is not a surprising finding, since undercounting of infant deaths is common in many countries. What is noteworthy is that the government was open to discussing the discrepancies and finally accepted the methodology proposed by the VPA team (Maldives 1998).

Official statistics are also important for ongoing poverty monitoring. In Gambia, the National Poverty Monitoring framework envisages the use of administrative records from the public sector (central administration, local governments and state-owned enterprises), supplemented by the records generated by non-governmental organisations. The latter includes the schools, hospitals and clinics run by charitable organisations (Gambia 1997).

Household surveys

Information obtained from a number of household and sector specific surveys was a major component in most of the PSI studies. In particular, household budget surveys were used to calculate money metric measures of poverty, while child and maternal health surveys provided anthropometric and other data for estimating mortality rates. Labour force surveys have also been an important database.

The living standards measurement surveys (LSMS) are a derivative of the household sample survey based on large, multipurpose questionnaires administered to households selected via a probability sampling methodology (Grosh and Muñoz 1996). Promoted by the World Bank, LSMS typically contain some measure of wellbeing based on income or consumption data, as well as standardised modules on demographic composition, access to services and employment. An interesting sampling modification to the standard LSMS design was tested in Lesotho, where the research team isolated and conducted additional interviews with specially designated vulnerable groups. These included street children, informal traders, piece job workers, construction workers and retrenched miners. People in these categories were approached at work, at shelters or in areas that they were known to frequent (Lesotho 1997). While there may be some problems with the methodology adopted in Lesotho, the notion of an approach that targets specific sub-groups of the poor does have considerable merit.

Another interesting methodological innovation was used in Latvia (Trapenciere et al. 2000). The survey design was premised on a purposive sampling methodology. All the communities in Latvia were first ranked along a scale of high to low living standards in a manner that represents the different local economies, extent of urbanisation, geography, social structure and demographics of the various areas. The ranking was undertaken according to four categories: average earnings per capita, retail turnover per capita, number of cars, and number of telephones per 1,000 people. This exercise led to the determination of three 'welfare regions'. Interviews were then administered to poor people in the capital, main cities, towns and rural areas within each of these three regions. Municipalities and parishes in selected districts of the three regions were chosen so as to reflect the country's diversity. The interviews were clustered around municipalities to enable an examination of community relationships and dynamics within certain areas. The households interviewed were chosen according to factors such as age and sex of household head, ethnicity, marital status, nationality, and education. Based on existing poverty data, special efforts were made to include large numbers of pensioners, disabled people, unemployed, families with children, orphans, former prisoners and other categories of people presumed to be at greater disadvantage.

Other useful methodological adaptations included:

- Conducting the 1996-1997 Palestinian Expenditure and Consumption Survey over twelve months to avoid seasonal variation (NPA 1999).

- Using multiple-stage sampling techniques, whereby certain areas and groups are purposively selected to ensure that highly vulnerable, but often hard to reach groups such as the homeless, are included. Apart from Latvia, this approach was followed in Grenada, where the size of the household was used to stratify the sample, based on the assumption that the poor households as a rule are larger (Kairi 1998).

- Using census data to elaborate profiles of the clusters in which sampling will take place, and integrating these data into the analysis (Lebanon 1998; Maldives 1998).

- Combining specially designed household surveys administered by official statistical agencies with the data generated by surveys carried out by various government departments. In Gambia, for instance, the Central Statistics Department, as well as the ministries of Agriculture and Health, which collect poverty relevant information on a regular basis through the National Agricultural Sample Survey and the National Nutritional Surveillance Survey, were all included as important sources of data (Gambia 1997).

Participatory poverty assessments

Participatory rural appraisal methodologies (PRA) draw upon various traditions of research, including applied anthropology, participatory action research, rapid rural appraisal, and agro-ecosystems analysis. Although the origins of the methodology are predominantly rural and generally related to participatory planning of natural resource management, they are increasingly used in a wide variety of contexts, including urban and poverty research. The methodology places a great emphasis on local people acting as analysts rather than as informants, while outsiders serve merely as facilitators. Instead of interviewing specific individuals, group contexts are used, with visual sharing of information and methods for ensuring that weaker or marginal members of communities are empowered to participate in the research process (Chambers 1994a, 1994b, 1994c).

Qualitative research methodologies were used for example in Uganda, where a series of Participatory Poverty Assessments were carried out applying a standard case study approach with a combination of PRA and other techniques. These included unstructured or semi-structured interviews of key informants, participant observation, focus group discussions and PRA tools such as resources, social and mobility mapping, time lines, wellbeing rankings, transect walks, and gender matrices (Uganda 1998a, 1998b, 1998c).

In Grenada, the poverty assessment carried out in 1998 applied a combination of quantitative survey and qualitative participatory methods. To select the communities for the national survey, all villages in Grenada were ranked based on a living conditions index developed from the 1991 census. Villages were then classified and given a value according to a ratio of 'met' to 'unmet' needs for all the households in a village. This ratio was then normalised to produce a percentage for each village, and the villages were ranked accordingly. Using this ranking and other secondary information available, the twenty poorest communities were selected along with two communities that had managed to escape from poverty. These communities were then interviewed using a Survey of Living Conditions questionnaire to generate the information required for the selection of the final 14 communities that took part in the participatory component of the study. The households to be interviewed were chosen on the basis of systematic random sampling, and workshops were run with these households in each of the survey communities. During these workshops, which applied a full range of PRA tools and techniques, people were given the opportunity to describe and analyse the type, level and degree of poverty that exists in their communities. This allowed the views and perceptions of the locals to be fed into and combined with the results of a national survey, so as to obtain a more thorough understanding of the poverty situation in the country (Kairi 1998).

A number of problems were identified with the application of the PRA approach. The reliance on translation from local languages was a frequently encountered difficulty as field researchers, including nationals, often were unable to speak all of the local languages. This may have resulted in a loss of important information, or of nuances in the views offered by the community. The representation of minority views proved to be difficult in most cases. The attendance of women and youth, for instance, was often reported to be poor. Even when they attended, they did not in many cases participate fully in the PRA sessions.

This problem relates to a frequently reported lack of clarity about the nature and dynamics of 'participation'. Concerns include the failure to account for issues of local-level power that inevitably shape the outcome of these exercises, the danger that dominant views are interpreted as universally accepted within a community, or the assumption that those present at a meeting are the true representatives of the community. All of these issues can mask critical differences and conflicts that may exist within communities and households.

Furthermore, PRA techniques appear to be difficult to undertake in urban settings due to the 'heterogeneity and business mindedness of urban dwellers' (Lesotho 1997). Participants from urban settings were reported to be unwilling to devote the time required for the PRA exercises and, in some instances, seemed to object to the type of methodology being followed. In general, PRA was characterised as time-consuming, especially when there was a heavy reliance on visualisation techniques (Kayateh 1997b).

Spatial measurement and mapping

A number of studies have attempted to incorporate a spatial representation of poverty. This provides a valuable tool for informing governments' as well as donors' decisions for prioritising interventions and targeting investments to specially deprived areas. The National Programme for Social Action, Employment and Youth of Mozambique is a good example of how social and economic goals can be integrated, while retaining the local political context of development. The programme identifies specific target groups and priority areas, where it seeks to integrate its three components (social assistance, employment creation, and youth) with a view to making its interventions in support of the designated target groups

Box 4. The Spatial Development Index of Mozambique

As part of the pilot phase of the implementation of a National Integrated Programme for Social Action, Employment and Youth, an index was developed to assess the potential of each of the country's provinces. The main components of the index are:

- Economic potential, comprising four indices that reflect the material base of the province, its economic potential, population stability and food security, respectively.
- Access, comprising three indices, respectively of access to the province, road conditions and removal of land mines.
- Institutional means, comprising census data on selected occupation categories, availability of training centres and distribution of governance structures.
- District development, based on a composite indicator of infrastructure.
- Community collaboration, based on the involvement of handicapped children in a community service programme, the distribution of community run schools, and experience in community collaboration.
- Donors and international NGOs, based on the distribution of such institutions and their projects.
- Mozambican associations based on the distribution of local organisations working in social action and credit provision.

more effective. Using secondary data, a geographic strategy was developed for the implementation of the pilot phase of the programme. The strategy utilises a Spatial Development Index, which is based on seven indicators, some of which themselves are composite indices (Thompson 1998).

In Maldives, both the composite index of vulnerability and its 12 discrete components have been mapped into an Atlas using a Geographic Information System (GIS). The Atlas depicts the atolls that are most in need, as well as the nature of their need (Maldives 1998).[10] Similarly, all of Lebanon's districts (*mohafazats*) and settlements (*kadas*) were ranked according to the aggregate score of the Living Conditions Index of households in the area. Once again, the components of the aggregated index are depicted geographically, and the distribution of the population is overlaid onto the index in order to show the scale of deprivation by region (Lebanon 1998).

Multiple techniques and triangulation

One important aspect of many studies lies in the use of multiple approaches and techniques for analysing poverty. Researchers drew on a mix of primary and secondary data, adopted a broad range of conceptual frameworks, and made great efforts to combine quantitative and qualitative research methodologies. With varying degrees of success, the results of these multiple techniques were compared and triangulated in an attempt to corroborate or refute findings obtained with the use of particular research instruments.

The poverty assessment report of Grenada provides an interesting example of the successful use of multiple assessment techniques. The study consisted of three components. First, a national survey of living conditions was carried out to obtain quantitative information on the country's households. This was supplemented by a community situational analysis, which collected qualitative information from 14 communities. Finally, in-depth interviews were conducted with representatives of a number of governmental and non-governmental organisations and agencies operating in different spheres of economic and social life (Kairi 1998).

Latvia combined different quantitative techniques on the basis of three measurement instruments, two of which were applied to each household in the sample (Gassmann and de Neubourg, 2000). First, all Latvian households were interviewed, using a poverty survey that consisted of four modules. The first part asked about perceived changes in standards of living since the country's independence; the second one about the coping strategies adopted by each household; the third asked about social assistance services; and the last section about education of children, health and related issues. In addition to the national household survey, a household questionnaire following a LSMS format was administered to roughly one third of the sample, in conjunction with a consumption diary. Then a recall survey was conducted with approximately two thirds of the sample. This survey included a questionnaire identical to the previous one, with a recall component substituted for the diary, in which informants were asked to recall the value and quantity of food and non-food items bought or received over the period of one month.

This is taken further in a proposal for the establishment of a poverty monitoring system in the Gambia, which recommends the collection of qualitative information to complement the quantitative data that will be generated by various government departments. The type of qualitative information to be collected using audio recordings, as well as other techniques, includes the perceived value of formal education, household perceptions of food security, and people's attitudes towards the environment (Gambia 1997). Given that the proposed monitoring system will rely on triangulating information from various government agencies, it seems that a coordinating body will be necessary to ensure the smooth functioning of the system. This body could also serve as a focal point or clearinghouse for contacts with other actors, since gathering information from non-governmental organisations is likely to be difficult unless they know with whom they are supposed to interact in government.[11]

Despite the obvious advantages of triangulating information obtained from multiple sources, several studies acknowledge that analysing and integrating the results of different research techniques is difficult, especially given the lack of coordination and capacities that characterises many countries. This problem suggests that this form of experimentation needs to be approached with care. Triangulation itself can lead to contradictory results, rather than providing supporting information from different sources. Resolving these contradictions then becomes an important challenge in itself.

Conclusions

Despite some important commonalities among national studies, it is far from clear that a consensus on how poverty should be conceptualised and measured is emerging. The efforts in many countries to adapt and expand upon standard definitions and methodologies belie the notion of a budding consensus. Usage of poverty lines and income proxies is quite widespread. But at the same time, there is a much larger concern for the relationships and dynamics of poverty than is suggested by the international literature. This concern is informed by a desire to reflect local realities more accurately than conventional definitions would allow. Emphasis is placed on understanding the social and relational dimensions of poverty, as well as the wider determinants of capability fulfilment, which money metric measures do not convey adequately. As the limits of economic definitions and measures are recognised, there is a corresponding search for viable alternatives.

The studies reviewed in this chapter have opened a window on some important but neglected analytical issues. Perhaps the single most relevant issue concerns the exclusion and isolation that accompanies poverty. Studies in extremely diverse situations note the loss of social contact, humiliation and stigma experienced by the poor. This has both a social and economic impact, cutting the poor off from opportunities and support. This dimension of poverty has received little attention from international agencies, although concepts of social exclusion have had a long history in poverty research in the industrialised countries. In view of our findings, it appears that similar analyses seem warranted in developing countries as well.

A second important theme relates to the impact of war and conflict. The risk of exposure to violence is a valuable modification to current conceptualisations of poverty, which have tended to focus on its economic dimensions to the neglect of the political circumstances that lead to hardship. Our findings from national studies are a forceful reminder that a large proportion of the poor are affected directly or indirectly by conflict, which implies the need for integrating the political context into the analysis of poverty. In addition to the physical hardship associated with war, conflict typically results in a shattering loss of assets, massive displacement and constrained economic opportunities for vast numbers of people. Conflict also results in serious damage to infrastructure, collapse of social service provision and under-investment in major economic sectors.

Given the relevance of safety and security for the conceptualisation of poverty, it appears that more research into these issues is needed. At present, the analysis of the problems is underdeveloped in many countries, compared to the severity and resilience of conflict. A closer linkage with the issue of ethnicity also seems warranted, as ethnicity not only is a major dimension in conflict, but also often overlays closely with the distribution of poverty. The addition of a conflict indicator, such as gunshot mortalities per capita, into an HDI based index could therefore be of great value by highlighting regions in which lack of safety may contribute significantly to poverty.

Two other issues in which further analysis seems justified are gender and AIDS. Both are covered in some of our studies, but not sufficiently. Gender issues are sometimes subsumed into an assessment of female-headed households, but this overlooks the situation of the majority of women in most countries. Furthermore, while abundant research has questioned the usefulness of the notion of headship for poverty analysis, none of the studies reviewed here echoes this concern. An area of further inquiry, which could benefit greatly from support from donor agencies, relates to the development of innovations in the analysis of the gendered dimension of poverty. These might include an examination of intra-household bargaining and decision-making processes, as well as the distribution of resources and income flows within households.

With regard to AIDS and its impact on poverty, future analyses need to ensure that apart from reporting on its prevalence, an effort will be made to identify the second level effects of infection. These would include both the macroeconomic and microeconomic consequences of AIDS, including its impact on labour markets, health spending, loss of productive labour, AIDS orphans, and the time required to care for infected people.

Our findings also reveal that there is a fair amount of experimentation in relation to the methodologies employed for the measurement, analysis and interpretation of poverty data. In an attempt to capture the multidimensional nature of poverty, most studies have tried to combine different data sources (censuses, household budget surveys, maternal and child health surveys, participatory community assessments, etc.) into the analysis and, in a few instances, into the establishment of an integrated poverty information system. Macroeconomic and fiscal data have been combined with information about social service facilities and infrastructure, to allow for a comparison between financial inputs and human development outcomes. Efforts have also been made to depict the spatial distribution of poverty and vulnerability in a few countries, for example by ranking atolls (Maldives) or districts (Lebanon) according to their level of deprivation.

The integration and standardisation of multiple data sources seems worth supporting. Further experimentation needs to be encouraged, as the new insights that emerge often are invaluable. International agencies should consider the possibility of providing technical and financial assistance to countries for the integration of databases on various aspects of poverty and deprivation. In some instances, this might require the development or dissemination of software packages that convert data into different formats, or that edit data fields to assist the merging of data sets.

However, care must be taken to ensure that standardisation does not obscure the specific circumstances of poverty in individual countries. In search of synthetic measures, many countries have development composite indices following the example of the Human Development Index introduced by UNDP in 1990. However, attempts to capture the multidimensionality of poverty with the help of composite indices have often been vitiated by the problem of arbitrary weighting of its components. In some cases, the individual components that make up a composite index are not well correlated, suggesting that they may refer to aspects of poverty that affect different groups in many diverse ways. While this need not be a serious problem when those indicators are reported separately, critical differences may be concealed when they are combined into a composite index. For this reason, rigorous testing is required if these measures are to be used as a reliable and unambiguous source of information on which policy decisions will be based.

Most importantly, development agencies must be willing to invest in creating a sustainable research infrastructure in developing countries, with the purpose of enabling them to carry on the statistical, analytical and policy work related to poverty after the withdrawal of external support. Statistics in many of these countries are often incomplete, inconsistent and of poor quality. Consequently, building national capacity for the collection, processing and interpretation of official statistics is an important first step for adequate policy analysis and monitoring to occur.

Mechanisms are also needed to ensure that local researchers are equally equipped to make use of the data, whether in universities, non-governmental organisations or government agencies. Only in this manner will it be possible to ensure that the results of the analytical work carried out by the statistical offices is integrated into processes of public debate and advocacy. This, in turn, will improve the prospects for reabsorbing those results into the design and implementation of policies for poverty reduction. ■

Notes

Julian May is Director of the Population and Poverty Studies Programme, School of Development Studies, University of Natal, Durban. He would like to thank Alejandro Grinspun, Rasheda Selim and Siddiq Osmani for their comments on an earlier version of this chapter.

[1] Different types of occupation were assigned different scores. Senior officials in the government and the private sector were given the maximum score of 2, while unskilled workers were given a score of 0.5. Each individual in the household was given a score, and a mean calculated for the total household. While this methodology may be useful in the cases in which no income data is available, the scoring process used in Lebanon seems unrelated to the scale of salary differentials across occupational categories. Moreover, a strong case can be made for using the maximum score of the household values rather than the mean.

[2] One of the advantages of the poverty dominance theory is that it relies on a sensitivity analysis using a low, medium and high poverty line to test the ranking of whatever unit of analysis is chosen (atolls in the case of the Maldives). These are then mapped onto cumulative distribution frequencies of the chosen indicator. If the frequencies of the indicators for different groups do not intersect below the maximum possible poverty line, then one group can be definitively considered to be poorer than the others. Second order dominance tests can be used if the cumulative distribution frequencies do intersect below the maximum possible poverty line (Foster and Shorrock 1988; Maldives 1998).

[3] The poverty gap index (PGI) is obtained by multiplying the headcount measure by the average income shortfall of the poor (i.e. the distance below the poverty line). This is one of a class of poverty measures known as the FGT set of measures, after the names of the economists Foster, Greer and Thorbecke (Foster et al. 1984). A possible extension of the composite threshold approach followed in the Maldives would have been to square the PGI in order to give greater weight to areas in which poverty is deepest. This method follows the logic of the FGT approach that underpins much of the analysis undertaken in many of the studies sponsored by UNDP. With the exception of Grenada, however, refinements of this kind were not explored

in any of the countries under review.

[4] One example is the capability poverty measure (CPM), an index developed by UNDP that is composed of three indicators that reflect the percentage of the population with capability short-falls in three basic dimensions of human development. The three dimensions refer to people's capacity to live a healthy and well-nourished life, to have access to safe and healthy reproduction, and to be literate and knowledgeable. The CPM differs from the HDI in that it focuses on people's lack of capabilities, rather than on the average level of capabilities in a country (UNDP 1996).

[5] For example, the presence of households without electricity results in a penalty of one point, which is then weighted by the percentage of households who report that they do not have elec-tricity. In some instances, such as transport, the indicator used affects the entire population in an island. As a result, the penalty points are effectively weighted by 100 per cent (Maldives 1998).

[6] Wasting and stunting are considered to exist when observations fall outside of two standard deviations from the distribution applicable to the world's population. General malnutrition is expressed in terms of low weight for age. Chronic malnutrition is reflected in a low height for age (stunting or linear growth retardation), while acute malnutrition corresponds to a low weight for height (wasting), which could be the result of a recent illness rather than malnutrition.

[7] In cases in which some data for calculating regional or state indices are missing, a common solution has been to use an amount that is constant and equal to the national figure. This has been the case, for instance, with the income component of the HDI, where sub-national infor-mation is often unavailable. This seems, nonetheless, to be a reasonable option in low-income countries, in which social indicators tend to make the largest contribution to the index.

[8] To some extent, the methodology adopted in the *Vulnerability and Poverty Assessment* of the Maldives rests on rests on the Basic Needs approach. Such basic needs may be thought of as comprising material and non-material needs, with clean water and primary education as exam-ples of the former, and political and judicial rights as examples of the latter. Composite indices developed from these basic needs indicators are in many respects similar to other social indi-cators, although attention is specifically placed on a bundle of core needs where lack of satis-faction is considered to provide an indication of poor living conditions. An important advan-tage of a basic needs indicator over other composite measures is that it can be calculated at the household level, and need not require cluster or regional level data. Unsatisfied basic needs mapping also has the potential to feed more directly into sector policy analysis.

[9] Nevertheless, the relatively low correlations found between the components of Lebanon's Living Conditions Index are a cause for concern. Only the education and income indicators show a Pearson's correlation coefficient greater than 0.3, suggesting that the different dimen-sions of the poverty index are largely unrelated. A further problem derives from combining indicators of goods or services that are publicly provided, like water supply, with those that require both public and private action (e.g., educational attainment requires schools, the abil-ity to meet the costs of education, and willingness to learn).

[10] The VPA calls for further analysis of its data set. Specifically, it recommends the use of mul-tivariate techniques to explore correlations and possible causal linkages between the many

variables that have been calculated, which would further enhance the preparation of intervention strategies. The report also calls for content analysis of the many open-ended questions asked during the household and cluster level surveys. Finally, it notes the existence of other datasets for the Maldives, and recommends their integration into a national Geographic Information System.

[11] Available capacity is very limited in the Gambia. While indigenous capacity is built, therefore, it is proposed that small ad hoc surveys be conducted by donor agencies and non-governmental organisations as a stopgap for information. Furthermore, in the interest of limiting the costs of data collection, it is also proposed to limit surveys to particularly impoverished areas to be identified using the results of the 1993 Household Economic Survey.

CHAPTER 3 Private Adjustments: Households, crisis and work

Mercedes González de la Rocha and Alejandro Grinspun

C hanges in the labour market have led to the erosion of work and a growth of informality in many countries. These developments, combined with cutbacks in public provision of social benefits and services, have forced households to organise their labour, time and other resources so as to protect and, if possible, increase their consumption. Their capacity to adapt and ward off vulnerability varies with factors such as household size, composition, and its stage in the domestic cycle. Many cope admirably, in no small measure because of strategies devised by women. However, the pressures faced by millions of poor households are stretching these capacities to their limits. Short-term coping strategies cannot totally offset the consequences of economic change. In some cases, they may even undermine a household's ability to recover and move permanently from vulnerability to self-sufficiency. There are increasing signs of breakdown in family and community support systems, along with social isolation, alcoholism and drug abuse, all of which should seriously concern policy-makers.

This chapter is based on a review of a sample of country studies financed by United Nations Development Programme (UNDP) from 1997 to 1999.[1] Drawing lessons from these studies is fraught with methodological problems. First, the review covers a highly heterogeneous group of countries, ranging from small island economies to the fourth most populous nation in the world. Second, few of the reports offer the kind of ethnographic material that permits detailed exploration of the coping strategies and livelihoods of the poor. In addition, the time period, quality of data, analytical approaches and methodologies differ from one study to another, precluding close comparability. These limitations notwithstanding, the studies contain a wealth of information on household responses to economic and social transformation.

The chapter is organised in five sections. The first demonstrates that wage income constitutes a major element of poor people's livelihoods and presents cross-country evidence of a growing deterioration of wages and work conditions. The second section discusses a number of factors that impinge upon the capacity of households to respond effectively to those changes. It also analyses the differential impact of change on individual household members, showing how declining livelihood opportunities typically impose unequal costs and burdens. Section three analyses a range of domestic responses undertaken by poor households that have been forced to undergo private adjustments in order to cope. The final section highlights the importance of social exchange and reciprocity networks for people's survival, but calls attention to the crumbling of such networks under the pressures of poverty.

Household resources and economic opportunities

The innovative strategies and resourcefulness that poor people use to survive economic change derive largely from 'private' initiatives implemented at the household and community levels. Labour plays a critical role.[2]

Work needs to be considered in all its forms — formal wage employment, informal work for cash, unpaid labour and subsistence production — because all of these permit individuals and households to mobilise their labour power so as to secure their livelihood. Even in countries where subsistence livelihoods prevail, wage employment is a crucial element for survival. Indeed, wages make the largest contribution to household income in countries that range from Latvia — where wages account for over 60 per cent of total household income — to Grenada, where most households derive their earnings from either wages or self-employment in small-scale agriculture and the services sector (Kairi 1998; Gassmann 2000). In Lebanon, where wage earners make up more than two thirds of the labour force, the majority of the poor also depend on wages or are self-employed (Lebanon 1998).

It is not surprising, then, that poverty is often closely associated with unemployment and low wages. Wage trends are the single most important factor explaining changes in wellbeing in Bulgaria (1998a), while in Latvia households whose main breadwinner is looking for a job face the highest poverty risk[3] (Gassmann 2000). In Palestine, too, the poverty incidence of households whose members are not in the labour force amounts to 33 per cent. By contrast, full-time employment is the strongest indicator that a household is unlikely to be poor[4] (Palestine 1998). There is also a strong association between unemployment and low satisfaction of basic needs in Lebanon (1998), while in Angola employment makes the largest positive contribution to consumption levels, especially in households with working wives (Wold and Grave 1999).

Even where formal wage employment is scarce, labour still constitutes the main asset of the poor. Like other household resources, labour does not exist in a vacuum. What matters is people's ability to convert those resources into assets that can lessen vulnerability and improve wellbeing. Vulnerability can result from a change in the amount or quality of the resources a household possesses, or in the opportunities it faces — or both. Understanding vulnerability thus requires focussing simultaneously on the characteristics of households, their endowment of resources, and their structure of opportunities, particularly in their relationships to the market and the state.

Ample cross-country evidence points to significant transformations at the household level that stem from a process of economic and societal change characterised by the erosion of work. Families have been especially hard-hit in countries in transition to a market economy, which have seen a substantial rise in unemployment and in casual work. In Mongolia, the transition has resulted in widespread unemployment and underemployment, coupled with falling real incomes. Mongolia's population is very young, and the lack of job opportunities has resulted in a 40 per cent unemployment rate among people under 25 years of age. Once a person loses a job, she will probably remain unemployed for some time. This sets in motion a cycle of cumulative disadvantages that narrows the prospects of large sections of society to secure a decent livelihood (Mongolia 1997).

In Bulgaria, swift, radical economic reforms cut wages and social benefits drastically, pushing many workers into the informal economy. Data shows that Bulgarian people are working harder to make ends meet, often with little success. Casual employment has not only mushroomed, but is concentrated in the lower tiers of the labour market where incomes are low and insecure (Bulgaria 1998c). Similarly, many Latvian households are turning to self-employment and subsistence production following a substantial decline in the relative importance of wage employment since the onset of transition. Discrimination in hiring practices, wage arrears and temporary and precarious forms of work have become commonplace, and increasing wage dispersion contributes further to social stratification. The chronically unemployed tend to become self-employed in very unproductive subsistence activities in agriculture. This has resulted in a substantial movement of the Latvian population away from the urban-based cash economy (Gassmann and de Neubourg 2000).

Elsewhere, the erosion of work can be attributed to the effects of economic crises and the adjustment policies implemented in their wake. The growth of unemployment and precarious jobs due to closure of firms, rising labour flexibility, the weakening of labour unions and the decline in public sector employment has reduced the prospects of many Uruguayan families for building their future through stable jobs (Uruguay 1999). Labour flexibility is also rising in South Africa, increasing the share of low-paid and less secure employment. This in turn exacerbates social stratification, as the bulk of the self-employed tend to be concentrated among the African, rural and female population (South Africa 1998).

East Asian countries have also experienced a growth in informality. In Indonesia, one the countries most severely affected by the 1997 financial crisis, real wages dropped by 33 per cent between August 1997 and August 1998, pushing a large number of people who had been formally employed in 1996 below the poverty line. While unemployment in Indonesia is traditionally low, partly because poor people cannot afford idleness, as much as 70 per cent of all poor household heads were self-employed in 1998, whereas only 28 per cent were wage earners (Indonesia 1998). Even in South Korea, where steady employment growth has provided the basis for the country's remarkable record in reducing poverty, half of all urban employment in 1993 was in the informal sector, and unemployment rates were relatively high, particularly in slum areas[5] (Korea 1998).

Formal employment is acutely scarce in most poor countries, and is typically performed by men. Because the poor cannot afford the luxury of unemployment, they are forced to survive on extremely low earnings, with long working hours and harsh working conditions. In Grenada, for example, wage labour has dropped as a result of government downsizing and a steep decline in agriculture, in which wage labour had prevailed. Both small farmers and rural labourers now exert pressure on urban employment, where light manufacturing for export has failed to fill the gaps due to comparatively high wage levels. A large part of the adult population is able to find only casual jobs in the informal economy(the only sector that has grown in recent years[6] (Kairi 1998).

Unemployment is also a growing phenomenon in Sudan, affecting largely women, the young and the rural labour force. Sudanese women, in general, appear to be more vulnerable to job destruction and less prone to benefit from job creation (Sudan 1998). In Angola, the urban informal sector shelters not only the poor, but also the better-off. In nearly three out of every four households in Luanda, at least one member works in the informal sector, mostly in commerce where women predominate (de Sousa 1998).

As informal activities proliferate, casual labour becomes a critical source of income for households. Casual labour, however, is characterised by very low and irregular wages, especially in urban areas where the market is saturated and competition for jobs is keen. It is therefore no surprise that in Kampala, employment was ranked among the three main priorities in participatory assessments carried out in four communities. As elsewhere in Uganda, almost everyone capable of physical work is engaged in producing for his own subsistence[7] (Uganda 1999a).

Household determinants of vulnerability

As labour market opportunities shrink, some people find refuge in the informal sector, which constitutes a crucial ingredient of their livelihood strategies. Often, however, the informal sector is as saturated and stagnant as the formal economy. In such circumstances, people are forced to adjust in order to forestall vulnerability. These changes, however, do not affect everyone in the same way. Households are typically endowed with different amounts of resources, which equip them differently to cope with change. The ability of a household to combine resources is affected by its size, composition and type, its stage in the domestic cycle as well as

Box 1. Unemployment, informality and poverty in South Africa

Unemployment in post-*apartheid* South Africa encompasses up to 30 per cent of the economically active population. It is highest among Africans, women, youth, the rural population, and those with no work experience — often as high as 55 per cent of those in poor households, who typically rely on multiple income sources to reduce risk. Livelihood strategies include a combination of agriculture and fishing, self-employment in small and micro-enterprises, wage labour, and claims against the state (pensions, unemployment insurance and state child maintenance), employers (pensions) or individuals (private child maintenance). Other critical income-earning and income-stretching activities include domestic labour, illegitimate activities (drug trafficking, prostitution and petty theft), the sale of household assets and the use of natural resources for cultivation, grazing, fishing.

In agriculture, the standard wage falls well below the subsistence minimum and the labour market is little developed. Mining relies largely on poor rural workers. Community and domestic services are mostly informal and performed by women. Of the 1.2 million people now in the informal sector, 86 per cent is African and 7.6 per cent coloured. But informality is not homogeneous. While informal wage employment provides an average income above the poverty line, mean and median incomes among the self-employed amount to half and one-ninth, respectively, of the mean monthly income across all informal categories. Moreover, income dispersion among the self-employed hides a large majority of people far below the poverty line. At least 45 per cent of those self-employed in informal activities earn less than the Supplemental Living Level (SLL), which is set at 35 per cent of the poverty line. Africans, young people aged 15 to 24, women and rural inhabitants constitute 76, 67, 60 and 46 per cent, respectively, of the self-employed earning less than the SLL. Eighty per cent of those with all 'markers' (African women aged between 15 and 24 in rural areas) belong to this category.

by factors related to headship, all of which determine the number of potential contributors to the household economy.

Households are commonly defined as social and economic units consisting of one or more individuals who live together and share both the 'roof' and the 'pot', that is, dwelling and food. As long as this element of 'sharing' exists, a single household can comprise several conjugal units. However, because this 'sharing' is often taken for granted, it is seldom discussed.

In reality, households encompass a complex array of relationships involving economic, social, cultural and political aspects of reproduction. They are social units organised not only around a 'shared' house and a 'shared' pot of food, but also around the complex task of generating incomes and managing labour — that most important livelihood ingredient for the poor. Analysing vulnerability requires opening up the *household* so as to assess how resources are generated and used, how they are converted into assets, and how the returns from these assets are distributed among household members.

Most studies of households have emphasised their ability to adapt to worsening employment, goods and services markets by means of increasing their effort. In so doing, households have not only been able to survive, but also to retain their basic form of social organisation, the family, which itself guarantees the physical and social reproduction of the poor. But this premise obscures the fact there may be limits both to the adaptive behaviour of poor people and to the viability of households as such. In addition, this premise masks the different impacts of economic crises and restructuring upon individual household members. These differentials tend to vary most significantly with gender and with age.

Household size and composition

The size of a household, its structure and the availability of income earners are crucial elements of vulnerability. In general, poverty is more prevalent in large households with few income earners. Findings from Uganda (1999a, 1999b) show a clear association between household size and access to land, work and food. Polygamy, for instance, is frequently linked to failure to meet basic needs. Polygamous families tend to be more prone to disease and to lack preventive health care (including mosquito nets) and enough food, as well as proper clothing and adequate housing. Large households in Lebanon (1998) are also reported to have lower levels of income than the average, while in Palestine the poverty rate increases consistently with household size, beginning with two-person households. The largest Palestinian households, with ten or more members, have the highest poverty rate (34 per cent in 1997), followed by single-person households (31 per cent). Poverty is also deeper in these households (Palestine 1998).

Even in Latvia, where households generally average of 2.47 members with a mere 0.52 children, recent data show that poverty ratios increase with each additional household member. Households with only one person have the lowest poverty risk (less than two per cent are below the poverty line), while almost 20 per cent of the individuals living in households with four or more members are poor. The larger the household, the deeper the poverty: poor households have three members on average, compared with only two members in non-poor households (Gassmann 2000). By contrast, in South Korea large family size is not associated with low income. According to data of 1982, poor households in Seoul were smaller than the national average (Korea 1998).

Our review thus provides some evidence of greater poverty characterising large households, but the association between the two variables is not always clear. A large household with only one provider and many small children will differ from a household that has an equal number of members, but a larger proportion of adults who are in a position to participate in income-generating activities.[8] Better-off households may also be more capable of staying together than poorer ones, which would result in smaller household size among the poor. Variables such as a household's dependency rate, rather than size alone, must be taken into account in assessing the degree of vulnerability of particular households. Size *per se* is not the issue; a combination of several factors, notably the availability of household members to generate incomes plays a critical role.

Sex of the household head

Female-headed households have increased almost everywhere as a result of demographic and socio-economic changes. Conventional wisdom holds that they are poorer, more vulnerable and more prone to transmit disadvantage to the next generation than households headed by men. Particularly when the head is a single mother, female-headed households are also the objects of stigma and discrimination in many societies, especially those that regard the nuclear family with a male breadwinner as the desired norm. A heated debate has developed in recent years between those who support the idea of a close association between female headship, poverty and vulnerability, and those who see these households as economically and socially viable. Our review of findings from several countries leads us to conclude that there are no grounds for arguing that female-headed households have a greater incidence of poverty or vulnerability than other single- or two-parent households.

Households headed by women are poorer in Bulgaria, Lebanon, Palestine and South Africa. The poverty rate among South African households with a female head is 60 per cent, compared with 31 per cent for male-headed ones (South Africa 1998). In Lebanon, the percentage of households below the poverty threshold is 40.3 per cent for those headed by men and 57.7 per cent in the case of households with a female head. This disparity is due, first, to the greater probability of widowhood or divorce in households headed by a woman, which implies the loss of a major source of income from the work of the former husband. Second, greater poverty among female-headed households can be explained by the lower wages obtained by women, whose mean wage is 78 per cent of that earned by men (Lebanon 1998). Likewise, households headed by women in Palestine constituted about eight per cent of all households in 1997, but 11 per cent of those living in poverty. Predictably, the poverty incidence is much higher among female- than male-headed households (30 per cent vs. 22 per cent). In poor households alone, 73 per cent of those with a female head, compared to 63 per cent of those headed by a man, suffer from 'deep poverty', which entails an inability to satisfy their minimum requirements of food, clothing and housing (Palestine 1998).

By contrast, findings from Angola, Indonesia, Latvia, Maldives, Sudan and Uganda show that households headed by women have equal or even higher incomes and consumption levels than their male counterparts. The presence of children in the household, its structure and composition, and the age of the head have a stronger influence on the probability of being poor than female headship. For instance, Latvian households tend to be poorer if they have children, regardless of whether a man or a woman heads the household (Gassmann 2000). Nor is female headship always the unwanted consequence of male desertion; it is often the outcome of women's own desires and decisions (Maldives 1998).

Recent data from Sudan also cast doubt on the thesis that female-headed households constitute a homogeneous group that tends to be poorer than those headed by males. Households with a woman head have a smaller number of members and therefore are less crowded. They also have a much higher per capita income than those headed by men in both urban and rural areas. At the same time, whether a household is headed by a man or by a woman has no statistical significance in its total level of income (Sudan 1998).

Gender and age of the household head are major poverty risk factors in Angola. But contrary to the stereotype of the 'feminisation of poverty', female headship is relatively more prevalent among better-off households and less prevalent among poor ones in urban areas than is the case with male-headed ones — although both types are equally represented among the extremely poor. In the countryside, though, female-headed households have the highest poverty level and the highest food budget share (Ceita 1999).

Results from the Uganda poverty assessment show that, in all the communities studied, female-headed households are characterised by higher consumption of food and medical treatments. This observation is in line with the well-documented fact that when women have control over an independent source of income, they tend to give priority to spending on food and other basic necessities that have a positive impact on family wellbeing. Thus, even if households headed by men may be richer in income terms (which is not always supported by the evidence), those that are headed by women appear to be better off in other respects because of their greater emphasis on welfare-enhancing consumption practices (Uganda 1999a, 1999b, 1999c).

The importance of the domestic cycle

Households are not static, but very dynamic social units. They evolve over time and are exposed to varying levels of vulnerability as they go through different phases in their domestic cycle. Capturing this element requires a longitudinal perspective that takes into account the various stages in the developmental process of households. Each of these stages is conducive to particular social arrangements that influence their ability to mobilise their labour and other resources in the face of change.

The *expansion* and the *dispersion* stages are critical times for poor households in terms of their exposure to vulnerability. These are the stages in the domestic cycle when the pool of household labourers relative to its dependants is lowest — fewer members are available to generate incomes for the domestic unit.[9] This is particularly prominent among the growing numbers of old people in Latvia and Bulgaria, where the state has reduced old-age pensions and child benefits following the collapse of communism (Bulgaria 1998a; Gassmann and de Neubourg 2000). Data from Lebanon (1998) and Palestine (1998) also suggest that households headed by young and old workers — in the early stage or the dispersion years of the domestic cycle — are much more vulnerable to poverty than those whose main providers are between 40 and 54 years old. Similarly, findings from a participatory assessment in South African corroborate the life-cycle dimension as a key determinant of the movement of households and individuals into and out of poverty (South Africa 1998).

Other studies document the presence of 'critical age groups' such as children, youth and the elderly. In Grenada, for instance, women and children are most severely affected by poverty. But elderly people are also vulnerable. Neglected by their adult children, they are often forced to depend on the charity of friends or the

---

**Box 2. Coping with protracted crisis:
Bulgarian households during transition**

Bulgaria's transition began with swift, radical economic reforms that drastically reduced minimum wages and social payments. Real wages and social assistance declined by an estimated 65 to 70 per cent between 1990 and 1998. By 1997, the minimum wage purchased only 33 per cent of the minimum subsistence basket. The share of total household income devoted to savings fell from ten per cent in 1989 to three per cent in 1997, when real consumption represented less than a quarter of its 1990 level.

Bulgarian families have resorted to various strategies to stave off poverty. Many households are removing their children from school. Second jobs and home-based production rose significantly. Only 25 per cent female-headed households have a person with a permanent job, compared with 75 per cent in those headed by men. One million people now work in the informal economy — which, according to a recent World Bank study, accounts for more than 40 per cent of Bulgaria's GDP. Now on a par with the private formal sector, the informal sector has become one of the driving engines of the Bulgarian economy. Growing absenteeism in numerous enterprises seems linked to more time spent on second jobs. Declining opportunities and the rise in casual work have increased pressures to migrate. Romany families have resorted to clan networks to secure jobs in distant places, while Muslim families tend to move from rural areas to the cities. People are now producing larger amounts of goods for their own consumption — including growing food, raising animals and producing basic textiles and garments for family use. The shift to subsistence production encompasses urban as well as rural families.

church (Kairi 1998). In Uganda, too, old age is frequently associated with poverty, particularly in situations where the aged are sick and lack support from relatives (Uganda 1999). And in Lebanon, the percentage of households below the poverty line is higher among heads aged 55–59 years, as well as 39 years or less. Workers earn higher wages for only about ten years of their working lives (Lebanon 1998).

Gender relations and household differentiation

Households are best conceptualised as a site of not only cooperation, but also of conflict and negotiation. They often constitute an arena of confronting interests and unequal burdens and access to resources, in which women, children, youth and the elderly are in the weakest position. A commonly held assumption is that households constitute a 'melting pot' in which differences among its members merge and disappear. If this were true, household dynamics could have a moderating influence on the conditions that women face in labour markets, to take only one example. But if the household itself is a locus of inequality, intra-household relations will add another layer of inequality to that created by markets. Social inequality will thus increase rather than diminish. It is therefore important to 'open up' the household and examine its internal dynamics and social organisation. As long as households are treated as a 'black box' in which the distribution of resources and capabilities is assumed to be equitable, we fail to understand the real impact of economic change on poverty and vulnerability.

In fact, household restructuring in response to declining opportunities and adjustment has not affected every member in the same manner. In many countries, women appear to be paying the highest cost of household transformation. They are working harder and longer hours, without any significant positive change in their status. Angola provides an example of women's increasing role as breadwinners during economic crises. In terms of their contributions to the household economy, poor women are now on an equal footing with men, yet continue to bear the burden of domestic chores assisted only by their children. Data from time-budget studies in urban Angola show that women have longer working days as a result of their double role as breadwinners and housewives. The same data reveal that men are not contributing to household chores to the extent that women have become breadwinners. Women, for instance, collect most of the firewood needed by the household. Collecting water also consumes many hours of women's time — and although men are doing more shopping than in the past, they still seldom take part in other domestic tasks (Ceita 1999; Wold and Grave 1999).

Data from Mongolia provide evidence of women's 'double burden' as an outcome of the transition. In the past, the state supported women in their childbearing and child-rearing functions through the provision of generous benefits. These were largely withdrawn in the early 1990s, as a result of which the number of day-care facilities dropped from 441 in 1990 to 71 in 1996. Yet women's perceived roles as 'care-givers' continues. As a result, many now face a work burden that encompasses their responsibilities both within and outside the household. This double burden often creates role conflicts that lead to lower career mobility for many women who try to balance the different demands they now face. Indeed, far from gaining control over their lives, women seem to encounter greater conflicts as they gain a footing in the paid sphere without being able to shed some of their traditional domestic responsibilities (Mongolia 1997).

In other countries, too, women's participation in wage employment and other income-generation activities has not produced equality in gender relations. In Uganda, women perform as much as 50 per cent of the work involved in cotton production, but do not control the money they earn. They also participate very little in the process of decision-making at the household or community levels. Men alone are involved in the transport business, in which women are not allowed — although in practice, they often carry heavy loads of goods from one place to another on foot. The marketing of produce is also mostly a male domain. Women can only participate with their husbands' permission and, if they do, they are allowed to handle only very small quantities of goods. Even then, women are expected to declare the outcomes of their transactions, as well as account for the money they spend for household consumption. Wives may be entrusted with money to keep, but have no right to spend it unless their husbands permit them to do so (Uganda 1999a).

Differential access to resources and discrimination against women and girls are common in many countries. Reluctance on the part of husbands was among the main reasons given by both men and women to explain the low female labour-force participation rate in Maldives. Ironically, men's control over women's lives seems to be an obstacle for the mobilisation of some key household resources, such as women's work. Stunting and wasting are especially prevalent among girls, partly because of the high incidence of infections and the acute anaemia suffered by many mothers (Maldives 1998).

Likewise, boys are said to be more valued than girls in Uganda, where families prefer to keep boys at school if they cannot educate all their children. Women who took part in the participatory assessment carried out in that country reported they felt 'at the mercy of their men' and had 'no voice even when the man is misusing the money' (Uganda 1999c). They also stated that their husbands beat them for attending meetings, and prevent them from using family planning services because they do not approve of such practices. Women's heavy workload, together with lack of ownership and limited access to land and other valuable resources, makes them not only poorer, but also more vulnerable in facing hardship and economic crises. In both rural and urban areas of Uganda, men control the most important household assets, including land, livestock, housing, TV sets, radios and vehicles. Perhaps the clearest indication of women's subordinate position is the fact that, upon a husband's death, widows are bequeathed to their husband's brother, together with all their household assets (Uganda 1999a).

Even though poverty and insecurity at work seem to be eroding men's traditional role as the family's main provider, the resilience of patriarchal systems of authority has prevented the changing roles of men and women in the productive sphere from translating into more equitable gender relations within the household. Indeed, as feelings of inadequacy on the part of men increase, the maintenance of patriarchal norms and values is leading to severe strains between the sexes. According to qualitative data from Uganda, being poor has severely eroded men's self-esteem and 'undermined their manhood'. Out of frustration, many men are said to resort to drugs, crime and violence (Uganda 1999a). In Grenada, too, lack of male self-esteem and feelings of inferiority, shame and frustration are associated with long-term unemployment and are leading many men to become engaged in illegal activities to support their families. Increased violence, crime and prostitution, as well as a deterioration of family life are reported as outcomes of job insecurity and lack of economic options (Kairi 1998).

Altogether, though, gender identities appear to be enormously resilient, even in the face of rapid change. In some cases, this resilience may serve as a buffer against extreme hardship, while in others it may constitute a serious handicap. The most revealing data come from Latvia, where unremitting economic pressure has led to pervasive feelings of depression, ranging from mild apathy, constant insomnia and stress to an obsession with suicide. Women, though, reported that their concern for their children has prevented them from even considering the possibility of committing suicide — which, together with drug and alcohol abuse, is much more prevalent among men, whose identity seems to depend heavily on their ability to earn money (Trapenciere et al. 2000).

This leads to the very interesting and largely unexplored area of masculinity and the impact of economic change on men's lives. Reversing our ignorance of these subjects is critical to improving our understanding of processes of social transformation in a truly gender-balanced manner.

Coping strategies and social reproduction

Labour market trends have triggered important changes in livelihood strategies. As a growing number of individuals experienced unemployment or had no other alternative but precarious jobs or subsistence agriculture, they have had to mobilise other sources of income to protect their consumption. In responding to these changes, the poor have displayed remarkable ingenuity and resilience. But the acute and protracted nature of the crises that have beset many countries seems to be eroding the resource base of the poor, straining their capacity for survival.

It is useful to distinguish between two different types of household strategies. A *reproduction strategy* involves a series of economic and non-economic activities aimed at ensuring the long-term reproduction and wellbeing of the household unit and its members. A *survival or coping strategy* is typically a short-term response to shock and stress, implemented to cope with the expected and unexpected hardships of everyday life. Short-term coping strategies may be further distinguished between *household work strategies* aimed at protecting or increasing household resources and *restrictive practices* based on cutting down or modifying household consumption of goods and services. The former are implemented mainly through a process of intensification of work performed by members of a household, whereas the latter often result from a failure of work-based strategies to prevent the erosion of a household's resource base — and are therefore a clear sign of decreasing household capabilities.

The distinction between the two is mainly analytical, since in actual practice many strategies have an element of both. It is sometimes difficult to know when an alteration in consumption stops being a coping mechanism and instead leads a household into destitution. Some changes in consumption patterns (like eating more cereal instead of meat) can be understood as coping strategies, while others (curtailing total consumption, dropping out of school or not visiting a doctor) are rather an indication of a failure to cope.[10] Both, however, are a response to constraining conditions, as households have to make tough choices within a binding budget limits. These choices often involve very costly tradeoffs. In general, a strategy can be said to exist as long as a household has the ability to choose. Once this capacity is lost, it is no longer possible to strategise.

Our review of country findings provides substantial evidence of a growing tension between short- and long-term livelihood strategies. In many countries, coping strategies are not only proving insufficient to offset the consequences of economic crisis and change, but may also undermine people's ability to recover in the future. This implies that there may be limits to the adaptive behaviour of the poor and that a survival strategy that relies on an intensification of household resources cannot be sustained permanently.[11]

Household work strategies

People adapt to worsening conditions by increasing effort. This often involves a twofold strategy consisting of more, as well as more intense, work. When incomes fall, households react by placing more members in the labour market and raising the share of informal and family-based work for cash, including the use of unpaid labour of women and children. Female labour-force participation rates have increased in almost every country, while men's traditional role as main family providers has declined in importance. Children's labour, which is seen as a resource to be invested in short-term strategies for survival, has also been on the rise. Household members who are already in the labour market tend to take second jobs and work longer hours, even as the total number of household income earners rises. As a rule, precarious and low-paid activities have increased at the expense of formal employment and income from wages and salaries. For many families, the informal economy now provides the basis for their livelihoods.

Mobilisation of additional household members

Since wages are a vital component of livelihoods, households' capacity to place their members in the labour market is one of the most crucial mechanisms for coping with economic hazards. According to evidence from many countries, households seek to compensate for an income loss by expanding their pool of income earners. This often involves adding members who had never been active economically (such as women and children) or had already stopped participating (like the elderly). In Indonesia, for instance, the dramatic fall in real wages from 1997 to 1998 was accompanied by a 3.5 per cent increase in the labour force. This increase was largely due to higher participation rates by women, especially married women with children, who decided to enter or return to the labour market after a period of absence (Indonesia 1998).

Mobilising additional household labour is critically important because it helps reduce dependence on a single source of income, which constitutes a key determinant of vulnerability. The economic position of Latvian households is directly related to the number of wage earners (Gassmann 2000). By contrast, the vast majority of Palestinian households depend on a single earner, largely the male head. This may help explain why, in the absence of female labour to supplement the income of the male breadwinner, poverty rates increase consistently with household size (Palestine 1999).

It is important to not only expand the pool of household earners, but also diversify the sources of income by drawing, when possible, from both wage and non-wage sources. This is one of the most typical strategies deployed by households seeking economic alternatives to protect their incomes. Both in Uruguay (1999) and Korea (1998), women and children work on a regular basis for extra household income, mostly in casual and informal jobs with a high degree of irregularity and instability. Poor Korean households are characterised by a higher number of workers, an indication that intensifying the use of labour is one of their mechanisms to make ends meet. In Bulgaria, too, the rise in second jobs, informal work and subsistence production means that more household members are working and that they do so for longer hours (Bulgaria 1998a). Likewise, between 13 and 19 per cent of Indonesian households have had to add the work of previously inactive members in their survival strategies since the beginning of the crisis (Indonesia 1998).

Family-based work for cash

In places where labour markets are not well developed and subsistence activities prevail, family members contribute to the household economy by participating in a mix of family-based cash and subsistence activities. This is the case in many poor countries where rural self-provisioning is the norm. Nevertheless, subsistence production is limited neither to agriculture nor to rural areas. A small but growing number of non-peasant families, including in some middle-income countries, are shifting to home-based production for lack of cash income, even in urban sites.

Where livelihoods depend on a single source, such as in many fishing communities of Uganda's Kalangala district, they are at greater risk (Uganda 1999b). To reduce this risk, people mobilise the collective efforts of all household and community members. Thus, although different in kind from formal wage employment, rural livelihood strategies also rely on mobilisation of household labour and the diversification of income sources for their survival. In rural Grenada, the majority of the poor do not have access to land, and even those who do lack the necessary resources to turn it into an asset. For this reason, the bulk of poor Grenadian households rely on 'backyard gardening', producing their own food for both consumption and sale or exchange (Kairi 1998). A similar situation is present in Indonesia, where a large number of agricultural households can be found in urban areas surviving on a combination of subsistence farming and family-based informal production and trade (Indonesia 1998).

In Uganda, too, subsistence farming is the main livelihood activity in rural communities, where very few people depend on paid employment or trade. Farming systems in Kapchorwa cover a wide range of food and cash crops, underlining the importance of having different sources to draw from. Women participate actively in the household economy, particularly in farming and petty trading, while boys and young men are becoming increasingly involved in casual work such as brewing, collecting firewood or grinding millet. Self-provisioning agriculture is also present among Uganda's urban inhabitants, who tend to poultry and goats and grow yams, bananas, potatoes and legumes in their gardens (Uganda 1999a, 1999b).

Traditional livelihoods in Papua New Guinea include subsistence gardening, river and seabed fishing, hunting and gathering. Everyone capable of work contributes to the household and village economy, from children as young as ten years old to elders aged seventy. When fishing or hunting is done for subsistence purposes, villagers use traditional techniques that inflict no harm upon their natural habitat. But as people increasingly need cash income to pay for school fees and services, they are intensifying their production in order to sell their catch or prey for cash. Lacking other means of earning incomes, villagers are also turning to cash cropping. This involves clearing large tracts of forest to create space for farming, hunting larger amounts of wildlife, and fishing more frequently, in larger quantities and farther away from the seashore. People's increased dependence on the cash economy is illustrated by the fact that in 1990, 43 per cent of rural households were involved in coffee production and 36 per cent in copra production (Papua New Guinea 1998). This example highlights the tension between short-term survival strategies and long-term social reproduction, as the intensification of the use of natural resources poses a serious danger to the sustainability of people's livelihood strategies in the future.

Intensification of work

Households are also responding to income shortfalls and job loss by intensifying the total amount of work performed, both by individuals who were already working and by the household unit as a whole. This applies to formal wage as well as non-wage employment. Evidence from Bulgaria, Indonesia, Uruguay and other countries shows people working longer hours, taking on additional jobs and increasing home-based production in an attempt to prevent the erosion of their incomes.

Indonesian families, for instance, coped with the recession that began in 1997 through a process of intensification of work. In a survey conducted in 1998, more than one third of urban poor households and half of rural poor households had taken additional jobs, while 34 and 42 per cent of poor households in urban and rural areas, respectively, were working overtime. Middle-class households also increased their work effort in order to prevent a slide into poverty. Despite all these efforts, poverty rates increased steeply after August 1997 (Indonesia 1998).

Second jobs also gained in importance among Bulgarian workers. From 1990 to 1998, the share of wages from the main job in total household income dropped from 58 to 53 per cent, while that of second jobs rose nine-fold, from 0.4 to 3.6 per cent. They comprise mostly temporary and part-time jobs, as well as undeclared services performed on the side, meaning that Bulgarian wage earners have been pushed into the informal or 'black' economy where consumption has increased remarkably (Bulgaria 1998c).

In Uruguay (1999), men as well as women and children are important agents in the household work intensification strategies that have accompanied structural reforms in that country. Men engage in self-employment, work longer hours or accept jobs that may require fewer skills and pay less than their earlier ones. Women and children take on precarious jobs to complement family income. For both of them, this normally entails a heavier workload, as women retain their domestic responsibilities and children struggle to keep up with their schooling.

Women's contributions to the household economy

Women's labour has become a crucial asset for household survival and reproduction. Women participate in income-generating activities in growing numbers, while men are encountering mounting problems to carry out their role as providers. Rising female participation rates in the labour force are an indication of these trends, although lack of jobs and the general contraction of the wage sector in many countries often limit women to low-paid, casual work in the informal economy. Predictably, women play a pre-eminent role in many of the work substitution practices implemented by households by shifting to home-based production of goods previously acquired in the market.

In countries like Latvia (Gassmann and de Neubourg 2000), households with a female breadwinner are evenly spread across social strata and constitute a majority of all households (56 per cent). The significant rise in labour force participation in the wake of the 1997 crisis in Indonesia can largely be attributed to higher participation rates among women, many of whom entered the labour market for the first time (Indonesia 1998). In Angola, almost half of all economically active women participate in informal activities, contributing substantially to household income. This large female presence is associated not only with a lack of job opportunities in the formal economy, but also with women's need for flexible work hours to balance wage employment with household and child care responsibilities[12] (Ceita 1999). In Uganda, casual labour is performed predominantly by women, who participate actively in petty trading and the marketing of produce, as well as in the production of cassava, potatoes and cotton. As in Angola, women's participation in the generation of household income is so important that households with only male income earners are reported to be among the poorest in Kampala (Uganda 1999a). In spite of this, many Ugandan men place restrictions on female participation in economic activities, especially on married women in rural villages.

Even though women's work is a crucial ingredient of the livelihood strategies of poor households in many countries, they still face severe discrimination in labour markets. Sudanese women, for example, are said to be the first to suffer from job loss and the last to benefit from job creation (Sudan 1998). Women who participated in focus groups in Grenada reported that they had a regular source of income, but their wages were usually very low and insufficient to meet their families' needs (Kairi 1998). In Bulgaria, only 27.6 per cent of female-headed households had at least one person permanently employed, while the corresponding figure in households headed by men was 74.6 per cent (Bulgaria 1998b). Even in South Korea (1998), where female participation rates are relatively high and their role in labour-intensive industries has been a crucial ingredient of the country's economic success, discrimination and stigmatisation of women entering the labour market are common. Women are concentrated in agriculture and the services sector, and those who work in light manufacturing for export tend to receive very low wages. As a result, women constitute one of the few 'pockets' of poverty that remain in the country, together with the elderly and single-headed households.

The dismantling of social programs in countries undergoing adjustment or transition has further affected women's position in the work arena. Mongolia (1997) dismantled publicly financed day care centres precisely at the time when labour burdens were shifting in many households towards greater female participation as wage earners. This has left Mongolian women no choice but to take on the double role of breadwinners and care-givers within the family. Given women's critical contribution to the household economy in so many countries, curtailing social programs presumed to benefit only women is bound to have an impact far beyond them.

Children's labour

Children have been particularly victimised by the declining trend in economic opportunities described earlier. There is ample cross-country evidence that, in responding to confining conditions, households have not spared children from their work intensification strategies. As a consequence, many are not attending school or drop out to contribute their labour to the household economy. They do this either by performing unpaid work or selling goods or services to supplement family income.

Child labour seems to be of crucial importance for subsistence livelihoods in Papua New Guinea, where children at the age of ten years start contributing to the household and village economy (Papua New Guinea 1998). Ugandan households protect their paltry incomes by pulling boys, and especially girls, out of school to help with domestic chores, forcing young girls to marry in exchange for bride price, and sending children and youths to perform casual jobs for food and income. Many children in Kampala have been forced to look for jobs at an early age in order to support themselves and help their families. As the number of street children has increased over time, they are turning to illegal practices like stealing or to the exchange of sexual favours for money to survive. Sex work is also common among women in the Kisenyi Parish (Uganda 1999a).

The use of child labour is not restricted to poor countries with subsistence economies. Many Bulgarian families are removing their children from school to put them to work (Bulgaria 1998a). Korean children also contribute an extra household income regularly by working at all kinds of casual and informal jobs (Korea 1998). In Indonesia (1998), about one out five poor households relied on children's unpaid work a few months after the financial crisis. While child labour has risen throughout the country, it is particularly high among urban boys from low-income families.

Although children's work has been mobilised almost everywhere as a response to declining incomes, it is not clear if it enhances household wellbeing. Yet the consequences for children can be devastating, imperilling their health and curtailing their educational opportunities. The need to use child labour for survival is one of the most important obstacles to education in Angola, where attendance rates among young children from families in extreme poverty are a dismal 49 per cent of their school-age cohort (Wold and Grave 1999). By contrast, data from Korea (1998) do not indicate that working children are necessarily being withdrawn from school. Nevertheless, one can presume that children who are asked to work regularly end up by dropping out of school and devoting their time to looking for work.

Expenditure-minimising and other restrictive practices

We have reviewed a number of work intensification strategies implemented by households so as to protect or increase their pool of resources in the face of declining opportunities. Often, however, such strategies are not sufficient to cushion the poor from the impact of unexpected shocks and change, forcing them to adopt a range of restrictive practices aimed at protecting the basic consumption of the household. In most cases, the latter implement a mix of both strategies. As they both seek to increase the household's disposable income, their net effect is often the same. Yet it is useful to keep the analytical distinction between the two, as restrictive practices tend to be implemented when work strategies do not suffice to offset the erosion of the household's resource base and are a sign of diminishing capabilities that may lead a household towards destitution. As a rule, these practices involve cutting total spending, changing consumption patterns and liquidating household property and savings.[13]

Cutting food consumption

Poor people in most countries have responded to shrinking opportunities by modifying the structure of their consumption, as well as by reducing it in absolute terms. This applies first to non-essential items, but very often to food staples as well. The proportion of households reducing both the quantity and quality of food consumed is very significant in Indonesia, where almost two out of five poor households cut expenditures on food after the onset of the crisis (Indonesia 1998). Urban households in Uganda, particularly in Kampala, have reduced food consumption to the point of having only one meal a day. They have also changed their shopping habits. Instead of purchasing small amounts of sugar, maize flour or beans on a daily basis, they now buy larger quantities for use over several days. This allows them to pay lower prices than they had earlier. Buying on credit has also become a regular practice (Uganda 1999a).

As households' budgets shrink, the share of expenditures devoted to food rises in many countries. In Bulgaria, food expenses as a share of total spending rose by half, from 36.3 to 54.4 per cent, between 1990 and 1997 (Bulgaria 1998a). A similar trend was observed in Mongolia after the transition, especially among households headed by pensioners or workers on fixed wages, who have slipped into poverty because of drastic declines in their purchasing power. This has led to a

Box 3. Coping with a sudden shock:
Domestic responses to crisis in Indonesia

To assess the impact of the crisis on poor households, Indonesia's statistical office conducted a nationally representative survey in 1998, covering 10,000 households spread over
27 provinces. The survey found that although the crisis impacted all households, rural as
well as urban, the poor were most seriously affected; many were found on the brink of survival. During the six months prior to the survey, Indonesian households resorted to the following practices to compensate for rising prices and declining purchasing power:

- **Doing additional jobs.** Almost 37 per cent poor of economically active persons in
  poor urban households and 49 per cent in poor rural households had to take on additional jobs to supplement their falling incomes.
- **Working overtime.** One third of poor households in urban areas and almost half in
  rural areas were found to be working overtime. Those employed before the crisis
  were working more hours, and even many middle-class families had to increase
  their work effort in the aftermath of the crisis.
- **Sending children to work.** Eighteen and 22 per cent of poor urban and rural households, respectively, were relying on child labour. The incidence of child labour was
  highest among low-income urban families.
- **Asking other household members to work.** Fourteen per cent of poor urban households and 19 per cent of those in rural areas were including the work of other household members — often people either previously inactive or retired from the labour
  market because of advanced age or motherhood. Many married women with children entered the labour market for the first time.
- **Reducing the quantity of food.** As many as 40 per cent of poor households had to
  reduce total food consumption after the crisis.
- **Switching the quality of food.** Vegetables, fruits, fish, meat, eggs and milk were the
  main items cut from people's diets. Nearly 60 per cent of poor urban households and
  half of rural households substituted rice and cereals for more expensive food staples. Non-poor households were no less affected — almost 40 per cent of them were
  eating more cereal and fewer protein-rich foods.
- **Withdrawing children from school.** Because the poor in Indonesia value education
  highly, only 2.3 of poor households in urban areas and 3.3 per cent in the countryside
  had pulled children out of school. But protecting children's education normally
  meant cutting back on other essential needs.
- **Reducing medical expenses and purchases of clothing.** People were forced to curtail health care visits and purchases of medicines to the obvious detriment of their
  health. Almost 73 per cent of the urban poor and 67 per cent of the rural poor also
  cut their expenditures on clothing.
- **Cutting expenses in recreation and transportation.** About half of poor urban and rural
  households, and more than 40 per cent of the better-off cut expenditures on trans-

portation, thereby reducing not only their capacity to work and generate incomes, but their ability to maintain social interactions with networks of relatives and friends. Two thirds of poor households reduced their expenses in recreation as well.

- **Withdrawing savings.** Almost one out of ten families, including 18 per cent of better-off households, had to withdraw savings in the wake of the crisis — typically a last-resort measure that poor people take in an effort to avoid cutting food consumption.
- **Pawning and selling valuables.** More than 7 per cent of poor urban households pawned some of their valuables, while 10-15 per cent had to sell them to obtain income for current consumption. The corresponding figures for rural areas were 9 and 8 per cent, respectively.
- **Borrowing from others.** In urban areas, as many as 40 per cent borrowed money and goods, generally from friends and relatives — compared with 31 per cent in rural areas. On average, one out of four non-poor households also had to borrow from others to make up for income loss.
- **Consuming own production.** While borrowing seems to be most common in urban settings, consuming one's own production includes a greater share of rural households, ranging from half of all households among the poor to over one third among the better-off. Among poor urban households, the proportion reached 19 per cent. Many urban families moved back to the countryside in search of an alternative livelihood source.

severe deterioration of people's diets, despite their efforts to protect food consumption. Daily calorie intake per person in Mongolia was 25 per cent lower than in 1989, and still remained 15 per cent short by 1996 (Mongolia 1997).

Changing dietary habits

People have also modified their consumption patterns in an attempt to save money. The consumption of bread and meat, once traditional staples in Latvian diets, has decreased in recent years. As people try to buy the cheapest food, potatoes and other vegetables have become the main items in their diet, together with cheap fish (Gassmann and de Neubourg 2000). In Mongolia, too, the quality of people's diets has suffered since the economic reforms began. Consumption of cheaper substitutes has led to serious nutritional imbalances, undoing the improvements made over a period of two decades that started in 1970 (Mongolia 1997).

Consuming food of lower quality has also been a common response to crisis in Indonesia. Almost half of poor households in rural areas and six out of ten in urban areas are eating smaller amounts of vegetables, fruits, fish, meat and other protein-rich foods, which they have replaced with rice and other inexpensive cereals. The poorest urban households in particular were consuming twice as much cereal as a proportion of their diets in 1998 as in 1996 (Indonesia 1998).

Reducing health and education expenses

Another symptom of people's increased vulnerability is that poor households are cutting expenditures on basic necessities other than food. As a rule, the poor spend a much larger share of their income on health and education than the better-off do. Still, they often cannot afford the cost of schooling or health treatment.

For instance, Angola's poor devote half as much of their budgets to educational expenses compared with the non-poor. Households with high dependency rates face the toughest situation (Wold and Grave 1999). In Uganda (1999), the cost of secondary education is said to be prohibitively high for poor families or youths without support. To send their children to school, poor families have to sell household assets or curtail other essential expenses, such as rent or medicines. The cost of seeking health treatment, together with inadequate services, leads people to resort to self-medication, traditional healers or untrained birth attendants. Likewise, a large number of Mongolian children have experienced disrupted schooling in recent years. The privatisation of Mongolia's education system following the demise of communism has shifted the costs of schooling from the public sector to the family. This has resulted in lower enrolment and completion rates among children from poor households (Mongolia 1997).

By contrast, the poor in Latvia and Indonesia have so far managed to protect children's education, although only at the expense of other basic needs. Education is highly valued among Indonesia's poor in rural as well as urban areas. Consequently, while a growing number of children have been withdrawn from school since 1997, only a small proportion of families have been affected (Indonesia 1998). In Latvia, many people have had to forego satisfying other critical needs to keep children at school. This applies, for example, to medical care, which in Latvia as in other former socialist countries used to be universally provided by the state and is now a private service that must be purchased. Poor families can no longer afford medical treatment. They tend to avoid seeing a doctor as much as they can, relying instead on home remedies, over-the-counter medications or advice from professionals with whom they are acquainted — who for this reason will not charge for their services. This means that in obtaining health care, people's entitlements have been replaced by personal connections and the exchange of favours (Trapenciere et al. 2000).

Cutting non-essential expenditures

Expenses on transportation, clothing, leisure and housing are among the first to be cut in times of distress. Although these consumption items are obviously not as critical as food or health care, their significance in people's wellbeing should not be underestimated.

Many Ugandan families are unable to afford decent accommodation in urban areas, where rents typically consume a large proportion of family income. To save on rent, people stay in bad housing with no toilets, water connection or electricity, often situated in areas that are prone to floods, where they share their living quarters with many other households (Uganda 1999a). The reduction of spending on transport, recreation and clothing among Indonesian families was both drastic and immediate when recession struck in 1997. Almost two thirds of poor urban households slashed expenses in recreation, while three out of four reduced purchases of clothing only a few months after the crisis began (Indonesia 1998).

In Latvia, many households cannot afford the high cost of rent, services and utilities, especially if the head is unemployed. To cope with rising costs, families economise in various ways, substituting cheaper for expensive fuel, foregoing housing repairs, or paying only part of their rent or their telephone, gas and electricity bills to avoid eviction or disconnection of services. Although these practices have helped Latvian families cope in the short term, their standard of living has deteriorated as a result.

Drawing from savings and borrowing

While poor people's capacity to save is limited, they still manage to do so when members of the household have access to regular income. Examples of such practices can be found in the Mexican *tandas*, the *tontines* of West Africa and several other savings schemes that serve as community safety nets for occasional expenses or emergencies. It seems, however, that the capacity to save has been eroded in many countries because people no longer have steady sources of income. In a context of need, savings are an asset to be consumed.

Consuming savings and going into debt was commonly observed among households in transition countries. In Mongolia (1997), unemployment — an outcome of labour market liberalisation and enterprise rationalisation — has led people to use long-term savings for daily consumption. In Bulgaria (1998a), savings as a share of total household income dropped 70 per cent from 1989 to 1997, at which time 97 per cent of household income was being devoted to consumption. In Latvia, many people lost their life savings with the collapse of state banks, currency reforms and the hyperinflation of the early 1990s. Unable to afford the rising cost of housing and services, a large number of families have become indebted by accumulating unpaid rent and bills (Trapenciere et al. 2000).

Data from a survey carried out in Indonesia (1998) 16 months after the beginning of the crisis showed that people without regular jobs were relying on their savings as a first step before cutting consumption. Almost ten per cent of poor urban households had withdrawn savings during the six months prior to the survey. The figure for non-poor households, which have more savings to draw upon, was even higher at 18 per cent. Borrowing money and goods was another common practice, generally from friends and relatives, but also from moneylenders who normally charge exorbitant interest rates. Unsurprisingly, this practice was most common among the poor in both rural and urban areas.

Box 4. Latvia: Adjusting to a new reality

Because Latvia's economy was closely intertwined with the Soviet market, the breakdown of the Soviet Union and the ensuing economic crisis and hyperinflation forced many Latvian households to adjust to a new reality that included unemployment and a precipitous fall of real wages, accompanied by the dismantling of a system of public subsidies for housing and a wide range of services. Suddenly, utilities became a heavy burden not only for pensioners and the unemployed, but even for salaried workers. Some pensioners were found to be cutting on food, since they were not willing to go into debt as a result of the accumulation of unpaid utility bills.

To keep up with housing rent as well as utilities, many Latvian families cut back on necessary expenses when their debts become so large that they risk losing services, even their apartments. Some close off rooms or substitute cheap fuels for expensive alternatives — or simply live without heating or electricity. Many children spend longer hours at school instead of studying by candlelight at home. Many poor Latvian households limit their phone calls to urgent matters or make these calls from their office — or cut off phone service altogether. Often, they pay just a portion of their rent or utility bills to show good faith and thus prevent eventual eviction or disconnection of services.

Homes have deteriorated. Roofs leak, toilets no longer flush, gas heaters smoke, along with other problems that are publicly invisible, but no less real to those affected. Despite strenuous efforts to economise, many families have been evicted and resettled in substandard housing, where conditions are often even worse.

Pawning and selling valuables

The liquidation of household assets and the pawning or sale of jewellery and other valuables are other last-resort actions that households are forced to take to protect their consumption. The sale of household items was observed among the poor of South Africa and Sudan, where previously acquired wealth was being consumed in exchange of current income for survival (South Africa 1998; Sudan 1998). Poor urban households in Indonesia have also resorted to pawning or selling valuables as a coping mechanism, while in Latvia a majority among poor households have sold much of their furniture or moved to substandard housing in order to pay off debts and afford food and other necessities (Indonesia 1998; Trapenciere et al. 2000). Few manifestations of poverty among Latvians are more telling than the empty, dark, unheated apartments in which many now live.

Home-based subsistence activities

Income from home production is one of the livelihood sources most subject to household management. It rises and falls with short-term economic swings. It is common for poor households to react to falling incomes by increasing their consumption of goods produced at home. Relying on informal production for sale and saving on goods previously bought in the market have enabled the poor to protect their consumption levels. This strategy is by no means limited to rural households. Many city-dwellers have moved back to live with relatives in the countryside, and even those who still live in cities are engaging in subsistence activities like backyard gardening and raising animals.

Evidence from Bulgaria, Latvia, Mongolia and Indonesia points to the growing importance of home-based production for family consumption. In Bulgaria (1998a), the share of home production in household income doubled, from 14.1 per cent in 1990 to 27.5 per cent in 1995. The substantial increase in the non-monetary share of household income since the beginning of the reforms derived large from this shift to household production. While farmers who used to produce for local markets have moved to large towns or cities, a rising number of urban people are now engaged in subsistence activities producing garments and food for family use.

Another transition country that has experienced a large increase in subsistence production is Latvia (Trapenciere et al. 2000). The dismantling of collective farms after independence affected agricultural wage labourers severely. Those left without a job perform various kinds of wage and self-employed work. But because these multiple activities do not provide year-round incomes, many unemployed people are forced to undertake subsistence work to survive. As the relative importance of the wage sector in the Latvian economy has declined, the country is witnessing a substantial movement of population away from the urban-based cash economy towards subsistence agriculture. This particularly affects the chronic unemployed, many of whom have moved away from the cities where they could not afford the rising cost of living. Some subsistence production takes place in urban areas as well. In addition to extensive backyard and pot gardening for food, animals are raised in apartments for consumption at home.

In Indonesia, which has undergone rapid urbanisation in recent history, the crisis has triggered movements back to agriculture. Instead of borrowing, a predominantly urban practice, consuming one's own production is most prevalent among rural households, both among the poor (50.3 per cent) and the better-off (37.1 per cent). Yet nearly two out of five poor urban households consume goods produced at home (Indonesia 1998). Likewise, widespread unemployment in Mongolia has led more than 95,000 people to move into herding from other economic sectors during the early 1990s to seek an alternative livelihood (Mongolia 1997). Mounting economic pressure is thus transforming the demographic landscape of many countries, whether as a consequence of long-term transition or of sudden shock.

Marginal and illegal activities

A varied and disparate number of activities best described as 'marginal' have proliferated as a response to enhanced vulnerability. Sometimes these occur in a context of pseudo-legality or in direct infringement of the law, and are as often an attempt to cope with adversity as an indication of a failure to cope. This does not imply that these activities did not exist before poverty set in or that they are confined to poor households. But faced with an increasingly hostile environment, some people have had to resort to whatever means possible to survive, which are often found in the interstices of the economy and society.

The heterogeneous mix of activities included in this category range from cheating at work to engaging in production or consumption in the black market, or undertaking illegitimate and even illegal actions. In Bulgaria (1998c), the same factors that are pushing workers towards informality also foster informal consumption in the black market. Unbilled services, undeclared activities and rents, and the hiring of illegal labour for construction and household repairs have become frequent among people who try to avoid sliding into poverty. There is also growing absenteeism in many Bulgarian firms because of people's need to moonlight. Petty theft at work for sale in the black economy is on the rise in Latvia. Some poor households, striving to make a living, engage in the illegal production and sale of alcohol, and alcohol abuse has become a matter of growing concern (Gassmann and de Neubourg 2000).

In Grenada, women who took part in focus groups discussions said that they often had no choice but to prostitute themselves. Selling their bodies was the only option they saw to obtain money to feed their children (Kairi 1998). Findings from participatory assessments in Uganda and South Africa also showed young girls and adolescent boys frequently engaging in prostitution to survive. Drug trafficking and stealing were other illegitimate activities often associated with poor youths and street children from these countries (Uganda 1999a; South Africa 1998). Apart from being a symptom of declining capabilities, illegal and marginal activities often result in social exclusion and stigma, further restricting the opportunities people may face in the future.

The limits of coping: Reciprocity networks in crisis?

The significance of what some authors call 'social capital' has been increasingly recognised in recent years. Social bonds and networks based on principles of trust and reciprocity enable people to pool resources and services in mutually beneficial arrangements, by encouraging economies of scale in purchasing or cooking, or the voluntary exchange of labour for harvesting and housing. They also provide an essential buffer, allowing the poor to borrow from neighbours or move in with relatives in times of need.

For these reasons, kin and friendship networks are a vital support mechanism, since the poor rely on them for the mutual exchange of goods, services and money. In Grenada, such self-help practices permeate society through the *marron* system, an arrangement in which people share their time and labour to help one another with house repairs and the planting or reaping of crops. Friendship networks also provide daily mutual assistance and support in difficult times, involving even exchanges of water, food and shopping essentials (Kairi 1998). In Papua New Guinea, the *wantok* system, based on kinship ties and other relationships among people of the same language group, operates like the *marron* for social exchanges sanctioned by the community. It not only constitutes a crucial ingredient in rural livelihoods, but links rural and urban areas through an elaborate system of reciprocal obligations that binds those who have already moved towns and cities with people of their own background in the countryside (Papua New Guinea 1998).

Other examples of the importance of reciprocity networks emerge from rural Uganda, where many families derive a large part of their livelihood from close relatives, friends and churches, as well as Latvia, where most people engage in exchanging goods and services with other households. Some poor households in Uganda, especially those that are female-headed and lack support from an estranged husband or his family, draw as much as 70 per cent of their livelihoods from relatives and friends (Uganda 1999b, 1999c). In Latvia, it is estimated that over 30 per cent of the households in the richest quintile give cash, goods or services to other families, while over 50 per cent of all households rely on networks of mutual help for short-term emergencies or long-term crises (Trapenciere et al. 2000). In Palestine, too, people lacking old-age security rely on support from family members, without which they would be unable to manage (Palestine 1998).

Yet however important these social networks and mutual support may be, the fact remains that such 'community' aspects of survival are limited. These resources

Box 5. Social networks, central to people's livelihoods

Kinship ties and community networks based on social exchange and solidarity allow not only for the pooling of resources and services that make people's undertakings more efficient or productive, but provide them with a crucial buffer during emergencies and crises.

People consider their social networks a critical ingredient of wellbeing. In Mongolia, the herder households ranked as poorest and richest in qualitative assessments were those that had the weakest and strongest social bonds in their communities. Poor households tended to have few social contacts, compared with the dense web of connections maintained by better-off households. In Maldives, the progressive replacement of the extended-family system by the nuclear family seems to be one of the main causes of the increasing hardships faced by many families in the poorest atolls. In Uganda, too, people associated poverty with reduced cooperation in the family, increased social isolation and a process of 'every one caring for oneself'.

are finite — and, apparently, diminishing under the pressures of poverty itself in several countries. Under conditions of extreme hardship, reciprocity may cease to be possible. Growing stresses on kinship and neighbourhood ties can erode and eventually exhaust these relationships of mutual help and solidarity that provide critical safety nets for the poor. This, in turn, can result in increasing social isolation, a phenomenon that has received little attention despite the fact that it appears to be an important outcome of poverty.

Evidence from Uganda (1999b, 1999c) confirms that worsening standards of living are straining traditional safety nets of mutual assistance and support. The *wantok* system in Papua New Guinea is also showing some fissures resulting from growing stress. Under its system of reciprocal obligations, urban *wantoks* are responsible for supporting rural people who move to the city. But the magnitude of *wantok* obligations has expanded to the point where some urban households can no longer fulfil all their duties, and are forced to withhold support from members of their kin groups (Papua New Guinea 1998). In Latvia and other Baltic states, people accustomed to depending on social networks have had to curtail their socialising; poverty has reduced their ability to maintain those networks at precisely the time when they are most needed. Moreover, as people become more isolated, they cut themselves off from the sources of information and assistance that could help them overcome their problems (Trapenciere et al. 2000).

Unsurprisingly, people without family or neighbourhood support face greater day-to-day livelihood difficulties. Isolated households are found to be more prone to poverty than those that can count on supportive social networks — yet another indication of the importance of these networks to wellbeing. Old age and widowhood, for example, are frequently associated with poverty, particularly when combined with lack of support from relatives. Female-headed families that are left-behind are also strongly represented among the poor, especially when remittances from a husband or male relative are low or uncertain. In Maldives, a country with one of the highest divorce rates in the world, women face great economic hardship in caring for their children, since many men fail to provide for their family's sustenance. The progressive replacement of the extended-family system by the nuclear family seems to be one of the main causes of women's increasing financial hardships (Maldives 1998).

Mounting pressure on households sometimes leads to the premature separation of family members, as in Uganda, where girls are forced to marry young for 'bride price' that can sustain ageing parents and other family members, particularly in times of need (Uganda 1999b). Migration in search of work, a common practice among poor people, may also lead to the gradual disintegration of family ties. In South Africa (1998), poverty has been linked with the fragmentation of family relationships and alienation from the community. Social cohesion has been severely affected by the forced displacement of poor communities, which has destroyed their support networks. Rising violence and crime have further contributed to the spread of fear and mistrust, undermining cooperation and solidarity in the poorest communities, which, ironically, are those that need them most. Evidence of deteriorating family life, domestic violence and separation or divorce is also found among the poor in other countries, together with a growing incidence of alcoholism, drug abuse and suicide.[14]

It is worth noting that the weakening of social bonds is associated not only with unemployment and insecurity of livelihoods, but with the burdens of excessive workloads that limits people's time for social interaction. For example, since the closure of publicly provided day-care centres in the early 1990s, Mongolian women are forced to accommodate both the demands of a job and their child-rearing responsibilities[15] (Mongolia 1997).

Because of the curtailing of social relations, the nuclear family has emerged in some countries as people's only shelter. In-depth interviews in Latvia show that families under stress either disintegrate or become more united, though a decision to remain together is sometimes dictated simply by scarcity. Many women with children choose to stay with a husband to avoid the greater distress they may face on their own, taking care of children while also working. The erosion of networks and the resulting atomisation of nuclear households have contributed to feelings of depression and low self-esteem (Trapenciere et al. 2000).

This shows that poverty and social isolation are closely related. Emphasis on the agency of the poor must not ignore the effects of severe stress on their resilience and adaptability. The 'protective' and cushioning functions of family and social networks cannot be seen as infinitely elastic. They have definite limits, and may erode to the point of exhaustion if stretched beyond those limits.

Conclusions

Research on households has made critical contributions to our knowledge of the impact of economic and societal change on people's lives, and the ways in which they organise themselves to cope with adversity. We now have a better understanding of the processes leading to vulnerability and the strategies deployed by poor households to keep it at bay. Households are very sensitive to economic and social change. Given their dependence on wage employment for survival, their organisation is intimately affected by trends in the labour market. Policies that impinge on the dynamics of the labour market are thus a major determinant of wellbeing. To comprehend the changing nature of vulnerability, we need an approach that combines the microanalysis of households and the analysis of policy and institutional change at the macro- and meso-levels.

This chapter has provided ample evidence of the shrinkage of opportunities for the poor, characterised by a decline of wage employment and people's growing difficulties in mobilising their labour as an asset. This has major implications for the economy and social organisation of poor households, affecting their division of labour as well as their income-generating strategies.

Work strategies for coping include sending more household members into the workforce and engaging in a range of cash and subsistence activities. Women's contributions to the household economy become more important as men's capacity to generate a sufficient income declines. Work hours become both longer and harder, jobs increasingly precarious and low-paid. Children, too, become income earners. As a result, the relative weight of informal work in the household economy tends to rise, as does the share of goods produced and consumed at home.

Work intensification strategies are often supplemented by other domestic responses aimed at shifting consumption and reducing total household expenditures. Normally, these responses take place when the mobilisation of additional household labour fails to protect family wellbeing or to forestall vulnerability. Indeed, the shifting and cutting of consumption are clear signs of vulnerability that become manifest when strategies to stretch household resources are no longer effective. The reduction of food intake, in particular, is a last-resort measure. When restrictive mechanisms go beyond minimising expenditure to the liquidation of household property and savings, the household's total resource endowment declines — yet another indication that a household is failing to cope successfully.

This points to an important finding of this chapter. The much-celebrated resilience of the poor has its limits. We need to revisit analytical models based on the assumption that the poor can always adapt to changing conditions and still survive. Emphasis on the agency of the poor should not blind us to the fact that the actions implemented by the poor to secure a livelihood take place in a context of structural constraints — and that under that certain conditions, these constraints can be crushing. The 'private adjustments' of households may become too costly for sustaining their wellbeing and reproduction.

As we have seen, household restructuring typically imposes unequal burdens on its members. The accumulated evidence suggests that women bear a particularly heavy share of the cost produced by adjustment and change. By increasing significantly their participation in the labour force, they have expanded further their already vital contributions to the domestic economy, often becoming main breadwinners. This, however, has not improved their position within the household. There, they continue to play a subordinate role.

Households are dynamic entities. As they evolve, their capacity to mobilise labour and confront vulnerability varies. They are a locus of 'cooperative conflict', in which interests merge and reinforce each other as well as compete for access to rights and resources. Together with reciprocity networks based on kin and friendship relations, households constitute an essential mechanism for the survival and reproduction of the poor. As their internal organisation and their capacity to engage in social exchange erode, poor households are cut off from vital sources of support and may disintegrate. Social isolation, that critical and often neglected outcome of poverty, increases people's vulnerability, accelerating a process of cumulative disadvantages that may further impair their ability to recover and climb out of their traps. ■

Notes

Ms. González de la Rocha is Senior Researcher at the Centro de Investigaciones y Estudios Superiores en Antropología Social (CIESAS), Guadalajara, Mexico. Alejandro Grinspun is Social Policy Advisor at UNDP, New York. The authors are highly indebted to Agustín Escobar from CIESAS for his valuable inputs during the research for this chapter.

[1] The review comprises 22 reports from 15 countries (Angola, Bulgaria, Grenada, Indonesia, Latvia, Lebanon, Maldives, Mongolia, Palestine, Papua New Guinea, South Africa, South Korea, Sudan, Uganda and Uruguay). The studies were sponsored by UNDP through the Poverty Strategies Initiative (PSI).

[2] Human capital (health, education and skills), natural resources, productive assets, time, family cohesion, claims and entitlements, and social and institutional networks are other important household resources that can be mobilised against vulnerability. Here the analysis centres on labour, not only because it is a resource that poor people have abundantly, but also because their success or failure to put labour to work is a central issue regarding vulnerability.

[3] Having access to wages, income from self-employment or pensions is associated with the lowest poverty risk, compared with households depending on income from agriculture or other social transfers. One third of the individuals in households that depend on social transfers other than pensions live below the poverty line of 24 Lats, while agriculture predominates in the two lowest quintiles of the income distribution. In contrast, private sector employment is heavily concentrated in the highest quintile, which also has a large proportion of families with at least one member with a public-sector job. While access to social assistance and unemployment compensation help some households rise above poverty levels, they are not universally available, partly because of the growth in informal sector activities.

[4] Employment is a much more significant factor than labour force participation rates in explaining poverty rates in Palestine, even though low wages are still a better predictor of poverty levels. Only 16 per cent of the households in which the head is employed full time are poor, as opposed to 34 per cent of the households in which the head worked only part of the previous twelve months.

[5] The poor in South Korea are classified in five categories, almost all of which are related to employment. They comprise those who are unable to work because of age or disability; those

who are unemployed but able to work; the underemployed; those who are employed but unproductive; and those who are employed but carry a heavy burden of expenses for housing, education and health care.

[6] By and large, women sell fruits and vegetables, but fishing, small-scale cattle raising and street vending are other activities typical of this sector. Although found among all social strata, unemployment is particularly high among the youth and older, unskilled workers, particularly women, and is strongly associated with household poverty.

[7] Casual labour normally involves piece-meal work in one's community, as well as work performed by migrants in other cities or areas of Uganda. Manufacturing is a male activity, but many women participate in petty trading, especially as 'verandah traders' and in the 'evening markets', which started when urbanisation took place and many people migrated from the countryside. Although marketing of produce is mainly the responsibility of men, some women participate, albeit only with their husbands' permission. Women also predominate in the production of cassava, potatoes and cotton, where they perform as much as 50 per cent of the work.

[8] Research conducted in Mexico during the economic crisis of the 1980s found that extended households were better-suited than nuclear households to implement labour-intensive strategies, especially if they were at a stage in their domestic cycle in which children were able to participate as income earners. Extended households were characterised by greater flexibility and the availability of a greater pool of members devoted to income-earning activities (Selby et al. 1990; González de la Rocha 1994). Chant (1991) also found that extended households are more conducive to women's participation in the labour market and to higher levels of income.

[9] The expansion phase refers to the situation where the domestic unit grows and increases its number of members through the birth of new members. The dispersion phase, in turn, starts when the members of the household begin to separate from the household of origin to form and organise their own units (González de la Rocha 1994).

[10] Sending children to work may also serve to protect households' income and ensure their reproduction during a crisis, but it also curtails children's life prospects and often contributes to the transmission of disadvantage to the next generation. This further highlights the contradictory nature of many household strategies, some of which may severely limit the possibility of longer-term actions.

[11] Research on the impact of economic crisis in Latin America during the 1980s documented the process of adjustment within poor urban households. One major contribution was the emphasis on the 'agency' of the poor and the rationality of their behaviour as they struggled to adapt to changing conditions. This challenged a long tradition of research that gave pre-eminence to structural factors in the analysis of social change. However, an excessive emphasis on poor people's capacity to adapt runs the risk of overlooking the fact that households' resilience is not infinitely elastic. Coping normally involves a delicate balance between short-term strategies for survival and long-term social reproduction, and the result of this tension is not always sustainable. Protracted crises, in particular, may erode and eventually deplete the resource base on which people's livelihoods depend. It is therefore important to introduce the concept of 'sus-

tainability' into the understanding of how people cope with structural constraints.

[12] The positive contribution of women's work to household consumption in Angola derives from several factors. First, a working wife often has a working husband, while the opposite is not as frequent; secondly, wives often earn more than their husbands; and thirdly, they tend to spend a larger proportion of their earnings on the consumption of basic necessities.

[13] We have included home-based production and migration to the countryside among the restrictive household practices, even though the former involves an element of work substitution and the latter is often driven by a search for work. While home-based production for own consumption involves a decision by a household on how best to deploy its labour power, this decision normally does not involve the mobilisation of additional household labour. Its main rationale, furthermore, is not to increase household resources but to reduce expenses on goods previously purchased in the market. Migration, in turn, can be interpreted as a strategy to enhance household resources by sending family members to work in cities or abroad for extra income. The emphasis here, however, is on movements away from the urban-based cash economy to rural-based subsistence activities, implemented in many countries to minimise consumer spending and protect basic consumption.

[14] Drinking is a major problem in Latvia, where it is considered both a cause and a consequence of long-term unemployment and poverty. Chronic unemployment is reported to have significant consequences for the persons involved, who become apathetic, depressed and prone to abuse alcohol in their search for an escape from the stark reality of their lives (Gassmann and de Neubourg 2000). Alcohol abuse is also common among poor men in Uganda, while Bhangi smoking has become popular among youths in the slum settlements of Kampala (Uganda 1999a).

[15] Changes in the intensity of social relations are also related to changing work patterns and organisation of production. Before the transition, socialist collectives offered considerable opportunities for social interaction, while job security resulted in employment within the same organisation for long periods of time. Both of these disappeared from the life of the Mongolian people after the transition. Higher travel costs, in turn, have weakened the ties between rural and urban members of family networks, as people are no longer able to afford a visit to relatives as often as in the past. It is precisely the unemployed and the poor who possess the fewest social contacts in present-day Mongolia.

4 Rural-Urban Linkages and Poverty Analysis

Alf Morten Jerve

Most developing countries today are undergoing a process of rapid urbanisation and are seeing a dramatic movement of people to towns and cities. Concurrently, circular migration between the rural and urban spheres has increased, as has the number households and families — many of whom are poor — who operate in both spheres. In Africa it is estimated that half of the poor will live in cities within 10 years from now, up from 35 per cent in 1996. The trends are similar in Asia, whereas in Latin America the situation appears to be more stable. The biggest wave of urbanisation in this region has already taken place and currently, about 75 per cent of Latin Americans live in cities. Nevertheless, rural forms of poverty are not declining in importance. While there are incidences of disenfranchised, poor, rural families filling urban slums, there is also evidence that support from the rural base constitutes an important element of the livelihood of the urban poor.

Most national planners and politicians are cognisant of the different challenges posed by rural and urban development. It is generally acknowledged that what happens in one sector influences the other, but there is no consensus on how these dynamics work. As a result, countries invariably have developed distinct policies for what are often considered as two separate sectors.

There is also a common understanding that the problem of poverty manifests itself in rather different ways in rural and urban environments, but poverty studies vary a great deal on how they analyse these differences. While the rural-urban dichotomy appears in most poverty statistics, the analytical significance of this distinction is less apparent. There is seldom a focus on how rural and urban poverty may be interlinked, and this may have consequences for the understanding of processes of impoverishment, as well as the formulation of policies to address them. Many researchers even go as far as questioning whether it is meaningful to treat rural and urban as two distinct forms of poverty. There is a danger that a dichotomisation of poverty may draw the attention away from the dynamics of the rural-urban interface, blurring important interdependencies between the two.[1]

It is our contention that the dynamics of poverty in the rapidly urbanising countries of the developing world have to be understood in the interplay between the rural and the urban spheres. A better understanding of the rural-urban interface is critical to the formulation of national poverty reduction strategies, particularly in countries experiencing rapid urbanisation or escalating rural-urban disparities. We need to comprehend such issues as:

- The patterns of migration between rural and urban areas;
- How intra-family resources flow across the rural-urban divide;
- The role of rural-urban links in strengthening poor people's capabilities for collective action;
- Whether our definitions of households as economic units grasp the realities of rural-*cum*-urban livelihood strategies, and therefore correctly depict incidences of poverty;
- The potential for achieving broad-based economic growth through an improvement of linkages between rural and urban spheres.

In this chapter we shall examine a sample of reports sponsored by the Poverty Strategies Initiative (PSI) of the United Nations Development Programme (UNDP) in nine countries: Angola, Lesotho, South Africa and Zambia in sub-Saharan Africa; Maldives, Nepal, Palestine and Papua New Guinea in Asia; and Latvia in Eastern Europe. The reports generally contain an analysis of rural and urban poverty, and present policy recommendations related to urban and rural development. The chapter is based mainly on a review of documents sponsored by the PSI programme and does not claim to be representative of the full range of poverty research in the countries selected.

We start by briefly discussing how rural and urban issues have been treated in the development literature, including more specifically in the analysis of the determinants of poverty. We then present some of the empirical findings contained in the PSI studies, which confirm that there is no emerging consensus on how rural-urban dynamics work. We first look at how the prevalence of poverty is presented and the explanations of rural-urban discrepancies. Then we proceed to show how this is translated into policy prescriptions. Throughout, our main objective is to distil particular insights on the rural-urban interface in these countries and identify critical lacunas in the analyses, in order to draw lessons that may be of general relevance for analysing poverty.

Why the rural-urban interface matters

The rural and urban in development theory

Many of the central debates in development literature have centred on the relationship between the rural and the urban spheres. These debates demonstrate how theoretical and methodological biases in development research may produce findings that overlook important aspects of social dynamics.

The hegemony of certain biases has indeed had a direct bearing upon development policies and aid priorities. During the immediate post-war period, most governments encouraged urban development. This was, in fact, a core element of the post-colonial nation-building project. Until the 1960s, the mainstream development theory of modernisation emphasised industrialisation — which was closely associated with urban growth — as the engine of economic and social development. The rural population was mainly perceived as a labour reservoir for industry and commercial farms. Rural development was promoted only to the extent needed to reproduce labour, and later to stem the exodus of rural poor to the cities. This notion of a dual economy came to dominate development strategies in many regions of the world. In its most extreme form, it served as the economic rationale for the mining industry and the *apartheid* state of South Africa. The less extreme interpretation was the 'trickle down' perspective, according to which the modern and mostly urban sector eventually would penetrate and transform backward rural areas.

The development assumptions of this two-sector growth model were severely critiqued by the dependency school of the 1960s and 1970s. The dependency theorists argued that the growth of urban centres was based on the exploitation of rural areas, which prevented them from taking advantage of their own development potential. This would eventually lead to underdevelopment rather than growth. The 'urban bias' thesis, presented by Michael Lipton (1977), showed that the tariff, trade, taxation and sector investment policies pursued by most governments had deprived rural areas of resources and infrastructure. This thesis became mainstream development thinking in the 1970s and 1980s.

In response to this radical critique, development agencies began to redirect their priorities towards rural development well into the 1980s. These attempts to make up for decades of rural neglect were accompanied by two important shifts in development paradigms opposing the post-war modernisation and trickle-down economic theories. First, across the East-West divide, the international community formulated a rights-based approach to human welfare, as reflected in the UN Covenant on Economic, Social and Cultural Rights. This was supported by the doctrine of 'basic needs', which held that the international community was responsible for ensuring universal coverage of primary social services. This implied that the needs of a rural person no longer had less priority than those of an urban person.

As a concurrent trend, development researchers advocated the role of the agricultural sector as the engine of growth in developing countries. The success of the Japanese and later the South Korean economy was believed to rest in a large measure on the modernisation and surplus production in agriculture. The land reforms that took place in those countries ensured a more equitable distribution of land, which served as a major catalyst for the impressive economic performance that followed. The improvements in wellbeing gained through land reforms initiated by revolutionary governments in China and Cuba also strongly influenced this view. Agricultural surplus production, it was argued, is not merely a means to feed a growing urban population. It also generates demand for industrial products and know-how, which stimulates economic growth and urban development. In this perspective, the picture is reversed: urban development is seen as contingent on rural development.

It is interesting that both the old dual-economy paradigm and the agricultural growth model represent theories of rural-urban links. The biases are definitely different, but both theories bring the rural-urban dynamics centre stage. It is the very nature of this relationship that represents the prime developmental force. This has led researchers to focus more directly on the interdependence and symbiosis of the rural *and* urban spheres.[2] These shifts in paradigms and perspectives have had important consequences for the study of poverty.

The rural and urban in poverty research

The analysis of poverty has been running in tandem with this broader development debate. But contrary to the development theories outlined above, the poverty discourse has to a much lesser extent focussed on the rural-urban link. Studies have tended to present a static picture of two categories of poverty, urban and rural. Surveys have recorded household-related socio-economic data, classified according to the place of residence of the household (notably the dwelling where the interview takes place) in a manner that distinguishes between rural and urban domicile. Survey designs have been ill-equipped to capture the fact that family units in societies under stress or rapid change may adopt a wide range of strategies, including that of having one foot in a rural economy and the other in an urban, or foreign, economy.

The statistical unit — a household, defined as a group of people sharing the same roof or pot at a specific point in time — may not represent a significant unit of analysis for social and economic decision-making. It may well be that the unit surveyed is only one branch of a larger household or family concern. Surplus in one branch may subsidise others. For example, low per capita consumption in one branch, such as a rural village, may in fact be a deliberate decision to funnel resources to another branch (for instance, family members pursuing education or work opportunities in an urban area). Such relationships, as well as the transient nature of many households, are critical factors for understanding poverty. A certain statistical pattern of rural and urban poverty can therefore disguise substantial dynamics embedded in rural-urban links. Where attempts have been made to incorporate these dimensions in surveys, it has been difficult to get reliable information on intra-family transfers.

The need for different poverty lines has long been recognised in poverty measurements. At the same time, there is also a strong case for treating the rural-urban divide as a continuum, rather than a sharp divide.[3] One would expect rural-urban linkages to be particularly prevalent in countries with rapid urbanisation. These linkages would normally involve seasonal labour migration, remittances, divided households, market exchange, flow of critical information and education opportunities, among others. New economic hardships have also resulted in the strengthening of rural-urban linkages among the poor in many transition economies.[4] In spite of this, measurements of poverty based on conventional definitions of household income or consumption tell little about how people manage under such circumstances, a perspective that is necessary to develop well-targeted public policy.

Rural-urban issues in poverty measurement and analysis

Research on poverty has typically treated the rural and urban spheres as two distinct categories of analysis, presenting a somewhat static picture of each and neglecting important interdependencies between them. This pattern, which has important implications for policy design, is also found in the analytical work carried out in our nine countries with support from UNDP.

In this section, we examine the main findings from these analyses, both with respect to the measurement of poverty and the identification of its causes. We focus first on the four countries in our sample that, according to the Human Development Index (UNDP 1997), are classified as having a low level of human development: Angola, Lesotho, Nepal and Zambia. Then we present two special cases: the archipelago of the Maldives and the archetypical dual economy of Papua New Guinea. These six countries have a sizable proportion of their population living in rural areas. Finally, we look at the three cases characterised by a relatively higher level of urbanisation: the Palestine territory entirely dependent on the Israeli economy, the transition economy of Latvia, which has experienced a major collapse of rural enterprises and the post-*apartheid* state of South Africa.

Angola, Lesotho, Nepal and Zambia
Angola

Poverty analysis becomes particularly difficult in Angola, a country ridden by 30 years of liberation and civil wars. The economy consists of four 'sectors', with widely different ramifications and rules of operation. The offshore oil exploration controlled by government is an enclave operation, an almost closed economic system with few direct linkages to the remaining economy. The largely informal urban sector supplies the bulk of goods and services in the cities and, foremost in Luanda, is fuelled indirectly by oil revenues and international aid. Due to the war and damaged infrastructure, the third sector, the rural hinterland, has for most practical purposes ceased to function as a regular economy. Commercial linkages with the urban economy are weak or completely cut off. The remaining 'sector' is the war economy of the areas controlled by UNITA, financed through the export of diamonds. The four 'sectors' are politically constituted by the logic of the war, which leaves very little room for a functional integration of rural and urban development.

Poverty measurements in a situation of war will have wide margins of error.

Families are artificially split and markets are highly distorted. Large rural populations have fled or been forcibly evicted from their homes, and migration to the capital city has been formidable. In spite of this, urban poverty is measured at half the rate of rural areas: 37 and 78 per cent respectively. Had it not been for the large number of refugees fleeing to the Luanda region, the contrasts would have been even greater. This reflects enormous differences in resource flows as well as the impact of war. Many rural areas and secondary towns in Angola largely correspond to the war zone, while Luanda, and to a lesser extent other cities, are safe havens.

The study financed by UNDP provides only indirect evidence of rural-urban linkages (Wold and Grave 1999). The data presented in the study are based on surveys from urban areas. They depict a vibrant urban economy in Luanda, where 40 per cent of the work force is involved in the informal sector. Two-thirds of those engaged in informal activities are women. The level of education of female heads of household is presented as the single most significant contributor to poverty reduction. This underscores women's important role as breadwinners in the urban economy. Analysis of rural household data does not reveal any similar role of women, probably because production for the market is very low in rural areas.

Little is said about the extent of rural to urban migration, although it would have been interesting to know how many in Luanda are regular labour migrants and how many are refugees uprooted from their rural homeland. One could expect, for instance, that labour migrants and displaced people will have different coping strategies once they arrive in the capital city. It would also be useful to have information about the extent to which urban dwellers and immigrants are able to send remittances to their home villages, especially in the war zone. Since there are few reliable surveys on rural livelihoods in Angola, we cannot determine how important is the contribution made by remittances from urban areas.

An important question for post-war development policies in Angola would be whether women in rural areas could play roles in the rural informal sector similar to those they are playing in the cities. This will be partly determined by the extent to which women today engage in the trade of rural produce. Evidence from several countries in Africa shows that that women are particularly active in rural-urban trade. They bring rural produce to urban markets and take consumer articles like second-hand clothing back to their villages and hamlets. It would thus be important to examine further any such role of female entrepreneurs in urban Angola.

Lesotho

Lesotho is a country with a low level of urbanisation. Only 20 per cent of its population of about two million people live in towns. At six per cent per annum, however, the current rate of urban growth is high and exceeds that of its neighbouring countries.

The rapid influx of people to the capital city of Maseru and other towns stems more from a deterioration of rural agriculture and the mining industry in South Africa than from a growing urban economy that offers new employment opportunities. Agriculture's share of GDP is steadily declining. The rural poor typically rely on agriculture as the primary source of income, while the better-off derive much of their income from labour migration and remittances. Any downturns in the South African economy may severely affect the over 140,000 Basotho males working in the mines, causing a further push towards rural-to-urban migration. Retrenched mine workers will first seek their fortune in urban Lesotho and, depending on circumstances, other family members may follow. As a result, Lesotho must expect a rapid increase in urban poverty, already estimated at 27 per cent of the urban population.

It is against this background that UNDP commissioned an *Urban Poverty Assessment* in 1997. The study starts with the problem of drawing clear boundaries between urban and rural areas. Many of the country's officially gazetted urban areas resemble large villages. As everywhere, there is a continuum in terms of population density from scattered hamlets to city centres, and setting the dividing line between rural and urban tends to become a political rather than a technical decision.

For this reason, distinguishing urban poverty as a category separate from rural poverty is problematic. Linkages between rural and urban areas mean 'that the problems of the urban and rural sectors are bound up with one another and cannot be considered in isolation from each other' (Lesotho 1997). This notwithstanding, poverty in urban environments, such as the capital Maseru, has certain attributes that are less evident in the countryside. The urban poor are typically more dependent on money to fulfil basic needs. Their income generation is more susceptible to the vagaries of the market. Social cohesion is weaker, meaning that poverty is more 'individualised' in urban settings. One example of this is the ticking social time bomb of increasing numbers of 'free-floating', retrenched mineworkers with problems adapting to the economic realities at home. The urban poor also have greater exposure to environmental risks, as well as a relative lack of personal safety as a result of crime, which constrains economic activity.

Urban poverty has been underestimated in earlier statistics that used conventional money-metric measures based on income or consumption. If non-income indicators reflecting entitlements and vulnerability are used, the number of the urban poor, and of poor people in general, definitely increases. Moreover, the application of a uniform poverty line across the country does not account for the fact that 'an urban household would need a higher cash income than rural households to avoid poverty' (Lesotho 1997). All household surveys concur that urban poverty is less severe than rural poverty, but interviews with urban poor indicate more mixed perceptions. People are almost evenly divided about whether life is better in urban or rural areas. As a rule, the urban poor appear to be more vulnerable, although on average they do better economically than their rural counterparts.

Registering household members can be difficult and, if not done correctly, may introduce severe distortions in per capita-based poverty measurements. The average size of the households surveyed by UNDP was 4.2 members, which included absentee members working in South Africa.[5] Two-thirds of the household heads have their roots in the rural area, and half of the households report that their relatives live in the countryside. This indicates fairly recent urban settlement.

The urban poor rely heavily on petty trade and casual labour for their cash income, but remittances also play a role. It is likely that receipts in kind are under-reported in the UNDP study, since only 13 per cent mention this as a source of income. Surprisingly, there is no mention of the economic importance of prostitution, which appears to constitute a valuable source of income for many single women in urban Southern Africa. It is also difficult to draw any firm conclusions regarding the size of inter-household transfers. About 40 per cent report that they never or rarely give or receive economic assistance to and from relatives. If this is the true pattern, it corresponds to similar findings from studies of urban poverty in Namibia, where a core of urban poor (generally the poorest) has lost ties with their rural home area (Tvedten and Nangulah 1999). This underscores the fact that the vulnerability of poor urban residents increases when they no longer are in a position to maintain relations with the home village.

The incidence of female-headed households is high, at 28 per cent, according to a survey conducted in 1987. The share among poor households is even higher. The UNDP assessment puts this figure at 35 per cent, of which half are widowed and the rest divorced or unmarried. Per capita income of female-headed households is less than two-thirds of households headed by men. The main differentiating factor is that men have access to better paid jobs, especially in South Africa.

Failing to get such employment, a man often becomes more of a liability than a resource for the household. This is especially the case in an urban context, where the man cannot assume his traditional role in agriculture and livestock farming. There is ample evidence that many women break off relations with men who no longer function as breadwinners, and that the general picture of female-headed households as a social malady has to be qualified. From the point of view of the woman and her dependants, she may in many circumstances stand a better chance of coping with poverty by staying free of conjugal obligations to a man and his family.

Low-cost housing areas in Lesotho towns conceal great variation in household incomes, which indicates that city life is regarded by most as temporary. Obtaining a plot of suburban land has been relatively easy through allocation of communal land controlled by the chiefs. Even the poorest households hold land and own homes almost as frequently as wealthier households do.

People seem reluctant, however, to invest in improving their urban house, and also to engage in urban community affairs. For the many first generation urban residents, 'life in the city is regarded only as a temporary necessity, and not as a permanent departure from the rural village' (Lesotho 1997). This attitude is further exacerbated by the widespread disillusionment with local municipal authorities. In the peri-urban areas of Maseru, allegiance to the local chiefs is apparently strong. These popular resentments, and the continued existence of links back to the village, may be a vital resource in stemming urban migration, but only if and when policies for sustainable rural livelihoods can be developed.

Nepal

Despite the fact that Nepal is a stable country, its rural-urban contrasts are no less striking than in Angola. Nepal's population of about 20 million is overwhelmingly rural, with only 12 per cent living in cities and towns. More than half of the urban population is concentrated in Kathmandu, whose population has tripled between 1971 and 1991.

Nepal's level of per capita income is among the lowest in the world. Urban income is more than double the rural income levels and, for Kathmandu, average household income is four times the rural average. The country depends heavily on agriculture, but the growth in agricultural production is outpaced by population growth. As a result, the services sector today, which is mainly urban-based, equals the share of agriculture in GDP. Public as well as private investments are highly urban-biased.

Ample evidence of the rural-urban dichotomy is presented in the *Nepal Human Development Report* (HDR), published in 1998. Unfortunately, the report does not contain a definition of what is understood as urban areas. Presumably statistics are based on the distinction between administratively defined urban and rural local government units.

There is great variation in measurements of the *income* poverty headcount, depending on the definition of the cut-off point. It ranges from about 30 per cent based on minimum subsistence consumption levels, to 70 per cent based on US$150 per capita per year. Common to all measurements, however, is that the headcount is much lower (from half to one-third) for urban than rural areas. In other words, the incidence of rural poverty is about 2.5 times higher than in urban areas, although income disparities are significantly greater in the latter.

Furthermore, the Human Development Index for rural areas is two-thirds that of urban areas. Rural households rely mostly on agriculture for their income (65 per cent), much of which is retained for domestic use. In fact, only 40 per cent of total income is in the form of cash. Still, studies have shown that wage income accounts for almost 30 per cent of total rural income. This indicates that many rural households depend heavily on agricultural wage work or other manual jobs to supplement their own cultivation, and reflects a situation of extreme scarcity of cultivable land, unequal land distribution and a large number of marginal farmers. As many as 40 per cent of

farming households own less than 0.5 ha of land, which accounts for the strong correlation found between size of landholding and household income (Nepal 1998).

Measurements of poverty using indicators of human *capability* (child nutritional status, female literacy, and quality of reproductive health care) reveal an even
bleaker picture. People are much more capability-poor than income-poor, and contrary to expectations, relatively more so as one ascends the income scale. Access to
economic resources alone has obviously not enhanced wellbeing significantly.
Urbanisation may improve income-earning opportunities, but this is not automatically translated into improved livelihoods.

The relatively better status of urban areas does not reflect itself in the status of
women. In fact, female participation in the labour force is higher in rural areas, and
shows even a declining trend in urban areas. It thus seems plausible that urbanisation has impacted adversely on women's income earning opportunities. On the
other hand, surveys do not corroborate the generally held belief that female-headed households are worse-off. The reason appears to be that households headed by
women receive remittances from migrant male household members. If this is the
case, it is an important effect of migration.

The Nepal HDR strongly argues that the worsening poverty trends, both in
absolute numbers and relative terms, are linked to failed agricultural development.
The marginal growth per capita in the 1980s and 1990s was highly skewed in
favour of the non-agricultural sector and urban areas. The market-oriented economic policies put in place from about 1990 did not make a dent in poverty, as was
projected. Rather, 'the withdrawal of subsidies, mass retrenchment of civil servants,
wage freeze, deregulation of administered prices and upward revision in the prices
of the goods and services delivered by public enterprises have had an adverse effect
on the situation of poverty' (Nepal 1998). These factors overshadowed any benefits that may have accrued from macroeconomic stability and reduced inflation,
particularly in the agricultural sector.

There are several causes for low agricultural productivity and its weak effect in
reducing poverty. The single most important factor seems to be the highly unequal
distribution of land and the failure of successive governments to effectively embrace
agrarian reform and maximise the number of viable landholdings. Other factors
relate to inadequate investments in physical infrastructure, especially in irrigation.
Access to credit for rural farmers is a third major problem, which has only been
aggravated following the deregulation of the banking sector in the 1990s.

Zambia

Post-independence Zambia has continued the urban-led development path established under British colonial rule. Its economy is highly dependent on the extraction
and export of copper, which generate revenues that are largely funnelled to urban

areas. Even today, Zambia's copper mining sector accounts for over 80 per cent of the nation's foreign currency receipts. The downturn in the copper market paved the way for a structural adjustment package, negotiated with the International Monetary Fund (IMF) in the early 1990s. Although the economy has seen some recent signs of recovery, poverty has been steadily increasing, reaching a level of almost 80 per cent by the end of the decade. Income distribution is extremely skewed, with 5 per cent of the population accounting for almost half of the national income.

The country's history has been one of rural neglect. The urban population, especially the mineworkers, have been a dominant political force, pressing governments to retain subsidies to vital consumption goods. Besides draining the public coffers, this policy worsened the rural terms of trade. These problems have continued even after the liberalisation of the economy. With the removal of input subsides and escalating marketing costs, many rural smallholders in recent years have returned to mainly subsistence farming, as they are no longer able to make a profit on cash crops (especially maize).

Given this situation, the government of Zambia decided to formulate a national strategy for poverty reduction. A framework document was developed in 1998 on the basis of a thoroughly consultative process, which was assisted by UNDP. Although the document presents no in-depth analysis of poverty, it does emphasise the existence of a vast rural-urban gap and the gravity of massive deprivation in the countryside, where poverty rates double those of urban areas (Zambia 1998).

Regrettably, there is no analysis of possible inter-linkages between rural and urban areas. With a continuous decline in the rural economy, it is likely that a growing number of Zambians will be forced to seek opportunities in the urban economy. For policy-makers, therefore, it would be of interest to know what role remittances from the urban economy play in the form of a safety net in rural areas. It is equally important to know whether support to the informal urban economy could provide a mechanism for harnessing urban-rural transfers for reinvestment in agriculture.

Maldives and Papua New Guinea
Maldives

The geography of the Maldives archipelago represents a unique case where nature itself sets absolute limitations on urban expansion. The country consists of twenty-six natural coral atolls comprising a total of 1,190 islands, of which only 200 are inhabited. The total landmass is very small, and a population of only 250,000 people creates a density as high as 480 persons per square kilometre. There are islands with more than 500 persons per hectare, but it is only in the capital city of Male' that a typical urban environment has developed. Male' is the centre of an economy that has experienced sustained growth over the past two decades, averaging almost 8 per cent per year, based on a rapid increase in tourism and the doubling of the total fish catch due to the introduction of new technologies. This development spurred rapid urbanisation and one fourth of the population now lives in Male'.

Although living conditions have improved considerably over the past decade, poverty — characterised by wide urban-rural disparities — is still found throughout the archipelago. It is in connection with this situation that in 1998, the Ministry of Planning and National Development decided to undertake a *Vulnerability and Poverty Assessment* (VPA) in cooperation with UNDP. The terms 'urban' and 'rural' are not used explicitly in the report, but the statistics presented generally distinguish between Male' and the atolls, which is the only urban-rural distinction that matters in Maldives. Male' is reported to have average incomes twice as large as the rest of the country, and four times the level of public services. It appears nonetheless that income inequality has stabilised in recent years.

Given the extreme variability present across the islands and atolls that comprise the archipelago, defining a single poverty line applicable to the entire country proved to be impossible.[6] Instead, the VPA tests the robustness of poverty rates for three different poverty lines. The lowest one is defined as half of the median household per capital income, which corresponds to approximately US$ 0.65 per person per day and can be used to identify the level of extreme poverty. Fifteen per cent of the national population is extremely poor. Of these, 15 per cent live in Male', which has a headcount ratio of only 7 per cent (Maldives 1998).

Extreme poverty is most prevalent in five atolls (Meemu, Lhaviyani, Baa, Faafu and Thaa) located in the middle north and the middle south of the archipelago. This finding is unexpected, since it implies that there is less poverty in the atolls situated furthest away from the capital. From a regional development perspective, the obvious question would be whether this is simply a reflection of natural variation in resource endowments, or whether there is some causal relationship between proximity to Male' and poverty. The VPA, however, does not probe into these questions.

Beyond identifying the geographical distribution of income poverty, the VPA makes little use of the survey data collected. It seems, however, that potential rural-urban linkages have not been adequately covered. There is no mention of migration patterns or level of remittances, and no tracing of household members living elsewhere, whether in Male', the tourist resorts or abroad (particularly in Australia and Sri Lanka, which are the preferred destinations for many migrants). This seems an important gap, given that households are dynamic social units, in which regular fusion and fission processes to cope with shortfalls in domestic labour and seasonal labour migration can cause significant errors in the measurement of per capita household income. Tourism and fisheries, the two booming sectors of the local economy, are also sectors that typically have seasonal fluctuations in labour demand.

In addition to the household survey, the report presents analyses of island specific information on public services, employment, nutrition and health. The purpose

Table 1. Living standards and poverty in the five poorest atolls of the Maldives

Living standard dimension	National average	Meemu	Lhaviyani	Baa	Faafu	Thaa	Correlation with poverty
Electricity[a]	9	4	4	4	10	15	No correlation
Transport[b]	26	3	47	0	0	4	No correlation, but generally better than average
Ownership of radio[c]	55	77	71	68	36	65	Correlation is fairly high
Education[d]	38	0	0	11	32	31	Educational services are better than average
Health[e]	10	28	0	0	8	7	Only one atoll is below the average standard
Drinking water[f]	-	-	-	-	-	-	None of the five atolls is ranked as having severe problems
Population density[g]	25	29	95	51	20	51	Some correlation: three of the atolls are significantly above average
Mal-nutrition[h]	49	28	49	37	76	33	Only one atoll with a severe problem
Employment in agriculture[i]	99	1	0	0	0	0	Strong correlation: no agricultural employment in four of the atolls
Vulnerability ranking[j]	-	6	12	11	2	9	Poverty is only partly covariant with vulnerability

(a) Percentage of atoll population on islands with no access at all. The highest possible score is 24.

(b) Percentage of atoll population on islands with more than 100 persons per boat. The highest score is 100.

(c) Percentage of atoll population with no radio. The highest score is 77.

(d) Percentage of atoll population on islands with more than 50 students per teacher. The highest score is 82.

(e) Percentage of atoll population on islands with no access to health worker. The highest score is 41.

(f) Reports on 'insufficient' and 'unsafe' drinking water.

(g) Percentage of atoll population on islands with more than 50 persons per hectare. The highest score is 95.

(h) Percentage of girls (1-5 years) with stunted growth.

(i) Percentage of national agricultural work force.

(j) Based on the Human Vulnerability Index across 21 atolls. A score of 1 denotes highest vulnerability.

is to calculate development indices to help locate the most vulnerable islands. A new composite index of poverty and vulnerability, the Human Vulnerability Index (HVI), especially tailored to an island state like Maldives, is presented. The index includes a measure of relative poverty, but only as one of 11 other living standard dimensions. According to the HVI, the highest vulnerability is found in the smallest islands. Interestingly, the islands with the highest incidence of extreme poverty are not necessarily among the most vulnerable.

Regrettably, the VPA does not examine correlations between poverty incidence and the other dimensions that comprise the HVI with a view to identifying possible causes of poverty. To do this, we have looked at the data that correspond to the five most poverty-dominant atolls (Table 1).

The emerging picture is far from conclusive. Income poverty is correlated with private ownership of a radio, which is quite plausible. The strongest correlation appears to be in relation to agriculture. There is no or insignificant agriculture in the five atolls. But surprisingly, we do not find a similar pattern for malnutrition. It may well be that the poor in these atolls survive reasonably well on subsistence fishing but, for unexplained reasons, are not able to generate much cash income. One can only speculate what role intra-household transfers and remittances might play. Given the fact that these atolls are closer to Male', is it possible that family members working there are the main breadwinners, but their level of remittances is just enough to keep other family members in the home village above the subsistence minimum? It seems appropriate to address these and related questions before the formulation of poverty reduction policies.

Papua New Guinea

Papua New Guinea represents another extreme case of rural-urban inequality. As much as 90 per cent of the population of about 4.7 million live under rural conditions. The remaining 10 per cent are mainly concentrated in three urban areas, of which the national capital, Port Moresby, is by far the biggest. There is significant migration between regions, with the capital experiencing the highest positive influx of migrants. Yet, in spite of a highly mobile population, the urban enclaves are poorly integrated with the rest of the economy.

Most large and medium-sized companies in the country are foreign-owned and cater mainly for the limited market of the small urban enclaves. Oil and mineral exploration, which constitutes the largest source of government revenue, generates little in terms of regional development effects. The industry is highly capital-intensive and depends on imported inputs, including foreign skilled labour. Public investment, in turn, is extremely urban-biased. More than half of the total national electricity is consumed in Port Moresby alone.

The rural economy, by contrast, still relies overwhelmingly on subsistence activities. It is estimated that three quarters of Papua New Guineans continue to rely on traditional farming and fishing as their main means of livelihood. Cash crop production has been increasing, but the main source of cash in the rural economy comes as remittances from relatives employed in the formal urban sector. It is this duality of 'Western' lifestyles in the urban centres, coexisting side by side with ancient tribal cultures, which constitutes the core development challenge of Papua New Guinea.

The *Papua New Guinea Human Development Report* of 1998 states that the average per capita income level of Port Moresby is ten times higher than in most rural areas. Through a series of participatory rural appraisals, the report documents 'the factors that support and undermine the sustainability of rural livelihoods' (Papua New Guinea 1999). It shows that while rural poverty is not rampant, due in large part to the widespread reliance on traditional fishing, hunting and gathering activities, most villagers nonetheless have experienced a decline in wellbeing. Many are pessimistic about the future, due to the growing pressure on their traditional way of life stemming from population growth, degradation of the natural environment, and urban cultural influence.

The present pattern of rural livelihoods is supported by a number of factors, which paradoxically also constitute an important source of vulnerability. The traditional land tenure systems are probably the single most important factor. The strength of these systems is that they are based on a flexible system of ownership, user rights and allocation rights, which has prevented both the concentration of land in the hands of few, and the emergence of a class of landless. The problem, however, is that pressure toward more effective land use and cash crop production, combined with population growth, is currently undermining traditional tenure.

Many of the young generation are not properly inculcated in traditional livelihood skills. In a quest for reaping short term benefits, the qualities of old techniques inherited over generations, for instance for maintaining soil fertility, are being lost to more extractive forms of land use. Uncontrolled logging and mining, for example, are causing major environmental degradation.

A strong feature of the traditional culture is that family and clan members are required to support each other in times of need. This works through broad networks, called *wantok*, involving virtually the entire population. This redistributive system links rural and urban areas through cash remittances from urban wage earners. Villagers also make use of their urban *wantoks* to market their produce and get information on work opportunities. There is considerable evidence that the *wantok* system is now under stress. Many urban kinfolk, in particular, are unable to meet all of their *wantok* obligations, causing major social insecurity. Although rural life is still held by most people as the 'good way of life', symptoms of a breakdown of traditional social cohesion are found in many rural communities, which for the first time are witnessing rising crime and violence.

Palestine, Latvia and South Africa

Palestine

Poverty in Palestine cannot be understood without reference to the extreme volatility of the political situation. The faltering peace process, border closures, security problems and unresolved territorial disputes have made coherent and long-term national development planning virtually impossible. The political need of the Palestine Authority (PA) to accommodate various factions and interest groups among the Palestinians within the emerging state has, more often than not, been overriding development concerns. The single most important factor causing a deterioration of living conditions is the restrictions on Palestinians seeking employment in Israel and on Palestinian businesses dependent on the Israeli economy.

In 1998, the National Commission on Poverty Eradication carried out the first comprehensive analysis of poverty in the Palestinian territories, with support from UNDP. Using household expenditure data as the basis for measuring poverty, the study shows that about 25 per cent of households in the West Bank (excluding Jerusalem, where the situation is more favourable) and Gaza Strip fall below the poverty line. Although living conditions appear to be deteriorating, extreme poverty and destitution are not a major problem.

Box 1. Wellbeing in Papua New Guinea

According to qualitative information collected in a series of participatory rural appraisals in 16 districts in the country, people describe the lack of wellbeing (*sindaun i nogut*) as involving:

- Land shortage;
- Land disputes;
- Tribal fights;
- Environmental degradation;
- Poor or destroyed gardens;
- Absence of water;
- Lack of transport;
- Poor nutrition;
- Absence of health care and shortage of drugs;
- Complications at childbirth;
- Lack of money;
- Early marriages;
- Abuse against women, polygamy, adultery, violence, and divorce;
- Hard work, especially for overburdened women;
- Disobedient children;
- Absence of children in family;
- No traditional 'men's house'.

Since most households depend on some form of salaried work, income poverty is closely associated with unemployment. Surprisingly, *capability* poverty, measured in terms of access to basic social services, is not congruent with income poverty. This is different from the situation found in most developing countries, where capability poverty generally reinforces income poverty. The discrepancy is also probably a reflection of the substantial influx, in per capita terms, of various forms of humanitarian support to the PA. Furthermore, *life cycle* poverty, caused by factors changing through a lifetime, characterises many of the permanent poor, who are the main beneficiaries of social assistance programmes. Those factors typically relate to age, illness and marital status (Palestine 1998).

Despite its small size, there are widening regional disparities within Palestine. There is no distinct urban-rural divide, however. In terms of population density, the refugee camps are the most 'urban'. The highest poverty rate is found in 'urban' Gaza. Its refugee camps have the highest proportion of poor people, while in the West Bank, poverty is essentially a rural phenomenon. Agricultural plots are generally small, the land is marginal and water for irrigation, which is controlled by Israel, is a major constraint. Access to land, therefore, is a critical determinant of poverty rates. Nevertheless, few families rely on the rural economy alone, as the vast majority of the heads of poor households are labour force participants.

The report sponsored by UNDP places the main determinants of poverty in the political context and history of the Palestinian struggle for statehood. Besides the psychological and physical effects of war and civil uprising (*Intifada*), the major causes stem from Israeli confiscation of land, strictures imposed on Palestinians seeking employment in Israel, and a sharp drop in remittances from family members working abroad (Palestine 1998).

During the Israeli occupation, the West Bank and Gaza turned increasingly into a labour reserve, with more than one third of the work force employed, legally or illegally, in the Israeli economy by early 1990s. The Gulf War in 1991, which led to the expulsion of thousands of Palestinian workers from Kuwait, combined with the faltering peace process after the Oslo Accords, had dramatic effects. The rapid increase in public investment following the creation of the Palestine Authority has cushioned this effect to some extent. Most of the public investment, however, is funded by donor agencies and the domestic private sector remains underdeveloped and constrained by the prevailing political uncertainty.

Latvia

Latvia is a highly urbanised country in which 70 per cent of the population live in cities and towns. Since gaining independence in 1991, it has undergone dramatic economic and social changes. The GNP nose-dived to half its pre-transition level, and started a process of slow recovery only after 1997. Latvian industries lost both their sources of raw material and their main market with the collapse of the Soviet Union. Farmers on newly privatised land were unable to compete with imported products. As a result, poverty rose spectacularly in the limited span of a few years.

Starting in 1998, UNDP financed a number of studies to inform policy-makers about the extent and characteristics of poverty. One of the studies analyses data from the 1996 household budget survey conducted by the Central Statistical Bureau. The survey collected information on monthly household expenditures and, using different per capita poverty lines, found that about 12 per cent of the population is 'very poor', defined as those who are below 50 per cent of the mean value of expenditures. The figure, however, rises to 40 per cent if the official minimum wage is used as the cut-off point, and to 67 per cent if the benchmark is the official minimum subsistence level calculated by the Ministry of Welfare (Gassmann 1998).

Numerically, there is more poverty in urban areas, which accounts for 67 per cent of all poor people. Nevertheless, poverty is more widespread (higher headcount ratio) and deeper (higher poverty gap ratio) in rural areas. The capital, Riga, has the lowest rates of all regions, but also the highest concentration of poor people. Although the values of expenditure items have been adjusted for regional price differences, the same poverty lines are used for both urban and rural areas.[7] Yet, the consumption patterns of rural and urban households are quite different. Rural poor households get 35 per cent of their food from own production, compared with only 6 per cent for the urban poor. In turn, urban households have substantially higher costs related to housing (house rent, payment for heating, electricity and water), which on the average makes up one third of the expenditure of all poor households.

The analysis also shows that 'the presence of children in a household increases the poverty risk' (Gassmann 1998). Although the average household size is 2.5 members and only three per cent of Latvian families have three or more children, poor households tend to be bigger and to have more children than the rest. This finding deserves to be examined in a broader comparative perspective on the relationship between household size and per capita income levels, given that it contradicts the pattern found in many rural societies where larger households generally are better off than smaller ones.[8] Patterns of household fission and fusion are likely to vary depending on the household's asset bundle, livelihood and work opportunities. Without time series data, there is no basis for ascertaining whether the high proportion of small (one and two-person) households is a legacy from the Soviet era of economic growth and industrialisation, or rather a pattern strengthened by the recent process of pauperisation.

The 1996 household budget survey has no data on inter-household transfers and relations. This precludes an assessment of the extent to which the mobilisation of urban-rural links represents an important coping strategy for the urban unemployed. It seems plausible that relatives in the countryside could provide a safety valve for urban residents, for instance as a source of cheap food or a place to send children and other dependants (pensioners and disabled) for shorter or longer periods. But the data, unfortunately, do not allow for an analysis of possible linkages between urban and rural households.

In a second study supported by UNDP, a total of 400 poor households were interviewed using a qualitative approach. The study confirmed that 'old' and 'new' poverty coexist side by side in today's Latvia. Whereas poverty during the Soviet period was associated with personal failure and outright shame, the new poverty of the transition economy can be explained more accurately as resulting from structural conditions: declining real wages, high costs of public utilities, loss of lifelong savings due to collapse of state banks, and lack of public resources capable of maintaining previous standards of social benefits and pensions (Trapenciere et al. 2000).

The study reports certain commonly held stereotypes regarding conditions in rural and urban areas. Many urban residents see the situation in the villages as a poverty trap with no improvement in sight, characterised by widespread unemployment and alcoholism. Rural respondents, however, tend to perceive their situation as less vulnerable, given the availability of cheaper food and lower utility costs. The picture with respect to inter-household dependency seems to be mixed. Many Latvians report having received 'considerable help from family members and relatives living apart', but the effect of poverty on household and family relations is more complex, and can have varied effects. 'Either it brings family members together (in some case, even couples on the verge of divorce) as they realise that solidarity is the only way to cope with their economic [situation], or the daily stress of financial problems splits families apart' (Trapenciere et al. 2000).

The qualitative assessment confirms the previous finding that large families are more vulnerable. This appears to be an urban problem, in particular associated with the higher housing and utility costs faced by city dwellers. The costs of medical treatment and education have also gone up dramatically, especially with the proliferation of bribes and unofficial contributions at better-quality hospitals and

Box 2. Collapse in the rural economy

In Viesite, a rural district in Latvia, a number of enterprises have closed over the last years. These include a large agricultural factory, whose former employees now have a markedly high rate of alcoholism; a diesel factory that collapsed along with its Soviet markets; a sewing factory which employed fifty women, and an industrial firm. There are only a few remaining enterprises, which operate with a very reduced labour force. The majority of the rural population survives on private or leased land and some forestry work, both of which frequently rely on manual labour.

schools. As a result, the health and education systems are becoming divided into two tiers, depending on people's ability to pay for adequate services. In the rural areas particularly, people complained of deteriorating services.

The study reports several forms of rural-urban linkages, including the move from city to country to take up farming. Often only the parents move away, leaving children in town with relatives to finish school. Many town and city people, even from Riga, do farming on a weekend basis if they have access to land. Two issues impacting urban employment are of note. First, discrimination in the labour market against non-Latvians, who make up half of the country's population, is mainly an urban problem. Second, there was also a general opinion that personal connections are needed to find well-remunerated jobs. The latter would work to the disadvantage of people from rural areas, unless family networks can be mobilised.

The upshot in Latvia reveals that processes of social differentiation have been deeply entrenched during the period following the collapse of the Soviet Union. Former systems of redistribution based on employment guarantees, universal coverage of social services and social security systems have been abolished or no longer function properly. The trauma of impoverishment has led to a dramatic increase in alcohol-related health and social problems. Latvia is becoming a divided country, which is witnessing 'the emergence of patterns of discrimination that may carry the danger of excluding certain portions of the population from the economic mainstream' (Trapenciere et al. 2000).

South Africa

Post-*apartheid* South Africa still retains most of its former socio-economic features. Inequality remains high, with the richest 10 per cent receiving over 40 per cent of national income. The racial bias is still considerable. Sixty-one per cent of Africans and 38 per cent of coloureds are poor, compared with 5 per cent for Indians and 1 per cent for white South Africans. Inequality within race groups is also substantial.

The *Poverty and Inequality Report*, published in 1998 with partial funding from UNDP, highlights a strong correlation between income poverty, unemployment, and human welfare indicators, such as low education and poor health. The severity of the country's poverty problem is illustrated by the fact that 'three children of every five in South Africa live in poor households and many children are exposed to public and domestic violence, malnutrition, and inconsistent parenting and schooling' (May 1998).

Poverty is overwhelmingly a rural problem. Whereas only 45 per cent of the population live in rural areas, they contain as much as 72 per cent of the total number of poor people. With the lifting of the *apartheid* restrictions on the movement of black people, urban poverty is also on the rise. Nevertheless, the main challenge for poverty reduction in South Africa unquestionably lies in the former Bantustans.

The former 'homeland' areas evolved under the three-pronged strategy of *apartheid*. This strategy was guided by the need to secure the best agricultural land for white-owned commercial farms and ensure the reproduction of cheap labour for the modern sector, while creating a political 'solution' for race-based separation of ethnic groups. This resulted in unsustainable farming, oscillating labour migration, poor quality of social service provision, and virtually no productive investment by the private sector. Only one quarter of rural African households owns land, and the same figure applies to the ownership of livestock. This makes agriculture less important than remittances and wage work as a source of rural livelihood. The dominant picture is one in which people in rural areas suffer from a 'poverty of opportunity', which is very difficult to escape.

Yet, given the dependence of rural families on remittances and wage work, the solution to the poverty problem cannot be found in the rural economy alone. As the report stresses, 'any attempt to spatially demarcate the South African poverty challenge would be a crude analysis, because the impact of the migrant labour system has been to link the rural and urban economies through the movement of people' (May 1998). This has generated a number of policy initiatives to improve rural-urban linkages, which we shall review in the next section.

Rural-urban issues in policy formation

We have seen that, in a majority of cases, a thorough assessment of urban-rural linkages and their impact on development is conspicuously absent both from the measurement of poverty and the analysis of its determinants. We now turn to a review of the policy prescriptions that have been put forward in the countries covered in this chapter. As will become apparent, there is no overall consensus concerning how to address the problems associated with rapid urbanisation and growing disparities between rural areas and urban centres. More specifically, countries diverge widely with regard to how to develop the agricultural sector and stem the tide of rural poverty.

Both Angola and Zambia are characterised by extraordinarily high rates of rural poverty. The same applies to Lesotho and Nepal, the other two countries in our sample with a low level of human development (UNDP 1997). It is noteworthy, therefore, that a set of radically different policy prescriptions for confronting the problem has been advanced in each case.

In Angola, the low and fluctuating prices for crops indicate that the market in rural areas does not work effectively. A sharp improvement of the crop market is thus seen as a precondition for dealing with rural poverty. Besides rehabilitation of the dilapidated transport infrastructure, it is recommended that the government introduce a minimum guaranteed price for main agricultural products and ensure the buildup of provincial storage centres. This should be accompanied by improvements in the outreach of credit programmes for both farmers and traders. The expectation is that the introduction of subsidies for rural producers will slow down out-migration, thereby lessening the pressure on the urban economy. In turn, the urban poor should benefit from a targeted price subsidy of food items commonly consumed in low-income households, such as maize meal. If this scheme is linked to the buildup of grain depots in rural provinces, it could become a 'win-win' strategy favouring both the urban and the rural poor (Wold and Grave 1999).

Whereas the adoption of redistributive policy instruments, such as government guaranteed purchases and price subsidies, is prescribed for Angola, Zambia's national strategy for poverty reduction endorses a much more orthodox approach to economic policy-making to stimulate smallholder agriculture and reduce poverty rates by half within five years (Zambia 1998). This is probably a reflection of the constraints imposed by the ongoing IMF programme, which does not allow the Zambian government much room to depart from economic orthodoxy.

Zambia's anti-poverty strategy puts agricultural development centre stage. The government recognises that investment in agriculture is essential for poverty reduction, and that 'agriculture and rural development are critical areas for achieving broad-based economic growth and ensuring food security at national and household levels' (Zambia 1998). As a result, the strategy outlines a number of measures to create an enabling environment for the individual farmer: improved land tenure rights, access to credit, appropriate technology and improved seeds, and access to market information. These measures would be supplemented by stepped-up public investments in infrastructure, particularly rural roads and storage facilities.

The key policy objective is to increase the farm gate price on agricultural products relative to the costs of production, so as to bring Zambian smallholders back from subsistence farming into the market. However, it is far from clear whether the policies outlined above will enable individual smallholders to beat structurally determined economic disadvantages. The question of how to tilt the terms of trade in favour of rural smallholders, particularly in the absence of state interventions in the market, remains unanswered. How can investments, productivity and growth in the smallholder sector be promoted without government subsidies and protection against imports and large commercial farms? Furthermore, given the lack of analysis of urban-rural linkages, the possibility that support to the urban informal sector might create ripple effects in the rural economy is not explored. For instance, facilities such as micro-credit could arguably be more effective if targeted to urban informal producers, provided transfers between the urban and rural areas can be harnessed for reinvestment in agriculture.

The Nepal HDR also espouses the view that agricultural development is the engine of growth and poverty reduction. Nevertheless, it calls for policies that stand at the opposite end of the ideological spectrum in comparison with those advocated in Zambia. The report severely criticises the current economic policy regime, questioning its ability to turn the tide of rural impoverishment and create a solid basis for development. Dissociating themselves from the policies of successive governments, which have sought to create a turnaround in the urban economy through market reform, the authors ask rhetorically 'what is to be done with and for the 88 per cent of the population that resides in the rural areas, more or less divorced from the "national" economy, while the rest is presumably integrated with the globalised market and its associated development process' (Nepal 1998).

A key premise of the HDR is that Nepal has 'no institutional foundation to permit the economy to move automatically towards industrialisation and export-led growth'. It therefore advocates the need to rise above the 'trickle-down rhetoric on the relationship amongst the market economy, growth and poverty alleviation' (Nepal 1998), calling instead for a comprehensive reform package aimed at the radical transformation of agriculture. This transformation is preconditioned on a far-reaching land reform, combined with increased public investments in irrigation, rural infrastructure and rural credit. Citing the experiences of China, Japan, South Korea, Cuba and Iraq, the HDR argues that land reform will not only transform agriculture by reducing vast inequalities in land ownership, but also 'help achieve faster industrialisation, enhance growth and alleviate poverty in both rural and urban areas' (Nepal 1998).

Notwithstanding the importance attached to agriculture, the HDR is weak in its analysis of rural-urban linkages. It blames the government for the adoption of a dual-economy approach, which has relegated the rural areas to the role of a labour reserve for the expansion of urban-based industries and services. But in doing so, the report stands to be criticised for an equally strong rural bias. In fact, it is questionable that rural Nepal today is 'more or less divorced' from the urban economy. However weak, the links that exist in terms of flow of goods, money, people and ideas will have to be inputted into any proposed reorientation of agriculture.

Furthermore, the report recommends that the government should promote national agro-industries, rather than the export-oriented textile industry, which utilises imported raw materials and, in some cases, imported labour as well. While the poverty reducing effect of textile manufacturing has been small, the HDR is silent on the question of what farmers should produce and for whom. This, in fact, represents the rural-urban linkage likely be the Achilles' heel of the reform programme outlined for Nepal.

The main development challenge is quite different in another landlocked country, Lesotho, whose economy is hugely dependent on long-distance labour migration to South Africa. With the integration of South Africa in global markets, the future for Lesotho is at best uncertain. Efforts in the past to develop a protected indigenous industry, reduce the dependency on South African imports and promote food self-sufficiency did not succeed. Rather, they contributed to rising budget deficits, foreign debt and inflation, paving the way for a World Bank/IMF structural adjustment programme in 1987. This resulted in a turnaround of the economy, which achieved GDP growth rates as high as 10 to 13 per cent annually during the 1990s. However, a similar effect on poverty reduction is yet to be seen. Reliable data show that poverty has continued to rise in both rural and urban areas.

Considering the many analytical findings of the 1997 poverty assessment financed by UNDP, which explicitly linked urban and rural development, it is somehow disappointing that its policy recommendations take a rather narrow view. Addressing pressing urban problems, the study recommends (1) investing more in urban infrastructure; (2) developing a functioning urban land market by abandoning the traditional system of user rights and allowing for private ownership of land; and (3) improving urban governance through enhanced local participation and increased revenue collection by a more progressive tax system.

It is unclear, however, why these measures should improve the situation of the poor, and not merely of the better-off. Implementing urban land titling, including in the peri-urban areas where most of the urban poor live, may well benefit those who have a plot today. But it is unlikely that commercialisation of urban land will affect those who are still to come, fleeing from a rural livelihood characterised by declining agricultural productivity and fewer opportunities for migrant workers abroad. There seems in fact to be very little evidence to support the assertion that a liberalised land market will ensure 'greater access for the poor' (Lesotho 1997). On the contrary, despite its undesirable effects in terms of uncontrolled peri-urban sprawl, the traditional system of land allocation has proven to be a great advantage for poor people coming in from the countryside. It certainly played a major role in ensuring that, unlike most cities in other countries, access to land appears not to be a major differentiating factor in Lesotho.

In contrast to the Nepal HDR, the Lesotho study sees no need for a radical policy shift. It acknowledges that 'structural adjustment policies have brought about economic growth, but with very little "trickle down effect" for the poor'. Nevertheless, its main recommendation to the government is to stay on course, that is, to 'continue its commitment to macroeconomic stabilisation policies and disciplined financial management, while at the same time enabling the private sector to flourish and create jobs' (Lesotho 1997). There is no advice on how this is going to be compatible with poverty reduction and the much needed, but not yet observed, redistribution. In particular, the report is silent with respect to the enormous challenge of reintegrating former miners and arresting degradation of agricultural land, both of which influence rural and urban poverty at the same time. The continuation of current economic policies may well represent the only feasible political option for Lesotho today.

But the jury is still out whether the urban as well as rural poor Basotho will stand to benefit from it.

The same policy ambiguity characterises the *Human Development Report* of Papua New Guinea, a country with a classic dual economy with small urban enclaves that are poorly integrated with the rest of the economy. Essentially, the HDR refrains from drawing any concrete policy conclusions. It emphasises that 'without adequate and equitable services, the rising sense of grievance in rural areas may see Papua New Guinea fracture into a jigsaw of well-serviced urban areas and under-serviced rural areas' (Papua New Guinea 1999). But it then struggles between a view that acclaims the virtues of the traditional rural life and one that sees the urgent need to modernise the rural economy to bridge the gaping rural-urban divide. The report also recognises that rural out-migration is inevitable, and even desirable, given the growing pressure on natural resources. But it also laments the fact that migration deprives the villages of the most able-bodied persons. And, in a similar vein, it states that reforming the land tenure system by introducing formal titles will lead to more efficient land use, but will also most likely exacerbate rural poverty.

Unfortunately, the Papua New Guinea HDR offers no guidance on how to strike the best possible balance between these contradicting development forces.[9] Clearly, the challenge of stemming the progressive transformation of a traditional rural life, characterised by a high degree of wellbeing and low material wealth, into a situation of 'modern' rural poverty with a strong feeling of deprivation and increasing social differentiation, will not be easy. It is rather likely to be very conflictual, challenging major vested interests in the current urban-biased development model that prevails in the country.

Achieving a more balanced regional development has also been a long lasting concern in the Maldives, owing to the strict limitations that its peculiar geography imposes on urban expansion. Besides the limited physical capacity of the archipelago for further urban growth, the authorities fear that if it continues unabated, the growth of the capital Male' may exacerbate regional disparities that could even threaten the stability of this homogeneous country. Yet the search for appropriate policy tools has been difficult despite sustained economic growth. Since the early 1980s, the government has taken various initiatives to curb the pressure on Male', including atoll-based integrated rural development projects and, more recently, the promotion of regional growth centres under the Selected Islands Development Policy. The results so far have been mixed, and Male' continues to be the focal point for migration from other islands. Most atolls are beset with serious problems relating to lack of productive employment, especially for women, and inadequate services and communications, as well as periodic food shortages.

Against this background, the 1998 *Vulnerability and Poverty Assessment* (VPA) takes the challenge of achieving balanced and equitable regional development centre stage. The report highlights the limited success of the 'regional growth centre' programme in fostering forms of centre-periphery linkages that may compete with the pull towards and dependence on Male'. In fact, the VPA was carried out as a response to the overwhelming need for improved island-specific information for 'finely-tuned development programmes geared to the specific needs, problems and opportunities of individual atolls and islands' (Maldives 1998).

The VPA does meet the objective of compiling detailed development-related information, but is weak in terms of analysing ongoing development processes. Using a broad range of single and composite development indices, it gives a well documented, but static picture of inter-atoll and inter-island differences. Certain assumptions about development causality are made: for instance, that improved distribution of electricity and access to transport will reduce vulnerability and poverty in the most isolated islands. Whether deliberately or not, there are nonetheless few attempts at addressing the causes of urbanisation and regional disparities. The assumptions made in the report with respect to the islands with the highest incidence of poverty and vulnerability are not tested, thereby depriving policy-makers of vital information for redirecting existing initiatives, such as the Special Islands Development Policy. This failure to analyse the reasons behind the pull exerted by Male' makes the VPA appear to underwrite current policy wisdom.

The case of Maldives demonstrates the need to understand better the relationship between development in the capital city (or any regional growth centres) and the outer areas. This issue is taken up in the *Poverty and Inequality Report* of South Africa, which focusses on the role of secondary towns in promoting rural economic growth. South Africa contains a broad spectrum of many small towns and secondary cities within the spatial continuum from remote rural areas to the four large metropolitan areas (Gauteng, Cape Town, Durban and Port Elizabeth). Various surveys show that the smaller the urban settlement, the higher the incidence of poverty. This finding is of great significance, since it highlights the importance of promoting small town development. This is necessary not only to alleviate the poverty that is already concentrated there, but also to absorb more of the rural poor through employment creation.

As long as a major growth of South African agriculture is not likely, the only feasible alternative seems to be to promote smaller-scale industrialisation in secondary towns. Agricultural growth depends largely on the implementation of a major land redistribution scheme, which appears politically and economically unrealistic at the moment. In addition, there are apparently few Africans who perceive themselves as large-scale commercial farmers. There is certainly a high demand for farmland among rural Africans. But according to surveys, most people want smaller plots that can be developed in conjunction with other forms of income generation.

This has led to a focus on peri-urban smallholder farming. The land reform programme has been stumbling, and the pace of tenure reform and land transfers has so far been very slow. Still, the challenge is to avoid the growth of mega-cities, which could attract the bulk of private and public investment capital, as well as the poor rural families' dislodging themselves from the rural slums created by *apartheid*. There are already in place several programmes to stimulate public and private investments in special regions and secondary towns, including tax holiday schemes.

Another development challenge created by the spatial dimension of *apartheid* is the existence of a limited revenue base to support local level service delivery. The low levels of tax collection and service payment, typical of black townships, confound the government's ability to deliver on the commitment to provide universal services on an equitable basis. The consequence, according to the South African report, might be that government policy could 'inadvertently "freeze" in place the spatial structures inherited from *apartheid*... leav[ing] the poor with little choice other than to continue under the harsh commuter and migrancy system established under *apartheid*' (May 1998).

Like South Africa, it is highly unlikely that rural development and growth in agriculture can provide the main thrust for reducing poverty in Palestine. The prospects for promoting other forms of income generation, however, are widely different. While the *Palestine Poverty Report* states that 'poverty eradication requires addressing the roots and reasons behind poverty, not only alleviating its manifestations' (Palestine 1998), it is not able to follow up in terms of concrete recommendations. One fairly obvious reason is that most of the roots of poverty are determined by factors outside the influence of the Palestine Authority. But even within these limitations, there are a number of measures that could be directed toward the numerous vulnerable groups and impoverished areas identified in the report.

The only major recommendations put forward, nonetheless, relate to the creation of a countrywide social security system. This implies mainly an extension and formalisation of existing programmes administered by the Ministry of Social Welfare, which are not geared towards enhancing the income-generating capability of poor households. There is no mention, for instance, of any policy measures that might ease the entry to the labour market of women, especially of female-headed households, which on average are more vulnerable to poverty. Nor are there references to any agricultural or land use policy to improve socio-economic conditions in the poor villages of the West Bank.

The rural-urban interface was not a major development concern as long as the Palestine territory functioned essentially as a labour reserve, but it is likely to become a critical factor with the ascendance to nationhood. The small territory of Palestine will remain dependent on its neighbouring countries for employment opportunities, and probably ought to invest heavily in strengthening its human capital to compete well in those job markets. In so doing, the Palestine Authority would be well advised to avoid the classic pitfalls of a development model biased toward the urban sector.

An equally daunting task awaits the Latvian authorities: to arrest a development trajectory from a situation of fairly equal opportunities to public social services, to one where economic status and place of living are giving rise to growing inequalities in term of access. People have lost the social security of guaranteed employment, and new coping strategies have emerged to confront rapidly deteriorating living standards. Some of these strategies include a strengthening of linkages between rural and urban areas. There seems to be much uncertainty, however, on how to stimulate rural economic growth to provide a safety valve for impoverished urban families.

The studies sponsored by UNDP in Latvia provide numerous insights on the characteristics of poor households and how they are responding to the changes around them (Gassmann 1998; Trapenciere et al. 2000). Both studies question the effectiveness of the existing social security system in targeting and reaching the poorest segments of the population, and advocate for policies that will reduce the costs of housing, medical treatment and education, and improve peoples' access to information about work opportunities and social rights. This is important in light of the fact that the employment opportunities being created in the new market economy do not seem adequate for absorbing the rising number of poor people. However, the core issue of ensuring equitable economic growth is not addressed in either one of the studies. The same applies to role of the rural areas, in particular the agriculture and forestry sectors, which could be instrumental in combating rural as well as urban poverty. But this issue is largely unresolved in Latvia's new deregulated economy, which is still struggling to find its course.

Conclusions

In the introduction, we identified five rural-urban issues that have a bearing upon the formulation of poverty reduction policies. Our review has shown that countries exhibit a great variation with respect to the patterns of rural and urban development and poverty. Rural poverty is a major concern in all countries. Without exception, the depth of poverty is more severe in rural than urban areas. The most extreme case is Papua New Guinea, where urban per capita income is ten times higher than the rural level. Papua New Guinea, in fact, represents a classic dual economy with urban enclaves poorly integrated with the rural economy, except through labour migration.

Rural-urban differentiation is also extreme in South Africa, which still retains the features of a post-*apartheid* economy. Seventy-two per cent of the poor live in rural areas, and typically it is not agriculture, but labour migration, that provides their main source of income. Lesotho resembles the former Homelands in South Africa in many respects. Those who receive remittances from work abroad are generally better off than the rest. Dependence on remittances is also high in Palestine, where poverty is closely associated with unemployment. Not surprisingly, the incidence of urban poverty appears to be correlated with rates of urbanisation. Thus, although poverty in Latvia is most severe in the countryside, it is in the cities that it is numerically higher.

Interestingly, evidence presented for Nepal questions the common assumption that poverty is more prevalent among rural female-headed households. It appears, nonetheless, that urban women do not benefit proportionally from the higher income levels of urban households. A somewhat different picture emerges from Angola, where it is noteworthy that women play an exceptionally important role in the urban informal sector, particularly in Luanda.

To various degrees, most of the country studies touch upon rural-urban issues, but they tend to be weak in prescribing strategies for better integration of rural *and* urban development. Moreover, there appears to be no overall consensus on how to address the problems associated with escalating urbanisation and growing rural-urban disparities. Some authors pin their hopes for a reduction in poverty primarily on further liberalisation, including through the creation of a market for urban land (Lesotho). Others advocate the adoption of 'interventionist' policies, for instance through a radical programme of land redistribution (Nepal).

Most frequently, agricultural development is seen as the primary means for achieving a reduction in poverty. Emphasis is placed, in particular, on stimulating smallholder agriculture. However, while in Angola it is proposed that the government should buy from farmers at guaranteed prices and subsidise the price of maize flour to urban consumers, the main policy thrust in Zambia points in the opposite direction. The main prescription in Zambia is to hold back the state from interfering in the agricultural market, despite the fact that the policies currently in place seem to have contributed to the marginalisation of a growing number of rural smallholders.

The failure of the agricultural policies of the 1990s is also blamed for the persistence of rural poverty in Nepal. This concerns especially the deadlock on all land reform initiatives, which has prevented a more equitable distribution of ownership in a country in which land is heavily concentrated. A similar pessimism concerning the prospects for rural development prevails in Papua New Guinea. In this case, however, the reason does not stem from the lack of modernisation and reform, but rather from the heavy pressure the latter exert on traditional values and skills, land tenure arrangements and social support systems. This pressure, if unabated, could lead to a deepening of rural poverty and a concomitant pressure on the country's modern urban enclaves.

Despite the calls for addressing rural poverty as a matter of priority, it is generally recognised that rural development is entirely dependent on improving the linkages with the urban economy. Only South Africa and Maldives seem to have made some progress in tackling urban *and* rural issues in an integrated manner. Maldives may have no other choice but to pursue a policy of balanced regional development, given its geographical constraints on further urban expansion. The case of South Africa is particularly instructive. In spite of its special history, South Africa's attempts to tackle the spatial dimensions of development by stimulating economic growth in secondary towns can provide valuable lessons for other countries.

In most developing countries, the pendulum typically has swung from one end of the spectrum (development of large urban centres) to the other (a narrow rural perspective). Most integrated rural development programmes of the 1970s and 1980s paid little attention to the promotion of small towns, even though this was supposed to be one of their core objectives. The example of South Africa, where the current pace of land redistribution provides little scope for basing poverty reduction on the growth of smallholder agriculture, demonstrates the potential of promoting secondary trade and industrial centres to create employment for the rural poor. Yet, this case also demonstrates that small town development requires more than investments in transport infrastructure. Equally important is to ensure active state intervention in directing and stimulating private investment. South Africa, in fact, was able to develop an interesting mix of spatial development policies by combining a long tradition of using public incentives and regulations to steer private investments with the need to reduce post-*apartheid* inequalities.

It is important to note that, in most countries, there is a continuum in term of population density from remote hamlets to the large urban centres. It is thus unfortunate that the conventional dichotomy of rural *versus* urban areas still seems to dominate development thinking and poverty research. Only in the Maldives, Latvia and Lesotho is the need to develop separate poverty lines for urban and rural areas raised. It is also worth noting, however, that even in a country as homogeneous as Maldives, constructing regional purchasing power parity indexes turned out to be impossible, as a standard food basket applicable across the country could not be found. This finding suggests that the 'rural' dimension may harbour wide interregional differences in many countries, a point that is frequently overlooked by analysts and policy-makers alike.

Furthermore, migration patterns are seldom reflected adequately in statistics on poverty and living conditions. Static measurements of per capita or household income, consumption or other indicators of wellbeing may conceal important cyclical patterns of movements of people and transfer of resources between households as well as within families. There are references to the importance of labour migration and remittances in many countries, including Lesotho, Maldives, Palestine, Papua New Guinea and South Africa. In Maldives, for instance, seasonal migration may be the primary source of income for many families left behind, explaining the discrepancy between the incidence of poverty and of malnutrition in the five poorest atolls. Angola, in turn, has witnessed a huge influx of refugees to Luanda due to the war, as a result of which Angola is experiencing a vibrant urban trading economy. In spite of these scattered references, we are missing detailed information about the pattern and magnitude of labour migration and rural-urban transfers, and how they may influence poverty statistics.

Because of this gap, we also find a lacuna in terms of policy advice concerning labour migration. In several countries, this is a major element of the coping strategies of poor households. This is the case even in highly urbanised Latvia, where impoverished families are coping with the drastic deterioration in living standards by establishing closer links between the rural and urban spheres. Notwithstanding this, there is a conspicuous ambivalence about how to harness the potential contribution of labour migrants to poverty reduction. Most authors hesitate between supporting households to increase their opportunities in urban labour markets, and developing rural-based alternatives for income generation.

This applies, of course, not only to internal migration, but also to the search for livelihood opportunities abroad. Particularly in Lesotho and Palestine, households are highly dependent on incomes generated in other countries. More generally, though, this relates to the new challenges that are likely to emerge with increasing globalisation, and the associated movement of people and goods across boundaries, which may further constrain the ability of governments to implement effective policies for the benefit of the poor. ∎

Notes

Alf Morten Jerve is Deputy Director of the Chr. Michelsen Institute, Bergen, Norway. He would like to thank Julian May and Alejandro Grinspun for substantive and editorial comments.

[1] In a much-cited article, Elizabeth Wratten (1995) argues that 'any such classification is intrinsically arbitrary. More importantly, from a structural perspective, the determinants of urban and rural poverty are interlinked and have to be tackled in tandem.'

[2] One entry point, for instance, has been the research on the role of small towns in Africa as a conduit for marketing, capital accumulation, and transfer and dissemination of technology (Baker 1990; Baker and Pedersen 1992).

[3] This does not negate the fact that certain aspects of urban poverty are conditioned on characteristics of the urban environment that cannot be found in similar degree in rural areas. This applies, for example, to some special environmental and health hazards, as well as the degree of social diversity, disintegration, dependency on market exchange, and exposure to government agencies and policies that is typical of urban settings.

[4] Both cases may differ from countries with more stable rural economies, in which the rural poor are less likely to build strong links with urban areas, while the urban poor may not need

to use the rural economy as part of their portfolio of coping strategies.

[5] The study contains no discussion of reporting problems, such as how to deal with the degree and duration of absenteeism of migrant labourers, and how to account for children temporarily living with relatives, which is a common practice in Africa. These factors would not only influence the calculation of per capita income, but information on them would have said something about the dynamics of household development.

[6] Income poverty is measured using household data collected through interviews of a sample of households in all 200 inhabited islands. The survey uses consumption as a proxy for income. The data are based on nominal prices and nominal consumption expenditures, not adjusting for regional differences in purchasing power of the currency. It turned out to be impossible to define a minimum common basket of consumption goods relevant in all islands. Although theoretically well-founded, establishing regional purchasing power parities met with too many problems in practice. Even in a country as homogenous as the Maldives, detailed knowledge about field level conditions revealed so much variation that the statisticians gave up on standardisation. It was not possible, for instance, to find a sufficient number of food items that are homogeneous enough across the country to provide the basis for a common food basket that could be used for determining a poverty line. The authors themselves argue that establishing an official poverty line in the Maldives is highly subjective, as 'efforts to objectively determine a basic minimum needs package for a household always lead to polemic results' (Maldives 1998).

[7] The report does not explain how the value of rural housing, where people do not pay rent, use wood for heating, and have their own water source, as well as own-produced food is computed. Nor does it explain why these factors do not warrant applying different poverty lines for rural and urban areas. It is plausible that a fixed amount in lat, the Latvian currency, can sustain a higher living standard in rural areas. As a consequence, rural poverty would be less widespread than what the official statistics depict. Surprisingly as well, the analysis shows that access to land in rural areas only gives a marginal reduction in the poverty headcount. In a situation of high food prices and massive rural unemployment from the closure of many small rural based industries, this finding does not seem very likely.

[8] The reason behind the relatively larger size of non-poor households is that poverty in agricultural based societies is often linked to marginal land and livestock holdings, which exercise pressure toward the splitting up of households into smaller units. Thus, it is only the better-off households that are able to stay together. Evidence from South Africa, on the other hand, shows that larger households do not have higher per capita incomes than the average household. This lack of covariance between size and income stems from the fact that poverty normally forces people to stay together (May 1998).

[9] The authors, in the end, merely resort to political rhetoric, stating that 'with well-targeted policies developed by policy-makers in broad consultation with all sectors, and agreed courses of action for all people to follow, most of these threats [to rural livelihood] can be countered and rural livelihoods in Papua New Guinea can comfortably sustain people far into the future' (Papua New Guinea 1999).

5 Participatory Governance and Poverty Reduction

S. R. Osmani

ood governance has recently been accorded a central place in the discourse on development. In some ways, this may seem to be a fairly self-evident proposition, but many issues need clarification. For example, what are the essential features of an appropriate governance structure, what are the problems involved in achieving good governance, and what actions need to be taken in order to tackle these problems?

Governance is a somewhat elastic concept. It has been interpreted in many different ways so as to encompass many different aspects of social organisation and the institutional framework within which social and economic activities are performed. Much has been written in the recent past on all these questions. The latest UNDP publication *Overcoming Human Poverty* is devoted largely to exploring the multiple relationships between good governance and poverty reduction (UNDP 2000). The World Bank, other international agencies and many individual researchers have also addressed these dynamics. A number of country studies sponsored by UNDP from 1997 to 1999 as part of its Poverty Strategies Initiative (PSI) have also dealt with different aspects of these issues in their specific country contexts. This chapter seeks to synthesise the ideas and lessons that emerged from the PSI. It focuses on one specific aspect of the institutions of governance — namely, governance at the level of local communities. This focus entails a range of concerns involving decentralisation, people's empowerment, and the involvement of community-based organisations in local affairs, as well as the relevance of all these reforms to poverty reduction.

The first section begins by noting the multiplicity of meanings that the term 'decentralised governance' seems to have acquired over time. People's participation at the grassroots level is an integral part of this notion of decentralisation. The value of participatory decentralisation is demonstrated by drawing upon various examples contained in the studies sponsored by UNDP. Two sets of problems are then identified that stand in the way of establishing truly participatory decentralisation. They relate, on the one hand, to the devolution of power from the top and, on the other, to genuine involvement of the poor from the bottom. The first set of issues is discussed in the following two sections of the chapter, in the light of the empirical evidence presented in the PSI studies. It is then argued that a crucial precondition for tackling both these problems is the creation of an environment that can empower people, especially the poor, so that they can exercise their voice in the affairs of governance. We then take up this issue by examining various approaches to empowerment. Finally, section VI brings together the major findings of the paper.

Decentralisation and people's participation in local governance

'Big government' is often blamed for the persistent woes of the poor in the developing world. It would be more accurate to say, however, that the problem lies in the wrong kind of government, such as a governance structure that meddles too much into the details of economic activities that are best left to the market, but provides too little support on 'public' matters that genuinely require non-market mediated governance. In the latter sense, one might even say that the rural people are actually undergoverned, as Thompson (1991) has suggested in the context of Sahelian countries.

Thompson's characterisation of the Sahel in this regard is generally valid for much of the developing world. While some activities affecting the rural poor are better left to the market, there is a large set of problems, characterised by market failure, that do require collective regulation or action by some sort of government(s) for their resolution. The problem of common property resource management is a prime example, as are public utilities and the provision of social and physical infrastructure. The reach and quality of governance in these spheres all too often fall short of requirements in part because government means a central bureaucracy preoccupied mostly with national or regional issues.

To some extent, voluntary groups and community organisations can deal with local problems, but there is a limit at which they can function effectively. The characteristic that most obviously distinguishes a voluntary organisation from a government is the absence of the capacity to make binding, non-voluntary decisions backed by legally sanctioned coercive power. In the absence of this capacity, all decisions are voluntary and have to be taken on the basis of unanimity. This can prevent collectively rational decisions from being taken.

Sometimes, local leaders assume governmental powers illegally, so as to achieve some specific objective. For example, Wade (1987) describes some illegal village governments in South India that were formed in order to manage local irrigation systems.[1] But the lack of legality of these pseudo-governments inevitably constrains their ability to perform the full range of functions that a legally constituted government could have done. Besides, it also makes them vulnerable to extinction, or at least impotence, in the event of a clash with the proper government. A classic example is provided by Yemen, where a rich tradition of community-based local governance that had emerged from the grassroots and evolved over time largely outside the official domain was suddenly destroyed by a government edict in the 1980s that sought to introduce government-sponsored decentralisation (Yemen 1988). It is, therefore, essential to first establish a legally sanctioned structure of decentralised governance within which the community-based organisations can then play a role.

There is also a profound lack of clarity on what 'decentralisation' is supposed to mean. The concept seems to have evolved over time and has by now acquired several shades of meaning (Mawhood and Davey 1980; Landau and Eagle 1981; Mawhood 1983; Conyers 1983, 1984). The first widespread use of this term in the development literature began in the 1950s, when a fairly consistent set of institutional changes were being introduced by the colonial powers (especially Great Britain) in preparation for granting independence to many African countries (Ostrom et al. 1993). This 'classic' decentralisation, as Mawhood and Davey (1980) described it, was organised around five principles:

■ Local authorities should be institutionally separate from central government and assume responsibility for a significant range of local services, mainly for primary education, clinics and preventive health services, community development, and secondary roads.

■ These authorities should have their own funds and budgets and should raise a substantial part of their revenue through local direct taxation.

■ Local authorities should employ their own staff, although in the initial stage the regular civil service staff could be employed temporarily.

■ The authorities would be governed internally by councils predominantly composed of popularly elected representatives.

■ Government administrators would withdraw from an executive to an advisory and supervisory role in relation to local government.

Classic decentralisation, however, rarely took place. Instead, the political leadership of developing countries usurped the term to describe very different types of administrative reorganisations. Because of these variations, it has rightly been suggested that 'decentralisation is not one thing; nor is it even a series of degrees along a spectrum or scale. For comprehensibility and utility in policy circles, the overarching abstraction "decentralisation" must be split into a host of separate, occasionally conflicting entities' (Cohen et al. 1981).

One classification scheme distinguishes four different forms of decentralisation (Rondinelli and Nellis 1986; Rondinelli et al. 1987; Blair 1995, 1998):

■ *Deconcentration* refers to institutional changes that shift the authority to make certain types of decisions from national civil service personnel in the capital to national civil service personnel posted at dispersed locations. In this arrangement, staff and resources are transferred from headquarters to lower units of administration under chief officers who can take operational decisions without reference to the headquarters.

- **Devolution** refers to reorganisation efforts that approximate 'classic' decentralisation most closely, insofar as significant amounts of independent legislative and fiscal authority are transferred to sub-national governments. Responsibilities and resources are transferred to these local governments with a large degree of autonomy to decide how to use the resources.

- **Delegation** refers to transfers of authority to public corporations or special authorities outside the regular bureaucratic structure. Agents not belonging to public administration are delegated by the central government to perform specific functions. The central government sets the objective of the delegated agents and transfers resources to them on the basis of approved plans and budgets, but the agents have a fair degree of autonomy in performing their functions and may even have autonomous sources of revenue, including borrowing from the capital market.

- **Privatisation** and **partnerships** refer to transfer of responsibility for public functions to voluntary organisations or private enterprises. The objective here is to mobilise the capacity and initiatives of civil society organisations (CSOs) working for social and economic development. Resources are transferred to the CSOs who enter into an agreement with the government on the basis of an indicative programme of work. Government does not interfere with their plans and budgets, but enforces *ex post* controls over the use of resources.

Of these four forms deconcentration amounts to the least amount of transfer of power to the local people. This type of administrative organisation can hardly be described as a move towards the development of local governance. Delegation, too, does not by itself transfer power to the local people, although the delegated agencies have scope for involving local people in their decision-making process. The two other forms, devolution and privatisation or partnership, provide the greatest scope for developing genuinely local governance based on popular participation.

It is arguable that people's participation in the process of governance is an essential precondition for successful decentralisation from the point of view of both efficiency and equity. One of the reasons is that it enables local services to be tailored according to local preferences.

But what is the mechanism through which local preferences are to be known? The only feasible way is to have an inclusive process of local governance through which each segment of the population can express and fight for their preferences. This point is underlined by Klooster (2000) in a revealing comparison between successful and unsuccessful cases of community-based resource management in Mexico. He has identified two distinguishing features of successful management. One relates to the presence of vigorous, regular and well-attended community assemblies. The other is the existence of accounting and reporting practices that provide community members with a healthy flow of information.

There are several other ways in which participation can improve the efficiency as well as equity of resource use (Adato et al. 1999b; Manor 1999). Thus, community participation has been known to improve the efficiency of irrigation systems by making use of local knowledge on soil conditions, water velocity and shifting water courses (Chambers 1988; Ascher and Healy 1990; Ostrom, Lam and Lee 1994). It has also improved the efficiency of water and sanitation projects, by ensuring that these are located where they are most likely to be used (Manikutty 1998), as well as of public work projects, by utilising local knowledge about safety hazards and vandalism (Adato et al. 1999a).

The value of participation for common property resource management is also highlighted in the human development reports (HDR) sponsored by UNDP in Madhya Pradesh (India) and Nepal. The Madhya Pradesh HDR gives a rich account of how participatory management of forests instituted under the Joint Forest Management Scheme (JFM) has begun to yield hope of halting the age-old process of forest depletion. The concept of Joint Forest Management has been defined as 'the sharing of products, responsibilities, control and decision-making authority over forest lands between Forest Department and local user group. It involves a contract specifying the distribution of authority, responsibilities and benefits' (Madhya Pradesh 1998). For a long time, the local people themselves were partly responsible for resource depletion, as they overexploited the forest resources for their immediate economic gain. JFM has sought to counter this tendency by vesting ownership of forest products to the people and by actively involving them in forest management. In this way, people can perceive a stake in the long-run preservation of their forestry resources, and apply their own preferences in deciding the rate and manner in which they are to be exploited. For this purpose, Village Forest Committees were set up for rehabilitation of degraded forests, and Forest Protection Committees were created to protect the well-wooded forests. By all accounts, these efforts, initiated in the early 1990s, are already beginning to have a visible impact on Madhya Pradesh's forest resources.

A similar approach to forest preservation has been adopted in parts of Nepal (Nepal 1998). Within the framework of Community Forestry Projects, forests are being handed over to community-based user groups for local management. By the end of 1995, about 200,000 hectares of forestland had been transferred to over to 4,500 user groups, with thousands of other user groups awaiting formal registration. The Forest Act of 1993 recognised forest user groups as 'autonomous and corporate institutions with perpetual succession' with rights to acquire, sell or transfer forest products. In 1995, the Federation of Community Forestry User Groups of Nepal was founded with the purpose of mobilising and articulating the interests of the user groups by increasing their awareness and strengthening their coordination. Available statistics show that this participatory approach to resource management has been much more successful than earlier top-down approaches when the Forest Department held supreme power.

Evidence from Nepal also points out the benefit of participation in water resource management. Two large-scale irrigation programmes, the Irrigation Sector Project (ISP), 1989-1996, and the Irrigation Line of Credit Pilot Project (ILCPP), 1988-1997, emphasised popular participation both in the design and the implementation of the projects. The ISP sought to organise farmers into water users' associations prior to project approval and to build up their capacity, so that their services could be utilised for upgrading the physical facilities and improving the performance of irrigation systems. While the ILCCP did not mandate that farmers organise themselves prior to project approval, it did nonetheless promote their participation at all stages of the project cycle. A recent evaluation report has found evidence of strong participation by user groups. Not only did they actively participate in the design of the project, but they also contributed handsomely in terms of both cash and labour at the stage of implementation (Nepal 1998).

Other research findings have confirmed the superior performance of farmer-managed irrigation systems. Thus, from a data-base of 127 irrigation systems, of which 86 were community-managed and 22 government-managed, the community-managed systems were found to be more efficient in terms of crop yield and cropping intensity (Ostrom and Gardner 1993; Ostrom 1994). The reason for this difference lies in the differing ability of the two institutional forms to ensure water during the winter and spring seasons when it becomes increasingly scarce. A higher percentage of community-managed systems were able to get abundant water to both the head and the tail of their systems across all the seasons.[2] Since water availability may depend on a number of physical factors that have little to do with institutions, Ostrom and Gardner (1993) carried out a regression analysis to isolate the effect of these factors and still found community management to be the superior institutional framework.

Apart from resource management, service delivery can also be greatly improved when carried out within the framework of participatory decentralisation. The Education Guarantee Scheme (EGS) of Madhya Pradesh is a shining example (Madhya Pradesh 1998). Its literacy rate is appallingly low, even by the low average standards of India. In January 1997 the government of Madhya Pradesh introduced the innovative Education Guarantee Scheme, which involved both a guarantee on the part of the government and a compact between the government and local communities for sharing the cost and managing the programme.

Under the Scheme, the government guaranteed the provision of a trained teacher, the teacher's salaries and training, teacher-training materials and contingencies to start a school within 90 days, wherever there was demand from a community without a primary schooling facility within one kilometre and provided this demand came from at least 25 learners in case of tribal areas and 40 learners in case of non-tribal areas. The community, in turn, had to identify and put forward a teacher and provide the space for learning. Local management committees were set up for taking responsibility for day-to-day management of schools, and in particular for ensuring regular attendance on the part of both teachers and students.

By all accounts, the Scheme has proved to be an overwhelming success. In the first year of its operation, more than 40 new schools opened each day, and after 18 months, the state could boast universal access to primary education. A good deal of work remains to be done in terms of improving the quality of education offered by these schools, but at least in terms of ensuring access to education, the Scheme clearly demonstrates the power of a decentralised participatory approach.

Yet another way in which participatory decentralisation helps is by creating a more conducive environment for resource mobilisation. For example, the Nepal HDR has noted how participatory water management projects have given the incentive to water users to contribute generously towards project costs. Nearly 72 per cent of the beneficiaries contributed cash, labour or both for the two farmer-managed irrigation projects mentioned earlier. In term of labour input, effective farmer participation was 51 labour days per hectare, and the farmers' total contribution, whether in cash or labour, amounted to 12 per cent of total project costs (Nepal 1998).

Another example comes from the Uganda Participatory Poverty Assessment Project (UPPAP) undertaken in the districts of Kumi and Kapchorwa under the auspices of UNDP and other donor organisations. Since people felt confident that locally mobilised resources would be used mainly for the benefit and according to the preferences of local people, they claimed to be more inclined to pay taxes to local governments than they otherwise would have (Uganda 1999a, 1999b).

The Education Guarantee Scheme of Madhya Pradesh also illustrates the resource mobilisation aspect. The scope for genuine participation by the local community has encouraged them to contribute materially towards the provision of primary education by providing for the school structure. By contrast, evidence from Tanzania shows how, in the absence of genuine of participation, top-down planning for education has failed to elicit physical and material contribution from the villagers (Kikula et al. 1999).

The value of truly participatory decentralisation has thus been firmly established. It should be borne in mind, however, that the history of attempts to institutionalise participatory decentralisation on a wide scale is replete with many more cases of failure than of success. A host of problems is associated with transferring power from the top downwards. Other problems involve organising people at the grassroots level so that all segments of the community, including the poorer and the weaker ones, can effectively participate. The following two sections take up these two sets of problems.

Transferring power from the top

Politicians have all too often used the slogan of participation and decentralisation as a rhetorical device to strengthen their own power at the centre of government. There are plenty of examples. In Senegal, decentralising reforms initiated in 1972 sought to encourage popular participation in the management of local affairs in the hope of countering the pervasive problem of peasants' refusal to repay government loans or otherwise cooperate with governmental programmes in rural areas. The affairs of each rural community were to be managed by a representative body, the rural council. But the councillors did not feel that their views were taken into account in the initiation and execution of local development projects. The reform, therefore, did not represent a major departure from French administrative practice, in which the state and its agents retained full supervisory control over all aspects of local level actions (Vengroff and Johnston 1987).

Over the last two decades, the Kenyan government has frequently affirmed its commitment to a policy of decentralisation and the involvement of people in local governance. But elected local government has been weakened during the same period because the *nyayo* philosophy of the President requires close linkage between local government and national policy, which is determined by the central leadership (Wallis 1990).

The experience of Tanzania has been a subject of controversy. The reforms embarked upon in 1972 included the creation of deliberative assemblies at all levels, which involved both elected representatives and the relevant government functionaries. Maro (1990) has concluded that this reform had the intended effect of increasing popular participation in drawing up village plans through the village councils and committees. By contrast, Slater (1989) observes that 'rationalisation and consolidation of centralised authority lay at the roots of the spatial restructuring of state power, so that decentralisation was more illusion or myth than hard institutional reality'. In a similar vein, Samoff (1990) concludes that in practice the administrative reforms in Tanzania served to reinforce central authority and converted village councils into development advisory committees dominated by administrators and technicians.

A number of studies sponsored by UNDP corroborate the general thesis emerging from independent research that the rhetoric of decentralisation frequently fails to match the willingness of the centre to relinquish power. Thus, the Tanzanian study notes that 'the commitment of many African governments towards a "bottom-up" paradigm of development based on people's participation has been conducted without any accompanying changes to the broad political and institutional environment. Local participation has been sought without any meaningful reforms of the power relations between government and local communities. Participation has been seen as a means to ensure the more efficient implementation of pre-conceived plans often through existing government structures' (Kikula et al. 1999).

The human development report of Nepal echoes similar views about the early attempts at decentralisation introduced in the 1960s. The *Panchayat* system of local governance was introduced at that time, but politically it was anchored in the premise that political consciousness and popular participation in politics were impediments to economic and social progress. Yet, 'people's participation' was 'an expression constantly used by political leaders and government functionaries. The strategy was to enlist the support of people in programmes envisaged at the centre and, through the process, gain legitimacy for the political regime' (Nepal 1998).

After restoration of democracy in 1990, efforts were made to reform the decentralisation process in order to enhance local participation. New local bodies, the Village Development Committees and District Development Committees, were created by the parliament in 1992. A high-level Decentralisation Committee, formed in 1996 to institute an effective decentralisation framework, pinpointed a number of faults in the existing system:

- Local bodies lack institutional and technical capacity;
- There is no clear delineation between the executive and legislative functions;
- The concept of people's participation in governance is not clearly stipulated;
- Field offices of line agencies exercise overriding influence over local government institutions.

Subsequently, a Decentralisation Law Drafting Committee was formed to frame legislative proposals in line with the recommendations of the report. However, with the change of government in early 1997, the draft law went into suspended animation. The new coalition government that came to power pushed through an ordinance to expedite the process of local elections, but without incorporating many of the substantive issues mentioned above. The resulting structure of decentralised governance does not appear to be very different from the pre-1990 arrangements. The composition of local bodies has changed somewhat, with greater representation of the weaker segments (especially women), but very little else has changed. Consequently, 'now as before, there is little indication of the political will manifesting to introduce substantive devolution measures in practice. Besides, the government at the centre is vested with statutory powers that are far too draconian to be consistent with the spirit of devolution. The government has the power to regulate virtually all components of the local government system, including its formation, boundaries, jurisdiction, membership, structure, composition and mode of elections, and, in addition, to suspend or dissolve local bodies, if deemed necessary' (Nepal 1998).

Recently, some isolated attempts are being made to build a more representative form of decentralisation through the Participatory District Development Programme (PDDP) taken up with the support of UNDP and other donor agencies. This new move will be discussed in more detail later. Suffice it to note at this point that Nepal's case provides a clear illustration of the difficulties inherent in transferring power away from the centre, without which genuine decentralisation must remain an illusion.

Recent developments in Mongolia give further illustration of the point. The collapse of communism in Mongolia has eroded the earlier structures of local governance based on collectives. The new political regime has made it clear that it intends to follow a strategy of instituting simultaneous reforms in economic and political spheres. While introducing a market economy to replace the old command economy, it also intends to replace the old centralised governance structure by a new democratic and participatory decentralised structure. This movement towards decentralisation has been driven, at least in part, by the reality of fiscal constraints. The loss of financial support from Russia has combined with the travails of transition to render the central government virtually bankrupt. In an effort to reduce the fiscal burden on the centre, the government has sought to establish local bodies that would be expected to finance local-level activities in social spheres such as health and education (Mongolia 1998).

Despite these efforts, very little power of governance has actually devolved to participatory local institutions. At each province (*aimag*), district (*soum*) and sub-district (*bag*) level, there are locally elected assemblies that nominate their governors. But the governors are chosen finally from the centre, and each governor is accountable to the one above rather than to their respective assemblies, with the *aimag* governor holding most power. As a result, the local bodies exist practically as mere branches of *aimag* administration. Even at the *aimag* level, only about ten per cent of the decisions are taken locally. The rest emanate from the centre.

Yet another aspect of the problems of instituting participatory decentralisation is illustrated by the experience of Yemen, which shows that the centre may actually throttle the effort at decentralisation when people themselves take the initiative to create and develop local institutions of governance without official assistance.

Yemen boasts a rich tradition of local-level governance based on community-based organisations emerging from the grassroots level. Community Associations (CA) started in Aden from British days, as charitable societies financed by workers, businessmen and others. Gradually they spread all over the country and went into services such as schools and welfare programmes, realising that the centre was incapable of providing these services in adequate quality or quantity. But resource constraints forced them to grow into larger bodies. The first Local Development Association (LDA) was established in 1969. Between 1974 and 1985, they covered all districts. The federating process proceeded further, first at the provincial level and then at the central level, culminating in the Confederation of Yemeni Development Associations (CYDA).

But this movement faced reversal in the 1980s, when Law No. 12 of 1985 ended the independence of local associations. The LDAs became Local Councils for Cooperative Development (LCCDs) and their general secretary became a state minister. All local taxes and incomes collected by them were brought under central government control by merging them with the central account. The central government then distributed funds according to its own criteria (Yemen 1988).

At the same time, the government was proceeding with a kind of decentralisation of its own. Semi-autonomous Rural Development Authorities (RDAs) and Rural Development Projects (RDP) were set up to undertake activities at the regional level, sometimes cutting across administrative boundaries. These entities have made significant progress in dealing with issues of integrated rural development, usually covering areas as broad as agriculture, extension, training, and especially infrastructure.

In spite of huge resources made available to RDAs and RDPs, however, many local communities were not reached and the benefits were confined to limited social groups. Landlords and influential people were appointed to the Boards of these agencies. The provinces served by these agencies are still among the poorest in the country.

Participation is not enough

If the unwillingness of the centre to relinquish or share power acts as one major impediment to effective decentralisation, the other stumbling block is the inability of the weaker sections of the community to participate effectively in the structure of local governance. In a recent study, Blair (2000) has attempted to identify the conditions under which truly participatory decentralisation can become a reality. To do so, he identified the common characteristics of six relatively successful cases (Bolivia, Honduras, Ukraine, Mali, the Philippines and the Indian state of Karnataka). His analysis points to two related conditions. First, participation must be extensive, bringing as many citizens as possible into the political process. Secondly, accountability must be ensured by setting up mechanisms that can hold the governors responsible to the governed for their actions.

On the first condition, experience suggests that special efforts will have to be made to enhance the participation of women and minorities, if necessary by reserving seats for them in village committees. If this is not done, they are likely to be excluded from the decision-making process in the normal course of things. As for accountability, Blair's study reveals that there exists a wide range of instruments or mechanisms through which citizens can exercise control over their officials. These include encompassing mechanisms such as elections, as well as fine-tuning mechanisms such as public meetings and opinion surveys. Any one of these mechanisms, on its own, may not be able to do much. But in combination, they can be powerful enough to ensure effective accountability.

However, these ideal conditions are seldom satisfied. As a result, the decision-making process often comes to be dominated by a combination of local elites and government functionaries. In a review of experience of African countries, a PSI study done in Tanzania notes that a major problem with the current efforts at decentralisation in the continent stems from the fact that 'the preoccupation with technical issues and the assumption of uniform community interests have resulted in insufficient focus on the socio-economic and cultural heterogeneity of communities. Differences in access to land, labour and credit resulting from village power relations, gender, age and caste tend to be overlooked. This has resulted in communities being dominated by local elite and the exclusion of certain groups' (Kikula et al. 1999). This finding is in line with a growing body of empirical research based on both past and recent history, which shows that weaker categories of users of common property resources are frequently excluded by dominant groups in order to achieve efficient use of resources (Allen 1992; Cohen and Weitzman 1975; Peters 1994; Andre and Platteau 1997.) This kind of governance structure may be decentralised in some sense, but it can hardly claim to be the kind of governance that is suitable for making a serious assault on poverty.

Different countries have tried to get around this problem in different ways. Zimbabwe, for example, has been groping for a strategy, first trying to bypass the local elite and then trying to co-opt them. In 1984, the Zimbabwean government introduced an institutional framework for local development, in which popularly elected Village Development Committees were designated as the fundamental planning unit. By 1989, however, the Minister for Local Government had to admit that the scheme was not working, since 'people were not sufficiently involved or active in the village and ward development committees'.

This lack of popular involvement could be explained at least partly by the fact that the new governance structure had tried to bypass the traditional structures of village organisation that still dominated the lives of rural people. Much of the legislation enacted since Independence has sought to extinguish traditional leadership. The chiefs, sub-chiefs and *kraal* heads together constitute the effective legal and administrative institutions, with historically defined areas and sets of rules that are clearly understood by the people. There was no place for them in the new institutional structure.

Predictably, the transition from traditional and chiefly authority (local, hereditary, and long-standing) to elected and bureaucratic (transient and possibly immigrant) has been a source of conflict. The Rukuni Commission report on land tenure, published in 1994, accepted this analysis. Following its recommendation, the government has introduced a Traditional Leaders Bill with a view to re-investing the traditional leaders with some of their former powers, by making them the leaders of village and ward assemblies. The resulting mixture of the traditional with the modern has apparently served only to foster further confusion (Kikula et al. 1999).

Similar confusion seems to prevail in Papua New Guinea. What has emerged in the wake of the 1995 Organic Law on Provincial and Local Level Governments is a superimposition of a new governance structure on an existing one, without any genuine attempt to integrate the two. This has resulted in a conflict between traditional and modern practices. For instance, the traditional system of governance allowed that if the local leadership failed to deliver a promised service, the aggrieved parties were entitled to seek compensation. This age-old principle is now being applied in many cases to the decentralised government agencies, which are not, however, empowered to provide any compensation. This has often resulted in discontent among the people, even leading to violence in some cases (Papua New Guinea 1999).

A more promising plan to work through the traditional village institutions is being attempted in Yemen, where UNDP has been supporting a programme known as Community-Based Rural Development (CBRD). The programme has been undertaken as part of the government's commitment to enhance the capacity of regional and local authorities to deliver social development services to the local clientele, and enable civil society actors and community organisations to engage in wealth generation and institution-building activities. Capacity-building at the grassroots level is thus an integral part of the programme. However, instead of building completely new structures, the government is trying to make use of the rich tradition of local cooperation that has characterised the Yemeni rural society for decades.

In particular, extensive use is being envisaged for two traditional institutions. One is the *sanduq*, a form of local community-owned fund. The other is the *musharaka*, a prevalent form of social cooperation for economic production in which different factors of production are owned by different people, but are managed jointly. The funds to be provided by UNDP for local development will be operated in the manner of a *sanduq*. In order to ensure efficient management of the funds, community animators and male and female elders will receive training and then form *musharakas*, which will be responsible for managing community funds and projects.

One component of the UNDP project involves micro-finance, as has now become the norm in many poverty reduction programmes. The distinctive feature of the Yemeni case, however, is that unlike in other developing countries, neither banks nor non-governmental organisations (NGOs) are being involved in administering the moneys. In recognition of the fact that Yemeni communities are still characterised by strong ties of solidarity and tradition, the funds for microfinance, like the funds for general developmental activities, are being designated as a *san-*

duq to be operated by the *musharakas* (Yemen 1998).

The results of this experiment are yet be evaluated. But the study sponsored by UNDP in Yemen notes some potential dangers of relying so heavily on traditional social structures based primarily on kinship and neighbourhood relationships. 'As experience shows, traditional socio-territorial units often appear to be coherent only in certain spheres of social life and united only in case of external danger and threats. These units are sometimes weakened by daily internal tensions and disputes between family lineages, and sometimes handicapped by excessive individualism and trends towards autonomy. Poverty may worsen these trends and force individual households to react only according to their own interest and their survival strategies. Therefore, an institutional approach to development needs to be prepared to apply a second principle: to confront existing organisations as well with new ideas, behaviours, and attitudes and to manifest the new ideas and attitudes where appropriate and accepted. Such a transition, when required, from purely kinship-based traditional groups to more adapted forms of problem-oriented "units of collective action" is not easy. The process needs time, incentives and stimulation' (Yemen 1998).

Other countries, like India and Nepal, have chosen the system of popularly elected village councils or *panchayats* as the vehicle through which different segments of the populations can work for their interests. The human development reports of Nepal and the two Indian states of Karnataka and Madhya Pradesh discuss at length the evolution, strengths and weaknesses of this system.

Both India and Nepal have a fairly long history of *panchayat* administration. At the insistence of Mohandas Gandhi, the concept of *panchayat* found a place in the Constitution of India. Article 40, one of the Directive Principles, states that 'the state shall take steps to organise village panchayats and endow them with such powers and authority as may be necessary to enable then to function as units of self-government' (Karnataka 1999). In practice, however, until recently the system was no more than either an appendix of the official bureaucracy or a vehicle for legitimising traditional village hierarchies.

A break from this tradition was first made by the Indian state of West Bengal. Beginning in the 1980s, the ruling Communist Party effectively used the village *panchayats* as a countervailing force against both the traditional elite and the official bureaucracy. At the same time, the central government tried to strenghten the system through new legislation geared towards making the *panchayats* more responsive to the needs of the weaker segments. The first round of *panchayat* elections under the new legal framework took place in Karnataka, followed soon by Madhya Pradesh.

There is a general expectation that the revamped *panchayats* will represent a much greater degree of participatory decentralisation than was the case with the earlier moribund system. First, the new legal framework has made it mandatory to ensure representation of the weaker segments by reserving seats for women and the lower castes. Secondly, the state governments have committed to transfer much greater power and resources to the *panchayats* than they had in the past. The same two features also characterise the recent attempt at resuscitating the village democracy system in Nepal.

The state of Karnataka has probably gone further than any other state of India in strengthening the *panchayat* system through legal means. The system acquired far more force in 1983 with the enactment of a legislation that transferred a wide range of powers from the state level to the lower levels. Furthermore, the new legislation made the leader of the *panchayats* the chief executive of the relevant administrative unit. This was a bold move intended to do away with the old system of government officials acting as the chief executive even when elected *panchayats* existed. The system was further improved by an act of 1993, which made the village assembly (*gram sabha*), consisting of all persons on the electoral roll in the village, the foundation of the entire structure of decentralised governance. This decision was aimed at ensuring that the elected members of *panchayats* cannot ride roughshod over the ordinary people at their whim. The assembly meets twice a year to review the accounts and performance of the village *panchayat* and identify beneficiaries for various development programmes (Karantaka 1999).

Apart from using the village assembly as a check against abuse of power by elected representatives, measures have been taken to broaden popular representation among the elected members themselves. The law stipulates that at least one third of the seats are reserved for women, apart from reservation for the scheduled castes (15 per cent), scheduled tribes (three per cent) and other 'backward classes' (33 per cent). In practice, the representation of the weaker groups has turned out to be somewhat higher than the minimum stipulated by the law. Thus in the early 1990s, some 43 per cent of village panchayat members were women, 22 per cent belonged to the scheduled castes, 9 per cent to the scheduled tribes and 35 per cent to other 'backward classes'.

Another important feature of the law is the reservation of a minimum number of chairpersons and vice chairpersons of different tiers of panchayats for the weaker sections. Thus, women must have at least one third of these positions, the scheduled castes and tribes must have positions in proportion to their population (subject to a minimum number), and other 'backward classes' must have one-third of the posts. The statutory reservation of seats for women and other weaker classes have clearly made a difference in ensuring broader participation. In Madhya Pradesh, more than one third of all *panchayat* members were women in the late 1990s. This is no mean achievement in a state where female literacy and other indicators of women's status are among the lowest in the country.

The Nepal HDR, while generally critical of the decentralisation process in the country, also acknowledges that mandatory reservation of seats for women has

Box 1. Village women speak out

The following story was reported in the diary of a resource person in Darhad, Karnataka (India):

'A tank was built in our village. It was inaugurated with great fanfare. The tank had taps on all sides but it didn't have a cover. It was left open. Leaves and seeds from the tamarind and banyan trees nearby would fall into the tank. Water in the tank became so contaminated that many children began to suffer from dysentery. The women's *sangha* in the village sent petitions and appeals to the *zilla* and *taluk panchayats* but there was no response. When they went to the *taluk panchayat* office, they were taunted: 'Why have you women have come to waste our time?' They shouted at the women and sent them back.

Some time later there were elections to the *taluk panchayat*. The women in the village decided that they would boycott the elections. They said they didn't need *panchayat* help for anything and would, therefore, not vote for anyone. Persons who came to the village to canvass votes got worried. They agreed that the tank should be cleaned and provided with a cover by the very next day. They gave a commitment to do so in writing.

What had actually happened was that the *gram panchayat* chairman had pocketed the money meant for the tank cover. Because of the condition laid down by the women and fear of an inquiry into the matter, the chairman took out a loan and got the tank covered overnight!'

facilitated much greater representation of women than would otherwise have been possible. The study also notes that while the elite classes still dominate politics in Nepal, the weaker classes have gained a better representation at the level of local governance compared to the national level (Nepal 1998).

All this no doubt represents a significant advance. But representation by itself is not enough. The question still remains: how well do the weaker segments really feel empowered vis-à-vis the traditional elite and official bureaucracy? Some isolated examples of empowerment that have ensued from the electoral process do exist (Box 1). But on the whole, there is still a general presumption that the elite domination of local government is far from over. A graphic description of this reality from the state of Karnataka is cited in Box 2.

The continuation of elite domination is acknowledged by all three HDRs from Nepal, Karnataka and Madhya Pradesh. As the Madhya Pradesh report notes, 'despite the limitations that such efforts at political decentralisation have in a context of unevenly owned economic resources, the emergence of a new leadership at the local level has had a dramatic impact in a churning of rural polity in Madhya Pradesh. The drama is still unfolding and the contestation between existing power structures of landlord-petty bureaucrat nexus with the new leadership is far from settled' (Madhya Pradesh 1998).

The same phenomenon is also found in Uganda. The Participatory Poverty Assessments in the districts of Kumi and Kapchorwa found that people were generally sceptical about the participatory nature of the elected local councils. The respondents in Kapchorwa alleged that the council members lacked accountability and transparency, and that they did not inform the ordinary people of the range of benefits to which they were entitled. The women respondents of Kumi felt that the local elite discouraged women from participating in the electoral process. They further despaired that even having a woman representative in the local council was not good enough, because she did not communicate with the rest of the women (Uganda 1999b, 1999c).

Evidence from the rest of the developing world corroborates these findings from the PSI studies. In Bangladesh, for example, it is well known that the chairman and elected members of the local government are drawn from the local elite, because of the influence of traditional patronage relationships. It has been argued that this has had a pernicious effect on social relations, because an authority that formerly entailed some reciprocity vis-à-vis ordinary people has been invested with official sanction and partisan support, thereby facilitating the ability of the local elite to further its own interests at the expense of the community (Khan 1987). Similarly, commenting on the Latin American experience of decentralisation, a recent study observes that the results have not been unequivocally satisfactory, partly because decentralisation has tended to lose effectiveness due to political patronage in the election of local officials (IFAD 1999).

Empowerment, civil society and the economic security of the poor

Deep-seated problems cannot be removed overnight simply by decreeing some system of decentralisation, whether it is done by co-opting the traditional social structure as in Yemen or by instituting a system of local democracy, with reservations for the weaker segments, as in India and Nepal. Nobody relinquishes power easily, be they the politicians and bureaucrats at the centre or the traditional elite in the village. Social forces must be created that would compel them to countenance sharing of power. An essential part of this social process is the gradual empowerment of the poor, so that they can convert their numerical strength into genuine bargaining power.

There are two essential elements of this process of empowerment. One is social mobilisation. Because of illiteracy, economic insecurity and a general lack of self-confidence, the poor cannot in general be expected to organise themselves entirely on their own without outside help. It is essential to make a conscious effort at social mobilisation with the help of change agents. But so long as the poor suffer from extreme economic insecurity, it is unlikely that they will be able to exercise effective bargaining power even with the help of social mobilisation. The process of social mobilisation must therefore be accompanied by measures to remove extreme insecurities of the poor.

The Nepal HDR cites one innovative experiment that seeks to make social mobilisation the cornerstone of the decentralisation process. Under the Participatory

District Development Programme, social mobilisation at the grassroots level has been combined with an ambitious programme of administrative decentralisation so that local governance can become truly participatory. The local authorities (District Development Committees and Village Development Committees) have been legally mandated to formulate district development plans and to manage the implementation of district and village level plans through community and user groups. UNDP is helping to mobilise community groups with the help of dedicated community organisers funded by the project, while at the same time trying to strengthen the planning and management capability of the staff of the local government. The overriding objective of the programme is to reflect the needs and priorities of the communities at all levels of development efforts. They will have a voice in formulating local-level infrastructure and income-generating projects and will also interact with local administration to access more effectively various public services such as health, education, extension, veterinary services and others. At present, community organisers funded by the project are acting as the catalysts of social mobilisation and group formation. Obviously, over the long term, others, presumably NGOs, will have to take over this responsibility (Nepal 1998).

A somewhat different model of social mobilisation has been adopted in Madhya Pradesh. There, the primarily responsibility has been taken up by a specially designed government institution called Rajiv Gandhi Missions, named after the late Prime Minister of India. There are a number of Missions, each of which is com-

Box 2. When speaking out is not enough

'I was supposed to become the chairperson because the seat was proposed to be reserved for a Scheduled Caste woman. But the landlord in our village didn't want me to become the chairperson. 'Why should she, an illiterate person, become chairperson?', they asked. Four or five men got together, convened a meeting and declared him chairperson — despite the seat being reserved for an SC! I didn't get elected because they couldn't bear to be superseded by someone from a Scheduled Caste. 'How can they be above us?', they asked.

But I fought them. 'Why deny me what is mine? You are not giving me anything that is yours. The government has given us reservation. So let us have it', I asked.

'We cannot do that, Sivanavva', they said. Then I asked them to make me vice chairperson, but that was a general seat. I said that just as they have taken away our reserved seat, they should give us the general one. They hushed up the matter for three months. After that the landlord produced a low-income certificate and was made chairperson. His wife was made vice chairperson.

There were three of us in the reserved category, two men and me. We remained members. The landlord and his wife became chairperson and vice chairperson'.

posed of senior officials from several ministries, works independently of line ministries, and is entrusted with some specific time-bound task — e.g., ensuring primary education for all, eliminating iodine deficiency, watershed development, etc. The officials of the Missions themselves go around organising user groups and other community organisations. The activities of these Missions have engendered a new wave of social mobilisation across the state. In this process, they sometimes, but not always, seek the help of local NGOs (Madhya Pradesh 1998).

Although the potentially important role of NGOs in supporting the decentralisation process is now generally accepted by most people, there remains some disagreement in the wider literature on exactly what role they ought to play. On the one hand, they are advised by some commentators to focus on their core functions, standardise their procedures and concentrate on maximising operational performance in the context of large-scale service delivery (Jain 1994, 1996). On the other hand, there are those who advocate for the flexibility to respond in different ways across a set of activities, with an underlying emphasis on grassroots level empowerment (Edwards and Hulme 1992, 1995; Fowler 1997). This tension between service delivery and social mobilisation is also reflected in some of the studies sponsored by UNDP. The studies on Kyrgyztan and Mongolia, for instance, have expressed concern that the emerging NGOs are far too concerned with service delivery to the neglect of the broader task of social mobilisation.

Recently, Edwards (1999) has tried to advance this debate on the proper role of non-governmental organisations by distilling some lessons from a number of successful NGOs operating in South Asia and also by drawing upon other studies on NGO performance in Asia, Africa and Latin America. He concludes that the NGOs are most successful when they adopt the three-pronged strategy of helping the poor to secure their livelihoods, attempting social mobilisation with the aim of empowering the poor, and trying to influence the overall political process by playing an advocacy role on behalf of the poor. This conclusion resonates strongly with an observation made by Esman and Uphoff (1984) in their path-breaking study on NGOs. According to the authors, 'the ability of rural residents to advance their... interests depends substantially... on their success in sustaining local organisations beyond the immediate tasks that precipitated them.' Non-governmental organisations can play a potentially powerful role precisely in this task of helping the poor to transcend the immediate tasks around which they initially happen to organise.

In view of the potentially instrumental role of NGOs in social mobilisation, their strengthening should itself be an important investment activity for agencies such as UNDP that value participation and decentralisation. Creating a civil society where none exists, and strengthening it where it does, is now an important part of their agenda. Many governments are also embracing this agenda with increasing vigour.

Several of the PSI studies take cognisance of this trend. The Yemen study, for example, notes that strengthening of the civil society is an integral part of UNDP's assistance for poverty reduction in that country. The studies on Kyrgyzstan and Mongolia also note how the state is trying to foster the growth of NGOs, at least partly with the intention of filling the political vacuum left by the collapse of communism (Kyrgyzstan 1998; Mongolia 1997).

But there may be a tricky problem here, as has recently been pointed out by Gray (1999). The problem concerns: what is really a civil society, what is its relationship with the state, and what kind of civil society organisations are going to emerge if the state wants to be their handmaiden?

Two rather different conceptions of a civil society are found in the literature. The first draws upon Alexis de Tocqueville's 1831 work *Democracy in America*, in which the civic associations that constitute the civil society are seen to be an important means for citizens to moderate the power of the state and assert their own interests (de Tocqueville 1831). In other words, the civil society is seen as a distinct entity that has an intrinsically adversarial relationship with the state. The other conception comes from Antonio Gramsci, who defined civil society as a social sphere or a public 'space' where political thought is transformed into action (Gramsci 1971). As such, this sphere is contested by all components of society, including the state. Gramsci believed that, in general, civil society functions as a vehicle for propagating the ideas of the ruling strata to the masses, in the process giving those ideas a legitimacy that they might otherwise lack.

Gray points out that the conception of civil society held by the World Bank and the UN agencies as well as many international NGOs corresponds to that of de Tocqueville, whereas in practice it could be a Gramscian phenomenon. He demonstrates this point by analysing the formation of local NGOs in Viet Nam, which in most cases have become the instrument of the state as opposed to being an adversarial entity. The Nepal HDR (1998) also points out that in the pre-1990 period, before restoration of democracy, the Nepalese civil society was mostly co-opted by the state. Non-governmental organisations were incorporated into a quasi-governmental framework under the Social Services National Coordination Council headed by the Queen. The Kyrgyz study also notes that the newly emerging NGOs are mostly institutions created from the top, often with state patronage, and with very little participation of people at the bottom (Kyrgyzstan 1998).

The question therefore arises: if state power belongs to the rich and the powerful, can civil society organisations really mobilise the poor so as to bring them into a harmonious relationship with the state? There is perhaps no unambiguous answer to this question. What is clear, though, is that the possibility of mobilising the poor as a voice to be counted in governance structures depends not just on the character of the mobiliser, but also on the attributes of the poor themselves. So long as they remain in an extreme state of economic and social insecurity, the prospects of mobilising them as an assertive force must be rather dim. Therefore, an important prerequisite of participatory decentralisation is the removal of extreme insecurities.

The studies on Madhya Pradesh and Yemen reveal that the drive towards social mobilisation in these countries take full cognisance of this requirement. Thus, when the local people are mobilised to preserve the forests or to develop water-sheds in Madhya Pradesh, the focus is primarily on the livelihood security of the poor. It is recognised that unless the poor can be guaranteed the security of their livelihood, it is unrealistic to expect them to mobilise themselves, be it for the preservation of forests or to develop water resources. Accordingly, the plan for resource conservation contains as an essential component an integrated livelihood strategy for all segments of society, including the vulnerable groups such as landless labourers and women (Madhya Pradesh 1998).

In Yemen, the approach to decentralisation has been consciously designed to achieve immediate economic gains for the people while engaged in participatory institution-building. Providing matching grants for productive assets or community infrastructure works will be the first step in a phased approach to community-based financing of income generating activities. Depending on their own choices, the poor may thus engage themselves in production intensification of food or cash crops, development of small-scale animal husbandry, input supply and marketing facilities, and micro-enterprises.

To initiate the process, a Regional Community Development Fund will be set up by UNDP. The fund will be initially set up at the national level and be operated at regional and community level. The fund will have two components:

- A Community Development Investment Fund (CDIF) providing matching grants for productive investments will be allocated annually to the community or sub-community level. It will strengthen the local *sanduq* systems.
- A Community Loan Fund (CLF) will be established and managed at the community level and provide loanable funds to community members or groups who have mobilised minimum levels of savings. The use of the funds and prioritisation of funding activities will be decided at the community level. The implementing institutions are qualifying community-based financial institutions.

An important aspect of this funding is the provision that no investment will be made in social services or other activities that do not directly produce income. The local committees (*musharakas*) will of course be allowed to use a part of the proceeds earned from productive activities for these purposes, and NGOs and other international agencies will be encouraged to provide social services. Nevertheless, the initial fund given by UNDP is to be used entirely for productive activities. This restriction presumably reflects the concern that social mobilisation will remain a distant dream unless the poor can escape from extreme economic insecurity.

Conclusion

The PSI studies, along with many others, have shown how genuinely participatory governance at the local level can yield benefits in terms of both efficiency and equity by giving the people a sense of ownership, by allocating resources according to people's preferences and by utilising their skills and knowledge.

But the goal of genuinely participatory decentralisation remains a distant one in most developing countries, despite the efforts made during the last half-century. This chapter has identified two major obstacles, based on evidence from several developing countries. The first obstacle lies in the reluctance of politicians and bureaucrats at the higher echelons of governance to relinquish power to the lower levels. The second one lies in the inability of the weaker segments of the population to make their voice heard in the face of elite domination of the traditional power structures.

Some countries have tried to tackle the problem of traditional power structure by introducing popularly elected democratic structures at the community level, fortified by a reservation of seats for the weaker segments. Some others have tried to work around the problem by coopting the traditional structure itself. Both approaches have had some success, but they continue to face many difficulties. The ingrained problem of elite domination has hardly been resolved.

It is inconceivable that the problems involved in achieving genuinely participatory decentralisation can be resolved without empowering the common people, especially the poorer segments of society. Neither the politician-bureaucratic nexus nor the traditional elite will voluntarily share power, let alone relinquish it, unless the poor themselves can exercise enough bargaining power to make them do so. The empowerment of the poor thus becomes the central agenda item in any programme for decentralising governance in a pro-poor manner.

Two components of a strategy for empowerment have been discussed in this paper. One component is to improve the economic security of the poor as an integral part of the drive towards decentralisation. The second is social mobilisation. The poor need to be organised so that their collective voice can overcome the weaknesses of their separate voices. International agencies, local and international NGOs, and civil society in general can play an important role here as the catalysts or change agents.

We have reviewed a number of studies that testify that this effort is taking place in many countries as an integral part of the move towards decentralisation. As a part of this effort, many governments have undertaken the responsibility of grooming and fostering a strong civil society. One potential problem here is that in the process of fostering the civil society, the state may feel tempted to co-opt it, to make it work as an instrument of the state, and to prevent it from playing an adversarial role. If this happens, it will defeat the whole purpose of empowering the poor. Much depends, therefore, on how much autonomy the state is willing to grant to civil society actors to organise themselves as a catalyst for social change.

This last consideration brings to the fore the question of the nature of the overall polity within which decentralisation is being attempted. After all, the politics of local government can hardly be divorced from the politics of national government. If graft, patronage and rent-seeking characterise the political process that determines the distribution of power in the centre, local-level government can hardly be an arena of popular participation just because it is local. There is ample evidence dating back many years that the characteristics of democracy at the local level resemble, to some extent, those at the national level (Bulpitt 1972). A more recent overview of current experience also confirms this view, suggesting that 'decentralisation is more likely to be thoroughgoing under liberal democratic/pluralist national regimes. Where the nation state is authoritarian/one-party, the mode of decentralisation tends to follow deconcentration, which effectively preserves central control. This applies equally to capitalist and socialist regimes, where small cliques have captured the power of the state. At the same time, however, the converse does not necessarily hold — democracy need not lead to decentralisation' (Klugman 1994).

Fortunately, however, the correspondence between national and local level politics is not exact. This implies that there exists scope for taking conscious action such that a reasonable degree of participation can be achieved at the local level regardless of the national polity. But this can only happen if the civil society can be strengthened enough to help the poor empower themselves. International agencies such as UNDP have an important role to play in order to help build a strong civil society, which in turn will help empower the poor. Hopefully, the empowerment process will eventually extend beyond the local level and begin to impinge upon the national polity as well to make it more responsive to the voice and the needs of the poor. Truly participatory decentralisation will then become a reality. ∎

Notes

S.R.Osmani is Professor of Development Economics, University of Ulster, UK. He would like to thank all members of the PSI evaluation team, especially Alf Jerve, and Alejandro Grinspun of UNDP, for their helpful comments an earlier draft.

[1] For other examples of indigenous governments with pseudo-legality, see D. Korten (1980, 1986), N. Uphoff (1982) and D. Curtis (1991).

[2] During the spring, when water is normally very scarce, about one out of four community-managed systems were able to get abundant water to the tail of their systems, while only one out of eleven government-managed systems were able to do so. Even in the high monsoon season, less than half of the government-managed systems got enough water to the tails, while almost 90 per cent of the community-managed systems did so (Ostrom 1994).

6 Poverty in Transition:
Lessons from Eastern Europe and Central Asia

Jaroslaw Górniak

Economic and political transformation in Central and Eastern Europe and the former Soviet Union republics provided a spectacular epilogue to a century marked by sacrifice on a large scale. Most of these countries now suffer from a severe and, in most cases, long-term transformation crisis triggered largely by three factors: the disintegration of the old economic system, a collapse in trade with other states in the region and an increasing need to adjust to the competitive demands of the world economy. Unemployment and a dramatic rise in poverty have appeared as the main social concerns in countries that were not accustomed to recognising, let alone confronting, these issues.

The Central European countries (the Czech Republic, Hungary, Slovakia and Slovenia) have made the most progress in disentangling their economic systems from planned to market economies. They have achieved relatively adequate living standards and are now applying for European Union membership. Despite continuing problems and challenges, the reforms introduced by these countries may be regarded as largely successful. Poland has achieved significant success in the economic sphere, but nevertheless has seen poverty emerge as a major social challenge.

The Baltic states (Latvia, Lithuania and Estonia) stood out positively from the rest of the Soviet republics even prior to the collapse of the Soviet Union. An internal 'border' appeared to mark them off from the other republics in terms of living standards and economic development. After they gained their independence, a process that strained relations with Moscow and on a number of occasions sparked armed clashes, these countries found themselves in a crisis from which they have only gradually extricated themselves. Estonia has been the most successful of the three and today is one of the leaders among the countries applying for European Union membership. All of them have nonetheless experienced varying degrees of poverty and are making noteworthy efforts to identify and solve these problems.

The other former Soviet republics have suffered the most from the crisis in the region. In some cases, the old order has collapsed entirely. These countries, however, do not represent a homogeneous group. Prior to the transformation they were characterised by different living standards and economic development. Differences have also become apparent with regard to the transformation strategy. The contrasts range from Uzbekistan, where the transformation process has been relatively gradual and peaceful, to Kyrgyzstan, which has adopted a market-oriented strategy burdened by serious problems, and Ukraine and Russia, which have suffered from long-term crisis and a dramatic increase in social stratification.

The countries of South Eastern Europe have been plagued by their own problems, particularly in the Balkans, as a result of civil conflict and ethnic wars. Other countries have been spared conflict, but have witnessed a sudden rise in poverty following economic breakdown. Such is the case of Bulgaria, which after a brief respite in the middle of the 1990s, has once again experienced a downturn from which the country is still trying to escape. The collapse in domestic demand caused by a sharp fall in real incomes poses a serious problem.

This chapter is based on the findings from policy work supported by the United Nations Development Programme (UNDP) through its Poverty Strategies Initiative (PSI) programme in 11 countries in the region: Armenia, Bulgaria, Estonia, Kazakhstan, Kyrgyzstan, Moldova, Poland, Russian Federation, Tajikistan, Turkmenistan and Ukraine. Although the analytical and policy work funded by UNDP varied in nature across countries, it provides a rich source of information for understanding the nature of poverty throughout the region and the challenges facing policy-makers. A clear diagnosis of the problem and its determinants should, after all, be the departure point of any public policy.

The chapter begins by presenting briefly the radical social transformation experienced in these countries, and the efforts supported by UNDP to raise public awareness of the magnitude of the problem. It then provides an analysis of how these countries are struggling to devise adequate tools to capture the extent, depth and profile of poverty. Finally, we present some of the answers that are emerging in the region, focussing on a number of programmes and strategies developed to address particular aspects of the poverty agenda.

The emergence of poverty as a public concern

The demise of the Soviet Union was an enormous shock for the region as a whole. Free of Soviet domination, the countries now had to develop their own political systems and market mechanisms. They managed to do this to varying degrees. Cooperative links that existed previously between countries broke down, traditional supplies of raw materials were interrupted, and the export markets of the huge socialist production plants collapsed because they were producing goods that failed to conform to the rapidly spreading patterns of consumption in market economies. In many places, short or more protracted armed conflicts broke out. This further exacerbated the severe economic crisis facing these countries, especially in the former Soviet republics.

As a consequence of this transformation crisis, the extent of poverty has increased dramatically, and so have income disparities. There has been a rapid improvement in the incomes of the top 5 to 10 per cent of society and a simultaneous fall in the incomes of the majority of the population in many countries. Social groups not previously affected by poverty, such as public sector workers, saw their salaries and living standards plunge. As a result of these developments, 60 to 70 per cent of the population in most countries currently earn fairly low incomes.

It is important to stress that poverty is not a new phenomenon that can be attributed exclusively to the transformation process. It did exist before in the Soviet Union and its satellite countries, even though political and ideological reasons obstructed its official recognition. This was particularly true in the republics of Central Asia, especially Turkmenistan and Tajikistan, where national income per capita was approximately two times less than the average in the rest of the Soviet Union. Even in Ukraine, international experts estimated that 11 per cent of the population lived below the poverty line in the late 1980s, although other sources put this figure at 20 to 25 per cent (Ukraine 1997a). In spite of this, inadequate attention was paid to ensuring proper analysis of living standards in the former socialist bloc. Until 1989, much statistical data was secret. This included the periodic family budget surveys, which contained a great amount of social information, as well as the existence of inflation and hidden unemployment. Attempts to conduct serious surveys of living conditions were forbidden and considered nationalistic propaganda. Soviet social policy was planned on a national scale, without taking account of regional peculiarities and imbalances.

Moreover, economic indicators during the pre-transformation period, which have served as a guideline when estimating the effects of the subsequent crisis, were often shaped by government optimism and the habit of recording on paper the performance of plans never intended for implementation. In addition to problems of economic growth, all the countries in the former Soviet bloc have poor records in environmental protection, life expectancy, health care, education and training. Although these problems have emerged largely during the course of the transformation crisis, some have roots in the old system. The transformation crisis merely intensified these problems. It did not create them.

The fact that poverty was never officially acknowledged explains why it was neither an object of public debate nor treated as problem of public policy. Politicians in most countries largely neglected the issue, even after its dramatic emergence following the transition. In an attempt to hide the problem, many people have willingly substituted various euphemisms for the word 'poverty'. Such behaviour often results from the fact that a person who is labelled as 'poor' or 'needy' risks being marginalised. A negative consequence is that social assistance may fail to reach those who need it because they are too ashamed to claim the benefits to which they are entitled (Trapenciere et al. 2000).

One key challenge for the region, therefore, was to increase awareness of poverty among both policy-makers and the public at large, and to identify the scale and structural causes of this phenomenon. This was one of the main functions of the projects financed by UNDP in the 11 countries covered in this chapter. Whether it was a qualitative poverty assessment in Latvia, a national strategy for improving public health in Kazakhstan, a study on women in poverty in Bulgaria, or a living standards survey in Tajikistan, a key objective of UNDP assistance to these countries set out to introduce the issue of poverty into the national public discourse.

Poverty in Eastern Europe and the former Soviet republics is still largely a problem caused by crisis-related factors. The radical political and economic changes unleashed by the demise of the Soviet Union have been accompanied by high unemployment, changes in the relative situation of large social groups (e.g. farmers), and a drastic drop in consumption levels as a result of changes in relative prices. This was further compounded by the inability of public services to satisfy basic needs and the reduction or removal of state subsidies on critical goods and services.

The key to solving the problem of crisis-induced poverty lies in guaranteeing stable economic growth and creating new jobs. One particular form of temporary poverty that has emerged in the region is associated with the difficulties involved in the 'full nest' syndrome, that period in the family cycle when children are still being brought up at home. During this time, the incomes of household earners, some of whom may be single parents, must be able to cover the expenditure of many people. Even if temporary in nature, the effects of such poverty can be inherited by children. They may be denied access to an appropriate level of education and be exposed to the dangers of biological underdevelopment due to malnutrition. At the same time, the prolongation of a crisis may result in the appearance of highly vulnerable social groups. It also increases the danger of long-term, structural poverty as a consequence of the emergence of a new competitive labour market and, in particular, the rising importance of education in market economies. Long periods of absence from the labour market can contribute to passivity and the development of a welfare dependency syndrome, factors that increase the likelihood of structural poverty.

Under these circumstances, the main challenges facing policy-makers in the region today are to limit structural poverty and mitigate its effects in the short term, while creating the conditions for empowering people and providing them with opportunities for escaping poverty. Particular attention needs to be paid to limiting the reappearance of poverty in later generations by ensuring that children receive adequate support and assistance. Given the strong regional character of poverty and unemployment in several countries (due, for example, to the closure of plants in many 'factory towns'), an additional challenge for public policy is to implement emergency packages of assistance to impoverished regions.

On the other hand, a number of factors inherited from the Soviet era led many people who suddenly found themselves below the poverty line to treat their situation as temporary. Among these factors are the presence of nearly universal literacy, an accumulated stock of goods, including a dwelling and domestic appliances, as well as the existence of a very active, skilled population prior to the transformation. This makes it possible, at least in principle, to mitigate poverty in the short term by creating jobs, raising incomes and improving the economic situation of the population.

Poverty measurement and analysis
Choosing a poverty threshold

To wage an effective attack on poverty, it is vital to identify its extent, nature and determinants. This requires, among other things, devising appropriate tools for gauging the scale of the problem, both for purposes of heightening public awareness and informing the design of policy. The first step is to determine which criteria or threshold should be used to differentiate between impoverished groups and the rest of the population. The method most frequently employed is to define a poverty line based on monetary or other indicators. Estimates of the extent and depth of poverty in a given society will be contingent upon the choice and exact location of the poverty line. The problem is that, to a large extent, all poverty lines are arbitrary. For this reason, all the countries covered in this chapter have been struggling with the need to come up with a set of measures that not only reflect accurately the incidence of poverty in their societies, but also are accepted politically as providing a sound basis for public action.

A review of the various surveys and assessments financed by UNDP in the region reveals that in the majority of countries, poverty lines were calculated on the basis of the value of income or expenditure per capita (or equivalent adult) in a household. Such poverty lines often were based on absolute criteria, such as the estimated minimum subsistence level or a social minimum. Other possibilities, however, were also examined. They included the setting of a relative poverty line, a subjective poverty line or a structural poverty line calculated on the basis of the share of expenditure per person assigned to food. The most frequent sources of data were the results of standard research into household budgets carried out by statistical offices or of special research projects investigating the problem of poverty, as was the case in Bulgaria, Latvia and Lithuania. Unfortunately, given the differences in methodology, the figures obtained in these studies cannot be compared across countries.

Poverty researchers in many countries were particularly sensitive about the methodological choices involved in setting poverty lines and equivalence scales. They often considered various alternative approaches, before recommending the one or two that seemed to be best suited for their country. The most prominent example in this respect is the Bulgarian report *Poverty in Transition* (Bulgaria

1998a), which grappled with the challenge of establishing a poverty line that would be theoretically sound, yet could also be used as a basis for social policy. The report presented a detailed analysis of the advantages and disadvantages of various poverty lines and estimated the percentage of households living in poverty using ten different methods for establishing the poverty threshold, nine of which had an upper and lower variant. The lowest line corresponds to the basic minimum income used to define eligibility to social welfare assistance (BLG 29,500 per capita a month). Based on this estimate, only 3.9 per cent of Bulgarian households were poor in 1997. This line, however, is administrative rather than analytical in character, and clearly underestimates the scale of poverty in the country. The incidence of poverty was significantly higher, ranging from 53 to 68 per cent of households, when other methods were considered. These figures, in turn, differed considerably from those obtained when variants of a relative poverty line were used. In the latter case, the incidence ranged from 4.2 per cent to 49.2 per cent of households.

Upon considering all the different alternatives, the authors of the report, which comprised a large team of national experts from academia, government agencies and the trade union movement, settled for a poverty line derived from calculating the share of expenditure on food per capita for each household unit.[1] Almost two-thirds (65.5 per cent) of Bulgarian households found themselves below this line (BLG 95,500) in 1996. The poverty headcount spread that emerges from different yardsticks is extreme. The challenge for researchers and policy-makers is to find one that meets the criteria of both theoretical legitimacy and fiscal feasibility, if it is to be officially adopted.

Other countries in the region have relied on multiple lines as well. In Latvia, the poverty profile was estimated on the basis of three thresholds, while in Estonia, a normative criterion was used involving a threefold classification: those who are poor, those whose ability to cope is in danger, and those who are at risk of becoming poor. According to this, more than half of the Estonian households is either poor or vulnerable to poverty. One-fifth of the population (the two lower income deciles) lives in direct poverty, while more than one out of three Estonians is below the poverty line (Estonia 1999).

In Poland, 5.4 per cent of the population is defined as living below the minimum subsistence line. If the official poverty line, which entitles people to welfare benefits is used, the incidence of poverty rises to 26.3 per cent and to 50.4 per cent if the threshold is set at the so-called social minimum line. Registered poverty, an administrative criterion that covers people already receiving social assistance and unemployed persons registered at employment centres (irrespective of whether they receive benefits or not), results in a poverty rate of 27.7 per cent of the population (Kabaj 2000).

Four poverty lines have also been proposed in Moldova. They are assessed at 30, 40, 50 and 100 per cent of the subsistence minimum. Twenty-one per cent of the

Table 1. The layered structure of poverty in Estonia

Poverty strata	Income level, Kr	Households		Individuals		Average income, Kr	Average consumption, Kr
		N	%	N	%		
Below the poverty line	Below 1,250	234,000	36.2	546,000	37.8	880	1177
In direct poverty	Below 1,000	117,000	18.1	314,000	21.7	698	1013
Poverty endangering coping	1,001-1,250	117,000	18.1	233,000	16.1	1132	1238
In poverty risk area	1,251-1,500	107,000	16.6	226,000	15.6	1369	1495
Outside poverty risk	1,501+	305,000	47.2	675,000	46.7	2828	2599

Source: Household Income and Expenditure Survey, 1997.

population is below the first line, which denotes a condition of extreme poverty or indigence, while 76.8 per cent live below the subsistence minimum. The poverty depth in Moldova is also large: 40 per cent in the case of the first line and 52 per cent in the case of the second. The share of expenditure on food in the poorest households is 66.4 per cent in the towns and 73.4 per cent in the countryside (Moldova 1998).

No precise data on the incidence of poverty is available for Turkmenistan. Nevertheless, it is still possible to infer the scale of the problem by comparing other indicators of deprivation across countries. Data on the share of food expenditure in household budgets are available from the Turkmenistan Living Conditions Survey, financed by UNDP. It shows that, on average, 68 per cent of expenditures in Turkmeni households are devoted to food (Turkmenistan 1998). This represents approximately the same share as that among Moldova's most impoverished households. While one cannot determine with precision the proportion of the country's population that is poor, the comparison with Moldova provides at least an initial indication of the magnitude of the problem in Turkmenistan.

Kyrgyzstan and Tajikistan are also among the poorest countries in the region. Sixty-two per cent of the Kyrgyz population lives below the poverty line, which represents the total monthly expenditure per capita required to ensure that a person consumes minimum calories for biological existence. The figure is even higher in the countryside, where it reaches 75 per cent of the population (Kyrgyzstan 1998). In turn, data from the Tajikistan Living Standards Survey, conducted in 1999 with funding and technical assistance from the World Bank and UNDP, shows that 87 per cent of households have a monthly expenditure of up to 20,000 Tajik roubles (less than US$ 12 at market rates). Slightly over one fourth of the Tajik households spend up to TR 8,000 (US$ 4.60). Other sources put the poverty rates at 70 to 96 per cent of the population (Turayev 2000). A recent report published by Goskomstat, Tajikistan's statistical agency, reveals that only 3.5 per cent of households have an expenditure greater than US$ 1 PPP per capita per day (TR 30,000 per month) (Goskomstat 2000). As can be seen, poverty is extremely high in Kyrgyzstan, Moldova, Tajikistan and Turkmenistan.

A number of countries examined the viability of establishing a relative, rather than an absolute, yardstick for measuring poverty. Relative poverty lines have various advantages. First, a relative poverty line accords with the observation that from the point of view of those who suffer it, poverty is primarily relative in character. In fact, people most often compare their present situation with that of others, with their own situation in the past or with their expectations for the future. As a result, they may not regard themselves as poor even when, by objective criteria, they are. By the same token, feelings of relative deprivation may increase during periods of rapid social change and dislocation.

A second important advantage of relative poverty lines is that they offer certain possibilities for cross-country comparative analysis. This is particularly valuable when contrasting methodologies and definitions of absolute measures make it impossible to compare poverty rates across countries. By setting a threshold at, for example, 50 per cent of the median income or expenditure per capita, one can at least compare the poverty profiles thus obtained in several countries at a time.

Of the countries covered in this chapter, five (Bulgaria, Estonia, Latvia, Lithuania and Poland) gave estimates of poverty using a relative line. The first four reported the poverty line at 50 per cent of median income or expenditure per capita or equivalent adult. This approach resulted in relatively low headcount figures, ranging from 6 to 7 per cent in Bulgaria (Bulgaria 1998a) to 7 to 10 per cent in Estonia (Estonia 1999), 10 per cent in Lithuania (Lazutka 1999) and 12 per cent in Latvia (Aasland 2000). The reason for such low estimates stems from the characteristics of the income distribution series in these countries. A large percentage of the population earns low incomes, and significant differences appear only in the upper half of the scale, especially between the top 5 to 10 per cent of society and the rest.

To correct for this distortion, the Central Statistical Office of Poland set the relative poverty line at 50 per cent of the arithmetic mean value of expenditure per equivalent adult in a domestic household. Approximately 15 per cent of the population was found to be living below this line, while poverty depth was estimated at nearly 20 per cent (Kabaj 1999). If a similar definition had been used in Bulgaria or Latvia, the estimates of poverty would have increased from 6 to 12 per cent in the former (Bulgaria 1998a), and from 12 to almost 17 per cent in the latter (Latvia 2000).

Despite the popularity and theoretical legitimacy of relative measures, experts in the region generally treat them with scepticism, largely because such measures, as explained above, are greatly influenced by the distribution of incomes in a society. Only in Lithuania does a consensus seem to be emerging among professionals that a relative poverty line, set at 50 per cent of the mean rather than the median equivalent expenditures, should serve as the basic criterion for determining poverty rates in the country.[2] Lithuanian experts prefer a relative line to normative criteria like the minimum subsistence level. They contend that although the latter are common, understandable and reflect the dynamics of poverty, they are also prone to be biased by subjectivism in defining the basic consumer basket. For this reason, they propose using instead a relative poverty line at constant prices for the purpose of monitoring poverty (Černiauskas 1999).

By contrast, Estonian experts do not share the same opinion about the merits of relative measures. Considering the country's comparatively low level of incomes, they feel that a relative measure would have limited practical significance for determining poverty rates. They propose instead a methodology for establishing an absolute poverty line, defined in monetary terms. The *income poor* are said to be those households whose income is less than the poverty line. In order to determine where such line should be drawn, a number of thresholds are examined using various methods. These thresholds correspond to various facets of poverty, and therefore can be thought of as representing different manifestations or components of the problem (Estonia 1999).

An important contribution of the Estonian study is that it recognises that poverty is not homogeneous. Thus, it is probable that determining its incidence on the basis of its various dimensions will not only result in different poverty rates, but also in different households being classified as poor. Estonian experts identify the following categories of poor people:

- The *food poor* are those households in which expenditures on food per consumption unit is less than the value of the basic food basket. Based on 1997 data, there are 29.9 per cent of such households in Estonia.
- The *consumption poor* comprise households whose consumption level is below half the median value of household consumption expenditures (700 kroons per month). According to this criterion, 8.5 per cent of Estonian households are poor.
- The *life style poor* represent households for whom expenditures deemed essential to survival, such as food and housing, account for more than 80 per cent of total consumption expenditures. Almost one in every four households (24.1 per cent) falls into this category.
- The *housing poor* are households who live in dormitory accommodation or who have half a room or less per household member, without counting the kitchen. Housing poverty affects 7.7 per cent of the country's population.
- The *subjective poor* are those who consider themselves to be poor.

In cases of long term, structural poverty, the correlation between insufficient incomes and other dimensions of poverty such as under-nourishment, inadequate housing or ill health normally is high. Subjective feelings of deprivation also tend to

Box 1. Drawing the line

Virtually all the former socialist countries have experienced a significant increase in poverty during the transition period. Estimates of its extent and depth are, nonetheless, contingent upon the choice of the poverty line that serves as a threshold for distinguishing the poor from the non-poor. Unfortunately, there is no simple solution to the issue of poverty measurement. All poverty lines are to some extent arbitrary, and therefore no simple, all-embracing definition of where the threshold should be located can be given.

For this reason, many countries have examined multiple poverty lines using a range of poverty criteria and definitions. Using multiple criteria for determining how to measure poverty may be fully acceptable for researchers. But policy-makers generally prefer to have one poverty line, which can be used for social policy purposes. The choice of one poverty line as a standard for determining eligibility to certain social benefits is fraught with problems, including the need to balance fiscal criteria and theoretical soundness. In the end, the choice is always political in nature.

Nevertheless, a combination of poverty lines can still be very useful, both for analytical purposes and for policy making. Ultimately, poverty is not a discrete concept, but rather a layered, multifaceted phenomenon that affects people in numerous ways. Differentiating between poverty layers has a vital socio-political importance, since poverty of varying intensity requires the implementation of diverse intervention strategies. This is especially relevant at a time of rapid economic dislocation, when people are subjected to various sources of social disadvantage.

correspond more closely with indicators of income poverty the longer people are trapped in such situation. However, in a context in which people become suddenly impoverished due to the convergence of various factors and poverty is, to a large extent, transitional, the correlation between its various dimensions is not necessarily strong. The data from Estonia, in fact, shows that the various poverty criteria correlate weakly with income poverty, independently of where the poverty line is set. This indicates, in the words of the Estonian experts, that 'all the poor households are not poor in the same way' (Estonia 1999). The question, therefore, is how to determine a poverty line that can capture all the main dimensions of poverty and represent the various categories of people who suffer from one or another kind of deprivation.

To do this, Estonians propose to determine the poverty threshold at an income level at which they can claim with at least 50 per cent certainty that any given household will also be poor in some of the other dimensions listed earlier. Hence:

In comparing various poverty criteria distributions, it became apparent that the lowest poverty line fulfilling all the conditions would be 1,270 kroons. Estimates show that 87 per cent of the consumption poor, 58 per cent of the life-style poor,

66 per cent of the food poor, *and 50 per cent of the* housing poor *are below a poverty line which is determined in this way (Estonia 1999).*

In other words, the poverty line is such that it covers all the poverty components that have been defined with recourse to a number of objective criteria that reflect the housing conditions, food expenditures and consumption levels of impoverished households. As can be seen, subjective assessments are not included in the determination of the poverty line. This, in fact, is indicative of the scepticism present in the region regarding the validity of subjective definitions of poverty based on respondents' self-assessment of their own condition. Although feelings of deprivation seem to be a natural indicator of poverty, their use in deriving a common yardstick is, to a degree, questionable. The scepticism that prevails in the region has been reinforced by the results of research carried out in countries such as Latvia, which show that people's assessments of their own deteriorating situation contrast with objective indicators of this situation (Gassman and de Neubourg 2000). Nonetheless, subjective criteria can still play a valuable role in poverty research. They can do this by providing a benchmark for checking the validity of the results obtained when using objective indicators for the determination of an absolute threshold.

The work carried out in Estonia contains a number of interesting insights that could be applied in other countries in the region. Most importantly, it shows that poverty is not homogeneous, but rather is a stratified problem that requires the adoption of several yardsticks for gauging its extent and character. By identifying different components or layers of poverty, policy-makers may be in a better position to devise different solutions for those who are directly affected by poverty, and those who are in less severe economic situations or are only at risk of becoming poor.

Our review of the analytical work financed by UNDP in the former socialist countries of Eastern Europe and Central Asia has produced several important lessons for poverty analysis and measurement:

- Poverty is a *layered* phenomenon. A combination of poverty lines based on several criteria gives a better picture of a country situation than the choice of a single poverty line, regardless of how the latter is determined. Multiple poverty lines can also be used for defining appropriate policies for particular target groups.
- Policy-makers, however, normally prefer a single solution, which could be easily used for administrative purposes. While the definition of such a unique poverty line must be grounded on a firm theoretical basis, it is important to stress that the choice, ultimately, is a political issue.
- Absolute thresholds seem to be better suited for monitoring poverty in poor countries as well as in countries undergoing rapid transition or economic

change. Relative poverty lines, on the other hand, may be better suited for richer countries where absolute deprivation, especially destitution, is less of a problem.

■ Nonetheless, both the absolute and relative methods of measuring poverty have advantages as well as disadvantages. The final choice of the approach to be followed must, therefore, be well justified. Making use of both approaches should also be considered, particularly for checking the reliability of the poverty rates obtained through the application of either one of the methods.

■ A number of interesting proposals have emerged from the transition countries. Of particular relevance are the approaches followed in Bulgaria (a modified version of the so-called Orshansky index) and Estonia (a layered concept of poverty based on absolute criteria analysed in multiple dimensions). These proposals should thus be considered for application in other countries where poverty data are inadequate.

The profile and determinants of poverty

One very important factor to note when addressing the issue of poverty in the countries of the former Soviet bloc is that impoverished people often experience financial difficulties as a result of external, independent factors. Well-educated people, including health service employees, teachers and other professionals, suddenly found themselves facing hardship as a consequence of low earnings. The same is true of many enterprise workers and employees, who earn low wages and regularly suffer from extensive wage arrears. Pensioners whose payments have failed to keep pace with inflation are in a similar situation. All of these groups have fallen into a state of poverty stemming from the economic crisis that has accompanied the transformation from socialism to a market economy. Feelings of deprivation have been heightened by rapidly widening gaps in incomes and living conditions between the majority of the population and the small, privileged elites who have benefited most from the privatisation process that took place in most countries.

With the exception of Central Europe, large groups of the population across the region have suddenly become innocent, random victims of poverty, regardless of the reform strategies adopted in a particular country. People have adopted an assortment of coping strategies in an effort to confront, and if possible escape from this predicament. There are normally two types of strategies. Some seek to generate additional revenues to supplement or make up for declining family income. Examples of income generating strategies include selling vegetables or cattle, engaging in casual or informal jobs, performing services and other paid activities. Many families have also resorted to a variety of activities that do not generate extra income, but rather seek to protect household consumption by cutting on non-essential expenditures. Examples of the latter are such activities as growing vegetables, collecting berries or mushrooms, sewing and knitting for family members, as well as other activities undertaken to provide goods or services to the household out of its own production (Gassman and de Neubourg 2000).

The causes of this dramatic and unprecedented rise in poverty are plentiful. A qualitative assessment funded by UNDP in Latvia found that respondents attributed the abrupt deterioration of social conditions to a multiplicity of factors: unemployment; low salaries, late pay, partially or in-kind; high cost of public utilities; hyperinflation and the collapse of the Baltija bank in 1995, which deprived people of their life savings; inadequate child benefits, which affected large families in particular; low market prices for agricultural production, coupled with the high cost of technology and inputs; and government's incompetence and indifference to peoples' wellbeing (Trapenciere et al. 2000).

The impact of the economic reforms introduced by the Latvian government shortly after the beginning of the transition process was also cited as a factor contributing to widespread poverty. The manner in which the privatisation of publicly owned enterprises took place, through the distribution of vouchers, prevented many Latvians from benefiting and led to a substantial concentration of assets and wealth. A large proportion of the population did not have the means to take advantage of the process by privatising land or houses. Others sold their vouchers to cover the cost of daily essentials. The massive reforms of the public administration also left people confused and intimidated by continuously changing regulations and demands.

Most of these factors were externally imposed on people. At the same time, alcoholism and a pervasive attitude of dependence on the state, inculcated during the Soviet period, contributed further to apathy and passivity. Alcoholism in particular is linked to unemployment, sometimes as a cause, often also as a result. Feelings of dependence, on the other hand, certainly had a strong impact at the beginning of the transition, when Latvians were still accustomed to a system in which enterprises not only functioned as production units, but also provided social assistance to their employees from cradle to grave. In time, most people gradually realised that they had to rely on themselves, their friends or relatives for their sustenance. Not everyone, however, has managed to adapt to the new situation successfully (Gassman and de Neubourg 2000).

A review of findings from a cross section of poverty profiles in the former socialist countries reveals that poverty occurs most frequently among:

- Large families, with three or more children;
- Single-parent households, especially those headed by single mothers, as well as households with a higher than average number of dependants in relation to income earners;
- Rural households, partly as a result of the prevalence of larger families in rural

areas in comparison with cities and towns;

- Families whose head or main income provider has a low level of education;
- Households headed by non-earners, such as unemployed persons or pensioners;
- Disabled people.

In most countries, the long-term character of the crisis has increased the danger of poverty being inherited by later generations. Long-term poverty may result in the emergence of what in other countries has been called an 'underclass' trapped in a 'culture of poverty'. This refers not only to the extreme marginalisation found among the homeless, although this too is a serious problem, but to the possibility that poverty may become consolidated and perpetuated among groups that are currently deprived of opportunities to support themselves, yet also lack the ability to change this situation. This problem particularly concerns children. For instance, one study found that:

> Children are the group most vulnerable to poverty in Estonian society. The younger the children are, the greater the probability that they live at a resource level which is below the poverty line. Of those up to 10 years old, 48 per cent live in poverty, while for those between 10 and 19 years of age, the figure is 44 per cent. One third of children live in direct poverty, and 13 per cent live in a situation that endangers coping. Therefore, on average, small children run a substantially greater risk of ending up in direct poverty than the remainder of the population (Estonia 1999).

In Poland, the only country in our sample with a relatively good economic situation, one third of all people living below the minimum subsistence level are children under 14 years of age, and almost half of this total are under 19 (Szukielojc-Bienkunska 1998). In the Russian Federation, the poverty rate among children under 15 stood at 46 per cent in 1994. For adults, aged 31 to 60 years old, the corresponding figure was 35 per cent, and for male pensioners it was 22 per cent. Even more disturbing is that a phenomenal 73 per cent of families with three or more children were impoverished in Russia (UNDP 1998).

This situation is alarming. Due to the impoverished condition of their families, massive numbers of children are in danger of being permanently deprived of key opportunities in life. Among other things, they may be denied full access to education, and suffer psychological or biological problems as a result of inadequate diet. Children from poor families may also suffer marginalisation from their peers, a fear that was echoed by many concerned parents in Latvia (Gassman and de Neuburg 2000; Trapenciere et al. 2000).

Together with high literacy and enrolment rates, the post-communist countries have inherited extensive, albeit poor, education systems. Nevertheless, in many countries, children from poor families now have restricted access to education due to the distance to and from school, the inability of their parents to cover travel costs, and the problem of child labour in the countryside. The enrolment rate in Kyrgyzstan, for example, is only 76 per cent, whereas in Moldova and Ukraine the respective rates are 87 and 83 per cent. One of the major tasks facing policy-makers in these countries should be to prevent the situation from deteriorating further.

In Moldova, the young age of people setting up domestic households is regarded as a major cause of poverty (Moldova 1998). The same happens in Armenia, where the labour market is very tight and favours workers with long employment records in enterprises to the detriment of young people, who are being made redundant (Armenia 1999). Pensioners also constitute a high-risk group in several countries. They are the most vulnerable group in Estonia, due to the country's low pension levels (Estonia 1999). Only in Poland, which boasts a relatively generous pension system, do pensioners enjoy a relatively good economic situation. The average pension in Poland amounts to 70 per cent of the average wage, and the state makes sure that no payment arrears occur.

Interestingly, many of our country studies do not find gender to be an important determinant of poverty risk. The situation is more complex, however. A study on the topic conducted in Bulgaria (1998b), found that four groups of women are particularly vulnerable to poverty: divorced women with children, single mothers, elderly single women, and women from minority groups (Muslims and Romanies). The authors of the study conclude that:

> Women are not inherently poorer than men, but the uneven distribution of the burden of crisis has formed groups of women who undoubtedly constitute the poorest population strata. They are being marginalised: temporary poverty grows into a way of life, not only for women, but for their children as well (Bulgaria 1998b).

Another study done in Latvia (Gassmann 2000) also contains a very interesting analysis of the relationship between poverty and gender. Women's poverty appear to be the outcome of their socially defined roles, including their child-rearing responsibilities, more than a function of lower education or of institutional obstacles to their professional carriers.

However, ethnicity does not seem to be a factor determining poverty. In Latvia, a country with a large Russian minority, the relationship between ethnic origin and poverty risk was found not to be very strong (Aasland 2000). The situation may be different in other countries, however, in particular in Southeast Europe. The vulnerability of Muslim and Romany women in Bulgaria has already been mentioned above.

On the other hand, unemployment certainly is a principal cause of poverty in the region. The main problems connected with the labour market relate to access to and quality of work, job security, wage levels, and wage arrears. Official statistics vary in accuracy from country to country and do not provide a full picture (Keune 2000). Statistics on employment do not shed light on the situation in the 'shadow econo-

Box 2. Being poor and being women

A detailed gender-based analysis of poverty reveals some differences between the risk for an individual to live in poverty depending on the characteristics of the breadwinner. Taking the official minimum wage as the poverty threshold, the headcount ratios for male and female-headed households are almost equal (39.9 per cent and 40.9 per cent, respectively). Whether a household has children or not makes a difference. With an increasing number of children, poverty rates are higher in female-headed households, although they are equal in case of no children. Regarding household size, four or more household members is a bad risk in both cases, although female-headed households have a significantly higher poverty rate (60.1 per cent to 51.5 per cent) in this context. The opposite is the case in single households. Female households do even better than their male counterparts. Only 15.4 per cent of single females are poor, compared to 23.6 per cent of single males. Then again, with increasing size, the risk for female-headed households to be poor is higher (Gassmann 2000).

my', where a considerable number of the officially unemployed and people seeking additional incomes have found work.[3] Moreover, non-working individuals are not always registered at employment centres, especially if registration does not entail any benefits. Hidden unemployment is especially high in the countryside. As a result of these factors, it is impossible to give a precise estimate of the scope of the problem.

If, however, we restrict ourselves to the official data, one very important fact to note is that young people are most at risk. This is particularly evident in Poland, where the unemployment rate among those aged 15 to 24 years old is almost 30 per cent, compared to an average unemployment rate of 12 per cent for the country (Kabaj 1999). The situation is similar, although less striking, in Russia and Ukraine, where the most vulnerable age group comprises those between 20 and 29 years. The table below shows unemployment rates for selected countries in the region.

Table 2 is a good example of the problems with official statistics in some countries. It is clear, for instance, that the low unemployment figures for Moldova, Tajikistan and Ukraine cannot be considered reliable. The national poverty alleviation strategy financed by UNDP in Moldova presents a different picture of the labour market situation in the country:

During the first half of 1997, over 110,000 workers (9.8 per cent of the total workforce) were sacked from enterprises, another 12 per cent (132,000 people) were on forced leave, and approximately 27,000 were transferred to part-time work due to reductions in the volume of production. As a result, 27,000 people were registered as unemployed in the month of October, of which 66 per cent were women. There was only one vacancy to every 11 unemployed persons, making their chances to get a job extremely limited. The purchasing capacity of the cash income of the population in 1996 constituted only 26.4 per cent of what it had been in 1990, and only 25.5 per cent in the case of salaries. The average salary in real terms, adjusted to the prices of previous years, was equivalent to the salaries of the mid 1960s, while in the sectors of education, health, and culture and arts, the corresponding salary was that of the late 1950s (Moldova 1997).

Similar problems are present in Tajikistan. The country was hard hit by the crisis in Russia and the other former Soviet republics, particularly by the collapse of the single market and the cooperative ties that bound those countries together. Tajikistan's crisis was further aggravated by the civil war that broke out after independence in 1992. As a result of the deep economic crisis that followed, men have become afraid to engage in commerce, which is often subject to racketeering. Women often play the role of main breadwinner, obtaining income through petty trading and other small-scale activities. Given this context, official statistics about unemployment are very misleading and should be treated with caution.

Labour market conditions are giving rise to a new social category alongside the impoverished unemployed: the working poor. Often these people work in simple, uncompetitive jobs and have to support other people in their families. It is difficult to estimate the number of working poor, as employees sometimes receive part of their wages 'under the table' in order to avoid paying income tax and insurance contributions that increase labour costs. This problem is compounded by the widespread prevalence of wage arrears in all 11 countries, especially in Russia, Ukraine and Moldova. The scale of this phenomenon varies, depending on the region, the branch of the economy, the sex of the employee and his or her competitiveness. In general, women as well

Table 2. Unemployment rates, selected countries (1990-1997)

	1990	1991	1992	1993	1994	1995	1996	1997
Armenia	...	...	3.5	6.2	5.6	8.1	9.7	11
Bulgaria	1.6	10.5	13.2	16.3	14.1	11.4	11.1	14.2
Estonia	...	...	...	5	5.1	5.1	5.6	5.4
Kazakhstan	0	0	0.5	0.5	8.0	11.0	13.0	13.5
Kyrgyzstan	...	0	0.1	0.2	4.1	5.7	7.8	7.5
Latvia	...	...	2.3	4.7	6.4	6.3	7.2	6.7
Lithuania	...	0.3	1.3	4.2	3.8	6.1	7.1	5.9
Moldova	...	...	0.1	0.7	1.1	1.4	1.4	1.7
Poland	6.3	12.2	14.3	16.4	16	14.9	13.6	10.5
Russia	0	0	4.8	5.7	7.5	8.8	9.3	9.0
Tajikistan	...	...	0.3	1.1	1.7	1.8	2.8	4.7
Turkmenistan	2.0	2.0	...	...	...	3.0	...	...
Ukraine	0	0	0.3	0.4	0.4	0.5	1.6	2.9

Source: Kolodko 1999 (based on official statistics).

as less competitive workers experience longer delays in being paid. Wage arrears have increased differences in pay and, therefore, income disparities among households. The alternative, however, would be unemployment for the less competitive workers, an option that they themselves would find even less attractive than lower wages.

Nonetheless, the low level of real wages in general, as well as the low level of incomes officially declared by enterprises, have had a devastating impact on people. The entire region recorded dramatic falls in real wages during the first five years of the transformation. The largest drops took place in Russia and Ukraine, where real wages declined by approximately 70 per cent. In Bulgaria, where there were major differences between the private and public sectors, real wages decreased to 30 to 40 per cent of their 1990 level and were still falling in 1998.[4]

Young people who are beginning their working lives are in a particularly difficult situation, especially if their lack of experience is combined with, at best, a vocational school education. The transformation has brought an end to the days when a vocational or technical training sufficed to make employees attractive to firms and every school graduate immediately found a job. Now, people with higher education have a better chance of finding employment than those with fewer years of schooling.

Education not only determines an individual's chances of securing employment, but also the level of her wages. Nevertheless, the situation varies from country to country. Education is a crucial stratifying element in Poland, where it explains income differences more than any other factor.[5] The same happens in the Baltic countries, whereas in Ukraine or Tajikistan, education is essential for managerial positions in the private sector, but is no guarantee of high earnings for other professionals, who are often less well paid than many factory workers. Despite this fact, as economies in the region become more market-oriented, it is likely that education will increase in importance as a determinant of life opportunities in every country. Individuals with less formal education can expect difficulties in finding employment and will be more at risk of poverty.

Geographical factors also have an important bearing on the labour market and therefore on poverty. Unemployment poses the greatest danger when it is structural and long-term, which usually takes place when the only large employer in a given area is forced to downsize or goes bankrupt. At the beginning of the transition, this was the case in Poland and other countries where state agricultural farms, which were often the main employers in the countryside, collapsed. This has led to the emergence of impoverished rural enclaves. Sociologists regard these poverty-stricken areas as the embryos of a new 'underclass' in places that had previously known none.

Given the multiple challenges facing the region to arrest the alarming rise in poverty, many countries have begun to develop policies and programmes to address the problem. We shall review a sample of them in the next section.

An evolving poverty reduction agenda

To varying degrees, all the countries in the region are struggling to address the sudden impoverishment of large segments of the population. They are doing so in a context in which jobs are being eliminated at an alarming rate, public services have been curtailed, and fiscal revenues are extremely limited. Another constraint is that most governments lack the knowledge and tools required for devising effective policies that are targeted at people in need.

Six countries have prepared comprehensive policy documents intended to serve as a basis for national anti-poverty strategies and programmes: Estonia, Kyrgyzstan, Latvia, Lithuania, Moldova and Poland. Others, like Bulgaria, Kazakhstan and Ukraine, have focussed on one particular aspect of policy-making with implications for poverty reduction. Most documents contain an analysis of the causes and consequences of poverty, along with a series of prescriptions aimed at promoting pro-poor economic growth, employment creation, education and human capital formation, as well as social protection and assistance to vulnerable groups. Only in one case (Kyrgyzstan) does the role of partnerships with civil society actors for social policy formulation occupy a central place in the analysis. Estonia has made a serious effort to identify specific target groups for social programmes, while Latvia has proposed a list of indicators for monitoring poverty and social stratification.

Despite the good intentions, most documents are too general to provide clear guidance for action. They normally contain a long list of very generic policy goals and directives, but with little prioritisation and virtually no systematic analysis of the relationship between various policies, the implementation conditions or the budgetary implications of poverty reduction. In most cases, policy goals are not quantified and neither the target groups nor specific interventions tailored to individual problems are spelled out in detail. The Kyrgyz Republic's poverty alleviation programme is the only one that contains some estimates of the expected cost of selected projects. Governance issues, furthermore, are missing in most analyses.

Nevertheless, as the presentation below will show, the governments in the region are making a first attempt to deal with the complex questions inherited from the Soviet era and aggravated during the transition process.

Bulgaria

In the early 1990s, the Bulgarian economy experienced a sharp decline from which it has yet to recover. Real wages plummeted to 30 per cent of their pre-crisis levels. Unemployment rose tenfold between 1990 and 1993, and stabilised around 11 to 14 per cent of the economically active population during the latter part of the decade. It is estimated that unregistered economic activities account for approximately 40 per cent of the country's GNP.

Against a background of rising poverty and widening income differentials, as measured by the Gini coefficient, Bulgarian officials and social policy experts engaged in a major debate on how to reform social welfare. As in other countries in the region, Bulgarian policy-makers face the dilemma of continuing with the system of universal benefits inherited from the communist era or adopting a system of strict targeting for those who are most in need. Clearly, the first option is fiscally untenable. It is also inefficient from the point of view of reducing poverty. On the other hand, strict targeting normally entails high administration costs, especially if it is based on complex means-testing procedures. Given the weak administrative capacity of public agencies in post-transition countries, a system of welfare provision based on means testing may easily become open to abuse. There is, moreover, a definite risk that groups that are entitled to certain benefits may not apply for them if the system is too complex or time- consuming.

To investigate these issues, a team of national experts, assisted by UNDP and the International Labour Organization (ILO), carried out a detailed analysis of the tradeoffs involved in adopting a targeted policy (Bulgaria 1998a). The study concentrates on the methodological problems involved in defining a threshold that can be used to determine eligibility for social benefits. This issue is closely related to how poverty is defined and where the poverty line is set. The Bulgarian authors suggest employing the basic minimum income level, which is based on energy expenditure and a basket of 22 consumer products, as well as a relative poverty line as the lower and upper poverty thresholds. Using a relative yardstick as a criterion for social policy is, however, questionable. Granting benefits to certain groups on the grounds that their position is relatively worse than that of other groups will not appeal to the latter, who may also see themselves as deserving of support.

Alternatively, ensuring a minimum subsistence income to all segments of the population seems unrealistic, at least in the short and medium-term. Budgetary resources are clearly insufficient to cast the welfare net too widely. Ultimately, any poverty line adopted as the official basis for an anti-poverty policy must be acceptable from a fiscal point of view so that public finances can cover the costs of the proposed programmes. The poverty line also needs to enjoy broad public acceptance if society is to cooperate in mitigating the plight of the poor.

While achieving such a consensus is essential, it is nonetheless important to realise that targeting is always a thorny issue. People who experience economic hardship, but do not meet the official criteria for receiving support, will question the legitimacy of a narrowly conceived policy. Targeting on the basis of income is particularly problematic in the context of economic transition in the region. Due to the explosive growth of the 'shadow economy', incomes declared officially are not a good measure of a household's material conditions. Means testing can also socially stigmatise those who apply for public assistance. Consequently, a policy of broad targeting appears to be a more attractive option, provided fiscal revenues allow for it. Non-income criteria should be considered for the allocation of benefits, including categorical indicators of need along the lines developed in Estonia (1999).

In the short term, reducing the size of the unregistered sector of the economy may help increase fiscal revenues and therefore improve the chances of success for public policies. This should be done with great care, however, given that many people use the 'shadow economy' as a means of coping with poverty. If it were suddenly reduced in scale, it would certainly undermine the situation of many families who are already struggling to make ends meet (Bulgaria 1998c).

Estonia

The Estonian government has produced a very comprehensive outline of a national poverty reduction strategy that contains basic principles and aims for guiding public policy. The emphasis of this official document, financed by UNDP, has been to clearly specify high-risk groups for whom particular sets of measures will be designed, according to the characteristics of each group.

Nearly half of Estonia's population lives in poverty or at risk of poverty, and consequently are potential subjects of specially designed initiatives. The official policy is to distinguish among three high-risk groups, depending on their location with regard to the national poverty line: those who suffer poverty acutely (below 80 per cent of the poverty line); those who are slightly below the threshold (81 to 100 per cent); and those who are at risk of becoming poor (up to 120 per cent of the poverty line). The government prioritises the first group as its main target for public policy. According to 1997 figures, 18 per cent of households fall into this category. It includes children and families with children, women, the long-term unemployed, the working poor, the disabled, the elderly and other individuals dependent on the social insurance system (Estonia 1999).

The main principle guiding Estonia's poverty reduction policy is that every social group should be guaranteed the basic human right to be actively involved in community life and to have a sufficient livelihood and social assistance for a decent living. In line with this principle, one of the government's key priorities is to actively reduce the social and economic vulnerability of families with children and to ensure their equal access to opportunities and resources. This entails, among other things, promoting their access to the labour market and expanding opportunities for combining work and child care; granting support through financial assistance and services; and providing housing on favourable terms and supplementary state guarantees for housing loans and essential durable goods for the household. Households most at risk will receive supplementary assistance to ensure their ability to manage economically. In the area of health, the policy prioritises families living below the poverty line and seeks to protect the health of the mother and the child, through health insurance for single pregnant women and guaranteed access to essential medical treatment and medicines. Children themselves are a major target for public policies, which will aim to minimise the risk of underdevelopment of children in poverty, protect their physical and mental well-being, and to expand the system of subsidised services for children from poor families.

Another set of measures is geared towards restoring the social and economic participation of the long-term unemployed through the implementation of proactive regional and labour market policies. The latter will focus on groups at greater risk of unemployment, such as the youth, rural inhabitants, single mothers, and disabled people. Measures to prevent discrimination or exploitation on the basis of age, gender, ethnicity, education or occupation will also be actively promoted. With regard to the rising number of working poor, the government's strategy is to reduce their economic insecurity by improving the quality of work, strengthening the social protection system, enforcing a minimum wage scheme, and instituting a system of employment and other types of insurance.

Estonia's policy also includes a number of proposals aimed at redressing gender imbalances. These proposals are based on the recognition that the causes and patterns of poverty differ for men and women, thus necessitating specific programmes to address their distinctive needs. A major priority is to enforce national policies to combat discrimination against women. Other measures will be geared to increasing the competitiveness of women in the labour market, expanding social security coverage for poor women, and improving the targeting of assistance directed to them.

Kazakhstan

The government of Kazakhstan developed a National Programme for the Promotion of a Healthy Lifestyle in cooperation with a large number of multilateral and bilateral organisations (Kazakhstan 1998a, 1998b). The document recognises that poverty is one of the main reasons for poor health standards in Kazakhstan. Other factors include an inadequate supply of good quality drinking water, the deterioration of sanitary conditions (e.g., overcrowding in schools), inadequate lifestyles (poor diet, smoking, alcoholism, drug abuse), pollution, the massive use of abortion as a contraceptive, and the spread of infectious and sexually transmitted diseases, including HIV/AIDS.

The programme presents a comprehensive set of measures aimed at improving the health status as well as the consciousness of the population regarding health issues. Emphasis is placed on providing better access to quality reproductive health and family planning information and services, promoting safe sex and preventing drug abuse and the spread of HIV/AIDS. Government bodies will collaborate with international and nongovernmental organisations in implementing the various components of the programme.

Many programme components are sensitive to the problem of poverty and seek to target low-income groups with special interventions. Poverty issues, however, are not addressed in an explicit and integrated manner. In particular, the initiative offers no specific public policy measures for alleviating poverty directly or for improving the material conditions of the same low-income groups targeted for public health interventions. This seems to be an important shortcoming, given the fact that poverty is acknowledged to be a major determinant of inadequate health conditions in the country.

Kyrgyzstan

One commendable feature of the national Poverty Alleviation Programme prepared in Kyrgyzstan (1998) is its emphasis on reaching out to community-based and non-governmental organisations (NGOs) and involving them as partners in the design and implementation of projects addressing poverty. Whilst encouraging, this also poses a formidable challenge to Kyrgyzstan and other former Soviet republics, given the weakness of their civil societies and the lingering mistrust of governments toward the voluntary sector, from which they fear competition for scarce resources for development projects. As a result, partnerships between government and non-governmental actors are still very weak.

As in other post-communist countries, Kyrgyzstan's voluntary sector is underdeveloped and highly dependent on foreign financing. Strengthening the role of civil society as advocate for the poor and their local communities will be a difficult, but essential task. Political and voter education is almost non-existent. There are virtually no institutions that provide free advice to citizens on their socio-economic, legal and other rights.

At the same time, public administration in most countries, particularly in Central Asia and the Caucasus, is also very weak, especially at the local level. This could make it more attractive to enlist the support of community organisations and NGOs in the fight against poverty. The flexible nature of development NGOs and their proximity to the people can enhance the transparency and community ownership of local development initiatives. This has the potential of improving their effectiveness and sustainability over the long run.

The Kyrgyz programme contains a number of proposals calling for the development of stronger and more effective social organisations. It also stresses the need to promote and popularise microfinance as a critical instrument for poverty reduction. Non-governmental agencies could play a major role in this area, building upon the experience of several international micro-credit programmes already in operation in Kyrgyzstan. Some of the challenges for mobilising civil society in support of poverty alleviation are:

- Support for the establishment and growth of grassroots-based organisations;
- Provision of training to non-governmental actors to enhance their advocacy and policy role with regard to poverty issues;
- Promotion of partnerships between development NGOs and local government authorities;

- Strengthening of information networks and non-governmental coordination mechanisms;
- Involvement of NGOs in the development of energy, time and cost-efficient technologies;
- Financial support through credits and grants to enable NGOs to initiate and implement poverty reduction activities.

Clearly, improved networking and coordination among development NGOs will be essential for capacity- building and avoiding duplication of efforts. While duplication is not a problem at present, it could become one as growing numbers of development organisations are set up at the community level. Sharing information on sources of credit and grants, credit users and their performance will also be extremely valuable. Over time, NGOs may become increasingly involved in the formulation of Oblast development plans and as subcontractors for public interest programmes.

Moldova

The wellbeing of children is essential to preventing poverty's passing from one generation to another. In Moldova, however, the situation of children is disturbing. There are at present 6,000 children aged up to 16 with disabilities, 11,000 orphans and bereft children, and more than 200,000 families with many children who represent the most numerous among Moldova's vulnerable groups. For many of these families, the main income source is a modest child allowance, which is often paid late. Recent years have seen a marked deterioration of nutrition standards among children from poor families, with adverse consequences for their health and cognitive development. It is estimated that children with physical retardation represented 9 per cent of the total number of children in 1995, rising to 19 per cent in 1996 (Moldova 1998).

Consequently, the government decided to develop a special programme to combat child poverty as part of the country's Short-Term Poverty Alleviation Programme. The initiative offers a wide range of measures aimed at instituting a social care system for orphaned and disabled children, as well as children from poor families. This includes the provision of material support to poor families, the distribution of in-kind allowances (clothes, shoes, textbooks and other goods) through the school system, supplementary feeding programmes, free access to essential medicines and training of family doctors, and an increased emphasis on pre-school education. One important goal of the strategy is to ensure that children continue to have access to education as a means of preventing the spread of illiteracy (Moldova 1997).

The government document contains a detailed timetable for certain priority tasks, along with the allocation of responsibilities to particular ministries in charge of preparing the legal and institutional measures required in specific areas. One major gap, however, is that the programme does not specify what material resources would be used when implementing the proposed actions.

Poland

Work supported by UNDP in Poland has focussed on the problem of unemployment, which is a major determinant of poverty throughout the region. An outline of a national programme against poverty and social exclusion has been produced, with a major emphasis on combating long-term unemployment through proactive policy measures rather than simply raising the benefit levels available under the current system. In fact, the chief recommendation of the authors is to eliminate the so-called 'Polish benefit syndrome' through a revamping of the social welfare system, which currently spends the bulk of its resources on passive measures while failing to improve the situation of the poor in any fundamental way (Kabaj 1999).

To achieve this, the programme proposes a set of measures for expanding employment opportunities and economic security for the unemployed through:

- Active labour market policies to increase the number of work places through public works projects, subsidised jobs and other temporary work based solutions;
- Training, vocational advice, job placement services and loans to help the unemployed reinsert themselves in the economic circuit;
- Promotion of small and medium-sized firms through greater access to credits, credit guarantees and tax relief on investments;
- Job-sharing schemes and other measures aimed at expanding short-term and part-time employment, while also improving the conditions of those who participate in these activities;
- Cash benefits and assistance in kind (leasing of tools, machines, etc.) to help people engage in independent economic activity;
- Close linkages between eligibility for social assistance and participation in training and employment, coupled with the removal of barriers that prevent people who receive benefits or allowances from engaging in paid work.

Because this author believes in the need to concentrate efforts and resources on a few key policy targets, he chooses to focus on the employment question at the expense of other aspects of poverty. The next step should involve the elaboration of a detailed action plan to guide implementation and the establishment of linkages between this and other poverty reduction programmes in Poland.

Ukraine

One of the challenges facing policy-makers in the region is how to improve the quality of the information used in the decision-making process, as well as their own ability to process and use this information for policy design. A project financed by UNDP in Ukraine made an important contribution in this respect. Commissioned by the Ministry of Labour and Social Policy, a study on 'social budgeting' was produced in cooperation with UNDP, the International Labour Organization and the World Bank (Ukraine 1999).

The study offers an accounting model for social expenditure planning that covers a period of approximately 20 years and includes financial forecasts based on alternative scenarios. It suggests various tools for planning future expenditure and assessing the resource needs of the existing social welfare system on the basis of several macroeconomic and demographic projections and offers simulations of the financial, economic and fiscal impact of possible social welfare reforms. Since the model takes feedback effects into account, it allows policy-makers not only to assess the impact of labour costs and possible budget deficits caused by social spending on employment and economic growth, but also to factor in the potential externalities that social expenditure might have on economic performance.

It is important to point out that the study presents only a model, not a solution that has been tested and applied in practice. Yet despite the fact that it is a simplified picture of reality, the proposed model does offer a systematic approach to decision-making, as well as a sophisticated method for calculating cost-benefits in the budgetary sphere. Another notable side effect of this project is that it entailed a close collaboration between a team of domestic experts and the foreign advisers provided by the multilateral agencies. This is a positive development from the point of view of transferring know-how to Ukrainian experts for the future refinement and application of the social-expenditure planning model.

Conclusions

Our review has shown that faced with a dramatic deterioration in living standards of vast segments of the population, Eastern European and Central Asian countries are making strenuous efforts to confront the problem as a matter of priority. While these countries were not prosperous before the transition from communism, they at least enjoyed developed social welfare systems and full employment. Both ensured an adequate standard of living for their people. The sudden rise of poverty after the demise of the Soviet Union has resulted from a combination of several factors: economic crisis, declining real wages and growing inequality, along with massive unemployment, irregular wage and pension payments and the breakdown of public services. In some countries, this situation was further aggravated by the outbreak of civil conflict.

Poverty was not recognised as a social problem under the previous system. Rather, it was considered an outcome of individual failure. This predisposition detracted from the perception of policy-makers regarding the urgency of tackling poverty during the early years of the transition. Only recently have governments begun to understand the need for improved tools for analysing the nature and scope of poverty as a prerequisite for designing effective public policy. The support provided by UNDP across the region must be credited with this achievement.

Research on the scope and depth of poverty undoubtedly performs an important function. By highlighting the extent of a problem, it compels politicians and the public to take steps to address it. Thus, in countries where poverty assessments have been conducted, the issue has crept into the public discourse and is now on the agenda of policy-makers. Admittedly, all poverty measures are somehow arbitrary. They are nonetheless essential tools for analysing and monitoring how well societies are performing, and for identifying measures to remedy the situation of those who are being left behind. An important criterion for selecting a poverty yardstick is that it should not only enjoy theoretical legitimacy, but also fiscal viability and political acceptance.

The incipient state of knowledge about the measurement, analysis and design of policies against poverty shows that there is still a great need for research and capacity-building in the post-communist countries. Measurement tools are still quite rudimentary, and policy measures need to be better tailored to specific problems and targeted more effectively to the groups they intend to help. In the future, therefore, donor organisations should put more emphasis on developing sound, country-specific methodologies for measuring poverty, and facilitate the international exchange of solutions among countries. This should take precedence over the concern with ensuring international comparability of poverty rates, which often comes at the expense of country relevance.

Poverty is clearly a layered phenomenon, affecting various social strata in different ways. This implies there cannot be a single, one-size-fits-all solution to all problems. Sophisticated policy tools must be developed to enable decision-makers to address the particular needs of specific vulnerable groups, based on a comprehensive poverty profile in each country. At present, most of the programmes and strategies formulated in the region are simple catalogues of good intentions, but lack concrete proposals for implementing the stated goals. The challenge, therefore, is to translate those general statements of policy into specific plans of action. This requires setting explicit timetables, identifying budgetary needs as well as additional resources that might need to be mobilised, proposing legal measures, and defining the institutional arrangements necessary for implementation.

Unquestionably, countries that are trying to build market economies under the conditions described here are experiencing hard times. For some of them, the worst is already behind. The majority, however, are still struggling to cope with the combined challenges of economic and political transition, a dramatic rise in poverty and burgeoning inequality. Their prospects for tackling these challenges successfully will depend largely on the quality of the strategies and action plans prepared today. Advice and support from foreign organisations are thus urgently needed during the policy-making process. This is undoubtedly a strategic entry point for future initiatives aimed at supporting the elaboration of national poverty reduction strategies in the region. ■

Notes

Jaroslaw Górniak is Adjunct Professor at the Institute of Sociology, Jagiellonian University in Kraków, Poland. Dr. Gorniak would like to thank Alejandro Grinspun for in-depth discussions and his editorial work, Rasheda Selim for her kind assistance, and Siddiq Osmani for valuable comments on an earlier draft.

[1] The poverty line was calculated on the basis of a modified version of the so-called Orshansky index, following the American Mollie Orshansky who, in the early 1960s, proposed a yardstick for diagnosing poverty in the United States. The Orshansky index, as originally formulated, was based on the assumption that poor American families spent one third of their income on food. Therefore, it pegged the poverty line at three times the cost of an administratively determined low cost budget for food, adjusted for family composition and rural-urban differences. This has provided the basis for the official poverty line in the US ever since. Other multipliers can be applied, nonetheless, in order to account for differences in the share of non-food expenditure in a household budget in other settings. In the case of Bulgaria, the authors chose to modify the Orshansky method by using a multiplier of 2.

[2] In 1997, 50 per cent of the mean consumption expenditures calculated at PPP dollars per day equalled US$3.95. This was extremely close to US$ 4 PPP proposed by international organisations as a poverty line for the former socialist countries of Central and Eastern Europe.

[3] The unregistered or 'grey' economy has grown in size throughout the region. In Bulgaria, unregistered economic activities account for approximately 40 per cent of GNP. The equivalent figure in Ukraine is 50 per cent, whereas the share of the shadow economy in Poland is estimated at 15 per cent of GNP, although the real figure is probably higher. The situation is very similar in other former socialist countries.

[4] This problem was addressed in a special report sponsored by UNDP in Bulgaria. The authors of the report point out that a major reason for the dramatic fall in real wages stems from the government's decision to maintain a restrictive system of centralised wage controls in the public sector and a low minimum wage. This has led not only to a dramatic deterioration in the material position of large groups in society, but also to a decline in budgetary revenue. It has also undermined the entire pension system. These trends are due to the fact that private enterprises do not declare wages significantly higher than wage levels in public enterprises, and tax rates have been adjusted in line with this low level of declared wages. The price liberalisation instituted at the beginning of the transition has led to major wage differentials between the private and the public sector. It has also undermined the state budget and resulted in a collapse in domestic demand (Bulgaria 1998c).

[5] This finding is based on the author's own analysis of the data contained in the survey of *Living Conditions of the Population in 1997*, conducted by Central Statistical Office of Poland.

CHAPTER 7

Financing Basic Social Services

Julia Harrington, Catherine Porter and Sanjay Reddy

The 20/20 Initiative, sponsored by several United Nations organisations and the World Bank, was adopted at the World Summit for Social Development held in Copenhagen in 1995. The Initiative proposes that in order to achieve universal coverage of basic social services, 20 per cent of budgetary expenditure in developing countries and 20 per cent of aid flows should on average be allocated to basic social services (BSS). The 20/20 Initiative is based on the conviction that the delivery of BSS is one of the most effective and cost-effective ways of combating poverty.

The assumption that 20 per cent of government spending would generally be sufficient to achieve universal coverage is based on calculations with regard to the current state of coverage in basic social services and the unit cost of providing these services. Among the assumptions regarding volumes of resource availability are that total government spending in developing countries will remain between 20 and 25 per cent of GDP and that donor countries will make progress towards the goal of allocating 0.7 per cent of their GDP to overseas development assistance (ODA). The numeric target of 20 per cent is simply a means to an end. The real goal is the reduction of poverty by providing basic social services to all.

Under the Poverty Strategies Initiative (PSI) launched by the United Nations Development Programme (UNDP) in 1996, a total of 27 countries received support for the preparation of country reports on national expenditure and the implementation of the 20/20 Initiative. These reports, which in many cases were carried out jointly with UNICEF, aimed first, to determine how much of the national budget and international aid flows are being spent on basic social services; second, to analyse the incidence of public expenditure on social services by income group; third, to establish the scope for inter-sectoral and intra-sectoral budget restructuring in favour of basic social services; and, fourth, to identify areas where the incidence and cost-effectiveness of BSS delivery could be improved.

Although all of the studies had common terms of reference, they vary widely in the data they provide. In some cases, this is because certain data were unavailable. Many country reports also had to completely recalculate budget figures to generate estimates of BSS spending. Nevertheless, this is in and of itself an important by-product of the exercise supported by UNDP, inasmuch as it makes it possible to assess the current availability of data on budget allocations to basic social services, as well as on final outcomes.

This chapter presents findings from 17 country studies on the current status of spending on BSS. It also examines the structure of public finances in these countries, with a view to finding ways of improving the quality and quantity of public expenditure on BSS in light of the 20/20 targets. The 17 countries covered in the chapter are Bangladesh, Benin, Burkina Faso, Chad, Colombia, the Dominican Republic, El Salvador, Guatemala, Jordan, Kenya, Lebanon, Morocco, Nepal, the Philippines, Uganda, Viet Nam and Zambia.

We begin by reviewing some basic concepts and methodological problems in the assessment of budget spending on basic services. Then we undertake an aggregate analysis of public finances in the countries under review, with a special emphasis on the level of allocation to the social sectors and to basic services in general, before assessing the role of ODA in the provision of basic social services in the sample countries. Finally, we provide a disaggregated analysis of social expenditures (education, health, water and sanitation), and conclude by drawing some key lessons for ensuring adequate financing of basic social service provision in developing countries. In order to analyse the extent of need and the potential for financing of basic social services, the chapter will examine existing indicators of poverty, education and health; the size of the national budget compared with GDP; total social spending; the priority given to basic social services out of the total expenditure on social services; and trends in the provision of basic health care and education.

Concepts and methodology

The definition of basic social services

The first methodological problem to be addressed is the definition of basic social services. The 20/20 Initiative defines basic social services as comprising basic education, primary health care and family planning services, low-cost water and sanitation, and nutrition programmes (UNDP et al. 1996).

There is a general consensus on what constitutes basic social services, but considerable variation in the specific definitions used in the countries under review. For example, budget data provided by governments may present expenditure according to level of education (i.e., primary, secondary, university), but the definition of 'basic education' proposed by the Copenhagen Summit includes adult literacy and non-formal education, which are more likely to be reported under other budget items. Even 'basic' formal education is not always defined in the same way. Most countries consider that primary education lasts for six years, but a few consider that primary education consists of as few as four years, while for others it may be as long as nine. Some countries include pre-school within their definition. As a result, it is difficult to accurately and consistently evaluate the total public expenditure on education with existing data.

Likewise, basic health care was defined by UNDP and UNICEF (1998) as including all community health intervention (epidemiological data collection, health system planning, health education, regulation, licensing, environmental health, prevention of communicable diseases, water and sanitation), all personal health services that are preventative in nature (including family planning, maternal and child health, infant nutrition, immunisation and treatment of communicable diseases), and curative care at primary and secondary levels (i.e. health centres and district hospitals). However, national health care budgets often do not differentiate between expenditure for preventative as opposed to curative care, or between basic and non-basic services.[1]

For a more accurate assessment of the progress towards 20/20 targets to be made in the future, some standardisation of national budgets will be essential. For the purposes of the present review, however, the only data available were those provided in the 17 country reports financed by UNDP. The lack of perfectly defined and comparable data will be an obstacle to the analysis, but not a fatal one, if these limitations are clearly understood. Knowing the general direction of progress is more important than the exact extent to which the 20 per cent targets have been reached. Also, the initiative is designed to be flexible in what is required of individual donors and countries. Universal coverage of basic social services, not the figure of expenditure, is the true goal, and the analysis of expenditures should be undertaken accordingly.

The problem of double counting expenditures

A second difficulty that may be encountered in assessing the extent of effort undertaken by the respective countries towards attaining the 20/20 goals is the problem of 'double counting'. Double counting of expenditure occurs when aid flows destined for social programmes are channelled through government development budgets and thus incorporated into the figures for government expenditure on social services, while also appearing in the total of foreign development assistance given for social services. This does not distort the final figure of the proportion of the total government budget expended on basic social services, but does give a distorted picture of the proportion of the government's *own resources* that are spent on BSS.

The country studies provide no way to avoid this distortion, since the reporting of aid expenditures is so inadequate, as is discussed in more detail below. For purposes of this analysis, we must simply be aware that whatever figures are reported for basic social services expenditure out of total government expenditure, especially in countries that receive considerable aid flows, the actual figures for government expenditure out of nationally generated resources are likely to be somewhat lower.

In some of the low-income countries, especially in sub-Saharan Africa, the development budget is entirely externally financed, which makes the issue clearer, even if the extent of the distortion is also larger. In such cases, the proportion of the government's expenditure on basic social services out of its resources is zero and only the recurrent budget should be included in the calculations. As a rule, the proportion of government expenditure out of nationally generated resources can be calculated if the proportion of basic social services expenditure out of ODA is known.[2] Therefore, the problem of 'double counting' is in principle wholly solvable, although the data necessary for this operation are only occasionally available.

Differences between budget allocations and actual expenditures

This review aimed to use actual government expenditures wherever possible. However, due to limitations in the data available from national governments and in the country reports, data on budget *allocations* have more frequently been relied on. There is some reason to expect a greater disparity between budgeted and actual expenditures in the social sectors than in other sectors of expenditure. One reason is that social sectors may often bear post-budgetary discretionary adjustments due to having weaker protecting interests than, for example, military expenditures and external debt payments. Additionally, the degree of illicit 'leakage' between allocated and final expenditures may arguably be expected to be higher in the social sectors for similar reasons of political economy. On the other hand, there may be contrary reasons for the degree of disparity to be lower. For example, the high proportion of non-discretionary wage costs in social sector expenditures may protect it from ex-post adjustments.

Other differentiating features of the social sectors are ambiguous in their implications. For example, smaller costs per final budget item in the social sectors could conceivably lead to superior (due to their small size and degree of standardisation) or inferior (due to their large number) ability to establish financial controls. Suffice it to compare the features of local contracts for school construction as against national contracts for the construction of bridges or the purchase of aircraft. Neither the country reports under review nor other information sources provide a basis on which to form strong judgments on this issue.

Aggregate analysis of public finances

In order to analyse the adequacy of public investment in basic social services, we begin with an overview of public finances in the 17 countries covered in this chapter. We are concerned particularly with the level and pattern of expenditure on social services in these countries.

It is important to note that our sample countries have very different economic and social situations. They have also experienced varying development in their economies and social indicators over the previous decade. Six countries are from sub-Saharan Africa (Benin, Burkina Faso, Chad, Kenya, Uganda, and Zambia), four from Asia (Bangladesh and Nepal from South Asia, and the Philippines and Viet Nam from South East Asia), three from the Middle East and North Africa (Lebanon, Jordan and Morocco), and four from Latin America (Colombia, the Dominican Republic, El Salvador and Guatemala).

Geographical differences in both economic and human development are immediately apparent. For example, the six countries in the sample with the highest child mortality are from sub-Saharan Africa. On the other hand, the highest achievers in terms of GNP per capita are mainly from Latin America. Countries can also be classified in terms of their social indicators by using the Human Development Index

Table 1. Economic and social indicators

	GNP/Capita $ (1998)	HDI[a] (1998)	HPI-1[b] (1998)
Medium Income			
Lebanon	3560	0.74	10.8
Colombia	2470	0.76	10.4
El Salvador	1850	0.69	20.2
Dominican Republic	1770	0.73	15.4
Guatemala	1640	0.62	29.2
Morocco	1240	0.59	38.4
Jordan	1150	0.72	8.8
Philippines	1050	0.74	16.1
Low Income			
Benin	380	0.41	48.8
Bangladesh	350	0.46	43.6
Kenya	350	0.51	29.5
Viet Nam	350	0.67	28.2
Zambia	330	0.42	37.9
Uganda	310	0.41	39.7
Chad	300	0.87	52.1*
Burkina Faso	240	0.30	58.4
Nepal	210	0.47	51.3

Source: UNDP, Human Development Report 1999, 2000.

[a] Composite index of three indicators: life expectancy at birth, educational attainment and real GDP per capita in Purchasing Power Parity US dollars (PPP$).

[b] Composite index measured by the percentage of people not expected to survive to age 40, the percentage of adults who are illiterate, and a combined indicator of access to safe water, access to health services and malnutrition among children under five.

* 1997 figures

elaborated by UNDP. With the exception of Viet Nam, all the countries classified as 'low income' also belong to the 'low human development' category. This includes all of the sub-Saharan African countries in our sample, plus Bangladesh and Nepal. The 'medium human development' group includes all of the Latin American countries, plus Jordan, Lebanon, Morocco, Philippines and Viet Nam.

The level of public spending on basic social services is determined by three factors: first, the level of aggregate public expenditure; second, the fiscal priority assigned to social sector spending; and finally, the priority of basic social services within total social sector expenditure. Governments are constrained in their absolute levels of spending by the size of the national economy, their ability to raise funds for expenditure from internal and external sources, and non-discretionary expenditure obligations in the form of debt service payments. Within the available budget, allocations are made to the major ministries such as health, education, social sectors, infrastructure, defence, and administration.

Thus, the share of spending on BSS to national product can be broken down into the following formula:

$$BSS/GDP = BSS/SS \times SS/PE \times PE/GDP,$$ where

- BSS/GDP refers to the 'human expenditure ratio', or the macroeconomic priority assigned to basic social services, expressed as the ratio of BSS spending over GDP;
- BSS/SS refers to the 'social priority ratio', or the allocation within social spending to BSS;
- SS/PE refers to the 'social allocation ratio', or the fiscal priority assigned to social spending; and
- PE/GDP refers to the 'public expenditure ratio', or the potential volume of resources available to government for allocation.

Due to data limitations in the country reports and other sources, we refer here only to central government expenditures. This may lead to some distortion (and, in particular, understatement) of estimated social sector expenditures, especially in larger countries that practice a degree of 'fiscal federalism'. Regrettably, however, there is no ready means available to correct for such error.

Public expenditure levels: The public expenditure ratio

The level of public expenditure, expressed as a ratio of GDP, is known as the public expenditure ratio. The public expenditure ratio shows the potential volume of resources available to government for allocation. A high level of public expenditure *per se* is not a guarantee of high levels of social spending, since the size of public sector spending may be driven by spending on items such as debt payments, military expenditures or subsidies to loss-making state enterprises. However, the public expenditure ratio shows the volumes of resources mobilised by government in total, and thus offers a baseline for discussing the scope for allocation of resources to basic social services.

Clearly, the extent to which the total resources available can be reallocated depends on national and international economic and political constraints, and thus varies widely from country to country. *The Human Development Report* 1991 suggests 20 to 25 per cent as a realisable public expenditure ratio in developing countries (UNDP 1991). The calculation of the 20/20 ratio of BSS/PE as the target for attaining universal access to BSS is based on the assumption that national budgets represent approximately 20 per cent of GNP.

Table 2 shows public expenditure as a percentage of GDP for the countries in the study. Only 7 of the 17 countries in the sample have a public expenditure ratio above the postulated level of 20 per cent. The average public expenditure of all the coun-

Table 2. Public expenditure as per cent of GDP

Country	Public expenditure (% GDP)*
Kenya	42.3
Lebanon	39.3
Jordan	35.3
Colombia	35.2
Viet Nam	23.0
Zambia	23.0
Morocco	21.2
Nepal	20.1
Uganda	19.3
Benin	18.8
Philippines	18.6
Chad	18.1
Burkina Faso	17.8
Bangladesh	17.0
El Salvador	15.3
Dominican Republic	14.8
Guatemala	12.6
Mean	**23.0**

Source: Khundker et al. 1999; Benin 1998; Burkina Faso 1998; Chad 1998; Sarmiento et al. 1999; Aristy 1998; Lazo 1999; Schneider 1999; Al-Bustany et al. 2000; Nganda 1998; Lebanon 2000; Akesbi 1998; Nepal 1998; Manasan 1994; Opio 1998; Viet Nam 1998; Zambia 1998.

* Figures correspond to the latest year available.

tries in the sample is 23.0 per cent of GDP, but this average is distorted by the four outliers in the sample, with public spending of 35 per cent or more: Kenya, Lebanon, Jordan and Colombia. These four countries are at least 12 percentage points higher than the next highest spender, Viet Nam, at 23 per cent. If these four highest-spending countries are excluded, the average for the remaining countries falls to 18.4 per cent. The lowest-spending country is Guatemala, at only 12.6 per cent of GDP. Two of the countries in the sample have public expenditures between 10 and 15 per cent of GDP, while another seven countries have public expenditures between 15 and 20 per cent of GDP. Thus, the countries represented reflect a wide range of public expenditure levels, although a majority are near or above the 20 per cent yardstick established by the 20/20 Initiative.

Overall, these figures suggest that the funds currently available for social services are quite limited, since public expenditure in total is generally low. Where it is high, this may be due to the fact that a country is incurring unsustainable debt finance or is a favoured recipient of ODA. While the question of reallocation will be addressed later, it is clear that social expenditure cannot be increased in absolute terms in most of these countries without economic growth, raising more revenue relative to the size of the national economy, increasing public debt, or a combination of these. Attempts to increase government spending may also directly conflict with fiscal austerity programmes required by international financial institutions.

Increasing expenditure without additional resource mobilisation is unlikely, since many countries are already running substantial deficits. Between 1990 and 1997, the average deficit of countries in the sample was 5.4 per cent of GDP. For the African countries in the sample, the average deficit was higher, at 7.4 per cent of GDP. Without dramatic GDP growth or revenue-generating measures, the existing high deficits are likely to prevent increased public spending.

Social spending relative to public expenditure:
The social allocation ratio

While the public expenditure ratio indicates the total government resource usage, the *social allocation ratio* (SS/PE) measures the fiscal priority assigned to social spending. Of public revenues and resources in any given year, the amount available for discretionary expenditure is what remains once non-discretionary payments, like debt services, have been made. Thus, the size of debt payments heavily influences how much can ultimately be spent on social services.

The countries in the sample are carrying a heavy debt burden of on average 23.6 per cent of national expenditure. Kenya and Chad spend 40 per cent or more of their budgets on debt payments, Colombia spends 39 per cent, Lebanon 33.5 per cent, and the Philippines, 32 per cent. In another three countries, debt service accounts for approximately one-fourth of the national budget. Only in Benin and Uganda does

Table 3. Expenditure on defence, debt, social services and basic social services as a share of annual national budget*

Country	Defence	Debt Service	Defence + Debt Service	Social Services	BSS
Chad	21.0	41.8	62.8	29.3	9.5
Lebanon	24.4	33.5	57.9	20.3	8.4
Morocco	25.6	26.8	52.4	40.2	16.5
Kenya	4.5	40.0	44.5	n/a	12.6
Zambia	4.8	39.0	43.8	28.8	6.7
Philippines	8.6	32.0	40.6	20.1	8.6
Jordan	16.6	16.6	33.2	43.6	15.8
Bangladesh	17.5	14.7	32.2	32.0	15.7
Colombia	7.0	23.1	30.1	43.2	16.1
El Salvador	7.1	22.1	29.2	23.8	14.2
Uganda	18.4	7.0	25.4	n/a	16.5
Benin	13.9	9.0	22.9	27.2	9.5
Nepal	4.7	14.9	19.6	29.2	17.3
Guatemala	n/a	n/a	n/a	46.0	13.6
Dominican Republic	5.4	n/a	n/a	38.4	8.7
Burkina Faso	n/a	10.2	n/a	27.0	10.4
Viet Nam	n/a	n/a	n/a	25.0	8.5
Mean	**12.8**	**23.6**	**35.7**	**31.6**	**12.3**

Source: Same as Table 2; IMF Government Financial Statistics.

* Figures correspond to the latest year available.

debt servicing consume less than 10 per cent of their national budgets.

Social expenditure surpasses debt in its 31.6 per cent average share of national budgets. In four countries (Colombia, Guatemala, Jordan and Morocco) social expenditure is over 40 per cent of the total national budget, and in two (Bangladesh and the Dominican Republic), over 30 per cent. In all the countries surveyed, social expenditure is over 20 per cent. Together, social expenditure and debt average over 50 per cent of national budgets in the sample, although the average figures across the sample are somewhat misleading, since they hide vast disparities among countries, especially with respect to spending on debt service. These figures suggest, perhaps surprisingly, that a low priority attached by national governments to social services in general is not one of the reasons for slow progress towards universal access to basic social services.

Of the 12 countries for which both debt service and social expenditure figures are available, debt is greater than social expenditure in four: Lebanon, the Philippines, Zambia and Chad. In these four countries the gap between debt service and social spending is at least ten per cent. With Kenya, these are also the only countries in which debt service consumes more than 30 per cent of the total budget. Although no aggregate social expenditure figure is available for Kenya, it is likely that debt service substantially exceeds social spending there as well, since debt service consumes 40 per cent of its budget, and in only three countries of the sample, none of which is in sub-Saharan Africa (Colombia, Jordan and Morocco), does social expenditure surpass this percentage.

In eight countries, social expenditure is greater than debt payments as a share of the national budget, and in five of these the difference is considerable (15 per cent or more). It must be noted, however, that the figures given for social spending are not perfectly consistent across country studies: in most cases, social spending includes health, education, social security and entitlements (i.e. unemployment benefits and pensions). As will be seen below in the analysis of basic social services in relation to total social spending, some countries spend a great deal on entitlement programmes that do not exist in other countries. In addition to this difference in actual *composition* of expenditures, there are differences in nominal *classification*. For example, some countries include spending on sanitation within their health budgets, while others may place it under capital expenditure on infrastructure. There are also other differences in the definition of social spending that may together account for a few percentage points in one direction or another.

Of the 12 countries for which both defence and social expenditure figures are available, only Lebanon spends more on defence than on social spending, though the trend in defence spending is downward. On average, these countries spend 12.8 per cent of the national budget on defence, compared with 31.6 per cent on social expenditure. Defence spending ranges from a high of 25.6 per cent in Morocco to 4.5 per cent in Kenya. Unfortunately, data for defence spending over time is unavailable, so we cannot conclude if there is a trend towards reallocating defence spending to other budget items, or vice-versa. Lack of commitment to social expenditure as such does not seem to be a reason for low levels of social expenditure, since a high proportion of discretionary resources seems to be devoted to them.

The social priority and human development priority ratios

While social spending occupies an important place in national budgets, the situation with respect to basic social services is much less favourable. The proportion of social spending devoted to basic social services is known as the *social priority ratio*. As illustrated by Table 4, spending on basic social services is usually less than half of total social expenditure: the average is 38 per cent. The proportions vary from a low of 22.7 per cent (Dominican Republic) to a high of 59.7 per cent (El Salvador). Of course, these figures must be interpreted cautiously in the light of the imperfect comparability of data on BSS expenditures across countries noted earlier.

As described previously, the definition of basic social services varies somewhat from country to country. Taking as given that this may cause a variation of a few

Table 4. Social expenditure and basic social services expenditure as a share of national budgets*

Country	Social Expenditure %	BSS Expenditure %	BSS/Social Expenditure %
El Salvador	23.8	14.2	59.7
Nepal	29.2	17.3	59.2
Bangladesh	32.0	15.7	49.0
Philippines	20.1	8.6	42.8
Lebanon	20.3	8.4	41.0
Morocco	40.2	16.5	41.0
Burkina Faso	27.0	10.4	38.5
Colombia	43.2	16.1	37.3
Jordan	43.6	15.8	36.2
Benin	27.2	9.5	34.9
Viet Nam	25.0	8.5	34.0
Chad	29.3	9.5	32.4
Guatemala	46.0	13.6	29.6
Dominican Republic	38.4	8.7	22.7
Zambia	28.8	6.7	18.6
Kenya	n /a	12.6	n /a
Uganda	n /a	16.5	n /a
Mean	**31.6**	**12.3**	**38.6**

Source: Same as Table 2.

* Figures correspond to the latest year available.

percentage points, we find that no country in the sample meets the target of 20 per cent of public spending dedicated to basic social services. The average expenditure on basic social services is 12.3 per cent of total spending. This figure is very close to that suggested in earlier studies (Mehrotra et al. 2000).

The six countries devoting the highest percentage of their total expenditure to basic social services are all spending between 15 and 20 per cent: Nepal (17.3 per cent), Morocco and Uganda (16.5 per cent each), Colombia (16.1 per cent), Jordan (15.8 per cent), and Bangladesh (15.7 per cent). The seven lowest-spending countries are all devoting less than 10 per cent of their total public expenditure to basic social services: Zambia (6.7 per cent), Lebanon (8.4 per cent), Viet Nam (8.5 per cent), the Philippines (8.6 per cent), the Dominican Republic (8.7 per cent), Benin (9.5 per cent), and Chad (9.5 per cent). These figures establish a very wide variation in the extent of progress needed to approach the 20/20 objectives, although it is evident that all countries must progress further.

It is interesting to note that there is not in fact any significant correlation between high social expenditure and high expenditure on basic social services. The highest spenders on social services overall (Guatemala, Jordan, Colombia, Morocco and the Dominican Republic) are second, fourth, fifth, eighth, and thirteenth in percentage devoted to basic social services. High social spending thus does not indicate either a lesser or a greater than average priority for basic social services. This important finding underlines the potential large gains to be realised from reallocation of social expenditure towards basic social services.

In fact, in 13 of the 15 countries for which data are available, the social priority ratio is less than 0.5; in other words, spending on basic social services accounted for less than half of total social spending. Only El Salvador and Nepal spent more than 50 per cent of their total social expenditure on basic social services, while the figure for Bangladesh is 49 per cent. As a percentage of total public budgets, spending on basic social services is on average over 20 points lower than total social spending. The low level of spending on basic social services compared to total social sector expenditure indicates its overall low priority.

As Table 3 above illustrates, in a majority of countries, levels of expenditure on basic social services are less than that on debt service. In five of these countries (Chad, Kenya, Lebanon, the Philippines and Zambia), debt service expenditure is greater than that on basic social services by over 20 percentage points. Uganda has the best basic social services to debt ratio, with debt receiving only 7 per cent of public expenditure in contrast to 16.5 per cent for basic social services. This favourable ratio is of course due to its having been an early recipient of debt relief under the Heavily Indebted Poor Country (HIPC) Initiative. In Benin, Bangladesh, Burkina Faso and Nepal, basic social services spending surpasses debt servicing by less than three per cent relative to total national expenditure.

In half of the countries for which there are data, expenditure on basic social services is less than that on defence. On average, basic social services take 12.3 per cent of national budgets, while defence takes 12.8 per cent. For most countries, the two figures are not very far apart. In only three countries (Chad, Lebanon and Nepal) does defence spending differ from basic social services spending by more than ten per cent.

This finding reinforces the lesson that major gains can result from reallocations of social sector expenditure towards basic social services. Comparatively small gains will be realised from the reallocation of discretionary expenditures towards the social sectors from other expenditure areas. Increases in discretionary resources through debt relief can free substantial resources for basic social services. Reductions in debt service and military expenditures are a critical component of any strategy to increase the provision of basic social services.

Reallocation and mobilisation of additional resources

From the above analysis of public expenditure, it is clear that basic social services are currently a relatively low budgetary priority. Basic social services expenditure will have to increase considerably if the 20/20 target is to be met. It might seem that the simplest way to increase basic social services spending is to reallocate resources that are already being spent on non-basic social programmes, since social spending is a large part of most national budgets. However, although social spending receives a large proportion of national budgets, it is more likely to be socially productive than is debt service or defence spending. While these are smaller items than social spending in most national budgets, they are promising targets for reallocation since they do not generally provide concrete benefits for the general population.

By taking such a large percentage of many national budgets, debt service has a negative impact on basic social services spending. Many efficiency and equity arguments for debt relief are today well known — and frequently rehearsed (Sachs 1999). The clear imperative to enhance human capabilities through increased spending on basic social services underlines the argument in favour of debt forgiveness, especially for those countries that already give priority to basic social services by minimising defence and other less productive expenditures.

Reallocation is only one approach to increasing basic social services spending. Given that in many countries public expenditure overall is very low, total resources available for basic social services are necessarily limited. Mobilisation of new resources is also needed in order to increase basic social services spending.

In principle, there are several strategies for mobilisation of additional resources. One is to improve the efficiency of tax collection. Another is to impose new taxes. However, both of these strategies face challenges in practice. Improving the efficiency of tax collection is made difficult by informational problems that are acute in developing countries. There is scope, nonetheless, for reversing the degree of leakage of resources within the tax collection system through appropriate restructuring of incentives (Klitgaard 1991). Tax rates in developing countries tend to be quite low. Resources can be raised in the short term by selling state assets and enterprises, but there remains limited additional scope for such gains in many developing countries and there is thus a need to identify new tax instruments and to employ existing ones thoughtfully.

In some developing countries, the dominant approach to adjustment is derived from 'first best' arguments that have overlooked the revenue-generating role of certain instruments. For instance, customs and excise taxes were a central source of tax revenues in many less developed countries, especially in Africa. In many cases, these taxes have been eliminated in order to facilitate gains from trade, although few alternative revenue sources may remain to the government. Gains in economic efficiency from such policy shifts should properly be balanced against the cost to social investment from the ensuing losses in revenue. Such a comprehensive approach to economic policy analysis has not been adequately pursued in the past.

Trends in basic social services expenditure

Only 9 of the 17 country studies reviewed for this chapter provide information on basic social services expenditure for three or more years. This sample is too small to draw any firm conclusions about general trends in basic social services spending. However, the pattern that emerges from this very small sample is that spending on basic social services tends to be stable. No country's expenditure varied by more than four per cent of total national spending over three consecutive years. All but two remained within two percentage points of where they began.

The greatest year-to-year changes noted are of just less than four per cent. Between 1996 and 1997, Uganda and Nepal increased their spending by this much. Given the very small yearly changes, countries tend to remain in similar relative positions. The highest expenditure recorded between 1994 and 1998 was by Colombia, which spent nearly 18 per cent on basic social services in 1995, but reduced this to 16 per cent by 1997. The sharpest fall is recorded by Chad, which reduced its basic social services spending from nearly 12 per cent to just below 10 per cent between 1995 and 1996.

In no country was the trend steady, even over the very short time period studied. All countries aside from Bangladesh (whose spending remained exactly the same for two years before declining) recorded both increases and declines in basic social services spending, although these may have been extremely slight. No country for which figures were available decreased its basic social services spending between 1996 and 1997.

Although the general trend seems to be one of gradual increases, the present rates of increase are so small that, even if they continued, it would take several years for most of the countries surveyed to reach a basic social services expenditure level of 20 per cent of national expenditure. Not only steady, but more significant increases in basic social services spending will be required if countries are to reach the 20/20 target.

Role of ODA in the provision of basic social services

The 20/20 Initiative is conceived as a compact between developing and industrial countries and thus targets donors as well as national governments. ODA should be monitored, as is national expenditure, to examine whether it is being used efficiently and equitably, and in particular as to whether the target of 20 per cent of resources devoted to BSS is being met. This section, therefore, reviews the extent to which aid flows are being channelled to the financing of basic social service provision.

Role of ODA in national economies

The influence that ODA spending has on conditions in a country will vary widely depending on how large a role ODA plays in the national economy. Table 5 ranks the countries surveyed according to the percentage share of ODA in GDP.

Table 5. The scale of ODA*

Country	ODA/GDP 1997 %	Public expenditure/ GDP %	ODA/ Public expenditure %
Zambia	19.0	20.1	94.5
Burkina Faso	13.0	17.8	73.0
Chad	13.0	18.1	71.8
Uganda	12.0	23.0	52.2
Benin	10.0	19.3	51.8
Kenya	5.0	17.0	29.4
Lebanon	10.4	39.3	25.4
Jordan	5.0	23.0	21.7
Viet Nam	4.0	18.8	21.3
Nepal	8.0	42.3	18.9
Guatemala	2.0	18.6	10.8
Bangladesh	2.0	21.2	9.4
Morocco	1.0	12.6	7.9
Dominican Republic	1.0	14.8	6.8
Philippines	1.0	35.3	2.8
Colombia	0	35.2	0
El Salvador	n/a	15.3	n/a

Source: Same as Table 2; UNICEF, State of the World's Children 2000.

* Figures correspond to the latest year available.

Public expenditure as percentage of GDP is given by way of comparison.

The level of ODA relative to the size of the economy varies widely, with one per cent or less of GDP in the highest-income Latin American countries, but ten per cent or more of GDP in the poorest five sub-Saharan African countries in the sample. In Burkina Faso and Zambia, ODA represents a larger percentage of the economy than discretionary public expenditure. Further, it finances anywhere between zero (Colombia) and 95 (Zambia) per cent of the budget. The 20/20 compact clearly has to be interpreted flexibly in light of these differing circumstances. In cases where the national budget is heavily donor-financed, it may be reasonable for donors to take a correspondingly larger share of responsibility for financing basic social services, as some other public responsibilities normally can only be financed nationally.

Is ODA meeting the 20/20 target?

The question of whether or not donors are meeting the 20/20 targets for spending on basic social services is partially answered by the data contained in Table 6. Only countries for which figures are reported for at least two years during the 1990s are included.

In very few instances, and only in one country consistently (Bangladesh), has

Table 6. ODA inflows to basic social services as a percentage of total in the 1990s*

Year/Country	1990	1991	1992	1993	1994	1995	1996	1997
Bangladesh	17.5	21.7	21.2	21.4	22.6	21.9	-	
Benin	-	-	-	10.4	14.0	14.1	18.4	-
Burkina Faso	15.0	12.7	13.5	15.2	18.4	17.8		
Chad	-	-	-	-	-	12.1	8.0	28.7
Kenya	7.8	14.7	9.6	11.4	17.6	22.4	-	-
Nepal	-	-	7.5	11.0	14.3	13.8	15.5	-
Uganda	-	-	-	27.5	21.6	17.1	-	-
Viet Nam	5.2	-	-	18.6	-	-	-	10.0
Zambia	11.8	55.0	2.8	21.7	-	0.8	0.2	4.3

Source: Same as Table 2; Authors' own calculations.

* Figures correspond to the latest year available.

basic social services spending constituted 20 per cent or more of ODA. The figures clearly indicate that donors need to increase their spending on basic social services in order to meet the 20/20 target, although it may be misleading to compare figures precisely across countries, since as noted earlier, there is as yet no clear consensus among donors on which development activities constitute basic social services. In some countries such as Benin, Chad, Kenya and Nepal, there appears to have been a sharp rise in the proportion of ODA devoted to basic social services over time. However, given the lengthy (decade-long) period over which growth in the share of ODA devoted to BSS is observed, it seems reasonable not to attribute this directly to the 20/20 Initiative, but rather to the broader growth in awareness of the importance of BSS, of which the Initiative is a part.

Prerequisite to ODA analysis: The problem of reporting

The greatest problem in discovering how much ODA is being spent on basic social services is that much information on aggregate ODA flows and composition is still unreported. While most donors describe basic social services as being an important component of assistance (OECD/DCD and UNICEF 1998), the country studies commissioned by UNDP under the PSI programme contain very little information on how much ODA is dedicated to social spending generally, and even less on the amount devoted to basic social services. There is only limited evidence on this score. For instance, data from Chad establish that a preponderance of ODA is directed towards investment, with basic health care representing 17 per cent and basic education 9 per cent of external assistance.

Donors keep records according to their own standards and policies. The first step towards monitoring and implementing the 20/20 Initiative with respect to

ODA will be to develop common standards for reporting on aid among donors. Clear, common interpretations of basic social services among donors will enable international comparisons to be made. It will be important to note not only the type of use to which ODA is directed, but whether the final recipient is government or non-governmental actors in order to make correct assessments of national government commitments towards BSS, in particular through correcting for the problem of 'double counting'.

There is already a trend in this direction: the Development Assistance Committee (DAC) of the OECD has developed a Creditor Reporting System (CRS) in which donors are beginning to participate. The CRS system sets out codes for different development activities, so that activities reported upon under the same codes are certain to be comparable. This system could be adapted to collect comprehensive data on external funding for basic social services. At the present time, there is a fairly clear consensus among donor governments, international agencies, and the DAC on the definition of basic education, which is the same as the 20/20 definition. There is also a general consensus among these parties on basic health: the definitions of the CRS, 20/20, and individual donors are quite similar. However, on nutrition, water and sanitation, there is much less agreement. These issues will have to be resolved if the CRS reporting system is to realise its potential as a tool for evaluating progress under the 20/20 Initiative.

Convincing donors of the validity of 20/20

Apart from the problems of lack of consistent reporting on funding of basic social services by donors, the 20/20 Initiative faces a few obstacles in being accepted by all donors. Donors may resent attempts by the international community to influence the pattern of their activities. Some donors appear to have misunderstood the Initiative to be a binding compact, and as such believe it is unrealistic. There are regular proposals for the improvement of development assistance, and donors may be cynical about the utility of new initiatives, particularly of such a systemic character.

In the 1990s, some donors have adopted 'Sector-Wide Approaches' (SWAps), bilateral agreements with recipient governments that cover an entire sector, such as health or education, in which the responsibilities of both the donor and the recipient country are set out. The objective is to integrate areas in which initiatives of both donors and governments have been fragmented, and to build the capacities of recipient countries. While SWAps are not incompatible with 20/20, they emphasise a sector-specific approach to development aid, which may or may not acknowledge the 20/20 targets that pertain to basic social services overall.

When 20/20 is interpreted formalistically, as a simple numerical target, it will not attract donor support and cooperation. Donors must understand that the goal of the 20/20 benchmark is universal coverage of basic social services, and that pursuit of the initiative is compatible with and even complementary to other development approaches.

Disaggregated analysis of social expenditures

The previous section allowed us to analyse the overall fiscal priority of social expenditure in the countries studied. This section will examine in detail the pattern of expenditure *within* the social services budget of these countries. In particular, it will analyse the priority awarded to basic social services, and if possible, draw conclusions on efficiency of spending. The analysis that follows will attempt to elaborate on the main finding of the previous section, namely, that although social services as a whole occupy a significant proportion of the government budget in many countries, allocation to basic social services remains a low priority. After a brief overview of the social service budget, a more detailed analysis of spending on the health, education, and water and sanitation sectors will provide information on the efficiency and equity of major components of basic social services expenditure.

Breakdown of social expenditure

Social expenditure is generally defined as including that on a subset of the following: education, health, social welfare, water and sanitation, employment, and housing. In some countries, the water and sanitation spending is included as part of the health budget allocation, and in others it appears in a separate category.

Education usually accounts for the most significant proportion of the social services budget. The average for the countries in this study is 44 per cent of the total. Health spending is much lower, at around 20 per cent. Health and education combined, as shown on Table 7 below, thus account for almost 65 per cent of the total social services budget.

In the middle-income countries of the data set for which figures are available, Colombia, the Dominican Republic, Jordan and Morocco spend around half of their social sector budget on 'other' social services including housing, social welfare provisions, and social security. It appears that Lebanon spends a notably high percentage of the social security budget on education and health, though the budgets calculated for the individual sectors include spending from other ministries that are not included in the total social services budget. The Philippines spends a relatively high proportion on health and education, though most notably on education.

The average for the low-income countries in the sample reveals higher overall priority given to education and health (around 70 per cent) as the range and level of social services provided is lower. This sectoral priority is likely to be appropriate in poorer countries, but must be supplemented by a high priority accorded to basic social services *within* expenditure on education and health.

Table 7. The pattern of social services expenditure across countries*

	As % of government spending			Health and education as % of social spending
	Total social sector spending	Health	Education	
Lebanon	20.3	5.3	12.4	87.2
Viet Nam	25.0	5.6	15.0	82.5
Bangladesh	32.0	6.2	18.2	76.3
Benin	27.2	4.72	15.6	74.7
Philippines	20.1	2.2	12.6	73.6
Nepal	29.2	5.3	13.9	65.8
Chad	29.3	5.3	13.3	64.8
Zambia	28.8	10.4	10.8	58.9
Dom. Republic	38.4	8.6	13.8	58.3
Jordan	43.6	9.2	14.6	54.6
Morocco	40.2	3.5	16.5	49.8
Colombia	43.2	8.6	10.3	43.9
Guatemala	46.0	n/a	16.0	n/a
Burkina Faso	27.0	n/a	n/a	n/a
El Salvador	23.8	n/a	n/a	n/a
Kenya	n/a	4.3	22.0	n/a
Uganda	n/a	6.3	22.0	n/a
Average	31.6	6.2	15.3	63.9

Source: Same as Table 2.
* Figures correspond to the latest year available.

Education expenditure

Education represents the single biggest spending item in the social services budget for most countries. The average expenditure on education is around 45 per cent of the social services budget, or 15.3 per cent of total government spending. However, high total education spending without efficient allocation is not sufficient to guarantee universal access to primary education, or to increase adult literacy. Indeed, it is well known that a large proportion of education budgets in some developing countries is taken up by higher-cost secondary and tertiary education that does not serve these goals (Watkins 1999). Basic education is defined as primary education and adult literacy by most of the country reports, although there are some differences in the length of primary education (which ranges from four to nine years), and some countries include pre-school education in their estimates.

Whereas the adult literacy rate for a country gives a good indication of the 'stock' of educational attainment accumulated over previous years, primary education enrolment rates provide a very concrete and current 'flow' estimate of governments' success in providing basic education. Enrolment figures, and in particular those for gross enrolment (which do not account for repetition of years), only provide information on the extent of access to basic education, and not on the quality of that education, which will of course have an important impact on future literacy rates.

Table 8 provides an overview of the share of education in the government budget, along with adult literacy rates and gross primary enrolment rates for the sample countries. It may be observed that the relation between the literacy rate and education spending either as a percentage of GDP or as a percentage of total public expenditure is weak, even after making allowances for the income group. This fact underlines the importance of factors unobserved at this level of aggregation (in particular, the internal composition of education expenditures and the quality of service delivery) in determining final outcomes.

The average literacy rate for the medium human development countries as a whole is 75.9 per cent. The average literacy rate for the least developed countries

Table 8. Selected education and expenditure indicators*

Country (Ranked by literacy rate)	Literacy Rate	Gross Primary Enrolment Rate	Education spending (% of total spending)	Education spending (% of GDP)
Middle income				
Philippines	94	117	14.6	2.71
Colombia	90	118	10.3	3.63
Lebanon	88	95	12.4	3.91
Jordan	86	94	13.8	4.87
Dominican Republic	82	103	16.5	2.44
El Salvador	76	94	n/a	n/a
Guatemala	65	84	12.6	1.59
Morocco	44	84	15.6	3.31
Low income				
Viet Nam	91	114	16.0	3.68
Zambia	78	89	13.9	3.20
Kenya	77	85	22.0	9.31
Uganda	62	73	22.0	4.25
Chad	48	65	13.3	2.41
Bangladesh	38	69	18.2	3.09
Nepal	36	110	13.9	2.79
Benin	32	76	15.0	2.82
Burkina Faso	19	40	n/a	n/a

Source: Same as Table 2; UNICEF, State of the World's Children 2000.

* Figures correspond to the latest year available.

as a whole is 48.5 per cent (UNDP 1997). It can be seen from Tables 7 and 8 together that Viet Nam, Kenya, and Zambia have high literacy rates compared to the average for their income or human development group, whereas Guatemala is under-performing in terms of literacy achievements compared to countries in its group at 65 per cent. The contrasting average for Latin American countries as a sub-group is 87.2 per cent. The high-performing poor countries have high spending on education as a percentage of GDP, whereas Guatemala has notably low spending. This suggests that absolute resource commitments as well as patterns of expenditure are important determinants of final achievements.

Burkina Faso is a striking example of a low-income country that under-performs in terms of literacy rates, with an extremely low average literacy rate of 19 per cent. The gross primary enrolment rate is also the lowest in our sample of countries. The objective of the government's current strategy for human development is to increase primary enrolment from 34 per cent to 60 per cent for boys, and from 30 per cent to 50 per cent for girls by the year 2005. Goals for improved literacy are also included in the strategy. However, there are other targets set for scientific and technical education, and quality of tertiary education, which may impinge on the availability of funds for basic education. Difficult choices in terms of the targeting of the available resources are in this case, as in others, inevitable.

Benin also has a low literacy rate, despite a respectable resource commitment to education. No time series is available for basic education expenditure, which stood at 5.2 per cent of total government spending or roughly a third of education spending overall in 1997. The increase in primary enrolment in recent years has resulted in higher pupil/teacher ratios, which has implications for the quality of primary education, in the absence of an increase in resources. Intra-sectoral reallocation is likely to be a key strategy in Benin, as elsewhere.

Nepal's literacy rate is well below the average for the developing countries, and even for the South Asian sub-region, which has one of the lowest regional averages in the world (48.4 per cent, excluding India). However, Nepal has achieved a high gross primary enrolment rate, even when compared to countries with much higher levels of economic development. The share of budget dedicated to education has increased from 8.8 per cent in 1991 to 13.9 per cent in 1997, and also the share of basic education within that budget is relatively high, at around three-quarters of the total. The efficiency of resource use is, therefore, a key issue. Efficiency of basic education expenditure can, in particular, be improved by lowering dropout and repetition rates in primary schools.

Table 9 shows the relative proportion of the education budget dedicated to basic education for the latest available data, as derived from the country studies under review. It may be observed that the relation between educational achievements and spending on basic education as a percentage of government expenditure is

Table 9. The relative importance of basic education expenditure*

Country (Ranked by literacy rate)	Literacy Rate	Gross Primary Enrolment Rate	Basic education spending as % of total public spending	Basic education spending as % of education spending	Basic education spending as % of GDP
Middle income					
Philippines	94	117	n/a	n/a	n/a
Colombia	90	118	7.5	72.57	2.64
Lebanon	88	95	7.4	59.7	2.33
Jordan	86	94	9.1	65.94	1.35
Dominican Republic	82	103	5.9	35.66	1.25
El Salvador	76	94	8.9	n/a	n/a
Guatemala	65	84	8.8	69.44	1.63
Morocco	44	84	14	89.74	2.63
Low income					
Viet Nam	91	114	5.3	32.81	0.62
Zambia	78	89	n/a	n/a	n/a
Kenya	77	85	10.6	48.18	4.48
Uganda	62	73	12.7	57.73	2.45
Chad	48	65	5.2	39.10	0.94
Bangladesh	38	69	n/a	n/a	n/a
Nepal	36	110	8.3	76.85	1.69
Benin	32	76	7.0	46.67	1.61
Burkina Faso	19	40	5.6	n/a	n/a

Source: Same as Table 2; Authors' own calculations.

* Figures correspond to the latest year available.

weak. The relation between educational achievements and expenditure on basic education as a percentage of GDP is stronger within each income group, even though there are still notable exceptions to such a relationship, underlining the importance of the efficiency of resource use.

Viet Nam has noticeably low spending on basic education as a proportion of education and high education achievements. However, the country has a long history of investment in education, and literacy rates are very high, with near-universal primary enrolment and low dropout figures. Spending on education appears to have been increasingly devoted to higher levels of education without impeding primary level enrolments. Yet there remain some regional and gender disparities that merit further investment in basic education. The Dominican Republic and Jordan also have reasonably high literacy rates at low levels of basic education expenditure, suggesting that the additional effort necessary to attain universal literacy may be low.

Especially in the African countries, the share of development expenditure in the education budget is extremely low. Where donors do not make up the shortfall, households are forced to foot the bill for textbooks, pay user fees, or contribute to capital investments. Chad and Benin, for instance, appear to be under-investing in basic education relative to the education sector as a whole, and to have notably low overall achievements as a consequence. In Chad, the education indicators are extremely poor. Enrolment rates are fairly low (60 per cent), and the pupil/teacher ratio is high at 65 students per teacher. The level of capital investment needs to increase, since only half of all classes take place in an adequate classroom. State spending on education includes only teachers' salaries, as development expenditure is financed entirely by donors. Around nine per cent of aid inflows to Chad are spent on basic education, which amount to approximately twice the state budget for basic education. To the extent that domestic constraints prevent the generation of additional resources, assistance from donors or debt relief directed towards BSS will be indispensable.

Taking into account all the countries in the sample, the macroeconomic priority assigned to basic education is on average just below two per cent. As noted earlier, this figure depends on three factors: the size of the public sector; the importance of the education budget as a proportion of the total public expenditure; and the priority assigned within the education budget to basic services. Relative to other basic social services, it is basic education that receives the greatest portion of resources, mainly because of the priority of education within total government budget relative to health and other social services.

Health expenditure

The level of government spending on health, as a percentage of both the social services budget and of total government spending, is appreciably lower than that of the education sector for all of the countries studied here, with the average level being just over six per cent of public expenditure. Within the health budget, resources allocated to basic health services vary considerably in their importance. Also, in many countries, government is not the only provider of health care, as there may also be the presence of the private sector and national and international non-governmental organisations (NGOs). The financing of publicly provided health care also frequently comes from not only general taxation, but also user fees, which have a potentially significant impact on access to primary health care (Reddy and Vandemoortele 1997).

Table 10 shows the relative importance of health sector spending in the sample countries, as well as their health status as indicated by child mortality rates. The average under-five mortality rate (U5MR) for the developing countries as a whole is 95 per 1000 live births. Thus, half of the sample countries have higher under-five mortality rates than the average.

Table 10 suggests a fairly strong rank-order relation between health expendi-

Table 10. Selected health and spending indicators*

Country (Ranked by U5MR)	Under-five mortality rate (U5MR)	Government health spending	
		% of total spending	% of GDP
Middle income			
Colombia	30	8.6	3.0
El Salvador	34	n/a	n/a
Jordan	36	9.2	3.2
Philippines	44	2.2	0.4
Dominican Republic	51	8.6	1.3
Guatemala	52	n/a	n/a
Lebanon	58	5.3	2.2
Morocco	70	3.5	0.7
Low income			
Viet Nam	42	5.6	1.3
Nepal	100	5.3	1.1
Bangladesh	106	6.2	1.1
Kenya	117	4.3	1.8
Uganda	134	6.3	1.2
Benin	165	4.7	0.9
Burkina Faso	165	n/a	n/a
Chad	198	5.3	1.0
Zambia	202	10.4	2.1

Source: Same as Table 2; UNICEF, State of the World's Children 2000.

* Figures correspond to the latest year available.

tures as a percentage of GDP and U5MR among the middle-income countries, which is perfect if the outlying case of the Philippines is discounted, and a weaker rank-order relation between these two statistics among the poorer countries. However, taking account of the presence of HIV/AIDS, which especially affects Zambia and Kenya among the sample countries, would be likely to greatly strengthen this relationship.

The Table shows that Colombia, Jordan, Lebanon and Zambia spend the most on health in relation to GDP. However, as they belong to different income categories, this comparison is not directly meaningful. Whilst Colombia, Jordan and Lebanon have relatively high health indicators in the group, Zambia is the country with the highest under-five mortality rate, at 202 per 1000 live births. The country also has very low indicators of health as measured by indicators of malnutrition, and water and sanitation. It is therefore encouraging to see that the latest figures (1997) show a relatively high percentage of spending devoted to the health sector (approximately ten per cent). In previous years, however, expenditure on health was low (around six per cent), and has increased only since 1994. The relative squeeze on health spending in the late 1980s and early 1990s was attributed to declining GDP due to external price shocks.

Looking at the countries with below-average under-five mortality rates shows that they devote relatively more resources to health than the other countries. A notable exception is the Philippines, which of all countries for which data are available devotes the lowest proportion of government resources to health, at only 2.2 per cent. This amounts to just 0.4 per cent of GDP, or less than $5 per capita. The country's tradition of pursuing social achievements, and the complementarity between high educational attainments and good health, may partially explain its high health achievements. With the exception of Zambia, the low-income countries in the sample devote approximately five per cent of government spending to health.

Countries also seem to be experiencing different evolutions of their health budgets. Of the countries for which a time series is available, Colombia, Jordan, Bangladesh, Nepal, Chad and Zambia show an increase in health care spending relative to the total budget over time. On the other hand, the Philippines, Kenya, Benin and Uganda experienced declines in their health care budgets, likely due to the increasing burden of debt payments, as discussed in the previous section.

The macroeconomic priority assigned to basic health care can be seen from the health expenditure/GDP ratios in Table 11. Of the countries under review, only Colombia spends more than a single percentage point of its GDP on basic health. Most countries in the sample are spending around 0.5 per cent. Given the health indicators for most of the countries in the sample, and the relationship examined above between health expenditure and outcomes, this is clearly not enough.

A common theme to emerge from the country studies is a lack of focus within health budgets on the most efficient forms of intervention. Most countries are spending too much on expensive tertiary and curative care. Of the ten countries for which detailed data on health expenditure are available, only four (Nepal, Uganda, Benin and Colombia) spend 50 per cent or more of their health budget on basic health interventions.

The Philippines, which has already been mentioned as having low absolute levels of health expenditure, also appears to devote resources to inefficient uses, with overspending on curative services, and high administration costs, when five out of six leading causes of death are infectious and therefore likely preventable. Usage of low-cost preventative and curative interventions is limited. Less than half of diarrhoeal cases of children under five are treated with oral rehydration therapy (ORT), an extremely inexpensive intervention. Also, spending on water and sanitation is very low, leading to an environment of high risk with regard to communicable diseases.

Jordan only spends 20 per cent of the health budget on basic health, and this figure also shows a decline between the years 1991 and 1997. Jordan has had a

Table 11. Basic health spending as a share of health spending, total government spending and GDP*

| Country | Government basic health spending | | |
	% of public spending	% of health spending	% of GDP
Middle income			
Colombia	4.3	50	1.51
Dominican Republic	2.7	31	0.40
El Salvador	4.1	n/a	n/a
Guatemala	3.8	n/a	n/a
Jordan	1.8	20	0.64
Lebanon	0.9	13.8	0.30
Morocco	1.4	40	0.30
Philippines	n/a	n/a	n/a
Low income			
Bangladesh	n/a	n/a	n/a
Benin	2.7	57	0.51
Burkina Faso	4.5	n/a	n/a
Chad	2.1	40	0.38
Kenya	1.3	30	0.55
Nepal	3.1	58	0.61
Uganda	3.6	57	0.69
Viet Nam	2.2	40	0.52
Zambia	n/a	n/a	n/a

Source: Same as Table 2.
* Figures correspond to the latest year available.

decrease in infant mortality, and an increase in available doctors, beds in clinics, and maternity care per capita. However, there has been a decline in the number of health centres and village clinics compared to previous years. Morbidity due to infectious diseases has also declined, though there has been an increase in the incidence of dysentery. There is still a lot of progress needed for Jordan to meet basic health targets. For example, immunisation of children is currently at 85.7 per cent. The main areas for freeing up expenditure on basic health appear to be wages and administrative costs. Clearly, restructuring of the existing health budget in favour of basic interventions is readily feasible and can serve to substantially enhance Jordan's basic health performance.

Chad spends a relatively small amount of its budget on basic health. At only 40 per cent, this amounts to just 0.38 per cent of GDP. Chad has extremely weak health indicators, and a very low level of coverage in basic health interventions. Life expectancy is low, even compared to the sub-region. Twenty per cent of infants are severely malnourished, and the total immunisation rate for infants under two years is just 13 per cent. ODA in Chad finances the entire development budget for health, and non-salary recurrent expenditure, including nutrition, water and sanitation. These expenditures amount to 16 per cent of international aid to Chad. Restructuring of expenditure in the health sector towards BSS is clearly a key imperative for Chad, as is an increase in the proportion of ODA devoted to health, which is currently below the 20 per cent level.

Nepal, with total health spending at only 5.3 per cent of public expenditure, has however managed to allocate a substantial portion of total health expenditure to basic health, and thus raised its level of basic health spending as a proportion of GDP above the average of the ten other countries with detailed data available. This is a considerable achievement, given that the total resources available for public expenditure in Nepal are lower than the average, and suggests what can be accomplished elsewhere even at low levels of total expenditure.

In summary, the countries studied spend relatively little on health. As a share of government spending, they average around three per cent. As a proportion of GDP, basic health represents just 0.4 per cent. This is mainly due to a lack of priority of health expenditure in national budgets. However, it is also true that within the health budget, most countries are not targeting low-cost, effective and efficient preventative interventions, but rather spend a disproportionate amount on expensive curative services. A majority of the countries in the sample for which data are available spend less than half of their health budget on basic services. Also, many of the country studies cite inefficiencies within the basic health system, such as over-centralisation, lack of proper accounting procedures, and over-reliance on expensive medicines.

Water and sanitation spending

Low-cost clean water and adequate sanitation are essential prerequisites for a healthy population, yet expenditure on their provision is low and falling in most of the countries in the study. Expenditure on water and sanitation is sometimes included in basic health expenditure, and sometimes separated. It is clear from the studies that water and sanitation occupy a low status within the government budgets. They also are little considered in the reports, likely because of lack of data.

Examination of expenditures in the sector in the countries for which information is available shows a declining trend in most of them. A notable exception is Viet Nam, which has increased the budget allocation to water and sanitation during recent years, though to a fairly low level of 0.5 per cent of total expenditure. The country has fairly poor levels of water and sanitation coverage compared to other social service indicators, revealing a comparative lack of commitment to these services in the past.

In Kenya, water and sanitation expenditures have declined severely as a proportion of the government budget, from 2.4 per cent to 0.4 per cent. In Nepal, government investment expenditure on drinking water has declined continuously in recent years, though the share of basic services within the water and sanitation sector has increased. Local NGOs are also reported to have played an important role in the provision of adequate drinking water. No disaggregated data are available on water spending for Chad. Benin, in turn, spends relatively high amounts (2.7 per cent) of its budget on water and sanitation, in the face of extremely low indicators of coverage.

Among the middle-income countries in the sample, we find that in Lebanon, the charge for clean water is higher in poorer rural areas, which also have a lower cost of basic provision. This implies that poor households are subsidising richer households. The standard of sanitation is also poor in the Philippines, where issues of effectiveness of water provision, and problems with pricing strategies and cost-recovery need to be addressed urgently. Latin American countries, as a rule, are spending low amounts on water and sanitation, despite these being the areas with the greatest shortfall in coverage among the basic social services.

Conclusions and recommendations

Most of the countries in this chapter have not reached a level of 20 per cent of public expenditure devoted to basic social services. Indeed, the average level for the group of countries studied is 12.3 per cent. Since government budgets are partially financed by ODA, the level of expenditure on BSS out of nationally-generated resources is even lower. This central fact underlines that the 20/20 targets are a worthy but still distant goal.

Social expenditure overall represents an extremely high proportion of discretionary expenditures (i.e. after debt service) for the countries in the study. This fact underlines that a lack of government commitment to social expenditures as such is not, contrary to popular perception, the primary reason for the failure to attain universal access to basic social services. A detailed review of social sector expenditures reveals nonetheless that there is substantial scope in most countries for reallocation of social sector expenditures towards basic services. Such reallocation, combined with a relaxation of government resource constraints through debt relief, reductions in relatively unproductive (e.g. defence) expenditure, and increased domestic and international revenue mobilisation can significantly promote the 20/20 objectives.

A detailed analysis of the health, education and water and sanitation budgets, and the allocations within each sector to basic social services in the sample countries, reveals that:

- Education expenditure enjoys budgetary priority over the health sector;
- In both of the major sectors, spending is not targeted well at basic services;

- The relation between overall social sector spending and social sector outcomes is weak in education, but stronger in health;
- These relations seem stronger when the focus is placed on basic social services expenditure;
- The allocation to basic interventions is generally lower for the health than for the education sector;
- In almost every country under review, there is a substantial scope for improved efficiency of resource use within the social services budget.

The level of public spending in most countries is below the level assumed in the original 20/20 estimate of the requirements to meet the goals of universal access to basic social services. As a result, attention to increased revenue generation is essential. Evaluation of progress towards 20/20 targets should therefore take place in the overall context of an assessment of national economic strategies, including mechanisms of tax collection. For heavily indebted countries, debt relief is an essential component of the pursuit of 20/20 objectives and should be treated as an integral element of the development and assessment of 20/20 strategies.

Other policy recommendations include improved monitoring mechanisms. There is an urgent need for more systematic recording of donor efforts by type and recipient, bound by a commonly accepted taxonomy. At present, in the absence of such a system, the database for evaluating the extent of donor and national government commitment to basic social services is weak. There is also a need to extend reporting of expenditures on basic social services to levels of government other than central government, in order to permit a more comparable and accurate understanding of the extent of national efforts, as well as the areas of most urgent need for the redirection of resources. At present, the data required to make such judgements do not exist.

The data reveal both an inadequate level and a very slow rate of growth of expenditures on basic social services. That higher expenditures on basic social services would be helpful to the attainment of the 20/20 goals is illustrated by the stronger relation that exists in the sample countries between such expenditures and human development outcomes than between poorly targeted overall social sector expenditures and final outcomes. More rapid attainment of universal access to basic social services will accordingly require both a relaxation of resource constraints and a reallocation of available resources to higher social priority uses, though the appropriate balance of these will depend on national circumstances.

Finally, no realistic analysis can afford to ignore considerations of political economy. Some of the structural changes envisioned here are more realisable than others. The formulation of appropriate strategies will in the final analysis depend not only on where the greatest opportunities seem to lie from the point of view of accounting, but also from the point of view of politics. In this light, existing budgetary patterns of strong support for social expenditure without a correspondingly strong support for basic level services should be read as revealing the past and present power of existing political constituencies. These are often of a broad-based or even mass nature, although they frequently exclude the poorest.

Realistic strategies will thus often involve forging workable compromises between the interests of these different groups, for example by sometimes favouring more universal over narrowly targeted approaches to provision. Such national compromises should be supported through the extension of debt relief to countries for which increases in basic social service expenditure are heavily obstructed by debt service obligations. The 20/20 vision is that progress towards universal access to basic social services will be attained not only as a result of moral concern, but also of the articulation of shared responsibilities and the pursuit of economically and politically well-designed and feasible strategies. ∎

Notes

Ms. Harrington is Executive Director of the Institute for Human Rights and Development in Africa, Banjul. Ms. Porter is a Fellow at the Overseas Development Institute, London. Mr. Reddy is Professor of Economics at Barnard College, Columbia University, New York. The authors wish to thank Alejandro Grinspun for his detailed and helpful comments on earlier drafts.

[1] The interpretation of basic services outlined here can be questioned. For example, curative care delivered even at tertiary levels is often 'basic' in nature (Reddy and Vandemoortele 1997). However, in this paper, we adopt without further enquiry the definitions provided here.

[2] Specifically, the share of nationally generated resources devoted to BSS is given by $(BSS - \theta \, ODA)/ DEVT$, where BSS, ODA and DEVT refer to the total levels of expenditure on BSS, ODA, and the development budget, respectively, and θ is the share of BSS in ODA.

PART 2 Country Cases

8 Angola

Mercedes González de la Rocha

P rior to the outbreak of armed conflict, Angola produced one of the most abundant harvests in Africa, which included maize, coffee, fruits and other agricultural products. More than two decades of war, however, have devastated the country's economy as well as its infrastructure and social fabric. Agriculture has suffered from an acute labour shortage because of the massive exodus of displaced persons migrating from rural areas into the cities as well as to neighbouring countries. As a consequence, production in the primary sector has experienced severe setbacks from which it has never recovered.

The protracted civil war dominates every aspect of Angolan life. No other priority receives so much attention from the government. The armed conflict siphons off resources from other sectors, diminishing the possibility of reviving the country's economy, which is heavily dependent on petroleum production. As the latter accounts for 60 per cent of GDP, any drop in the international price of crude oil causes a major loss of public revenues, squeezing the social sectors and making it extremely difficult to design and implement specific policies to combat poverty.

The government has had a reputation for designing sound development plans, but of being unable to implement them. Lack of continuity appears to be a major problem for government initiatives. The few programmes that the Angolan authorities have tried to implement were always abandoned within a few months. The consequence is that public policies have had a meagre impact on the lives of the poor.

It is against this background of very limited success in the implementation of development plans that in 1997, the United Nations Development Programme (UNDP) offered its assistance for the preparation of a series of studies on poverty and gender. As this chapter will show, the ability of donor-assisted initiatives to contribute to major changes in policy is severely constrained by the institutional fragility that characterises many developing countries. This calls for a major effort by donor agencies to invest in capacity-building and institutional development in these countries.

Poverty analysis

Given the particular situation imposed by the war, there have been relatively few studies and resources to carry out systematic analyses of poverty in Angola. For this reason, the possibility of drawing from technical and financial resources made available by UNDP through the Poverty Strategies Initiative (PSI) was very well received in some government circles. The UNDP office invited Angola's National Statistical Institute (INE) to serve as the focal point for the PSI project, which was perceived as an opportunity to undertake in-depth analyses that could be used as inputs for the formulation of public policies to combat poverty. The purpose was also to fill some critical information gaps that were believed to impede a better understanding of the phenomenon of poverty in the country. The choice of INE as the project's counterpart was certainly a strategic one, not only because INE is perhaps the only government entity with some built-in research capacity, but also because it is part of the powerful Ministry of Planning. This was seen as providing an important entry point for linking research results with policy-making and planning.

Based on several discussions between the staff of UNDP and INE, it was decided that the PSI funding would be used for the preparation of four studies related to poverty. The first study was an analysis of the policy measures required for alleviating poverty by pursuing equity and efficiency goals in tandem, rather than one at the expense of the other (Wold and Grave 1999). It was prepared jointly by INE and Statistics Norway as a first step to galvanise national efforts towards the preparation of Angola's first national poverty eradication strategy.

The second output was a study for the determination of a basic food basket for Luanda (Ribeiro 2000). It includes an assessment of the impact of inflation and exchange rate policy on living conditions, as well as a definition of a basic basket of goods linked to food security and estimates of consumer purchasing power. This study was intended to feed into the development and adoption of a database to monitor the cost of the basic basket of goods.

The two other studies were a profile of rural poverty and a socio-economic and demographic profile of labour in the Luanda province. The former contains a breakdown of poor and non-poor households in rural areas, a profile of the rural poor, and a definition of target groups for public programmes. The latter is an assessment of the evolution of employment and unemployment indicators during the 1990s (Adauta de Sousa 1998).

In addition to these four studies, a set of guidelines for the production of gender statistics was developed and used in training workshops conducted with mid-level government officials in Luanda, Lubango and Benguela, and a document on the role of women in Angolan society was produced and published (Ceita 1999).[1]

The policy study, together with the profile of rural poverty and the analysis of the role of women in Angolan society, are rich in information and analyses about poverty, labour markets dynamics, gender, employment, and the coping strategies of the poor. The same may be said about the study for the determination of a basic food basket for Luanda, even though this output was of a different kind and, unlike the others, was not expected to have a direct impact on the public debate. According to data compiled by INE, between 60 and 70 per cent of the population live below the official poverty line. Of these, 13.4 per cent live in extreme poverty. The flight of refugees from rural areas has been formidable, turning the cities into a refuge for the poor. Seventy per cent of the population in Cabinda, 68 per cent in Lubango, and more than 60 per cent in the other main cities (Luanda, Lobito and Luena) fall into the category of poor (Angola 1997a). The studies financed by the PSI confirm the findings from the national Human Development Reports (HDR) sponsored by UNDP in 1997, 1998 and 1999, which single out the impact of the war as one of the main determinants of the country's massive levels of poverty. High unemployment and extremely limited access to health services are also closely associated with poverty.[2]

In the face of extreme vulnerability, people have resorted to a multiplicity of survival strategies to make ends meet. Household survival strategies include women's and children's participation in the labour market, particularly in informal sector activities in which, according to various sources, almost 50 per cent of the urban population is engaged. In Luanda, for example, it has been estimated that 54 per cent of all families are linked to the informal economy (Adauta de Sousa 1998). Women have entered the labour market on a permanent basis, and are considered to be breadwinners on equal footing with men (Wold and Grave 1999). Although labour plays a central part in people's survival strategies mainly through work intensification practices, households have also been forced to adopt a range of 'restrictive' strategies to protect their level of consumption from further erosion. These include not going to the doctor in order to avoid the cost of health services, using cheap but less efficient sources of energy such as firewood, and incurring debt to pay for children's education (see chapter 3, this volume). These 'private' initiatives have flourished as a result of the lack of support that the poor get from the government, which is itself subject to acute pressures due to the protracted armed conflict.[3]

It is important to stress that the activities financed by the PSI programme were integrated into existing local initiatives for data-gathering and research. They also contributed further to strengthening the efforts that in recent years had been supported by UNDP, as well as the World Bank. In particular, the institutional collaboration between UNDP and INE dates back to the preparation of the 1997 *Human Development Report*, which was under way at the same time that the PSI studies began. This contributed to a fruitful fertilisation of ideas between both sets of analytical work, a process that was certainly aided by the fact that some key INE staff participated in both. Some of the statistical data on which the HDR is based came from the analyses carried out by the PSI studies, which also appear to have had a significant impact on the contents of the report. More importantly, the HDR clearly pointed out the need to undertake more in-depth and systematic analyses of poverty in Angola. This need was partly met by the PSI project. The latter thus fell on ground that had been prepared by the initiatives and activities that were being undertaken locally, even though with great difficulty and limited resources.

Perhaps the single most important analytical contribution of the PSI studies, particularly the one on anti-poverty policies, is the notion of poverty as an economic and political phenomenon (Wold and Grave 1999). The significance of this notion may be gauged only by considering that, by and large, poverty in Angola is perceived as being primarily a 'social' problem. By implication, it has been deemed to be out of the ambit of government action. A central purpose of the analytical work supported by UNDP, therefore, has been to emphasise the economic and political roots of poverty. Likewise, the analysis of the conditions of women has generated a fledgling debate in academic and policy circles on the importance of their role for society and the discrimination they face in the development process (Angola n/d).

Although, as we shall see later, one cannot be too optimistic about the probable impact of these studies, there are at least some indications of a greater awareness about poverty and gender issues among key policy-makers. It was encouraging, for instance, that at a press conference held in late 1999, the President of Angola dealt extensively with the question of poverty, using data produced by the PSI studies. It appears, furthermore, that both the national HDR and the PSI studies may have influenced the design of government programmes, although concrete evidence of such impact is hard to come by. The Medium Term Stabilisation and Economic Recovery Programme 1998-2000 deals explicitly with poverty issues. Among the broad objectives of the Programme are to 'combat social injustice and disparities', 'rehabilitate the economic and social infrastructure and equipment in areas in which refugees and displaced persons will resettle', 'revitalise the peasant agricultural sector' and 'ensure minimum levels of consumption of food and other basic necessities'. The social objectives of the Programme are to:

- Reduce unemployment and combat poverty;
- Increase food and other basic supplies to the population;
- Improve the provision of public health services and primary health care;
- Improve the provision of education and occupational training services;
- Upgrade the infrastructure for basic sanitation and drinking water supply to rural and urban populations (Angola 1997b).

There are, in short, positive signs that give some room for hope. Unfortunately, the problems of institutional weakness and lack of continuity that have plagued this war-ravaged country in the past seem to have once again doomed the prospects for translating the analytical outputs sponsored by UNDP into tangible policy outcomes.

Capacity-building

The development of local capacities was not a major objective of the PSI project, given its limited funding and its primary emphasis on advocacy and raising awareness. Nevertheless, it would not be correct to say that the project did not have any impact on capacity-building. Its main merit lay not so much in creating new capacities where none existed before, but in availing itself of those that were already available in the country and putting them to good use for carrying out systematic analyses of existing survey data on poverty and gender issues.

The PSI activities were undertaken on ground made fertile by existing policy initiatives, as well as a track record of collaboration between UNDP and the Living Conditions Monitoring Unit of the National Statistical Institute. To a significant extent, UNDP was able to benefit from the participation of a team of local experts who not only possessed solid academic training and specialised skills, but also the required competencies and experience for carrying out this type of work. This critical mass of expertise is rarely an abundant resource in countries such as Angola. Tragically, it is not uncommon that some of the best talents in these countries are forced to devote themselves to other activities or to migrate in search of more viable and attractive options due to the lack of incentives in their home country. This 'brain drain' deprives countries of some of their most qualified people, giving rise to serious capacity gaps that may take an entire generation to remedy.

In the context of low salaries, lack of continuity and insufficient resources faced by local researchers, the financial and technical support provided by international organisations over the years, albeit limited, has been critical for ensuring the development of a core group of highly qualified professionals. This also applies to the technical staff at INE, which has been the preferred local partner for the poverty surveys carried out in Angola with funding from outside sources, particularly the World Bank, as well as the national Human Development Reports sponsored by UNDP.

It is to UNDP's credit that it decided to collaborate with and support the core group of experts at INE. This was the appropriate institution to conduct the project activities both because of its access to data and the human capital and technical know-how it had accumulated over time. Besides, the fact that INE belongs to the Ministry of Planning offered, at least in principle, the possibility of establishing a direct link between the analytical findings and recommendations from the PSI studies and the political sphere. While the dialogue between UNDP, the INE experts and the government authorities has not been devoid of problems, there has nonetheless been a gradual process of accommodation that has enabled key local actors to become increasingly sensitive about the problem of poverty.

The emerging recognition of poverty as an economic and political phenomenon and, consequently, as an integral part of the economic policy responsibilities of the government, is no minor achievement in a country that until recently, had avoided dealing explicitly with the problem. Since many studies had already been carried out prior to this project, it certainly cannot be said that the PSI project by itself placed the subject of poverty and gender on the agenda of discussion. Nevertheless, the institutional collaboration that the PSI studies made possible allowed these topics to be discussed in broader circles as an instrument of dialogue and public awareness. The project was a fundamental step towards achieving a better understanding of Angola's poverty problem, and establishing embryonic links between the producers of data and decision-makers in government.

Equally important is the fact that the topics of poverty and gender are increasingly entering into the public arena. Findings from the poverty profile, for example, were printed in the local press, which is devoting more attention to these issues now because, for the first time, reliable data are becoming available. These and other findings were also discussed in seminars and forums in the city of Luanda and other urban sites, with the presence of government personnel, civil society members and academics. Although not as extensive as would have been desired, these dissemination activities nonetheless helped to create consciousness about the magnitude of the problems facing Angola. They also provided critical knowledge for understanding the policy challenges that these problems entail.

Moreover, just as the inclusion of the group of INE experts clearly benefited the PSI project, there was also a parallel process of institutional learning at INE itself. The implementation of the project activities, which revolved around the analysis and systematisation of survey data and their translation into policy relevant outputs, had important side benefits for both the institution and the experts who participated in the studies. In light of this, it is regrettable that changes that subsequently took place in the leadership of INE apparently aborted a process of learning-by-doing that had been in progress for several years. These changes will be discussed next.

Institutional weakness

The activities sponsored by UNDP produced a number of significant findings and recommendations that could have been used for the development of policy. Moreover, as we have seen, the decision to locate the PSI project in the National Statistical Institute was amply justified in term of its expertise and its critical bridging role between researchers and policy-makers. Unfortunately, and apparently without prior notice, a decision was taken in 1999 to change the Director-General of INE and other key personnel. These decisions have resulted in a change in the priorities of the institution. Understanding and analysing issues of poverty, employment, the informal sector and female labour, which had been priority concerns under the previous management, ceased to be given the same importance under the current management. The new Director-General has expressed little interest in the generation of 'social' statistics, which have now given way to the collection and processing of macroeconomic indicators.

Consequently, the existence of the Living Conditions Monitoring Unit, a critical space created for socio-economic analysis within the INE, is no longer part of the restructuring plans of the new management. What could have been a seed for new and innovative analysis — which is extremely important for the design of more effective development policies — has instead undergone a process of dismantling following the changes experienced since 1999. INE's best staff, who had pursued post-graduate studies abroad, specialising in survey techniques, applied mathematics and other relevant topics, have left the institution to take up jobs elsewhere. If the former Director had continued as head of INE, or if his successor had drawn upon the investment made in training its personnel, the PSI project could have been part of a process of enhanced capacities within the institution. Instead, a project that had enjoyed some success was dismantled, preventing its results from being fed into policy design and more ominously, discontinuing a process of learning and capacity-building that will take time to restore.

The case of Angola is particularly revealing in many respects. It clearly demonstrates the importance of institutional stability for the success of any initiative. Perhaps because of its limited size, the UNDP project has had a negligible impact in countering what is widely perceived as the weakness of Angolan institutions, characterised by frequent personnel changes, instability and lack of continuity. The direction taken by key agencies seems to depend in large measure on the interests of the individuals who head them, which is a clear sign of the absence of institutionalisation.

Thus, even though some institutional learning took place in INE as a result of the PSI activities, it is highly unlikely that the enhanced capacities generated by the project would be available for future initiatives related to poverty. The changes that followed the qualitative shift experienced by INE have very high costs, both personal and institutional. They not only affect the core group of individuals who were directly involved in the project and have now scattered in other directions. These changes also have a more profound impact in terms of the accumulation of knowledge, given the impossibility of pursuing a collective effort of compilation, analysis and interpretation of data for policy use in a context of institutional fluidity.

One other element in the Angolan case may have some important lessons for similar undertakings in the future in other countries. The absence of middle management personnel with high technical competencies in government ministries was a serious problem. Middle management has the potential to be a link between information and the applied use of that information. Any effort to influence the design of policies through the production of reliable information and analysis on important topics is impeded by the lack of capacity to make use of those inputs. This lack in Angola acted as a further constraint on the potential of the PSI activities to have a discernible impact on policy-making.

An important lesson to be drawn from this experience is the need to focus future efforts on the training of personnel in state secretariats and ministries. This training should cover such apparently simple skills as learning to interpret statistics, perceive the relationship between different variables, and translate analytical outputs into instruments for the design of policies. Without this institutional capacity at the government level, no study would be able to have an impact on policy design, no matter how good it may be. The same could also be applied to the personnel of civil organisations, where there appears to be a tremendous need for this type of training.[4]

Partnerships

Apart from their intrinsic value for ensuring local ownership of policies, the establishment of partnerships amongst social and institutional actors can serve as an antidote for the problems of institutional weakness discussed above. This applies both to the existence of coordination among international organisations and, most importantly, between such organisations and national entities.

With respect to the former, the case of Angola represents a missed opportunity for establishing close links between key international organisations present in the country. The World Bank, for example, has had many projects in Angola in recent years. Funding from the Bank facilitated the establishment of the Living Conditions Monitoring Unit of the INE, which was subsequently involved in the preparation of both the national HDRs and the poverty studies sponsored by UNDP. The World Bank also financed the household survey that furnished the raw data for the poverty studies carried out under the PSI project, as well as for a new national income and expenditure survey that was implemented in 1999-2000. The fact that the same core group of professionals at INE was involved in both sets of activities should have prompted UNDP and the World Bank to coordinate their assistance more closely. Instead, there was very limited connection between the two, and funding for each set of activities was independent from the other.

Clearly, one cannot attribute to the PSI project a seed role in terms of leveraging additional resources for poverty-related work. It is more than likely that given its long history of involvement in the country, financing from the World Bank for the latest household survey would have been made available even without the presence of the PSI project. It seems more accurate to say, instead, that it was the financial support of the Bank that enabled UNDP to achieve significant results in a short period of time, since the data used in the PSI studies had already been collected and were thus available for analysis.[5] What we find, therefore, is the simultaneous but uncoordinated efforts of two major international organisations, probably to the detriment of their Angolan partners.

Beyond the collaboration between UNDP and the INE expert team for the conduct of the studies, there is also no evidence that PSI activities led to enhanced partnerships involving national actors. Although efforts were made to circulate the project outputs among civil and non-governmental associations, and some workshops and forums did take place, no social group has claimed full ownership of the results of the project. This may partly be attributed to the fact that dissemination activities have been rather limited. They took place mainly through personal contacts of the researchers and the informal distribution of reports to government officials, local academics, and representatives from non-governmental and international organisations with offices in Luanda. Unless UNDP and INE make a deliberate effort to ensure that the results of the studies reach a wider policy audience, it is improbable that genuine national ownership will emerge. A specific target should be the Ministry of Planning, given its privileged role in economic policy-making.

Conclusion

Our review of the experience of Angola has yielded some valuable lessons for donor engagement in support of poverty reduction strategies. Probably the most relevant lesson relates to the negative impact that institutional fragility has on the accumulation of knowledge and capacities that may be utilised for policy change. This case illustrates that institutions in many countries are extremely vulnerable to political developments, and take different directions according to the interests of the persons leading them. All too often, the result is that policy initiatives are discontinued, capacities that were created with great effort are wasted, and precious time and energy are lost.

Angola is, sadly, a case in point. The sudden change of leadership at the National Statistical Institute doomed the prospects the PSI project might have had of influencing the government's policy agenda. The change meant that the collection and processing of poverty-relevant information ceased to be a priority for the INE, which led to the dismantling of a Unit that had acquired substantial expertise in the analysis and interpretation of survey data. In this context of change, there was no possibility that the PSI project could have some tangible impact in terms of enhancing local institutional capacities for policy analysis and design.

Before the institutional shake-up at INE, however, the PSI project had achieved some moderate successes from which lessons may also be drawn. Part of its success hinges on the fact that the project deliberately sought to build upon existing local initiatives involving the collection, processing and interpretation of survey data, thereby contributing to ongoing efforts to strengthen the country's indigenous research capacity for poverty analysis. Together with the work funded by the World Bank and other international organisations, the studies sponsored by UNDP were able to introduce new concepts, ideas and approaches that have helped to enrich the understanding of poverty and gender in Angola.

A key factor in ensuring the quality and policy relevance of the PSI studies was the participation of local researchers with solid training and experience. At the time the UNDP project was launched, the choice of INE as the main focal point was amply justified. INE had a small cadre of experts who, given their institutional location within the Ministry of Planning, could have played an essential bridging role between research and analysis, on the one hand, and their application on the other. These capacities were not created by the PSI project; they already existed within the INE. What the project made possible was taking advantage of the existing skills in order to carry out new analyses on topics that had not received adequate attention from policy-makers.

In fact, the analytical work commissioned by UNDP was intended to serve as a building block for the preparation of Angola's first national poverty reduction strategy. Had this process not been discontinued, it might have led to the development of a genuinely home-grown national anti-poverty strategy.

There are still some encouraging signs that the question of poverty has begun to gain greater recognition, both in policy circles and with the public at large. In this context, the PSI studies could still prove to be a valuable instrument with which to engage key decision-makers in a process of public discussion and debate. A major constraint, however, is the absence of technically qualified middle management personnel in government ministries. This may preclude the translation of analytical inputs into concrete policy and programme initiatives, and thus underscores the need to focus future efforts on training staff in the ministries and other government agencies in order to make a more substantive policy dialogue possible.

Furthermore, and given the fragile nature of government institutions described in the chapter, it would be useful to explore the possibility of targeting future initiatives to civil society actors as well. A central goal should be to strengthen their capacity for negotiation and advocacy, and to ensure that they become more actively involved as pressure groups in the process of triangulation between the experts and researchers who carry out the analytical work and those within the government who take decisions.

To make this possible, it is important to ensure that after the research phase of a project is completed, there is sufficient space for a period of reflection, analysis and absorption of its results by local actors. International organisations tend to operate under tight timetables, which normally conflict with processes that may take longer to mature and bear fruit. This often undercuts the possibility of achieving some tangible policy outcomes based on the research conducted.

Therefore, international organisations will need to make provisions in their project budgets and time-frame to allow this period of reflection and analysis to take place. Without it, it is unlikely that the knowledge generated by the research they support will be assimilated and applied in the policy arena. If government institutions lack the necessary capacity to translate the results of operational research into actual policies, then an effort must be made to ensure that this task is done elsewhere. Angola has a small but highly qualified group of academics who could play this role. But for this, they will need support, continuity, and space for critical thinking. ■

Notes

The author would like to acknowledge Alexander Aboagye and Joao Freire from the UNDP office in Luanda as well as Alejandro Grinspun, UNDP, New York.

[1] Although it appears that this 'package' of activities was overly ambitious, by the end of 1999 all had been completed. With the exception of the study on *Poverty Alleviation Policy in Angola* (Wold and Grave 1999), which was published in both Portuguese and English, all the other studies were produced in Portuguese alone. Even the workshops on gender statistics were organised and carried out within the limits imposed by the country's war environment, in other words, in areas where it was possible and safe to go. Other areas were apparently too dangerous to visit.

[2] The imbalances caused by the transition from a socialist to a market economy are also among the reasons for the increase in poverty. Under the previous system, people were assured of a minimum threshold of wellbeing that included health services, education and free housing.

[3] In 1994, for instance, defence and internal security absorbed 56.5 per cent of the public budget, administrative expenditures another 29 per cent, while the health and education sectors received 3.4 per cent and 2.6 per cent, respectively.

[4] According to the former director of the INE, most non-governmental organisations in Angola are engaged mainly in the provision of social services, where the practice of advocacy is practically non-existent. Consequently, these organisations cannot be considered to be real users of the studies sponsored by the PSI project. These studies are bound to be most useful for those who are engaged in advocacy activities on regular basis, which is not the case among local civil society entities.

[5] The PSI funding would not have been sufficient to conduct the household income and expenditure survey, which was very expensive. But that funding was nonetheless crucial for carrying out the analysis of the data furnished by the survey.

9 Mali, Mauritania and São Tomé e Principe

Pierre Hassan Sanon

Like many other sub-Saharan African countries, Mali, Mauritania and São Tomé e Principe face a huge debt burden that severely constrains their development prospects. The weight imposed by debt servicing drains scarce fiscal resources that could most effectively be devoted to financing programmes to address the vast scale of deprivation affecting a large portion of their population.

By many estimates, these countries are among the world's poorest, a fact that renders their high indebtedness even more poignant. The bulk of their foreign debt is composed of public as well as private debt guaranteed by the state. Servicing this debt makes it virtually impossible to balance the budget or the balance-of-payments account, and leaves very few resources for discretionary spending.

In attempts to meet their debt-servicing obligations while simultaneously addressing national financial needs, the three governments have had to constantly negotiate with their lenders the rescheduling of their debt. Having benefited from the debt reduction measures implemented since 1996 by the World Bank and the International Monetary Fund (IMF), Mali, Mauritania and São Tomé are now eligible for debt relief under the enhanced Heavily Indebted Poor Countries (HIPC) Initiative, announced at a Group of Seven meeting in Cologne, Germany, in June 1999. Central to the enhanced HIPC Initiative is the requirement that countries prepare a Poverty Reduction Strategy Paper (PRSP), which has to be endorsed by the Boards of the Bank and IMF before a debt reduction package can be approved. In addition to preparing a PRSP, countries need to establish a satisfactory track record of economic performance, normally over a period of three years, under the IMF's Poverty Reduction and Growth Facility (PRGF).

The three countries became eligible for debt relief during 2000: Mauritania was approved in February, Mali in September, and São Tomé in December of that year. In order to qualify for the enhanced HIPC, the government of São Tomé e Principe first had to negotiate a three-year lending agreement with the Fund under the terms of its PRGF facility, which was approved in April 2000. By taking advantage of the debt relief conditions set by the enhanced HIPC initiative, Mali, Mauritania and São Tomé should be able to free resources for the financing of development activities aimed at the reduction of poverty. However, to do so, they first need to have a full strategy in place, with clear and measurable targets as well as mechanisms for monitoring progress towards meeting them.

This chapter examines the experience, results and impact of the Poverty Strategies Initiative (PSI), a programme sponsored by the United Nations Development Programme (UNDP) to assist countries like Mali, Mauritania and São Tomé e Principe in the preparation of national strategies and action plans against poverty. The first section presents a general overview of the socio-economic and political situation in each of the countries. Next the activities sponsored by UNDP in these countries are described. Section three analyses the extent to which PSI activities have built indigenous capacity for policy design and implementation. The fourth section examines the processes followed in each country for diagnosing poverty and elaborating policy for addressing it. The chapter concludes by summarising the main results of the PSI projects and suggesting a role for UN agencies in supporting countries in the PRSP exercise.

Social and economic background

Although each country has a markedly different historical legacy, all three share certain similarities that have limited their potential for development and impacted poverty. Despite their huge size, Mali and Mauritania share a harsh climate and physical environment characterised by the encroaching desert, which occupies the bulk of their territory. As a result, they each have an extremely low population density of 7.7 and 2.3 inhabitants per square kilometre, respectively. The archipelago of São Tomé e Principe, on the other hand, is characterised by geographic isolation and a high population density of 135 inhabitants per square kilometre.

Apart from their high level of indebtedness, the three countries also have weakly diversified economic bases. Despite its inhospitable land, Mali relies heavily on agriculture, which employs about 80 per cent of the active population and provides 42 per cent of the gross domestic product (GDP). Cotton, the lease of cattle and, more recently, gold, provide the backbone of export revenues. Although agriculture and mining also play critical roles in Mauritania, its coastline permits deriving significant wealth from fishing and other maritime activities. However, because wealth is concentrated in the hands of a small elite, high levels of inequality persist. São Tomé, too, depends heavily on agriculture, notably cocoa and coffee production, although fishing, tourism and oil exploitation have also become important.

São Tomé e Principe experienced a negative growth rate of -1.1 between 1990 and 1998. Per capita income averages less than US$270 annually, about one third of the economically active population is unemployed, and almost half of the population lives below the official poverty line of $220. Mali's average income per capita of US$250 per year (1998) makes it one of the world's poorest countries.

Between 1990 and 1998, the GNP per capita average annual growth rate was estimated at 0.5 per cent, in part because of the ravages of recurrent civil war, which ended only in 1997, and contributed to the country's high unemployment. In Mauritania, where GNP per capita grew by a mere 1.1 per cent per annum between 1989 and 1999, the unemployment rate was estimated at 23 per cent in 1997 (UNDP 2000).

Given these factors, poverty abounds far beyond income parameters. In Mali, where a staggering 70 per cent of the population lives on less than $1 per day, infant mortality claims 144 deaths for every thousand live births, and adult literacy amounts to only 38.2 per cent. Similar indicators characterise Mauritania, where the percentage of people under the national poverty line is 57 per cent (UNDP 2000). Although life expectancy in São Tomé e Principe is 64 years and infant mortality stands at 60 per 1000 live births, the negative growth rate throughout the 1990s offers little hope of bringing the vast majority out of poverty.

Existing poverty, combined with high levels of indebtedness and misallocations of the state budget, have impacted levels of national spending on health and education. In both Mali (1999) and São Tomé (1997) only 10 per cent of the national budget goes to health care, while in Mauritania the figure is a low 7.8 per cent (1997). The spread of the HIV/AIDS pandemic could stretch under-funded systems to the breaking point.

As in most countries, poverty has pronounced gender and age dimensions. Malian women and children stand at greatest risk. Similarly, poverty in São Tomé e Principe particularly affects single mothers and their children, as well as the elderly. Another vulnerable group in both São Tomé and Mauritania is composed of people working in the informal sector. Although data are highly unreliable, it is estimated that as many as three out of five people in São Tomé work in such occupations. In Mauritania, just under half of the people involved in informal sector activities are poor.

Despite the dismal economic outlook, there are signs of hope in other areas. All three countries have re-established constitutional democratic regimes. Civil society — including unions, political parties and non-governmental organisations (NGOs) — has developed rapidly over recent years. In São Tomé and Principe, where multiparty elections took place in 1998, there were nearly one hundred community-based organisations, a blossoming particularly notable in the face of the lack of material institutional, financial and human capacity. In Mali, the military coup of 1991 that removed President Moussa Traoré from power cleared the way for reforms that have opened up possibilities for democratic change. Mauritania's adoption of a new constitution in 1991 was followed by institutional reforms that led to the establishment of a multiparty system, an independent press, presidential and congressional elections, and the establishment of republican institutions.

Tackling poverty

It has been argued that it is impossible to achieve any significant reduction of poverty in countries bypassed by economic growth. The programmes aimed at promoting socio-economic development implemented so far by governments and donors in Mali, Mauritania and São Tomé have generally failed to translate into concrete gains for their people. Given the severe constraints imposed by their limited natural endowments, these countries may have little choice but to invest in their people so as to lay the grounds for long-term development — rather than simply awaiting growth as a precondition of declines in poverty rates.

As one of the largest donors, UNDP has been involved in poverty reduction activities in these countries for many years. With their local funds, the UNDP offices have assisted their national partners in the formulation and implementation of a range of projects targeted at poor people. In recent years, UNDP has stepped up its involvement in poverty reduction and has increasingly shifted towards providing policy advice for the development of sector studies and programmes. The PSI programme reinforced this tendency by encouraging the UNDP offices to utilise a small amount of resources as an instrument for leveraging policy change. Such change should result from encouraging the design of national anti-poverty strategies and programmes under the leadership of the country's authorities.

In each country, PSI resources financed technical assistance for evaluations of existing programmes, compilations of poverty-related data and consultations with vulnerable groups — all of which should provide a basis for formulating nationally owned poverty reduction strategies. PSI activities aimed at building on what existed and vesting locally the analytical and policy work financed by the programme. National ownership, it was felt, was a necessary condition for achieving success in reforming policies in favour of poverty reduction. Without such ownership, it would be unlikely that national authorities would sustain their commitment to implementing the strategies and programmes developed. Establishing an institutional set-up with a clear mandate for coordinating, monitoring and evaluating public sector — and, in some cases, non-governmental — interventions against poverty was another key priority of the PSI programme.

Mali achieved the greatest progress in meeting these goals. There, the government approached UNDP for assistance in evaluating a national programme for poverty reduction that had been in place since 1994. After conducting a series of sector and other diagnostic studies to assess achievements as well as gaps in the implementation of the programme, the evaluation concluded by pointing to a number of critical issues that had hampered the success of the government's actions. The most important ones referred to an imprecise definition of programme priorities, weak implementation capacity, inadequate financing for key programmes, and an absence of mechanisms for monitoring poverty and feeding back data to decision-makers.

In addition to this evaluation, UNDP joined with UNICEF and UNFPA to assist the Ministry of Economy and Planning and a team of six national experts in the preparation of a social sector expenditure review. The study, which was carried out in 1998, analysed trends in public finances for the period 1986-1996, paying particular attention to the share of the government's budget devoted to financing basic services in health, education, nutrition, water and sanitation. The review also covered aid flows to assess whether donors — as well as the government — were meeting the targets set by the so-called 20/20 Initiative (chapter 7, this volume). Determining the scope for inter- as well as intra-sectoral restructuring of public expenditures and aid flows in favour of basic social service provision was a key goal of the expenditure review.

A separate study conducted jointly with UNICEF focussed on street children, particularly in Bamako. Forced by poverty to abandon their schooling, many children end up living in the streets where they become particularly susceptible to infectious diseases and other risks (chapter 3, this volume). The study interviewed some of these children to gather information on their needs and characteristics as an input to the design of programmes specifically tailored to meet those needs. Still a fourth output of the PSI project in Mali analysed the policy and regulatory framework for engaging civil society and community organisations as partners in the fight against poverty.

All of the above studies and the evaluation served as inputs into the elaboration of Mali's *Stratégie Nationale de Lutte contre la Pauvreté* (SNLP) — the country's official anti-poverty policy. Completed in 1998, the SNLP is the result of a two-year long process of consultation and validation involving a broad range of national actors — with the support of the entire UN system in Mali. The intensely consultative process followed in the elaboration of the *Stratégie* has undoubtedly contributed to creating a strong sense of ownership among Malian officials, who regard the SNLP as a home-grown document that responds to the country's needs and priorities. During a mission conducted in late 1999, officials from IMF and the World Bank were presented with the SNLP as the government's framework for negotiating Mali's access to debt relief under the enhanced HIPC Initiative. The elaboration of a Poverty Reduction Strategy Paper (PRSP) will therefore build upon the existing national strategy developed with assistance from UN agencies.

A similar project took place in Mauritania, where the government decided that it needed an evaluation of the national programme that had been implemented from 1992 to 1996 as the basis for a new anti-poverty programme. As in Mali, the evaluation noted a number of institutional lacunae that had obstructed coordination between public and non-public actions to address poverty.

The main outcome of the PSI project in Mauritania was the elaboration of a new government anti-poverty programme — the *Programme National de Lutte contre la*

Pauvreté (PNLCP), which provides guidance for the actions of the national authorities from 1998 to 2001. Unlike the previous programme, the new one specifies an institutional mechanism vested with the responsibility for coordinating the work on poverty in the country. Of particular importance in this respect was the creation of a *Commissariat des Droits de l'Homme et Lutte contre la Pauvreté* (CDHLP) with cabinet rank for the task of policy and programme coordination. Despite lingering doubts about the technical capacity of the *Commissariat* to perform these functions, a first step has been taken towards ensuring that poverty reduction receives a higher priority than in the past.

Mauritania's PNLCP has not only been used as a basis for discussions with the Bank and the Fund on the interim PRSP, approved in February 2000; it has also had a catalytic effect on the formulation of two essential projects in 1998. The first is the *Projet de promotion des initiatives locales*, which aims to develop micro-enterprises, build or rehabilitate schools and dispensaries, and improve the supply of drinking water. The second initiative is the establishment of a Social Fund for Poverty Reduction, which will provide grant funding for community infrastructure and equipment upon the submission of project proposals by local communities and non-governmental organisations.

Limited local capacities and a changing political environment have conspired against achieving similar progress in developing anti-poverty policy in São Tomé e Principe. On the basis of a representative sample of different categories of vulnerable groups located in various zones of the country, the PSI project financed a series of 'consultations' aimed at identifying their needs and gathering proposals for addressing them. A team of Belgian experts provided the technical know-how, and trained local staff in the use of participatory research methodology to enable them to conduct similar exercises in the future. As an additional input into the formulation of policy, the project also assisted in the compilation and consolidation of all data sources relating to poverty in São Tomé.

The next phase of the PSI project involved the elaboration of a strategic outline for poverty reduction, the *Cadre Stratégique de Lutte contre la Pauvreté*. The document is very succinct, and does not provide specifics on such important issues as the financing requirements, the implementation modalities or the institutional mechanisms required for managing and coordinating poverty reduction activities. It is possible that what the country needed most at that time was simply a framework document outlining a few policy priorities as a basis for a discussion with national authorities and a means of raising awareness about poverty. Clearly, the document could not have served as an instrument for guiding the implementation of anti-poverty actions.

At the time, São Tomé was embarking upon negotiations for an IMF loan and has since been approved for debt relief under the terms of the enhanced HIPC

Initiative. Given this context, the work sponsored by UNDP could provide the basis for the negotiations with the lending institutions. Much work is needed, however, before the government of São Tomé has a national anti-poverty strategy with clearly defined targets and concrete mechanisms for implementing the actions required.

Capacity development

Neither Mali's SNLP nor Mauritania's PNLCP or São Tomé's *Cadre Stratégique de Lutte contre la Pauvreté* constitutes an umbrella poverty reduction programme separate from and encompassing all other government actions. They are primarily strategic frameworks that seek to enhance coherence and coordination among the various macroeconomic and sectoral policy instruments implemented in each country, as well as to align the actions of the donor community behind nationally defined poverty reduction targets. Mali's *Stratégie Nationale*, for example, builds upon a range of sector-specific policies including a gender component (*Plan National d'Action pour la Promotion de la Femme 1996-2000*), an education component (*Programme Décennal de Développement de l'Education 1998-2007*), as well as additional components on health (*Programme Décennal de Développement Sanitaire et Social 1998-2007*), environment (*Plan National d'Action Environnementale*), and food security (*Plan d'Action National sur l'Alimentation et la Nutrition*). Similar components exist in Mauritania, and are being developed in São Tomé e Principe.

Because each of the anti-poverty strategies was conceived as a cross-sectoral instrument, these countries faced the need to develop adequate coordination mechanisms that could ensure a proper alignment of all governmental and donor interventions with the poverty reduction targets set in the strategies. For the same reasons, they had to establish nationwide systems for regular gathering and analysis of poverty data so as to enable a systematic monitoring of progress in meeting those targets.

Although the PSI projects were not primarily capacity-building exercises, they still made some contributions towards establishing the technical and institutional foundations for policy implementation. This was perhaps most prominent in relation to improving poverty-related data collection. In Mali particularly, and to a lesser extent in the other two countries, there is a great diversity of survey instruments and data sources on poverty. Harmonising existing socio-economic data so as to permit an adequate analysis and monitoring of poverty is a problem that hampers the development of policy. Solving this problem requires setting up a well-integrated system that collects data from various sources throughout the country.

Steps in this direction have been taken in all three countries. In Mali, assistance from UNDP had led to the creation of an *Observatoire du Développement Humain et Lutte contre la Pauvreté* in 1996. Staff from the *Observatoire* was involved in the PSI project, specifically in gathering and analysing data on poverty that fed into the elaboration of the SNLP. This participation strengthened the technical capacity of the experts from the *Observatoire*, and their expertise can now be put to good use with the decision to implement a Poverty Analysis and Monitoring Information System (*Système d'Information pour le Suivi et l'Analyse de la Pauvreté*, or SISAP) as one of the cornerstones of the PRSP.

A poverty monitoring system similar to Mali's is being set up in Mauritania — although in this case, there were no specific contributions from the PSI project. In São Tomé, as mentioned earlier, the compilation of data on poverty and its consolidation into a single document may be considered an essential first step towards rationalising poverty information in the country. Indeed, this work proved its usefulness as soon as it was completed. The African Development Bank was able to build upon it when assisting in the creation of a unit to monitor poverty within the National Statistics Office.

In Mauritania, as well as in Mali, UNDP assistance also helped reinforce existing mechanisms for coordinating the planning and implementation of the government's anti-poverty policy. In Mauritania, a department within the Ministry of Planning that had received assistance from UNDP for managing the government's poverty reduction programme from 1992 to 1996 was transformed into the newly created *Commissariat des Droits de l'Homme et Lutte contre la Pauvreté* and given ministerial status. Its new mandate encompasses the oversight, coordination and monitoring of the national anti-poverty programme covering the period 1998-2001. Although the decision to establish the *Commissariat* cannot be attributed directly to the PSI project, the latter certainly did play a role in convincing the national authorities of the need for a high-level government structure capable of coordinating the actions of other ministries as well as non-governmental entities. The *Commissariat* is also responsible for coordinating external aid to Mauritania — a fact that may facilitate the mobilisation of donor resources to fill the financing gaps of the new poverty reduction programme.

PSI activities in Mali maintained close collaboration with the two committees created by the government to oversee, coordinate and monitor the implementation of the SNLP — the *Comité d'Orientation* and the *Comité National de Coordination et de Suivi*, respectively. The institutional framework in Mali seems to be further developed than in Mauritania, and definitely more so than in São Tomé e Principe. Both committees have a tripartite composition that encompasses members from the government, civil society, bilateral donors and specialised agencies. In addition, 30 focal points located in the technical ministries, as well as in the country's main non-governmental and trade union organisations, provide yet another layer of coordination and validation that may prove essential to the implementation of the SNLP.

In contrast to Mali and Mauritania, there are no such coordination mechanisms in place in São Tomé, where the main impetus for the elaboration of a national policy against poverty came from donors rather than the government, which was facing presidential elections during the course of the PSI project. The Ministry of Finance has in the meantime assumed a lead role in the PRSP process. This seems a sensible choice, given the ministry's involvement in negotiating a PRGF loan from the IMF. To ensure proper coordination with other ministries, however, it may be advisable to establish an institutional framework that cuts across the respective jurisdictions and responsibilities of the various line ministries.

Consultation, ownership and partnerships

A truly national strategy requires ownership. Strategic priorities need to be chosen in consultation; actions proposed have to be validated; and efforts from all local partners must be summoned for implementing these priority actions. This is arguably the most important ingredient for ensuring the sustainability of policy decisions.

PSI activities set out to promote processes of local consultation in the elaboration of the respective national programmes and strategies in each of these countries. The expectation was that consultative processes would enhance local ownership, which in turn would establish the foundations for a balanced partnership between a country's authorities and its donors. The extent to which consultations took place, however, varied from one country to another.

Once again, Mali stands out as the most successful of these countries. The organisation of five regional seminars was one of the main contributions of the PSI project. High-level officials from the Ministry of Finance and specialists from the *Observatoire* conducted the seminars, which were held in the western city of Kayes, Sikasso in the south, Gao in the east, and Ségou and Mopti in the centre of Mali's vast territory. The seminars took place at different stages during the preparation of the *Stratégie Nationale* so as to garner the views of the local communities, authorities and non-governmental actors, validate the overall direction of the strategy and mobilise support for its subsequent implementation. Documents were translated into local languages and disseminated through the media and the written press. Inputs from these consultations were fed back into refining the policy thrust that the national strategy embodied, culminating in a national workshop at which the final document was presented to the public. Not surprisingly, the process followed in producing the SNLP has generated a strong sense of commitment from the entire spectrum of Malian society — and is highly regarded by all the actors involved.

The establishment of coordination mechanisms open to the participation of various actors gave further impetus to the sense of ownership emanating from the elaboration of the SNLP. By a decree of 1999, the government created the *Comité de Coordination et de Suivi* and the *Comité d'Orientation* for the steering and monitoring of the national strategy. Representatives from government, civil society and the donor community sit on both committees, which meet regularly to review the status of discussions with lending institutions as well as the implementation of SNLP priorities. As mentioned earlier, Mali has also instituted a system of focal points in each ministry, whose mission is to mobilise and coordinate the actions of all the relevant departments so that they conform to the goals established in the SNLP. At the local level, moreover, non-governmental organisations act as an interface between government authorities and the community in support of specific programmes.

Strong national ownership has provided a solid foundation for a partnership between Mali and its external donors. As a result of the social sector expenditure review sponsored by UNDP, UNICEF and UNFPA, the Ministry of Finance has set ambitious targets for budgetary allocations for primary education and health care, and identified financing gaps that Mali's donors could assist in meeting. The resources that the government is in a position to mobilise for the SNLP amount to only half of its financial requirements; without financial assistance from donors, the poverty reduction targets contained in the SNLP will not be achieved.

For this reason, Mali's aid consortium convened a Round Table meeting in September 1998 to review the recently completed SNLP and to pledge financial support for the government's plans. The 1998 Round Table was also the occasion for discussing a reform of the aid system so as to improve the targeting of external resources to support Mali's national priorities, most prominently the implementation of the SNLP.

PSI activities in São Tomé e Principe set out to promote a consultative process similar to that of Mali. The country, however, was in the midst of elections that ushered in a multi-party system — and this context proved much less conducive to a broad-based public debate on poverty. Nonetheless, UNDP sponsored five public events to discuss the content of the *Cadre Stratégique de Lutte contre la Pauvreté*. Four district workshops took place initially (three in São Tomé and one in Principe), culminating in a national seminar with the participation of government, civil society and donor representatives.

The results of the PSI project, it is claimed, have informed the formulation of policy both for the short- and medium-term. They were used, for instance, in the Public Investment Programme and the *Plan d'Actions Prioritaires* 2000-2002, as well as for São Tomé's Strategic Options for the year 2005, a document outlining a series of mid-term macroeconomic and sector priorities for the country. The government also presented the *Cadre Stratégique* to the IMF when negotiating a PRGF package prior to qualifying for HIPC debt assistance in December 2000. It is far from clear, however, that the activities carried out under the PSI project have enjoyed the same degree of local ownership that they have in Mali. Because of a lack of indigenous capacity, external experts were responsible for most project activities, even though some training of local personnel took place. The congressional elections of

1998, moreover, limited the involvement of government officials in critical phases of the project. These two factors combined to curtail prospects for vesting the policy process initiated by UNDP in the local context.

In Mauritania, too, the process of preparing the *Programme National de Lutte contre la Pauvreté* seems to have been less inclusive than in Mali. Some consultations took place during its preparation, and a national workshop gave all partners (central government, civil society, community groups, and bilateral and multilateral donors) an opportunity to debate the programme prior to its finalisation.

The government of Mauritania feels strong ownership of the PNLCP, which it used as the basis for the interim PRSP — and the *Commissariat* is fully committed to implementing the tasks it has been called upon to perform. Indeed, the country's donors have acknowledged the government's efforts by pledging financial support to the programme at the Third Consultative Group for Mauritania, which was held in March 1998. Further support came forth with the Bank's and the Fund's approval of Mauritania's qualification for debt relief in February 2000.

Nevertheless, the PNLCP lacks an institutional framework such as the one established in Mali for the SNLP. Despite the government's firm commitment, implementation capacities seem limited, coordination of policies set by the various line ministries inadequate, and systems for monitoring poverty underdeveloped. As in São Tomé and even Mali, these are clearly critical entry points for any future assistance from development organisations to these as well as other sub-Saharan African countries.

Conclusions

Donor organisations and lending institutions finance a substantial portion of the development budgets of Mali, Mauritania and São Tomé e Principe — as well as many other poor countries in Africa and elsewhere. Lending institutions also exert strong influence over the terms under which these countries can access external resources to finance their development needs. Donors therefore can hold enormous sway over poor countries' policies — and put this influence to good use or, alternatively, aggravate existing problems if they do not coordinate their actions.

Often, the pursuit of differing, even conflicting, agendas by individual donors has stretched the already limited capacities of these countries beyond their ability to function. This problem is further compounded when those agendas impose certain requirements and time-frames that may conflict with the planning frameworks set by the countries themselves. For this reason, one of the greatest contributions donors can make is to provide the space in which nationally driven processes of policy formation can develop.

PSI activities were valuable in this regard. Particularly in Mali and Mauritania, they built upon existing policy initiatives, whose strengths and weaknesses they helped evaluate as an input to the development of new policy. The PSI projects also sought to strengthen home-grown coordination mechanisms that could steer the policy process forward — and particularly in Mali, they endeavoured to foster nationwide consensus on the policy thrust put forward by the government.

Through public information campaigns (Mali and Mauritania), social mobilisation of vulnerable groups (Mali, São Tomé) and the organization of workshops and seminars with broad-based representation, PSI activities in all three countries helped create awareness of and commitment to the emerging national poverty reduction plans. The development of Mali's poverty reduction strategy took almost two years to complete. The end result was the *Stratégie Nationale de Lutte contre la Pauvreté*, a comprehensive document outlining eight priority areas that has provided the basis for Mali's interim PRSP and its qualification for debt relief under HIPC terms. The decision reached by the IMF and the World Bank in September 2000 to provide interim debt relief to the government of Mali will make it possible to release much-needed resources for essential programmes instead of repaying the debt. Further support from Mali's international lenders will be necessary, though, if the country is to come even close to addressing the vast scale of deprivation that affects as much as three-fourths of its population who survive on less than US$ 1 per day.

While less inclusive in its formulation, Mauritania's new *Programme National de Lutte contre la Pauvreté* represents the continuation of government efforts initiated in 1992. Evaluating the government's actions during four years of implementing anti-poverty actions provided the foundation for the PNLCP, paving the way for the Bank's and the Fund's approval of a debt relief package for Mauritania in early 2000. As in Mali, therefore, the assistance provided by UNDP proved critical during the negotiations with the Bretton Woods institutions. The respective governments simply had to validate their existing poverty reduction programmes with the World Bank and IMF before they could become eligible for debt relief.

São Tomé differs from Mali and Mauritania in many respects. The country's socio-economic and political context, combined with its extremely limited base of indigenous expertise, made it extremely difficult to make great strides on the anti-poverty policy front. These constraints notwithstanding, the assistance provided by UNDP resulted in the adoption of a framework document, the *Cadre Stratégique de Lutte contre la Pauvreté*, which subsequently served as an input into the elaboration of São Tomé's interim PRSP. On this basis, the country was first able to successfully conclude negotiations for a PRGF loan from the IMF, and subsequently to qualify for HIPC assistance following World Bank and Fund decisions adopted in December 2000.

After all the preliminary work conducted in the three countries, UNDP must continue to support the respective governments in their negotiations with IMF and the World Bank over the design and implementation of national anti-poverty strategies. Already in São Tomé, the government has requested UNDP assistance in the presentation of its case to the Bretton Woods institutions. In Mali and Mauritania, too, success in reducing poverty will depend on developing local capacities for policy analysis and implementation, including through the establishment of permanent poverty monitoring systems already in progress. Above all, the continued involvement of UN agencies, particularly those concerned with human development goals, will be critical to ensuring that macroeconomic agendas are fully consonant with the objective of poverty reduction set by the countries. ■

Notes

Mr. Sanon is a social development specialist who works as an independent consultant. He wishes to acknowledge the government and UNDP offices of Mali, Mauritania and São Tomé e Principe, as well as the staff of the former Social Development Division, UNDP, New York.

10 Lesotho, Uganda, Zambia and Maldives

Julian May

During the late 1990s, poverty was once again placed on the international agenda. This time, however, governments of poor countries are expected to take a far more proactive stance, preparing poverty profiles, developing policy frameworks, and implementing action plans and strategies for poverty reduction. These have become key requirements in a range of negotiations between poor countries and international donors. Most recently, the Heavily Indebted Poor Countries (HIPC) Initiative has made the establishment and monitoring of poverty reduction targets and the elaboration of a Poverty Reduction Strategy Paper (PRSP) a condition for obtaining debt relief and concessional assistance from the World Bank and the International Monetary Fund (IMF). Most PRSP countries are in sub-Saharan Africa, where the capacity to either formulate, implement or monitor a poverty reduction strategy is very limited. Assistance from donor organisations has also been limited, with few exceptions. One such exception was the Poverty Strategies Initiative (PSI), a programme implemented by the United Nations Development Programme (UNDP) to support the efforts of developing countries to diagnose poverty and develop policy for reducing it.

This chapter assesses the results and impact of PSI activities in three countries from sub-Saharan Africa (Lesotho, Uganda and Zambia) and one Indian Ocean country (Maldives). While different in many respects, the four countries share the formidable task of having to respond to the vast unmet needs of their population with scarce national resources and capacities. In the three African countries, the spread of HIV/AIDS has stretched their limited resources and capacities even further. The four cases differ with regard to the impact of PSI activities on poverty analysis and policy design. From this point of view, the comprehensive data-gathering exercise conducted in Maldives seems to offer valuable lessons for the three land-locked African countries.[1]

The first section briefly presents the context of each of the PSI projects. The following section describes the PSI activities in each country and examines their impact on poverty research and policy formation. Next we focus on three critical issues: capacity development, government ownership, and policy coordination, calling attention to the importance of revisiting the notion of 'government' as a unified whole. Finally, the chapter distils some lessons from the experience of these countries to inform donor policies for similar initiatives in the future.

Background

Lesotho has an extremely fragile economy based on subsistence agriculture, livestock and remittances from miners employed in South Africa. In 1993, nearly half of the population was considered poor. The crisis of the South African gold mining industry during the 1990s has led to large-scale retrenchments and a drastic decline in the number of mine workers, thereby increasing the vulnerability of remittance-dependent households. Many rural families have moved to the city, particularly to the capital Maseru, where informal activities have mushroomed — as evidenced by the growing numbers of street vendors who eke out an existence by selling their wares. Lesotho's rapid rate of urbanisation, which exceeds that of its neighbouring countries, has turned urban development into a major concern for the government. The uncontrolled expansion of urban shack settlements around Maseru is encroaching onto arable land and leading to the emergence of serious health problems, which the government has been incapable of addressing. Furthermore, riots broke out in the country's major towns in 1998, destroying 80 per cent of their commercial infrastructure.

Despite mounting urban problems, the bulk of poverty research in the past had focussed on Lesotho's rural poor. There were nine poverty assessments between 1991 and 1997, including two studies conducted by an indigenous institution and three by the World Bank. All of them concentrated on poverty in the rural areas, where 80 per cent of the population live. To fill the gap in knowledge about poverty in urban areas, UNDP decided to commission an *Urban Poverty Assessment* (UPA) in 1997. The assessment consisted of a quantitative survey, a qualitative research component and a policy review focussed on the capital Maseru and two other lowland towns (Lesotho 1997).

Uganda's resource base is much richer than Lesotho's. The country boasts substantial natural resources, including fertile soils, regular rainfall and considerable mineral deposits of copper and cobalt. For more than a decade, the government has sought to rehabilitate and stabilise a war-torn economy. Currency and civil service reform, price liberalisation on export crops, and removal of subsidies on petroleum products have combined to produce a remarkable economic growth rate of 6.5 per cent per annum during most of the 1990s, which was accompanied by a drop in the incidence of absolute poverty. Nevertheless, levels of poverty have remained high, affecting almost 55 per cent of the population. Poverty rates, moreover, vary widely from one region of the country to another, ranging from 28 to 59 per cent in 1997, and the poorest 20 per cent of the population actually became poorer between 1992 and 1996, especially in the countryside (Uganda 1999). This suggests that the policies introduced with substantial support from the international lending institutions have failed to benefit a large proportion of Uganda's poor.

In 1999, the government decided to carry out a poverty assessment to lay the ground for revising the national Poverty Eradication Action Plan (PEAP) prepared in 1997. The UK Department for International Development (DfID) provided the bulk of funding for the Uganda Participatory Poverty Assessment Project (UPPAP), which involved a series of district poverty assessments implemented in Kampala, Kapchorwa and Kumi (Uganda 1999a, 1999b, 1999c). The project was a collective undertaking. Oxfam UK acted as the implementing agency, recruiting local experts who were based in the powerful Ministry of Finance. UNDP's financial contribution was minor, yet critical to the project's success. It helped resolve the issue of where to locate UPPAP, and to disseminate the findings of the district poverty assessments and the government's anti-poverty plan. Both these contributions played a significant role in stimulating local ownership, as well as in linking poverty research and analysis with the design and implementation of policy.

Zambia, too, has high levels of human deprivation. According to the national *Human Development Report* (Zambia 1998a), over 69 per cent of the population fell below a money metric poverty line in 1996, rising to more than 80 per cent of the population in some provinces. Income distribution is extremely skewed: five per cent Zambians receive almost half the national income. If anything, standards of living deteriorated further during the 1990s. Life expectancy at birth has dropped, and most measures of mortality remain among the highest in sub-Saharan Africa. The prospects for economic growth are bleak, despite progress in privatisation and budgetary reform. The copper mining sector, which accounts for over 80 per cent of Zambia's foreign currency receipts, is still struggling to cope with declining production rates and slack world copper prices. The external debt is almost 200 per cent of annual GNP and, out of concern for the November 1996 elections, most donors cut their aid programmes, further worsening the country's economic prospects.

In 1997, the President mandated the Ministry of Community Development and Social Services (MCDSS) to coordinate the preparation of a policy framework for the reduction of poverty, transferring this responsibility away from the Department of Population in Development of the Ministry of Finance, which had until then been the government's coordinating mechanism. A committee was set up to develop, first, a National Poverty Reduction Strategic Framework (NPRSF) and, subsequently, a National Poverty Reduction Action Plan (NPRAP). Both activities received support from UNDP. Here, as in Uganda, the work sponsored by UNDP has provided a foundation for the subsequent negotiations with the World Bank and IMF for accessing debt relief under the terms of the enhanced HIPC Initiative.

Unlike the three sub-Saharan African countries, Maldives is a middle-income country that has experienced sustained economic growth over the last two decades, with an average increase in GDP of eight per cent per annum. Most social indicators such as infant mortality rates, life expectancy and adult literacy rates reflect a dramatic improvement during this period, which sets Maldives — a medium human development country — apart from the other three cases. Nevertheless, Maldives faces extreme environmental fragility, which makes its situation germane to that of many poor African countries. Its fragility stems from a number of attributes associated with the country's peculiar geography: small size, insularity, dispersed population and extreme paucity of land-based natural resources.

Maldives is an archipelago encompassing 26 atolls and 1190 islands, of which some 200 are inhabited. One third of the islands have less than 500 inhabitants, and only 33 are larger than one square kilometre. Not surprisingly, many areas remain under-serviced and have seen little improvement in their quality of life despite sustained economic growth. The government, therefore, is concerned that the benefits of growth have not spread evenly throughout the country, leaving its most remote and vulnerable communities further behind. In edition, erosion and global warming threaten this low-lying country, 80 per cent of whose area is one metre or less above sea level.

These conditions have given rise to various attempts to implement policies of balanced regional development over the years. Nonetheless, lack of reliable, spatially disaggregated data has time and again hampered the initiatives of successive governments. Responding to this situation, UNDP correctly identified the need for a new study as a critical entry point for policy. Thus, the *Maldives Vulnerability and Poverty Assessment* (VPA) was born.

Stimulating poverty research and policy

In every country, UNDP financed analytical work that addressed key current or emerging policy challenges: arresting the rise of urban poverty (Lesotho), promoting sustainable livelihoods (Zambia), redressing regional imbalances (Maldives), and empowering the poor through decentralised governance (Uganda). With varying success, this work helped inform policy-making and led to concrete plans and programmes whose implementation is now in progress.

UNDP financed two specific components of Uganda's Participatory Poverty Assessment project. Government officials, representatives from non-governmental organisations (NGOs) and academics were sent on a study tour to derive lessons from the Tanzania Participatory Poverty Assessment (PPA), which the World Bank had sponsored a few years earlier and was widely regarded as a model for exercises of this kind. The visit to Tanzania, however, revealed many shortcomings in the design of that country's PPA. The government, it was felt, was not utilising the results of the study for policy purposes. Furthermore, the poverty assessments failed to generate much public awareness beyond the small circle of government officials and researchers who had been involved in the project. The exposure Ugandan officials gained from the Tanzanian experience had a major impact on the institutional design of UPPAP, tilting the balance in favour of locating the project within the powerful Ministry of Finance, Planning and Economic Development. This decision turned out to be a crucial factor that facilitated the translation of UPPAP research results into policy design, particularly in the revision of Uganda's anti-poverty plan that the government began in February 2000.

In addition to the study tour, UNDP financed a series of dissemination activities aimed at validating the results of the district poverty assessments and enriching the PEAP review process. PEAP documents were synthesised and translated into the five major vernacular languages, and consultative workshops were held throughout the country with extensive participation from civil society leaders, district authorities and donor representatives. The impact of these workshops can hardly be underestimated. Although poverty had been known to affect a vast proportion of the Ugandan population, particularly in the rural areas, the vivid portrayal of people's predicament through their own voices impacted policy discourse in an unexpected and dramatic manner. The results of the participatory district assessments fed directly into the re-design of PEAP — an outcome that was greatly facilitated by the adoption of a highly inclusive approach for the formulation of policy.

A second stream of activities sponsored by UNDP (jointly with UNICEF) focussed on public and aid financing of basic social services. A team of Ugandan specialists received assistance for a social sector expenditure review, which went beyond simply tracking central government's expenditures in primary health care and basic education to examine a sample of district budgets as well (Opio 1998). The analysis concluded that the government was devoting a substantial proportion of its discretionary spending to the provision of basic social services, and was therefore largely on track to meeting the expenditure targets set by the 20/20 Initiative. At the same time, the report found that the donor community was lagging in some sectors (see chapter 7, this volume).

Despite the relevance of social sector spending for poverty reduction, the impact of the expenditure review on policy was rather limited. The main reason seems related to the timing of the study, which took place when the government's medium-term expenditure planning process was well advanced. By the time the study was completed, the Ministry of Finance had already made its budgetary provisions, thereby precluding the possibility of integrating the results of the expenditure review into its mid-term planning framework.

The formulation of Zambia's NPRSF and NPRAP followed a similarly participatory approach as activities in Uganda. When the government solicited assistance from UNDP, a series of provincial poverty assessments were already under way, with support from the World Bank. By 1997, however, the exercise was complete in only three provinces. The government thought it necessary to expand the consultative process to all provinces. Consequently, provincial workshops took place throughout the country during 1998, culminating in a national workshop with all the country's relevant stakeholders.

The main outcome of the consultative process was the definition of five priority areas for the NPRSF. A second team of consultants was then commissioned to quantify the five priority programmes, identifying the steps and time-frame required to achieve the objectives set in the NPRSF. This exercise resulted in the first draft of the NPRAP, which was submitted to further consultations before a third team of consultants, together with an advisory committee drawn from government and civil society, completed the final draft. The three teams of local consultants used in preparing the NPRSF and NPRAP reported directly to the Ministry of Community Development, given its mandate for coordinating all poverty-reduction work.

As in Uganda, UNDP also financed a social sector expenditure review to examine the share of the government budget and aid programmes spent on the provision of basic services in health, education, nutrition, water and sanitation (Zambia 1998a). A team of local experts carried out the analysis, led by a former Permanent Secretary of Finance. The finding that Zambia was spending a high proportion of its budget on the social sectors (between 25 and 30 per cent), but approximately only 7 per cent on basic services, suggested that the government was not devoting enough of its resources to those areas that benefit poor people most.

Indeed, improving the delivery of primary health care and basic education became key priorities in the interim PRSP the government presented to the Boards of the IMF and the World Bank in mid-2000. Despite increasing attention to those sectors, there remain serious gaps that prevent a systematic monitoring of expenditures on basic social service provision. The Ministry of Finance, for instance, felt the need for establishing a proper database for tracking expenditures from the central down to the provincial level. The same need arises on the donor side because of inadequate coordination amongst donors.

In contrast to Uganda and Zambia, PSI activities in Lesotho failed to link with ongoing policy initiatives, thereby missing an opportunity to assist the government in implementing more rational urban planning. The *Urban Poverty Assessment* began with an extensive review of the available research on poverty, including the three World Bank studies conducted during the 1990s. A questionnaire survey supplemented the literature review. To secure ownership by the government, the team of national and international consultants in charge of the UPA study sought to involve the ministries and departments concerned with urban planning. These were the Ministry of Economic Planning and the Ministry of Local Government, which acted as the project's implementing agency. The study was completed in three months and presented at a workshop convened to evaluate its recommendations. Surprisingly, however, the final report was never formally submitted to the government, which generated a sense of deep frustration among government officials who felt the UPA could have fed into several ongoing planning exercises.

One can only speculate about the reasons why the UPA study was not submitted formally to the authorities. The study clearly addressed an issue of rising concern for the country, which was given added urgency by the events of 1998. Nonetheless, the initiative had not come from the government, but rather from UNDP itself. Changes at the helm of the UNDP office shortly after the final draft was completed may have thus played a role in halting a dialogue that had barely started.

It is also possible that the criticisms levelled at the draft report persuaded UNDP to cancel the project altogether. Workshop participants and other government officials questioned the usefulness of the report. Its recommendations were considered too general for policy action — or, in some cases, too contentious. The report was said to contain serious gaps, focussing only on lowland urban poverty to the neglect of other equally important issues like the urban informal sector or urban agriculture. There was no information on land markets, nor an assessment of the existing policy framework for urban planning. These and other issues raised during the workshop still have not been resolved, and remain a point of contention within the country.

A debate on a new Local Government Act was taking place at the time of the study. The latter could have fed into this process and strengthened it by providing analyses to facilitate the process of establishing local authorities. It seems, however, that the UPA project was unable to develop strong linkages with some key departments such as Local Government and Housing, or with a central coordinating ministry with a mandate for anti-poverty policy. In light of this, UNDP may have deemed it inconvenient to release the urban poverty assessment while the debate on the Local Government Act was taking place. Whatever the reason, the UPA project evidently failed to forge close linkages with existing policy processes or a strategic alliance with some key government entity. In both respects, Lesotho differs from the other, more successful cases reviewed in the chapter.

The contrast with Maldives is especially marked. Here, too, the initiative for the PSI project came largely from UNDP. Due to the almost complete lack of indigenous research capacity, the design of the VPA report was entrusted to a team of international consultants. After a false start using a regional research agency, UNDP appointed a team of experts from the Netherlands who, as in Zambia, reported to a steering committee comprising government as well as UNDP representatives. Local experts, some of whom were in government service, participated at various points of the study as well.

The VPA team took special care in adapting the concepts and methodology used in the study to local conditions. In a country in which communities are widely dispersed over an area 820 km. long and where seasonal shocks can curtail people's livelihoods, conventional notions of poverty provide a poor instrument for policy. Consequently, the study used the concept of *vulnerability* as the starting-point and collected both quantitative and qualitative data for deriving 12 living standard dimensions which, when combined, would result in a synthetic measure of deprivation — the Human Vulnerability Index (HVI) (chapter 2, this volume).

The project began with a lengthy fieldwork procedure, with primary data collection on all inhabited islands of Maldives — making the VPA survey the most comprehensive one ever undertaken in the country, both in terms of geographical coverage and analytical scope. Apart from estimating 12 scalar indices and the HVI at the island and atoll level, the VPA introduced several other methodological innovations. Particularly noteworthy was the use of the opinions of islanders, Women's and Development Committees, and Island Chiefs to assign priority weights for the 12 deprivation indices of the overall HVI. The end result of the exercise was the publication of the VPA report (Maldives 1998), which was accompanied by an electronic database and an atlas of a wide range of indicators of needs and resources covering the country as a whole and each of its constituent atolls.

Capacity development

With the exception of Lesotho, where non-delivery of the *Urban Poverty Assessment* thwarted its potential impact, all PSI activities helped enhance indigenous capacities for policy planning and implementation in varying degrees. Capacity development was certainly not a key goal of the PSI projects — and it would not have been realistic to expect a major impact with such limited funds. Still, government officials and, in some cases, non-governmental actors, have gained a better understanding of poverty and are now better equipped for designing and implementing actions addressed to the poor — or to face complicated negotiations with donors and lenders.

UNDP engagement in Zambia initially aimed to support the Department of Population in Development of the Finance Ministry, which had received a mandate from the cabinet to assist other government departments with preparing action plans against poverty within their respective jurisdictions. The Department was also required to assist the provinces in the preparation of their own development plans. However, UNDP was forced to change tactics following a presidential decree of 1997 that switched this responsibility to the Ministry of Community Development (MCDSS). As MCDSS was ill-equipped to perform its new coordinating function, UNDP proposed a project to strengthen its capacities for anti-poverty planning and monitoring. Nonetheless, the project did not begin in anticipation that the coordinating role might shift back to the Ministry of Finance. Indeed, over the course of implementing the PSI project, the likelihood that MCDSS would retain its mandate to coordinate the NPRAP became increasingly dubious.

Despite this uncertainty, there was a broad consensus that the NPRAP design process had impacted the work of government officials. It contributed first and foremost towards a redefining of pro-poor policies, as reflected in the budget for the year 2000. Officials from the Ministry of Finance and MCDSS stressed that the NPRAP process helped them understand the distinction between the *reduction* and the *alleviation* of poverty. The main challenge for public policy was thus recast in terms of *who should be entitled to welfare assistance as opposed to receiving investment resources for productive endeavours.* Identifying the optimal mix of loans and grants became central, recognising that there is a threshold below which people cannot repay loans.

The NPRAP process also compelled other government departments to direct attention to poverty issues. The Department of Trade and Industry, for example, became aware about the poverty-reducing effect of the micro-enterprise sector. Ministries like Agriculture, which already knew about the relevance of their own work for poverty reduction, suddenly became aware of the role of other government departments. All in all, PSI activities succeeded in strengthening the resolve of Zambian authorities to find a solution to the poverty problem.

No such capacity-building impact resulted from the PSI project in Uganda, where a high level of skills already existed within the Ministry of Finance. Barring some training provided by the Institute for Development Studies, Sussex (UK), UPPAP relied entirely on local expertise. Instead of using external consultants, Oxfam recruited contract staff and placed it in the Ministry of Finance so as to facilitate its full involvement in the management of the project. This decision, it was hoped, would also facilitate the absorption of UPPAP findings into the government's decision-making process. It is worth noting, however, that the institutional design of UPPAP, specifically its location within the Ministry of Finance, was informed by the study tour that exposed Ugandans to the shortcomings of another country's experience (Tanzania). From this point of view, the study tour sponsored by UNDP can certainly be described as an important capacity development exercise in itself.

The UPPAP exercise had a more tangible capacity-building impact at the local level. The dissemination of the government's anti-poverty action plan and the participatory assessments empowered through community-level workshops empowered local actors to participate in the PEAP review process more effectively. The workshops also helped to strengthen district capacities for participatory poverty assessment and planning, contributing, for example, to the preparation of Community Action Plans based on the PEAP. During the next phase of UPPAP, UNDP envisages continued support to strengthening the capacities of district authorities and non-governmental organisations for poverty-focussed participatory planning and monitoring.

Maldives represents the most prominent example of capacity-building. Apart from the obvious skills acquired by the staff recruited for the VPA survey (school leavers), government officials in various departments clearly benefited from the exercise. The location of members of the research team within the statistical service of government was critical. Senior officials from the Planning Ministry were directly involved in the design and logistics of the study, while officials from the Ministry of Finance were also drawn into it and shared responsibility for the management of the project. Thus, even though the team of foreign experts undertook the bulk of the analysis, some transfer of skills occurred. Regular and extensive consultations between the project team and government authorities greatly facilitated this outcome.

Government planners are now better equipped to use disaggregated socio-economic data in support of policies seeking to redress regional imbalances — and to defend those policies against the reservations of other ministries. Data on the precise extent and distribution of vulnerability in the atolls were not available before the publication of the VPA. By providing an accurate picture of the enormous variability and segmentation between atolls and islands, the VPA has led to the realisation that geography is one of the principal determinants of poverty and vulnerability in the country. Extreme dispersal of population makes service delivery and transportation difficult, both in terms of cost and reliability. As a result, some communities are acutely vulnerable to livelihood shocks and unexpected events such as illness, especially those associated with childbirth. Difficulty in accessing information concerning markets and government services further compounds the isolation of many communities, constituting another important barrier to poverty reduction.

The VPA has provided a sizeable body of information on many aspects of human development. Used properly, information on government inputs could be linked to data on outputs and measurable outcomes so as to assess the effectiveness of government programmes. This would provide the authorities with a useful planning tool for future interventions. Already, the Health Ministry is revisiting its data gathering methods in order to improve the calculation of infant mortality rates. Some NGOs, in turn, are relying on VPA data for project identification. Both are a direct outcome of the VPA exercise, and a clear indication of its capacity-building impact.

Data-gathering and processing seem to be the highest priority for future skills development in all these countries. These skills remain in drastic short supply, despite relatively adequate levels of capacity in Zambia and Uganda. The adoption of a programme approach to poverty reduction will make the task of monitoring results even more challenging, since the data requirements are likely to be far more extensive than those required to assess specific projects. Countries such as Uganda and Zambia, both of which are engaged in a PRSP process, already face this problem. There are expectations that UNDP, as well as other UN agencies, will assist them in the complex task of monitoring the performance of their poverty-reduction plans.

Consultations and ownership

One of the salient features of PSI activities was their direct engagement with national processes of policy formation, particularly in Uganda, Maldives and Zambia. This engagement required flexibility on the part of the funding agency (UNDP), an emphasis on process as opposed to focussing simply on the delivery of outputs, and a willingness to consult, generate commitment and broker consensus among a wide variety of actors.

Despite the problems mentioned earlier, even Lesotho's *Urban Poverty Assessment* managed to bring issues hitherto neglected to the attention of policy-makers. Government officials admitted that urban poverty and planning had not received much attention until the UPA study, despite Lesotho's rapid urbanisation and the growing internal migration stemming from the absence of economic opportunities in rural and mountainous areas of the country. The study did contain many analytical findings, but was short on policy recommendations (chapter 4, this volume).

Part of the reason for the lack of specificity of the UPA seems related to the extremely short period for completing it — just three months. Some government officials associated the project's tight time-frame with its reliance on foreign expertise, which was only available for a limited period. This, in turn, constrained the opportunities for skill transfer, as well as for developing close linkages with key government entities or processing the abundant information that had been collected by the local researchers. The inability of the project team to respond to comments made at the workshop in which UPA findings were presented only compounded those problems.

Indeed, representatives from government, civil society and the research community went as far as questioning the notion that a consultant — or, for that matter, a donor agency — with no local presence could build local capacity — a notion they equated with the practice of top-down planning. Even when foreign experts are highly qualified, their knowledge of local conditions may be inadequate to ensure a correct identification and analysis of country problems. External agents, furthermore, often lack the sensitivity required to negotiate policy changes.

The combination of an inflexible deadline, weak linkages with local actors and lack of responsiveness resulted in the project's demise. The government has largely overlooked the study, whose findings have not been disseminated even though the issue of urban poverty has since been placed on the government's policy agenda. Many people now recognise that Lesotho may face a narrow window of opportunity for a rational urbanisation process, provided it is properly planned and implemented. The challenge is managing urban growth in the face of high unemployment and limited opportunities in rural areas.

Ironically, the urban poverty assessment could therefore still have an impact on policy-making. Government officials in the planning departments recognise the need to fill important gaps in their understanding of urban development issues. They are eager to review a simple list of policy recommendations drawing from international best practices on urban planning and management. Indeed, the Irish government agreed in 1998 to update the poverty mapping exercise in light of the recent changes in Lesotho's poverty profile, in particular the rising tide of urban poverty. UNICEF, in turn, decided to provide additional funding for the study so as to obtain health information, while the World Bank is contributing towards an education component. The World Health Organisation (WHO), DfID and UNDP also joined the new initiative. This suggests that if the UPA project had been better implemented, it could have been a very timely and policy-relevant intervention.

This was the case in Maldives, where the *Vulnerability and Poverty Assessment* has become a key document in planning exercises. Understanding the determining influence of geography on poverty and vulnerability has had a major impact on government policy. The spatial information contained in the VPA has proven extremely useful for the implementation of the settlement consolidation policy, which seeks to encourage the movement of people from remote, sparsely populated and under-serviced islands to nearby islands with higher levels of service. The study also dovetailed with pre-existing efforts to establish an integrated regional database that would collect statistics from all islands for purposes of policy formulation. While the physical data already existed, the VPA has now provided the socio-economic data necessary for planning.[2] This information, moreover, has become the backbone of a UN common database and is integrated into the development information system of UNICEF.

Since Maldives has no parliamentary standing committee in charge of debating poverty issues, the VPA report was presented to the Cabinet for discussion several times. This was a critical factor not only for overcoming official resistance to some VPA results that diverged from existing official statistics, but also for building a strong sense of ownership among government authorities. There are several indications of the importance the latter attach to the vulnerability study. For one thing, the government distributes the VPA to external agencies as representing the most accurate depiction of the current situation in Maldives. For another, it has successfully used the VPA in international negotiations to make its case that Maldives should retain Least Developed Country (LDC) status. These negotiations took place in Geneva during the Round Table Meeting (RTM) on LDC graduation in 1999. The VPA equipped government representatives with data to demonstrate that income levels in Maldives were far lower than the figures published by the World Bank — and that the country's main problem, at any rate, was not absolute poverty, but rather extreme vulnerability.

PSI results have similarly equipped the governments of Uganda and Zambia to negotiate with their donors on a reasonably solid footing, in this case for the preparation of the PRSP. In both cases, the national anti-poverty plans that UNDP helped design (Uganda's PEAP and Zambia's NPRAP) served as the basis for discussions with the Bretton Woods institutions.

In February 2000, the Ugandan authorities set out to review the country's poverty plan based on an assessment of the activities funded by UPPAP. To assist this process, UNDP decided to sponsor a series of consultative workshops so as to provide a forum for debating the existing anti-poverty plan as well as the findings from the district poverty assessments. District-level administrators and NGOs were drawn into these workshops, thereby contributing to broad ownership of the policy formation process beyond the limited confines of the government. Indeed, the emphasis placed on consultation appears to be an important feature of Uganda's approach to development planning, and has generated a sense of commitment among a wide range of national actors.

This sense of commitment and ownership was also fostered by the extensive and close collaboration between the UPPAP team and decision-makers in government, particularly in the Ministry of Finance, Planning and Economic Development. The Ministry commissioned the studies and was integrally involved in managing the project, whose results were utilised for the revision of PEAP.[3]

Both factors — government's involvement in the driver's seat and the intensely consultative nature of the PEAP review process — empowered Ugandan officials to negotiate with IMF and the World Bank the early approval of Uganda's qualification for debt relief under HIPC. From the beginning, Finance officials were very assertive in their views concerning the negotiations for HIPC status. PEAP was presented to the donor community as Uganda's poverty plan, implying that the PRSP requirement had already been met. Government authorities therefore expected donors to prepare their aid programmes using PEAP as their planning framework. Support outside the official poverty reduction plan would be discouraged.

Zambia, too, had been in negotiations with IMF to qualify for HIPC status. As in Uganda, the NPRAP was regarded as satisfying the requirements for HIPC, a view that the World Bank seemed willing to consider even though it had not been involved in its formulation and had some reservations about its quality. Of particular concern to Bank officials was the fact that the NPRAP budget was twice the country's gross domestic product (GDP). Other donors were equally critical, arguing that both the NPRSF and NPRAP could have been better conceived if there had been more extensive consultations with Zambia's development partners.

Unlike the government, which saw the NPRAP as the programme against which it would judge itself, opinions among NGOs differed. Some were generally positive about the extensive consultations that had taken place through the provincial workshops, which gave them an opportunity to review various drafts of the NPRAP as it was being developed. Other NGOs, however, did not share the same sense of ownership. They criticised the limited role of civil society in the steering committee that prepared the national plan. Some also felt that the document produced by the government simply reviewed well-known poverty trends in Zambia, but fell short on analysing policy priorities and budgeting procedures — both of which could have empowered NGOs to prepare advocacy programmes and identify their comparative advantages in the implementation of specific activities. These gaps were widely regarded as a potential constraint for NPRAP implementation, notably for the independent monitoring and evaluation of government actions by civil society.

Despite these reservations, the Zambian government planned to use the NPRAP to justify its request for IMF assistance. The plan's emphasis on health and education was in line with IMF and World Bank's recommendations, paving the way for using it as the foundation for the PRSP. The challenge for the government, therefore, was to integrate the NPRAP with the HIPC process, and identify concrete benchmarks for monitoring progress in reducing poverty.

Intra-government relations and policy coordination

The notion of government ownership presupposes a unity of purpose binding together the multiple branches that make up a government behind common policy goals. If this depiction were accurate, the only concern for donor organisations would be to finance work of the best possible technical quality. Its translation into policy should pose no serious problem, as long as some government agency takes ownership of such work. Evidence from our country cases, however, reveals that competing, sometimes even opposing, interests tend to permeate the government machinery of many countries. Such competition often complicates policy formation and coordination; it also implies that ownership by one branch of government does not guarantee ownership or even commitment from others.

Nowhere has this been more apparent than in Zambia, where frequent shifts in mandate between the Ministries of Finance and of Community Development have affected their ability to coordinate anti-poverty policy. Presidential decree, party politics, international agencies and personalities have all played a role. Changing opinions about the capacity of the Finance Ministry to coordinate poverty reduction activities led to the closure and subsequent re-establishment of a directorate of national planning within its jurisdiction. From 1995 to 1997, this unit was responsible for assisting other government departments as well as provincial authorities with the preparation of development action plans focussing on poverty. In 1997, however, this mandate was transferred to MCDSS. Despite UNDP efforts to strengthen the coordination capacity of this ministry, Zambian NGOs, other government departments and many donors doubted that it had sufficient clout to perform this task effectively.

As a result, the future location of the poverty coordination role remained uncertain even as the NPRAP was being prepared. There was a widespread expectation that the coordination function would shift back to the Ministry of Finance — an expectation that became reinforced once the PRSP process began. World Bank and IMF staff have insisted on a strong leadership role by finance ministries, and this view was shared by many Zambian authorities who expected the NPRAP to filter to all sectors instead of remaining as a stand-alone programme of one ministry. Officials in both Finance and MCDSS acknowledged the existence of a grey area in terms of policy coordination.

This lack of coordination became evident during the process of preparing the NPRAP itself. Relying on a large research team and extensive district level consultation produced an unwieldy document with little direct policy relevance. MCDSS recruited a second team of consultants to synthesise the original draft, which was then re-worked by a third team that was charged with the preparation of an action plan for implementation. Estimates of the cost of implementing NPRAP were far in excess of the country's GDP, which provoked a negative response from the donor community. Perhaps a more conventional approach like a Medium-Term Expenditure Framework led by the Finance Ministry would have resulted in a more realistic budget for the government plan.

Problems of intra-government coordination were also present in Lesotho and Maldives. In Lesotho, these problems were exacerbated by the ongoing debate on a new Local Government Act, which brought to the fore the question of coordinating urban management policy. While some departments were interested in extending the urban poverty assessment to three other cities and developing an action plan to implement its recommendations, the Ministry of Local Government felt that it had not been properly consulted and halted the process. UNDP was unable to broker an agreement between opposing views within government. Because the UPA team had failed to forge a strategic alliance with some key local actor, it was in no position to influence the outcome of this argument.

By contrast, UNDP managed to overcome the resistance of some government entities to findings from the vulnerability assessment carried out in Maldives. From the outset, some ministries like Health and Education were reluctant to engage in a new study on the ground that good baseline surveys were already available in the country. UNDP was able to persuade them that however well done, those surveys were not being used for policy formation. Eventually the Planning Ministry took the lead and assumed responsibility for the VPA survey.

Once the survey was completed, it took a long time before the government approved it. Some of its findings departed from official statistics, in particular infant mortality rates and unemployment figures. By relying on different survey instruments and indicators, the VPA was actually questioning the data-collection procedures used by other ministries, which made the sponsoring Ministry of Planning quite unpopular. Nonetheless, staff from the Planning Ministry was willing to confront these issues and respond to the concerns of others. The VPA team itself played a crucial role in brokering agreements between the various parties, explaining at length the assumptions of the study, allowing these assumptions to be tested, and identifying areas for further investigation.

As a result, at least some of the sectoral departments came to accept the results of the study and even began to re-evaluate their own data. The Ministry of Health, in particular, acknowledged the need to revisit the country's Vital Registration System so as to improve the calculation of infant mortality rates, which it is now doing with technical assistance from WHO.

The UPPAP project of Uganda represents the most successful case of institutional collaboration. The close partnership between the Ministry of Finance, Planning and Economic Development and an NGO (Oxfam), which was grounded on an underlying collaboration between DfID, UNDP and the government, worked to the advantage of all parties involved. Government officials strongly supported the UPPAP model — as did donors, who welcomed the willingness of the Finance Ministry to engage in this new form of institutional partnership.

Finance officials involved other ministries and government agencies, as well as civil society and other development partners extensively during the revision of PEAP. The location of UPPAP within a key government agency also facilitated the translation of the 'voices' of poor people into policy discourse. UPPAP results were used, for instance, in the formulation of the Plan for the Modernisation of Agriculture. At the same time, Finance officials were concerned about the lack of medium-term planning and budgeting at the district level, where capacities for policy design and implementation are extremely inadequate. This highlights the need to examine intra-government dynamics not only at the central level — that is, between line ministries with specific sectoral mandates — but also at different levels of government. As countries move towards a more decentralised governance structure, the focus of capacity-building programmes will need to extend beyond the capital city.

Lessons

Our review clearly shows that PSI activities have had a far greater impact than their limited funds would suggest. They introduced new themes into public discourse, like vulnerability in Maldives and decentralised governance in Uganda. They strengthened indigenous capacity for poverty analysis and the development of policy for its reduction. They also reinforced ongoing national policy initiatives, increasing the leverage of certain key ministries and enabling countries to engage more strategically in negotiations with international donors and lenders.

The vulnerability assessment of Maldives equipped the government with data for developing its settlement consolidation policy and for making a successful case before the donor community against LDC graduation. In Zambia as well as Uganda, UNDP assisted in the review or development of national anti-poverty plans, thereby equipping the respective governments with a policy instrument that they could present to the IMF and World Bank in the context of HIPC and PRSP negotiations. Even in Lesotho, the assessment sponsored by UNDP led to a revisiting of the issue of urban poverty, raising the awareness of policy-makers about the need for a rational urban management process. Lesotho's experience can best be described as a missed opportunity. Had the study on urban poverty been completed and submitted to the government, it could have greatly assisted in forming policy for an emerging problem for the country.

Successful outcomes depend on a number of factors that, to a lesser or greater degree, were present in Uganda, Zambia and Maldives. Their absence in Lesotho, on the other hand, may help explain the limited impact of the urban poverty assessment there. While these factors were specific to each of the four cases covered in the chapter, they may also be relevant to other countries embarking upon the definition of pro-poor policy.

Ownership

It is commonly acknowledged that local ownership of poverty analyses and policies is a fundamental component of sustainability. This notion of ownership is normally premised on extensive involvement of local actors in:

- Identifying the issues to be investigated;
- Designing the terms of reference and managing the project;
- Selecting the consultants or institutions that will be involved;
- Feeding into the project results and disseminating them.

The mechanisms used to develop local ownership were similar in all four countries. They involved workshops, the creation of steering committees with broad participation, and the circulation of information and draft reports for comments and validation. Workshops in particular were widely used as consensus-building and feedback mechanisms, which contributed to the refining of documents and to instilling a sense of commitment from a variety of actors. The iterative process followed in Uganda and Zambia — whereby a policy document is developed and reviewed at both the central and local levels — seems to offer a viable alternative to top-down planning.

However, workshops *per se* are no guarantee of ownership. Failure to translate workshop recommendations into policy undermined government ownership in Lesotho. If participation is perceived as merely instrumental or symbolic, as was the case with some Zambian NGOs, commitment to the process will also erode.

Perceptions of civil society must therefore be incorporated into the policy process, especially as governments increasingly turn to civil society organisations as development partners because of their role as delivery agents, as well as brokers and advocates for poverty reduction.

Strategic alliances

The experience of Maldives reveals that local identification of issues to be examined actually need not be a *necessary* condition for ownership. It was UNDP, and not the government, that first raised the need for a new study to inform the country's settlement consolidation policy. The government concurred, though only over the resistance of important ministries that questioned the need for such a study. UNDP also selected the research team and managed the project. The critical success factor in Maldives was the formation of a strategic alliance with key governmental actors who were willing to assume full responsibility for the project's outcome. Foremost among these was the Ministry of Planning, which needed data to support its policy of balanced regional development. High-level officials from the Finance Ministry and the statistical agency threw their weight behind the initiative, pulling in other actors along the way.

This underlies the relevance of understanding intra-government dynamics, which challenges the misleading notion of government as a unified whole endowed with a common purpose. Governments are often composed of a series of vested interests that operate neither neutrally nor unanimously. Competition and jurisdictional concerns may pit certain agencies against others, undermining the prospects for shared ownership. Indeed, intra-government dynamics emerged as a critical factor conditioning the success of PSI initiatives in all countries. PSI activities themselves were often used to enhance the position of some ministries *vis-à-vis* others.

To minimise the chances of a policy stalemate, strategic alliances should ideally be formed with an agency that commands the authority and leverage necessary for influencing and coordinating policy-making. Ministries of finance or development planning often seem best placed to perform these functions — and they offered the best entry points for PSI activities in Uganda and Maldives. Such ministries constitute a critical link in the governance chain that goes from political authority to local implementation, which may facilitate the formation of broad partnerships within government as well as between governments and other actors in civil society or the donor community.

This requires better knowledge of what might be called the 'tactics of coordination' — that is, the mechanisms through which a coordinating ministry with no direct responsibility for specific programmes can ensure optimal impact through the best use of limited public resources. The need for such coordination is not exclusive to governments. Donors must also coordinate their actions — a role that UNDP is called upon to play in most countries.

A strategic alliance with government agencies for developing anti-poverty policy must be premised on several factors:

- Government departments and other institutions traditionally involved in poverty reduction must shift from a notion of welfare assistance to one that emphasises livelihoods support and enhancement of capabilities.
- Donors must shed many of their conventional practices and procedures, which include inflexible financial cycles, *ex-ante* planning and centralised decision-making, adopting instead an approach based on shared learning, flexible funding programmes, *ex-post* accountability and partnered decision-making.
- Local stakeholders in civil society must go beyond their traditional functions of advocacy and brokerage, and see themselves as partners with a shared responsibility for the success of well-intentioned policy initiatives.
- Government agencies, in turn, must demonstrate a concomitant willingness to share information and decision making so as make partnerships effective.

If the lead government agency is a finance ministry in charge of budgetary regulation, it will have to transcend conventional notions of poverty reduction as the outcome of trickle-down effects, supplemented by handouts for those unable to participate in market activities. Recognising the positive contribution of poverty reduction to economic growth will require capacity development within finance ministries so as to make them more sensitive to poverty issues.

Capacity development

Globalisation has not simply brought about a movement of finance and commodities, but also knowledge. Even in poor developing countries, local experts are often in touch with recent thinking about poverty, and the technical capacity to undertake poverty analysis already exists. However, the resource-constrained environment of these countries may contribute to a fragmentation of technical services, as well as an absence of a critical institutional mass necessary to complete large bodies of work. International donors are therefore called upon to supplement or strengthen indigenous capacities — but not to substitute for them.

Consequently, the manner in which international experts interact with national researchers or institutions is of paramount importance. The short-term nature of consultancy work frequently conflicts with the long-term character of policy change. Foreign consultants may not be at hand for resolving arguments and brokering consensus among local actors; technical support may become staggered where it should be continuous; and the local absorption of technical inputs for the redesign of policy may suffer accordingly.

Nationals from many countries question the principle that an outside agency can build local capacities without engaging with local processes — and strengthening their own capacity along the way. Locating foreign experts within a key agency certainly facilitates the transfer of skills to locals. It may also facilitate the formation of alliances that could bring a policy initiative to a successful conclusion. A genuine partnership, however, requires more than a transfer of skills from one party to another. It must be premised upon a balanced relationship between both parties. Important though skill transfer may be, many countries expect donor engagement to take the form of shared learning between national and foreign actors. Achieving a balance in knowledge and influence reflects a spirit of shared responsibility for developmental outcomes.

National processes

Donor-funded policy initiatives have a greater chance of success when they are embedded in ongoing, nationally driven processes. Such initiatives tend to fit more easily into the country time-cycle in terms of budgetary and policy sequencing. It has to be recognised, however, that in-country timing decisions are themselves affected by the international development agenda, as the current concern with fulfilling HIPC requirements demonstrates. Nonetheless, donor funding cycles can bring in an unwelcome rigidity and undermine local ownership and sustainability.

Collaboration among donors is critical because of potential synergies and benefits from scale. The participation of various donors in a country-led initiative may also provide some form of independent monitoring function for the activities of one another. A coordinating agency with sufficient clout within the donor constituency is necessary, preferably one with country presence and access to national decision-making circles. If other donors perceive the coordinating agency as weak, they may not acknowledge its coordination function. This applies to the bilateral organisations as well. While Irish Aid seemed to be especially influential in Lesotho and DfID in Uganda, it was less certain which agency was playing a lead role in Zambia.

More generally, donors need to set realistic expectations about the possible impact of their initiatives on policy change. Countries are increasingly assertive about their own development strategies. They engage directly with their international donors in events like Round Tables or Consultative Groups, in which they use those strategies as a tool for mobilising aid. A flexible funding instrument like the PSI seems well-suited to further encourage this positive trend. ■

Notes

Julian May gratefully acknowledges the assistance and comments of the UNDP officers in each of the four countries visited: Mathasi Kurubally (Lesotho), Shaheem Razee (Maldives), Joseph Opio-Odongo (Uganda), and Delia Yerokan (Zambia).

[1] The country missions took place from 17-19 January 2000 (Lesotho), 30 January-4 February (Maldives), 7-9 February 2000 (Zambia) and 14-16 February 2000 (Uganda). The information used in the chapter derives from various documents and interviews with UNDP staff, senior and local government officials, representatives from non-governmental organisations, and local and international consultants in each of the four countries.

[2] Given the huge volume of information gathered during the VPA exercise, only ten per cent of the data has been analysed so far. Moreover, the report stressed the need for further analysis of the data that were collected. Officials from the planning department are already considering updating the VPA. This update is particularly important because of the sensitivity of many of the indicators used in the report and the possibility that the inter-atoll vulnerability ranking may have changed since its publication. The incorporation of data from the forthcoming census into the VPA database could provide a viable option for easily updating the information.

[3] This was not the case with the other activity sponsored by UNDP (the review of social sector expenditures), which seems to have generated less local ownership and, therefore, has had a more limited impact on policy. The need for the review was identified externally, and its timing conspired against the possibility of feeding its findings into the preparation of the government's Medium-Term Expenditure Framework (MTEF).

11 Nepal and the Indian States of Karnataka, Madhya Pradesh and Rajasthan

S. R. Osmani

Following the example of the global *Human Development Report* (HDR) introduced by the United Nations Development Programme (UNDP) in 1990, many countries have prepared national and even sub-national HDRs to highlight major disparities in development trajectories and help policy-makers prioritise investments that could enhance people's choices. A number of national and state level HDRs were financed through the Poverty Strategies Initiative (PSI) of UNDP. This chapter provides an assessment of the activities undertaken under the auspices of the PSI programme in India and Nepal.[1] It demonstrates how PSI activities played an important catalytic role in these two countries, and how the HDRs that resulted from those activities were used to influence policy-making.

The first section briefly describes the nature of the activities undertaken under the PSI programme in the two countries. The following section discusses the processes of preparation for the respective HDRs in Nepal and in the Indian states of Karnataka, Madhya Pradesh and Rajasthan. We are particularly interested in exploring the extent to which the process of preparation was inclusive, and identifying the actors that were involved in these activities. The third section examines how successfully the PSI activities have gained ownership by the relevant stakeholders, how well they have entered the mainstream of economic thinking and policy-making in the two countries, and how far they have helped to build the capacities of various actors involved in poverty alleviation. Next we assess the impact of the PSI activities on policy-making and advocacy, both inside and outside the government. The impact is assessed mainly in terms of the role these activities played in stimulating debate, leading on to further initiatives of a similar kind, and inducing concrete policy actions by governmental and non-governmental actors. Finally, the chapter focusses on the extent to which the PSI programme in India has been able to stimulate interagency collaboration in the field of poverty alleviation. We conclude by pointing out the strengths and weaknesses of the PSI activities and drawing some general lessons of wider relevance.

Promoting human development

The major component of the PSI programme in both countries was the preparation of Human Development Reports. There is, however, a significant difference in the nature of the assistance provided by UNDP in the two countries. In India, funds from the PSI programme were used mainly to catalyse a number of state-level Human Development Reports (SHDR), and only secondarily to fund them directly. By contrast, in Nepal, resources were used directly for the preparation of the national HDR of 1998.

The first SHDR of India was published in 1995 for the state of Madhya Pradesh. It was produced from the state government's own resources, without the help of external finance. The UNDP office in New Delhi assisted mainly by offering some advisory support. This pioneering effort, however, soon caught the attention of many agencies and the PSI programme enabled UNDP to take a lead role in helping to replicate the effort in other states.

To this end, UNDP organised a workshop in Bhopal, the capital of Madhya Pradesh, in late 1996 with funding from the PSI programme. The goal of the workshop was to disseminate the findings of the Madhya Pradesh SHDR of 1995 and to encourage other states to replicate the effort. The workshop was very well attended. In addition to the authors of the Madhya Pradesh report, officials from a number of other state governments, representatives of various donor agencies and national and international non-governmental organisations (NGO) and academics were invited.

Several of the representatives from other state governments who attended the workshop returned to their states convinced of the value of SHDRs. The workshop was a success in that Madhya Pradesh went on to produce a second report in 1998 while Karnataka produced a report in 1999. Rajasthan and Sikkim both scheduled publication of their SHDRs for 2000. Several other reports are at various stages of preparation. For instance, the state government of Assam is preparing its own SHDR with the help of UNDP and the Indian Planning Commission, which has earmarked additional central assistance for the exercise. The SHDRs for Uttar Pradesh and Goa were ready to get under way with the signing of agreements between the state governments and UNDP. The government of Andhra Pradesh and UNDP jointly organised a workshop in June 1998 to identify the outline and resource persons for the preparation of background papers for their own SHDRs. The governments of all these states have already requested additional central assistance from the Indian Planning Commission. The process of consultation and preparation of background papers has also been proceeding apace in several other states, like Himachal Pradesh, Arunachal and Tamil Nadu. The states of Bihar, Jammu and Kashmir, Meghalaya, Punjab, Kerala and Tripura have also expressed interest in collaborating with UNDP in this area, and discussions have also been held with Maharashtra, Nagaland and West Bengal.

In Nepal, the PSI programme assisted in the preparation of two reports. One is the *Nepal Human Development Report* (1998), which was the first and so far the only one of its kind to be produced in that country. The other is a social sector expenditure review, which was prepared in collaboration with UNICEF within the framework of the 20/20 Initiative promoted by the United Nations to increase financing for basic social service provision. Nepal has a proud history of being one of the pioneers of the Initiative. It was one of the first four countries that UNICEF chose in 1993 to carry out detailed case studies of public sector expenditures, which formed the foundation for the subsequent launching of the 20/20 Initiative. That early study had a visible impact on the country's public finances, as the proportion of spending on basic social services rose impressively for a few years. For instance, the human priority ratio defined as expenditure on social priority sectors as a proportion of total public expenditure, rose from 11.7 per cent in 1992/93 to 14.5 per cent in 1994/95. But this ratio, along with all other indicators of spending on basic services, has since stagnated. The recent expenditure review sponsored by the PSI programme was born out of the recognition that fresh efforts were needed to restore the momentum of reorienting public finances towards basic social services (Nepal 1998a).

Preparing the Human Development Reports

The PSI programme was launched with the expectation that it would have an impact far beyond its direct outputs. The content and the quality of work supported by the programme are important for this purpose, because high-quality work that is relevant for a country's poverty reduction efforts is likely to inspire other actors to carry forward the tasks. But, arguably, the process whereby these activities are undertaken is even more important. Even work of the highest quality will not have a major impact on policy or the public discourse in a country if it is undertaken in isolation and does not receive wide dissemination. If, by contrast, work of even moderate quality is undertaken in an inclusive manner, its ideas will stand a better chance of being translated into action and leading to new and better quality work. The process of preparing the national and state-level HDRs is thus no less important than their content.

A wide range of participants attended the Bhopal workshop mentioned above. The inclusiveness of the process and the wide publicity given to the workshop helped to strengthen the legitimacy of the notion of the human development approach to a wide constituency in India. It also encouraged several other states, which were inspired by the example of Madhya Pradesh, to follow suit with their own SHDRs.

The preparation of these subsequent SHDRs, however, varied somewhat in their degree of inclusiveness. The second Madhya Pradesh HDR (1998) was prepared, as in the case of the first one, mainly as a government enterprise. A dedicated group of senior civil servants, many of whom also had considerable academic credentials, were entrusted with the responsibility of drafting the report. A local research-oriented NGO called Sanket was also deeply involved and worked in close collaboration with the government team led by the Planning Secretary. Some academics were included in the advisory committee, but they played a relatively minor role.

The Rajasthan SHDR was also the outcome of collaboration between a team of senior civil servants and Sanket. By contract, the Karnataka SHDR was prepared almost entirely by a team of senior civil servants, many of whom (as in the case of Madhya Pradesh) had considerable academic credentials. A review committee, however, provided guidance to the state government team on substantive issues such as the calculation of district income using purchasing power parity norms, as well as district poverty estimates based on pooling central and state government survey samples. The review committee also was responsible for the inclusion of a chapter on the status of the statistical data system in the state.

In contrast to the Indian SHDRs, the government was hardly involved in the process of preparing the Nepal HDR. A local research institute called the Nepal South Asia Centre (NESAC) prepared the report with support from a few outsiders, in particular some academics drawn from the University. Interestingly, two major figures involved in the preparation of the report happened to be politically aligned to the two major political parties of Nepal, a fact that lent a considerable amount of cross-party neutrality to the report itself.

While the reports were written in each case by a small group of people in both India and Nepal, attempts were made to involve a much larger group in a process of consultation and interaction, both during and after the writing stage. The degree to which this was done varied, however. Perhaps the widest range of consultation occurred in the case of the Nepal HDR. As each chapter was written, a separate workshop was arranged to discuss its contents among academics and others having specific expertise on the subject matter of the chapter. Once all the chapters were written, a more encompassing workshop was held to discuss the complete draft. An even more encompassing interaction followed at the stage of launching the report, when in addition to the academics and experts, invitations were also extended to a large number of civil servants, politicians, NGOs, journalists and other civil society representatives. Once the report was complete, a series of discussion sessions were held between its authors and a number of government ministries to help the bureaucrats internalise the report's findings.

The process of consultation was less inclusive in the case of Indian SHDRs. Although an independent advisory committee was supposed to guide the work of the teams responsible for writing the reports, with a few exceptions the members of these committees did not play a significant role. In the case of Madhya Pradesh, the drafts were sent out to the elected leaders of local government (district *Panchayat*) for their views. This process of consultation was deemed important especially in view of the emphasis given to decentralised governance in both the SHDR itself and in the general policy framework of the state. It is not clear, however, how significantly any feedback received from the members of local governments contributed to the final output. The value of this consultation lay more in making the lower echelons of government aware of the notion of human development and its implications for economic policy-making.

Similarly, the HDRs in Karnataka and Nepal also laid a special emphasis on decentralisation and participatory governance, but unlike in Madhya Pradesh, there was no attempt to involve members of local government in the preparatory stage. In both cases, however, once completed, the document was disseminated to the district level and below. This was done most systematically in Nepal, where the HDR was translated into the vernacular for the consumption of local level governments and members of civil society.

The preparation of the report on social sector expenditures in Nepal (1998a) also involved the participation of other stakeholders. A retired official of the Ministry of Finance with detailed first-hand knowledge of the intricacies of government accounts was responsible for preparing the report. But in this task, he received constant support from the member of the Planning Commission in charge of public finances. Furthermore, a series of informal group discussions were held roughly once every six weeks during the preparatory stage in order to consult a wide spectrum of people.

Ownership and mainstreaming

One of the chief criteria to judge the success of the PSI activities is the extent to which they have been able to mainstream the ideas and activities supported by them. This issue is closely related to that of ownership, because unless a wide range of stakeholders beyond UNDP owns the ideas and activities promoted by the PSI programme, they are unlikely to become part of the mainstream of economic thinking and policy-making in a country.

Neither in India nor in Nepal did the PSI programme make any major breakthrough in terms of conceptual or methodological innovation in the analysis of poverty or the formulation of policy for poverty reduction. But in both countries, the activities sponsored by the programme made a successful bid to popularise the idea of human development and the particular approach to policy-making it implies. The global *Human Development Reports* have been doing this popularisation quite well over the last decade, but in order to mainstream the idea in a more concrete manner, work also had to be done at regional, national and sub-national levels. The South Asia Human Development Reports of the past two years have gone some way towards meeting this need in the region. The SHDRs of India and the HDR of Nepal supported by the PSI programme have carried that process forward to a significant extent.

In Madhya Pradesh, Karnataka and Rajasthan, the notion of human development has obviously become part of the mainstream thinking of policy makers — though not yet so much a part of their actions. Indicators such as the HDI (human development index), the GDI (gender development index) and the GEM (gender empowerment measure), which are essential parts of the human development vocabulary and toolkit, are now routinely employed in both oral and written communication among government officials.

The language of human development, as distinct from the conventional notion of 'development', has already been permeating the official discourse on planning and policy-making. At the same time, social sectors such as health and education are now receiving far greater attention, at least in policy statements, than they did in the past. Significantly, the HDRs seem to have succeeded in inspiring this reorientation of focus even in the higher citadels of power. For example, in his speech to the state assembly in 1999, the Governor of Karnataka cited evidence from the state HDR to draw attention to the problems of human development in the state.[2] In a similar vein, the King of Nepal used the language of the 1998 HDR in his speech to the national parliament. Although statements of this kind may be more rhetorical than substantive, it is equally true that all major new ideas enter the realm of rhetoric before they influence the practical world of policy-making.

One of the reasons why mainstreaming has been so rapid in the case of the Indian SHDRs is that in all three cases examined here (Karnataka, Madhya Pradesh and Rajasthan), the state governments have fully owned these reports. The tradition was set by the pioneering 1995 SHDR of Madhya Pradesh, which was produced wholly at the initiative of the state government and written primarily by government officials. Karnataka and Rajasthan have followed that tradition. The fact that the government was responsible for both the initiation and the preparation of the SHDR made it easy for the product to be owned by the government. This in turn made it easy for the ideas popularised by the SHDR to enter mainstream economic thinking in the official circle.

Active involvement on the part of the government creates an advantage in terms of local ownership. The danger is that this process may lead to just another government report, either bland or self-adulating, with very little honest and critical reflection. This did not happen in India, however. Perhaps this can be attributed to the exemplary tradition set by the 1995 SHDR of Madhya Pradesh, which was undertaken in a spirit of genuine soul-searching to examine why one of the most resource-rich states of India also happens to be one of the most backward in the economic and social spheres. This first report appears to have set the tone for the SHDRs that followed.

In all cases, the team responsible for the preparation of the SHDR was given considerable autonomy. Officials from the highest levels of the bureaucratic hierarchy were involved with the team, with the result that there was very little scope for meddling from bureaucratic quarters. It is interesting to note the contrast with another official report on intra-state disparities in Karnataka that was being prepared in parallel with the SHDR. The officials of the Karnataka government confided that unlike the SHDR, the other report bore all the hallmarks of an official document — bland and non-critical.

Unlike in India, the government of Nepal has not officially endorsed the *Human Development Report*, which is largely perceived as an independent research report prepared by a team of outsiders. There are two reasons for this. First, government officials were not directly involved in the preparation of the report, although the authors did organise seminars and workshops to consult officials. Secondly, frequent changes of government within a short period of time have rendered it difficult to ensure ownership or implementation of any kind of initiative in Nepal.

The fact that the report has gained wide popularity has nonetheless enabled it to influence mainstream economic thinking. This resulted partly from the fact that the main authors of the report were two highly respected intellectuals, who also happened to be aligned to the two major political parties in Nepal. According to a member of the Planning Commission, another factor is that the report was prepared under the auspices of the UN system, which is viewed by the government as more neutral and sympathetic than other multilateral and bilateral donor agencies. The end result is that even though the report itself is not fully owned by the government, the force of ideas expressed in it is widely acknowledged within the official circles. In fact, the first HDR ever produced in Nepal has inspired the government to produce a second report, which will be carried out in collaboration with UNDP.

Government decisions to produce new rounds of Human Development Reports in both India and Nepal demonstrates growing acceptance within the official circles. A similar process is also under way outside government circles. In Nepal, for instance, the HDR has already entered the curriculum of the Masters' courses in economics and sociology in the University. The trade union movement has also been using it as a learning resource in the training courses organised for trade union members.

Unlike the HDR, the report on public finances in Nepal had no difficulty in gaining ownership by the government. This is mainly because the Member of the Planning Commission responsible for public finances was deeply involved in an advisory capacity throughout the preparation of the report, although a retired civil servant did the actual analysis and writing. Another reason for the sense of ownership of this report is that it is seen as a continuation of the 20/20 Initiative, in which the government has a strong sense of ownership.

Capacity-building

The preparation of SHDRs in Madhya Pradesh, Karnataka and Rajasthan was an exceedingly valuable capacity-building exercise from the point of view of the respective governments. Although the NGO Sanket was deeply involved with the SHDRs of Madhya Pradesh and Rajasthan, the main responsibility was borne by government officials. It is true that report-writing is nothing new for the officials, who are routinely engaged in the preparation of different kinds of reports. But this was a report with a difference: analytical as opposed to being merely descriptive, honest as opposed to being economical with the truth, and self-critical as opposed to being propagandistic. A different kind of mental orientation and an altogether different level of intellectual effort were needed to produce these reports. Given proper incentives, this valuable training can be put to good use in a wide range of government activities.

Since independent researchers were responsible for writing the Nepal HDR, there was no such scope for capacity-building within the government during the process of preparation. But both in Nepal and India, the output of the process did create scope for capacity-building both inside and outside the government. In both countries, the district level analysis of human development indicators carried out by the HDRs has enhanced the capacity of local-level governments to formulate local plans in multiple ways, in particular by:

- Generating district-level statistics that can be used as plan benchmarks;
- Developing methodologies that local governments would be able to use for constructing similar statistics in the future;
- Clarifying what it means to adopt the human development approach to planning.

In Nepal, the inter-district ranking generated by the HDR has also enhanced the capacity of the government, as well as donor agencies, to target their interventions more effectively to areas that are most in need of support. The report on social sector expenditures similarly contributed to capacity-building. It has done so by equipping the government with a detailed statistical basis and by presenting it with a menu of policy options on which to build a programme for reorienting public expenditure towards basic social services.

Capacity-building of a different kind is also taking place in civil society. Clear evidence of the fact that the HDRs have enhanced civil society's capacity to play the advocacy role is that various disadvantaged groups, trade unions and political parties are liberally using the information generated by the HDRs to advance their respective causes.

In order to enhance the capacities of Indian states to undertake SHDRs, UNDP signed a three-year project for Capacity-Building for Preparation of State Human Development Reports with the central government.[3] Under this project, UNDP would support the states in the preparation of SHDRs by:

- Mobilising appropriate local expertise in the states;
- Carrying out assessments of existing needs and capabilities at the state level;
- Providing expertise to the state governments for improving data quality, collection and analysis;
- Providing expertise to develop and refine gender indicators, and for training and sensitisation of district-level personnel, especially those dealing with statistics, planning and administration of *Panchayat Raj* institutions;
- Developing action to improve existing delivery mechanisms with respect to basic services for human development, covering livelihoods.

To ensure common definitions and measures in the preparation of SHDRs, a network of national experts will be engaged to work closely with the state governments. The experts would refine concepts, evaluate statistical databases at the district level, and identify critical human development issues in select states, as well as bottlenecks that impede development among disadvantaged groups. Based on empirical knowledge and augmentation of the existing data, the experts would help finalise indicators tailored to the needs of specific regions, to be adopted for measurement of human development in Indian states.

The SHDRs catalysed by the PSI programme have led to further activities and have helped leverage additional funds for activities oriented towards human development goals. These activities support the ongoing attempts at sensitising the agencies responsible for collecting and analysing statistical data in India on issues of gender. In 1996, the government of India adopted the National Policy for the Empowerment of Women in response to the commitments made at the Fourth World Conference on Women, held in Beijing in 1995. One component of the Policy stated that 'Gender Disaggregated Data will be collected, compiled and published on a regular basis by all primary data collecting agencies of the central and state governments as well as research and academic institutions in the public and private sector'. An Interagency Working Group was set up in order to support the government in the implementation of this policy. The Working Group is intended to help develop methodologies for the construction of the Gender Development Index (GDI) and Gender Empowerment Measure (GEM), both of which were first introduced by UNDP in the *Human Development Report 1995*. The Group is led by UNDP, and other members are the Central Statistical Organisation, the Department of Women and Child Development of the government of India, ILO, UNICEF, UNIFEM, UNESCO, WHO and the World Bank.

Moreover, in 1996-1997 UNDP and UNIFEM joined hands with the Department of Women and Child Development and the government of Karnataka to support a pilot study aimed at disaggregating gender data in two districts each in four states (Gujarat, Karnataka, Tamil Nadu and West Bengal). One of the recommendations of the study was to expand databases with standardised formats for gender-based disaggregation, and to identify a group of core variables and indicators to be used for comparison across the country. In order to enhance the government's capability to undertake these tasks, UNDP signed with the government of India a project entitled Gender Audit at the State Level in September 1998. The project aims to support the Department of Women and Child Development and Central Statistical Organisation to review the methodology for the computation of GDI and GEM, and to identify the required district-level data to be collected and processed. Based on this, a national programme would be formulated to fill in the gaps in the existing data systems.

As part of this project, two brainstorming workshops were held towards the end of 1998 on developing gender indicators and establishing mechanisms for monitoring them at the state and district level. Among other things, these workshops discussed two background papers. The first paper, commissioned by the Department of Women and Child Development, focussed on 'en-gendering' official data systems in the states and districts of India. The second paper discussed a methodology for the computation of the human development and gender development indices (HDI and GDI), and was prepared by the Central Statistical Organisation (CSO). The methodology developed by the CSO, with the help of the Interagency Working Group, identified 18 indicators that need to be measured for the purpose of computing the GDI and the GEM. These indicators are already being tried out on a pilot basis on some districts in the state of Karnataka. UNDP and other agencies are closely monitoring this pilot project with a view to arriving at a final set of indicators. The work done in connection with the SHDRs has contributed enormously towards preparing these indicators. UNDP, other UN agencies and the government of India have all contributed resources for these activities.

Influencing policy and the public discourse

The PSI programme was conceived as a relatively small intervention backed by a modest outlay. On their own, therefore, the PSI activities could not have been expected to have a profound effect on the country's poverty reduction efforts. It was expected, however, that if properly conceived and executed, they would work as catalytic agents by stimulating public debate, introducing new ideas to policy circles, strengthening existing initiatives, and inspiring new ones. In this manner, the ultimate cumulative effect of the PSI activities would be much larger than their direct and immediate impact. In both India and Nepal, there are good reasons to believe that the PSI programmes has had discernible impacts both at the level of government thinking and policy and at the level of the civil society.

Prior to the workshop in Bhopal, a debate was taking place in India on whether a national HDR or a series of state level HDRs was the best way of advancing the human development perspective in India. The workshop helped to win the argument in favour of those who had envisaged that in a country as diverse as India, it made more sense to have a series of state level HDRs instead of a national one. Inspired by the workshop, two more states, Rajasthan and Karnataka, immediately embarked upon preparing their own SHDRs, and the government of Madhya Pradesh felt encouraged enough to produce a follow-up report. Many more states are following suit. Meanwhile, UNDP has convinced the government of India of the value of state-level HDRs, with the result that the central government has agreed to provide funds (to be supplemented by UNDP's own resources) for supporting the preparation of SHDRs for all the states of India in the coming years. In Nepal too, the first HDR has generated enough enthusiasm to convince the government of the need to produce a second HDR, with support from UNDP.

It is too early to make a full and proper assessment of the extent to which the HDRs have influenced actual policy making in the two countries. HDRs are not meant to be primarily policy documents. By their very nature, rather than formulating specific policies with well-defined targets and budgets, they focus on describing a country's socio-economic situation from the perspective of human development and indicating the general directions that the economy and the polity ought to take in order to make human development possible. It would, therefore, be unrealistic to expect a direct translation of the ideas contained in HDRs into immediate policy actions. What is more likely is that the particular way of thinking inspired by the human development perspective would gradually begin to mould the mindset of those in charge of making policy. This is a long-term process, but there are already signs that the process has begun.

The importance of SHDRs is being acknowledged at the highest levels of policy-making in India. In the 1999 annual meeting of the National Development Council, the joint empowered forum for State Chief Ministers and the Union Cabinet, the Deputy Chairman of the Planning Commission emphasised the role and relevance of SHDRs in the rationalisation of plan outlays and monitoring. The SHDRs were also credited with ensuring that indicators of human development relevant for policy analysis and action are readily available.

At a more concrete level, the clearest example of policy impact comes from Madhya Pradesh, which has had the longest exposure to SHDR so far among all the cases reviewed in this chapter. According to senior government officials, the conceptual framework underpinning some of the major policy initiatives undertaken in this state during the last five years has been deeply influenced by what they recognise to be three major tenets of the human development approach:

- Switching of government expenditure to activities that directly influence the wellbeing of the poor;
- Taking a multi-sectoral approach to intervention, because human development is an outcome of simultaneous improvement in many different dimensions of living;

■ Participation of the people themselves in the activities intended for their
wellbeing.

An outstanding example of how this recognition has influenced policy-making in
Madhya Pradesh is the Education Guarantee Scheme (EGS), which the government
introduced in January 1997 with a view to ensuring universal access to primary education in the shortest possible time. The scheme involves both a guarantee on the
part of the government and a compact between the government and local communities for sharing the cost and management of the programme. Under the EGS, the
government guarantees the provision of a trained teacher, the teachers' salaries and
further training, teacher-training materials and contingencies to start a school within 90 days, wherever there is demand, provided two conditions are met. First, there
must be no primary schooling facility within one kilometre of the community that
makes the demand. Secondly, this demand must come from at least 25 learners in
case of tribal areas and 40 learners in case of non-tribal areas. The community, in
turn, has to identify and put forward a teacher and also provide the space for teaching and learning. Local management committees are set up for taking responsibility
for day-to-day management of schools, and in particular for ensuring regular attendance on the part of both teachers and students.

By all accounts, the EGS has proved to be an overwhelming success. In the first
year of its operation, more than 40 new schools opened each day and, after 18
months, the state could boast universal access to primary education. This is indeed
a remarkable achievement for a state that has long suffered the ignominy of being
known as one of the most illiterate states of India. A good deal of work remains to
be done in terms of improving the quality of education offered by these schools, but
at least in terms of ensuring access to education, the EGS clearly demonstrates the
power of a decentralised participatory approach.

Other examples of the emergence of a new way of thinking in Madhya Pradesh
are the community-based programmes for forest management and watershed development. In both these programmes, community groups have been actively involved
in the preservation and management of resources, and a multi-sectoral approach has
been adopted to secure the livelihood of all groups of the poor, not just those who
would benefit directly from the use of forest or water resources. Recognising that
people would be more willing to conserve resources if they had a stake in their conservation, they have been given ownership as well as management responsibilities.
Furthermore, in recognition of the fact that the poor would refrain from over-
exploiting scarce resources only if they had alternative income earning opportunities, attempts have been made to create such opportunities by offering them credits,
skills and other inputs. In other words, the traditional top down approach of bureaucratic management of natural resources has been replaced by a community-driven
approach, in which the livelihoods of the poor rather than resource conservation for

its own sake is the primary goal. It is this community-based holistic approach towards livelihood security that the new thinking in official circles identifies as the distinctive feature of the human development approach. These programmes are quite new, and yet preliminary studies indicate that they are already beginning to bear some fruit (Madhya Pradesh 1998).

The impact on policy-making is less evident in Karnataka, which is not surprising, given the fact that the SHDR of this state is more recent. An additional problem was that the report was prepared when the *Janata Dal* party was in power in the state, but the government collapsed soon after it was completed. During the election campaign that followed, the opposition Congress Party used the findings of the SHDR in its election manifesto to draw attention to the plight of the people in the state. It also used the report's policy prescriptions to draw inspiration for its own programmes. Although the Congress Party won the elections, the transition caused by the change of government has led to a natural delay in translating ideas into action.[4]

Even so, the senior government officials who were responsible for overseeing the preparation of the report have carried the task forward during the transition period. In particular, the Chief Secretary of the government of Karnataka kept the process going by asking the line Secretaries to prepare policy papers for their respective sectors, with an understanding that these would be informed by the findings of the SHDR. Some of these papers have already been prepared. The one on rural development has focussed on assessing the quality and quantity of the estimated 200,000 water sources in the state, which was identified by the SHDR as a critical issue for the rural poor. Two inter-ministerial task forces have also been set up for education and health, following the report's recommendation to reorient the government's policy thrust towards these sectors (Karnataka 1999).

Another indication of a changing mindset, in both India and Nepal, is the broader perspective from which economic wellbeing has begun to be perceived. A common feature of the SHDRs of India and the national HDR of Nepal is the special effort that has gone towards obtaining a disaggregated picture of wellbeing, across geographical locations, ethnic groups, gender and occupational groups. For example, they have all tried to develop human development indicators at the district level. In so doing, they have gone beyond the standard measure of per capita income and tried to construct measures of other dimensions of human development, namely health and education.

As a result of these exercises, it has now become possible to rank all the districts in terms of a wide range of human development criteria. This ranking is being utilised for multiple purposes by a variety of actors both inside and outside the government. The government Madhya Pradesh, for instance, has been struck by the finding that some of the most advanced agricultural districts are actually near the bottom of the pile in terms of social indicators of human development such as health and education. By contrast, some of the tribal districts, which are known to be extremely poor in terms of conventional economic criteria, rank quite high in terms of social indicators. The reasons for such divergent performance in terms of economic and social indicators have become matters of serious inquiry both within and outside government circles.

In both India and Nepal, district authorities have begun to use the district-level human development indicators to their advantage. The poorest districts are using them as an advocacy tool to advance their case for greater allocation of resources from the higher echelons of government. Furthermore, all districts are using, or are being encouraged to use them as a benchmark in formulating their district development plans. This exercise in local-level planning has received a boost from the happy congruence of two separate developments. One is the construction of district-level indicators described above. The other is the move towards decentralisation of governance that has been proceeding strongly in Madhya Pradesh, Karnataka and Nepal since the early 1990s. The drive towards decentralisation has created the institutional imperative for formulating local development plans. At the same time, the Human Development Reports have come at an opportune moment to facilitate the formulation of these plans. They have done so first by guiding the orientation of plans, in particular by driving home the message that development is more than building roads and dams, and, secondly, by providing a regionally disaggregated statistical picture of human deprivation that the district authorities can use as their plan benchmarks.[5]

At higher levels of government, the most concrete use of these district indicators has so far been made in Nepal. During 1998-99, the government has launched three new programmes, the formulation of which has benefited directly from the disaggregated picture of human deprivation highlighted by the Nepal HDR. The Special Area Development Programme has been launched with a view to strengthening the poverty alleviation efforts in 22 backward districts. In identifying these districts, extensive use was made of the inter-district ranking in terms of human development generated by the HDR, supplemented by other information. The programme seeks to channel large amounts of national and international funds into infrastructure, education and health projects for the chosen districts, and to manage these projects with the help of local communities. At about the same time, the Disadvantaged Groups Development Policy and the Indigenous Population Development Policy were launched for the benefit of the untouchables and the indigenous populations respectively, both of which were identified by the HDR as the most deprived social groups in Nepal.[6]

The disaggregated picture of human deprivation depicted by the HDR has become a very useful advocacy tool for diverse social groups in Nepal. Civil society organisations representing the untouchables, the indigenous people, women, and workers have quoted frequently from the report in support of their respective causes. The trade union movement has used the analysis of the HDR to argue publicly against what it perceives to be the Western world's attempt to impose the ideology of 'globalisation as a panacea' for the ills of the developing countries. As already mentioned, the trade unions also use the report as part of the syllabus for training their members. Newspapers and other media use it all the time. Even the leader of an underground Marxist party (which is responsible for armed insurgency in the mountain regions of the country) has quoted from it to draw attention to the plight of the mountain people in his regular column written for the most widely read vernacular weekly of Nepal.

The Participatory District Development Programme (PDDP) supported by UNDP represents yet another case of the inter-district ranking generated by the HDR being utilised in policy-making. The objective of the PDDP is to strengthen the government's efforts to promote participatory decentralisation in Nepal. It was born of the realisation that decentralisation cannot work for the benefit of the poor unless people are empowered at the grassroots level and that such empowerment can come only if they are mobilised in autonomous community organisations. UNDP has helped in this regard by conceptualising and implementing the programme. This initiative, together with a similar one called Local Governance Programme (LGP), encompass both strengthening of the local government institutions and social mobilisation at the household level.

Under these programmes, a team of social mobilisers are employed to form settlement-wide community-based organisations (CBO), separately for men and women. The process begins by encouraging every household to join a savings group, in which they are required to deposit a fixed amount of savings every week. Once the discipline of regular savings has become firmly established, the CBOs are formed with a view to undertaking a wide range of activities. In order to ensure that the decision-making process is not usurped by a handful of people, the CBOs are not allowed to have any executive committee. Instead, all members of the organisation take decisions together.

After forming the CBOs, the members continue to mobilise small savings on their own and, in their weekly meetings, they take decisions on their investment. In addition to their own savings, funds also come from the Capital Credit and Seed Grant of the Project and from the Local Trust Fund with the District Development Committees (DDC). Since the PDDP intends to strengthen the local government institutions in an integrated manner, it has also been possible to accommodate the programmes of other donors within its management structure. For instance, NORAD provides seed money for Local Trust Funds in some of the districts, while UNICEF collaborates in child-related programmes in some other districts. SNV, a Dutch aid agency, has also been operating in collaboration with the PDDP. In response to a possible resource crunch after the withdrawal of project support, a Poverty Alleviation Fund has been created at the centre. The annual budget for the year 1999-2000 has set aside Rs. 100 million in order to set up this fund. Additional support will come from the Local Trust Fund at the sub-regional level.

By mid 1999, PDDP and LGP had together covered 40 districts. It is estimated that nearly half a million people have already been served by these two projects, and an independent evaluation shows that they have been served pretty well. First, the scheme has provided a mechanism for conflict resolution at the local level and, in the process, ensured that resources and privileges are not cornered by a powerful few. Secondly, it has provided a mechanism for ensuring that all developmental activities are undertaken in a genuinely participatory manner, thereby improving the likelihood that poverty reduction efforts will succeed better than in the past.

Inspired by these positive results, UNDP and the government of Nepal have decided to extend the PDDP approach to a larger number of districts. This extension will cover in the most backward districts, where intervention is most urgently needed. This is where the Human Development Report sponsored by the PSI programme has made a contribution. By ranking the districts in terms of human development, it has helped to identify the districts most in need of support. UNDP has decided to use this ranking to choose the districts for inclusion in the next phase of the programme.

Unlike the HDR, however, not a great deal can be said about the impact of the social sector expenditure review funded partially by the PSI programme in Nepal. The report, as it stands, is quite impressive. It was prepared by a local expert with deep inside knowledge of government finances and has been strongly supported by the National Planning Commission. The Member of the Planning Commission in charge of public finances has taken a keen personal interest in the study, and the final formulation of the document has benefited from a wide-ranging consultative process. The recommendations made in the report, in favour of reallocating government spending towards basic social services, raising additional revenue, levying user charges wherever possible so as to achieve greater efficiency, and devolving more fiscal powers and responsibilities to local governments, are all very sound (Nepal 1998a).

Despite all this, the actual impact of the study is not yet visible. The principal reason is that, although the report had been in the making for a while, it was finalised too late to input into the preparation of the annual budget for the year 1999-2000. As it happens, the final stages of the preparation of the study coincided with the final stages of preparation of the forthcoming budget for the year 2000-01. Moreover, the same Member of the Planning Commission was deeply involved in both these processes. There is, therefore, a general expectation that the recommendations of this exercise should inform the fiscal measures to be proposed in the forthcoming budget.

In practice, however, this may not happen. The government seems already committed to several large hospital projects, which will make it difficult to devote a larger proportion of health sector expenditure to basic health care services, as required by the 20/20 Initiative. This does not, however, rule out greater impact in the longer term; as the previous commitments are phased out, additional resources are mobilised through various means such as user charges, privatisation and general improvements in efficiency, and local governments are given more powers to raise and utilise additional fiscal resources.

Supporting interagency collaboration and aid mobilisation

The PSI projects in both India and Nepal have succeeded in promoting collaboration between the central government of India, various state governments, bilateral donors and multilateral organisations.

The main collaboration in the preparation of the Indian SHDRs has taken place between UNDP, state governments and the central government of India. But others have also been involved. The momentum created by the Bhopal workshop was further strengthened by two additional workshops, which UNDP organised in collaboration with other institutions. A national workshop on Poverty and Human Development was organised jointly by the Dutch embassy, the World Bank and UNDP in April 1998. Representatives from the government, NGOs, bilateral organisations and the UN system attended the meeting. The participants recommended the need to examine the human development situation at the level of localities, not national aggregates, and to make better use of the rich corpus of data that is currently under-utilised for policy and programme purposes. They further recommended the establishment of mechanisms to make the data user-friendly so that it can be used for decision-making. These recommendations reaffirmed the ideas that had emerged in the Bhopal workshop.

Subsequently, in July 1999, UNDP collaborated with the Indian Planning Commission to organise another national workshop on the Core Contents and Indicators of Human Development. The goal of the workshop was to discuss the suitability of various human development indicators with senior officials from the government of India, representatives of state governments and other resource persons. The workshop helped build a consensus regarding the core variables and issues that need to be covered in state HDRs. These instances of collaboration between UNDP and other agencies played a crucial role in adding legitimacy to the idea of state-level HDRs, culminating in the capacity-building project that UNDP subsequently signed with the government of India.

A second set of activities sponsored by the UNDP programme in India was even more directly aimed at promoting interagency collaboration and aid mobilisation. These activities sought to influence the policy dialogue between international donors and the government of India in the India Development Forum (IDF), the official name for the Aid Consortium group for India. Aid Consortium meetings, in which donors and the recipient country discuss development strategy, are typically organised by the World Bank by virtue of its status as a major donor in many countries. The same is true also for the IDF. But UNDP has been trying for some time to reorient both the content and format of these meetings, to make them more responsive to the perspective of human development in terms of content and more inclusive in format.

To these ends, the UNDP office in New Delhi prepared a position paper for discussion at the IDF meeting in Paris in July 1997 (India 1997). The purpose of this document was to push the donors, and the World Bank in particular, towards adopting the human development framework in their strategic thinking. Resources from the PSI programme were used to produce this position paper. In order to make the format of these meetings more inclusive and country-led, UNDP has been advocating the idea of holding preliminary meetings in India so that a wide range of stakeholders can participate in the process of deliberation. The World Bank itself has also been moving recently in that direction. In pursuit of this goal, the two institutions jointly organised the India Poverty Consultation Workshop, a kind of pre-IDF meeting, in New Delhi in January 1999. UNDP contributed a position paper, apart from organising this workshop (India 1999).

The PSI programme contributed both directly and indirectly in these activities. Directly, it provided funds for preparing background papers for the two position papers mentioned above. Indirectly, the SHDRs supported by the PSI programme provided essential resources, in terms of both data and analyses, for preparing the positions papers. Furthermore, the series of workshops organised in connection with these activities provided an opportunity to a wide group of people from academia, media and civil society to engage in debates and deliberation with both the government and the donor community.

Although these activities have fed into ongoing processes instead of initiating new ones, they have certainly helped to strengthen the existing interagency collaboration. The position papers prepared for the IDF meetings, as well as the workshops in which they were presented, have reinforced the growing collaboration between UNDP and the World Bank. They did so in manner that has served to redress some of the imbalance that typically has characterised the relationship between these two institutions.

The strengthening of existing collaboration between international organisations is also in evidence in Nepal. The most obvious case is the social sector expenditure review in which UNDP collaborated with UNICEF. The effect of the Nepal HDR has been somewhat indirect, but no less potent. While it would not be true to say that the HDR led directly to some new collaborative initiative, it is clear that the inter-district ranking produced by the report has been utilised by the UN agencies in their ongoing efforts to enhance interagency collaboration in Nepal. They have decided to concentrate their collaborative efforts initially in two of the most backward districts identified by the HDR — Achham and Baitadi, in the far-western mountainous region of Nepal. They have agreed, furthermore, to adopt the social mobilisation approach adopted by the PDDP for their future work in these districts.

The way this collaboration works is that whenever one of the agencies decides to undertake some programme for a number of districts, it would try to include one or both of these two districts. Thus both the PDDP, supported by UNDP, and the Decentralised Planning for the Child Programme (DPCP), supported by UNICEF, have Achham as one of their common districts. UNESCO has included these two districts in their programme for Enhancing the Role of Women in Development through Community Learning Centres (WIDE-CLC). The World Food Programme and UNDP have jointly devised a food-for-work programme for the two districts. The United Nations Environment Programme (UNEP) will collaborate with the United Nations country team for Nepal to produce a state-of-the art environmental study for the two districts, while UNDP and the Food and Agricultural Organisation (FAO) will join hands to identify critical food security concerns and opportunities.

The Nepal HDR is also helping to solve a problem of inconsistency that has often plagued the UN agencies in the past in the use of data. Different agencies have tended to use different data sources in their respective country assessments. Recently, they have decided to ensure greater consistency by adopting a UN Common Country Assessment (CCA). While the CCA still draws upon data from multiple sources, a decision has been taken to rely mainly on the consistent statistical database created by the Nepal HDR wherever a problem of inconsistency might arise.

Conclusion

In comparison to the millions of dollars spent by UNDP alone, not to mention other agencies and the respective country governments themselves, the PSI activities were a very small intervention in the context of both countries' efforts to reduce poverty. As such, it would be unrealistic to expect that they would have a huge direct impact. Those who conceived of the PSI programme did not expect it either. From the very beginning, the objective of the programme was to use the small financial outlay strategically so as to have a large indirect effect.

These indirect effects were expected to flow from the ability of the PSI activities to act as a catalytic agent, by raising awareness, by generating critical information, by supporting interagency cooperation, and by building capacities of relevant stakeholders. If this catalytic function is performed well, then the activities supported by the PSI programme can be expected to lead to new initiatives, perhaps by leveraging additional funds from other sources, or by strengthening existing initiatives. In either case, the ultimate effect would far exceed the immediate direct effect of those activities.

For this to happen, two conditions must be met. First, the activities must be chosen with great care, giving due consideration to the question of which kind of activities are likely to have the largest possible catalytic impact in the particular circumstances of a country. Secondly, the processes that are employed in undertaking these activities must be inclusive enough to generate a sense of ownership on the part of relevant stakeholders and to be able to create relevant capacities. This applies especially, though not exclusively, to the government of the host country.

It is from this perspective that the PSI activities in India and Nepal have been assessed in this chapter. In neither country has the programme been in existence long enough to fully assess its impact. Nevertheless, even for the short period it has been existence (four years in India, three in Nepal), we find enough evidence of a strong catalytic effect. In both countries, the Human Development Reports have been singularly successful in raising awareness about the value of the human development approach and the huge disparities that exist between regions and between different population groups. They have also succeeded in reorienting the strategic thinking of policy-makers, in building capacities both inside and outside the government, and in equipping local governments and civil society with concepts and information that they are capable of using effectively while playing their respective advocacy roles. In India, the activities around the state HDRs have also had considerable success in leveraging additional funds for carrying forward the tasks initiated by the PSI programme.

It would be presumptuous to claim that these changes have occurred directly as a consequence of the activities supported by the PSI programme. There is no doubt that gradual changes in the development paradigm that are taking place at the global level, helped to a considerable degree by UNDP's own global effort at pushing the human development agenda, must have played a big role in bringing about these changes. But it seems equally clear that the PSI activities in India and Nepal have contributed significantly towards bringing this global agenda closer to the attention of both policy-makers and civil society.

All the PSI activities undertaken in India have helped to strengthen interagency cooperation, both among the UN agencies and between the UN system and other multilateral and bilateral donors. Clearly, the position papers written for the India Development Forum have enhanced the capacity of both UNDP and the government of India to influence donor strategies, especially those of the World Bank, towards the human development approach. To a significant extent, interagency cooperation was also promoted in Nepal, if not as a direct outcome of the PSI activities then as a result of the inter-district ranking generated by the *Human Development Report*.

A number of factors can be cited for the impressive success of the PSI programme in both countries. First, the HDRs have gained wide acceptance among diverse segments of the population. This is in part because they have addressed issues such as hunger, livelihoods, literacy, education, and people's participation in governance, that are close to the heart of the people. Most importantly, in both countries these reports have been seen as honest attempts to understand and address the problems they face. The intellectual quality and analytical rigour of parts of these reports may be debated, but there is a general consensus about the intellectual integrity and genuine spirit of enquiry underlying the work. The absence of political and bureaucratic interference has played a crucial role here, which was a remarkable achievement given the fact that the Indian reports were prepared primarily by government officials. In Nepal, the attribute of political neutrality has emanated from the fact that intellectuals aligned with the country's two major political parties were involved in the preparation of the report.

Second, while the HDRs did not make any path-breaking innovation in conceptualising poverty or laying the theoretical foundations for poverty reduction strategies, they made a major empirical contribution in both countries. This has had a far-reaching effect. The SHDRs of India and the HDR of Nepal made a conscious effort to statistically delineate the disparities that existed within their jurisdiction, whether between districts, ethnic groups or sexes. Diverse advocacy groups have seized upon these statistical data in order to advance their respective causes. Almost any disadvantaged group can find something in these reports to offer concrete evidence in support of their grievances. As a result, the HDRs have not remained isolated intellectual exercises; they have entered the mainstream of political and economic discourse.

Third, in the context of the move towards decentralised governance that has gained momentum in both countries in the 1990s, the decision to support the preparation of HDRs has turned out to be an astute one. In India, decentralisation means, in the first instance, greater autonomy of the states in designing economic policies and allocating resources. In this respect, the state-level HDRs have proved an ideal vehicle for equipping the state governments with the statistical picture of human deprivation within their territories and for identifying policy priorities and critical bottlenecks. It is because of this potential contribution SHDRs can make to the cause of decentralisation that UNDP has been able to persuade the government of India to undertake a project for producing SHDRs for as many Indian states as possible.

In both India and Nepal, the HDRs have made a further contribution to the cause of decentralised governance by generating a statistical database disaggregated at the district level. Local governments utilising this database as benchmarks for formulating local development plans, as diagnostic tools for allocating resources to the most deprived areas, and as advocacy tools in asking for resources from the higher echelons of government.

In view of the support given by the HDRs to the cause of decentralisation, there is a good case for UNDP to continue to support these activities in both India and Nepal. National and sub-national HDRs could be a very effective instrument for policy and advocacy, given the fact that decentralised participatory governance has gained wide acceptance as the most appropriate institutional framework for advancing the cause of human development in both countries. Of course, the nature and content of these reports will have to evolve. The first rounds of reports were comprehensive in nature, surveying the whole field of human deprivation in their respective jurisdiction. Future HDRs will have to focus more specifically on crucial priority areas, and they will have to be much more policy-oriented.

Those who undertake these activities, whether government officials or independent researchers, may need technical support to able to rethink economic policies from the human development perspective. Particularly in India, similar needs of this type will be felt within each state, as every state undertakes to prepare HDRs of its own. There has been some discussion in India about setting up a resource centre to service these common needs and distil lessons from common experiences. Once in existence, such an institution could provide support to the efforts of other countries in the region to implement the human development approach to economic policy-making. The UNDP office in New Delhi has expressed an interest in such a centre for some time. This could prove an astute use of any future resources. ■

Notes

The author is especially grateful to the UNDP country offices in India and Nepal for providing excellent help and support during the field visits on which this report is based. He would also like to thank the many individuals and institutions in both countries who gave generously of their time and opinions.

[1] The assessment is based primarily on the information gathered by the author during his field trips (February 19-29, 2000 in India and April 1-5, 2000 in Nepal), supplemented by the reading of documents collected before and during the visits.

[2] The following excerpt from the Address of the Governor of Karnataka to the State Legislature (October 1999) quotes data directly from the *Human Development Report of Karnataka* 1999: 'My government is aware of the fact that despite our efforts made in the areas of primary education and literacy, rural female literacy is less than 35 per cent in many districts. There are still over a million children in the age group of 6 to 12 who are out of schools. Half of the children, who enrol in Class I, do not complete elementary school. My government thus proposes to launch a massive programme to achieve universalisation of primary education and raise the overall literacy rate of the state to 80 per cent by 2005 AD.'

[3] UNDP has committed US$ 500,000 out of its core funds for this project, which is far in excess of the US $150,000 that was initially committed out of the PSI programme to support the preparation of SHDRs. More significantly, the government of India has committed to spend up to US$ 1 million in each of the three years of the project duration. This project thus represents a successful case of a relatively small amount of PSI resources first leveraging a much larger amount of UNDP's own core funds and then going on to leverage even larger funds from outside UNDP, viz. the government of India.

[4] An interesting episode occurred in the Bellary district of Karnataka, which is a traditional Congress stronghold. Sonia Gandhi, the leader of the Congress Party and widow of the late Prime Minister Rajiv Gandhi, contested the election for the national parliament from this constituency in 1999. While touring Bellary during her election campaign, she was embarrassed by the journalists and opposition candidates who pointed out that despite decades of support given by the people of Bellary to the Congress Party, it had done little to improve the lot of the common people in the district. In support of this contention, the detractors pointed out that although the district ranked fairly high (7th) in terms of per capita income, it had a low rank in terms of the Human Development Index (HDI), a fact that had only recently been brought to light by the Karnataka SHDR.

[5] For instance, according to the Chairman of the District Development Committee of the Kavre district in Nepal, his district plan has taken the HDR figure of 37 per cent literacy rate for his district as the benchmark and is aiming to raise it to 60 per cent within the plan period.

[6] The member of Nepal's National Planning Commission responsible for these programmes stated that while the HDR alone was not responsible for the genesis of these programmes, it played a big role, first by drawing attention to the disadvantaged groups and locations and, second, by developing concrete indicators with which these groups and locations could be identified for the purpose of targeted policy action.

CHAPTER 12 Laos

Alf Morten Jerve

n late 1998, the Vientiane office of the United Nations Development Programme (UNDP) applied for funds from the Poverty Strategies Initiative (PSI) to assist the Laotian government in redefining its policies for rural development. The case of the Lao People's Democratic Republic (Lao PDR) illustrates some of the problems that donors and development cooperation agencies may encounter when trying to engage in a policy reform process in a context of weak institutional capacity and limited ownership.

Some governments find the concept of poverty ill-suited to their national political rhetoric, sometimes even potentially threatening. To date, the Laotian government has only reluctantly engaged in limited, mostly donor-driven, analytical work on poverty. This reluctance by no means constitutes a denial by either the government or the Lao People's Revolutionary Party that poverty is a serious issue, but it does reflect the fact that national unity has been the overriding concern in this multi-ethnic country. This concern gives rise to a political discourse that emphasises development rather than differences.

This political reality played a role in the type of work UNDP conducted in Laos. Two other factors influenced the focus of the PSI activities. First, poverty is overwhelmingly a rural phenomenon, which implies that it is not possible to address poverty without also addressing rural development issues. Secondly, the country's rural development strategy has been criticised for its treatment of ethnic minorities and its approach to local-level planning and development management.

In response to these factors, UNDP decided to place its work on poverty in the broader framework of rural development policy, and simultaneously address both rural development management and ethnic minority issues. This was done through the preparation of four studies and a follow-up conference at which the results of the studies were presented to government officials, Party functionaries and representatives from the donor community. UNDP also became involved in supporting two key actors. One is the Central Leading Committee on Rural Development, which is responsible for the supervision of the controversial Focal Site Strategy for the development of the country's remote areas. The other is the Lao Front for

National Construction, which has a mandate to oversee the government's policy towards the ethnic minorities.

Country context

Laos is among the least developed countries in the world, with life expectancy at birth of 52 years and a comparatively high degree of shared poverty.[1] More than 80 per cent of the country's 4.8 million inhabitants live in rural areas, and poverty is overwhelmingly a rural problem. There are 236 different ethnic groups, and the non-ethnic Lao — often referred to as ethnic minorities — make up 70 per cent of the population. These two features are more or less congruent, making poverty reduction a question of how to integrate ethnic minorities into mainstream national development, and how to develop economic opportunities for rural people, and ethnic minorities in particular. There is, moreover, the fundamental question of how to improve government service delivery in a sparsely populated country where large mountainous tracts have no road access.

With the enormous ethnic diversity and rural-urban disparities of Laos, it is virtually impossible to establish meaningful indicators of culturally acceptable minimum standards of living. For this reason, the country has no officially accepted poverty line. Based on minimum caloric requirement, it is estimated that 22 per cent of the population live in deep poverty — with 26 per cent in rural areas and only 8 per cent in urban areas. A Social Indicator Survey conducted in 1992-1993 estimated that 46 per cent did not have enough income 'to live decently'. A World Bank study from 1995 estimates even higher levels of poverty, especially in the rural areas: 26 per cent of rural Laotians do not have the income required to provide a minimum food intake. The situation is worse in the South. More than half of the rural population (53 per cent) falls below a higher poverty line, which includes allowance for non-food expenditures (World Bank 1995).

There is, moreover, no detailed information on the relationship between poverty and ethnicity. Mainly for political reasons, information on ethnicity has not been collected in population censuses and household consumption surveys. There is also the practical problem of no officially recognised terminology for categorising ethnic groups that corresponds to ethno-linguistic classifications or to what people prefer to call themselves. There are groups that live a secure traditional life in areas with abundant natural resources, but an increasing number of minorities experience environmental stress and a sense of deprivation in their inability to generate sufficient income and to benefit from social services.

Ethnic Lao dominate the government, civil service and the Lao People's Revolutionary Party. Despite a long history of peaceful relations with the various ethnic minorities, the government has pursued policies of 'stabilising' and resettling minority communities since independence in 1975. The government justifies

its policies in terms of a development ideology of modernisation and cultural evolution, as well as nation-building and a perceived security risk.[2] Hence, poverty
reduction, rural development and ethnic minority issues are by and large overlapping concerns, with strong political undercurrents that greatly complicate policy.

Against this background, the UNDP office decided to provide assistance to the
government for a refinement of its rural development policy. An equally important
objective was to help place ethnic minority issues on the country's policy agenda.

Rural development policy

Rural development has been a priority in the Lao PDR since a Party resolution
passed in 1994. The topic ranked high on the agenda of the Sixth Donor Round
Table meeting in 1997. One of the key objectives of the current policy is to 'alleviate poverty among rural populations in remote areas' (Lao PDR 1998b).[3]

To achieve this goal, the government elaborated a Focal Site Strategy for 1998-
2002, which was presented to the donor community at a meeting held in Vientiane
in 1998. Focal Sites are defined as rural areas in which the government concentrates its development efforts to alleviate poverty among its inhabitants. Village
consolidation is seen as the most cost-effective way of making development services available to scattered and remote communities that would otherwise not be
reached with the limited resources available in Laos. Village consolidation is also
officially expressed as a means necessary to reduce the adverse environmental
impacts of shifting cultivation in poor and remote areas. As a result of the Focal
Site Strategy, the term 'rural development policy' came to be associated with the
government's intention to develop rural growth areas, based on settled agriculture
and improved public services.

The Focal Site Strategy had been controversial from the beginning. Although
the government contends that the Strategy is based on voluntary resettlement, it
has set ambitious targets for its implementation. In several cases, more than 50 per
cent of the upland district populations, mainly in the South, are to be moved over
a period of five years (Goudineau 1997). The speed of the planned resettlement has
received criticism from several donors and non-governmental organisations, who
fear that the Focal Site Strategy could become an instrument used by the government for coercively resettling ethnic minorities from remote mountain areas to the
lowlands. Critics, not least within the donor community, argue that the development rhetoric behind the Focal Site Strategy, while making use of familiar concepts
of area-based development, community participation and bottom-up planning,
actually disguises a top-down, technocratic approach to development aimed at
enhancing control and influence over ethnic minorities.

In response to this criticism, in recent years it appears that the government has
taken a more cautious approach, realising that rushing ahead might cause prob-

lems. Nonetheless, there remain reports of overzealous local authorities applying pressure and coercion to meet targets. Even in cases where people moved voluntarily, adjustment to the new sites has turned out to be so difficult for most that quality of life and living standards have dropped.[4]

The Focal Site Strategy also met with a profound scepticism among donors with respect to the implementation capacity of government. A major weakness of the strategy is that it lacks a clear policy and guidelines on resettlement (Goudineau 1997). There is confusion between implementing agencies and lack of transparency and formalisation of rights and obligations in the relations between the state and those who resettle. A critical issue, for instance, is the right to land and the impending scarcity of quality land with the higher concentration of people in the new sites.

There is also incoherence in the process of designating sites. Some are identified by central government, others by provinces and districts. There are as many as 87 official sites, a large proportion of which lack budgetary planning. Part of the problem is an apparent rivalry over the coordinating and monitoring role, between the provincial Rural Development Offices reporting to the Central Leading Committee for Rural Development (CLCRD) and the Party, and the provincial Departments of Planning reporting to the State Planning Committee and Government. Various line departments execute projects. Since these agencies have their own planning processes and sectoral priorities, their programming is not well integrated with the Focal Site Strategy. In some cases, line agencies have dropped projects in localities designated Focal Sites, assuming other sources of funds will fill the financial gap. Management of the Focal Site Strategy, therefore, has become a critical issue.

This climate of confusion and distrust of government policy, in a context in which all parties otherwise agree on the critical importance of promoting rural development, led UNDP to apply funding from the PSI programme to pursue further analysis in two policy areas.[5] Studies were commissioned to serve both as an input into government decision-making and a means of rallying donor support for the implementation of rural development programmes.

The first theme covered by the studies is the rural development management process. This includes an overview of existing planning and budget procedures, data collection and monitoring systems, and resource mobilisation. Additionally, the model developed under the Integrated Rural Access Programme (IRAP) was reviewed at the request of the Swedish International Development Cooperation Agency (SIDA), the programme's main donor. IRAP is a pilot initiative undertaken with the International Labour Organization (ILO). It aims to prioritise investments and improve local-level planning based on an analysis of people's physical access to different services or basic needs.

The studies recommend a shift in government policies from investments in 'hardware' to investments in people, a reduced emphasis on studies, data collection and planning tools that has been typical of most donor projects, and greater attention to public sector reform, especially at decentralised levels of government (Taylor 1999). While endorsing the basic logic of the Focal Site Strategy, the studies nonetheless stress the need for more systematic planning and better coordination between the various players from government and the donor community (Tracey-White 1999a). IRAP is viewed as a useful approach to area development planning, provided it is modified in order to make it less expert-intensive and more geared to facilitating consultative and participatory methods of local level planning (Mercat 1999).

Surprisingly, none of the studies above grappled with the ethnic minority issue in assessing the political, participatory and technical aspects of decentralised planning, despite the multi-cultural context of Laos. In response to this, a separate study was financed by the PSI programme to document the impact of government policies on ethnic minorities and make recommendations on how to integrate these concerns into mainstream development planning (Chamberlain 1999). The main focus of this report is on Laos' Ethnic Minority Policy, which is found to conform to the spirit of the ILO Convention 169 on the rights of indigenous and tribal peoples. The policy, nevertheless, needs to be strengthened and made more explicit with regard to resettlement, traditional land use rights, the status and recognition of minority languages, customs, traditions and indigenous knowledge, and rural development planning.

In addition to these studies, the PSI project included a technical assistance component in support of the State Planning Committee and the CLCRD, and funding for a national workshop to discuss the findings of the studies with all the relevant stakeholders. A synthesis report was prepared in preparation for the workshop, which took place in October 1999. The report lists five policy areas that should receive priority attention from the authorities:

- Creating the right conditions for ethnic minority issues to be fully integrated with rural development planning and management;
- Improving planning processes, at both central and local levels;
- Creating the means for income and employment generation in remote rural areas;
- Expanding human resource development and training;
- Reforming public administration and strengthening of local institutions.

The synthesis report formulated ten potential project packages for the follow-up phase, of which the first two were adopted at the national workshop. They will provide institutional support to the policy-making agencies responsible for the policy on ethnic minorities and the Focal Site Strategy, respectively. Package 1 will assist the Lao Front for National Construction, which has an explicit mandate, given by the Party, to supervise the ethnic minorities policy and 'build solidarity in the population'. Its Department for Ethnic Groups and Social Class is very vocal on the minority issue and appears to be the best avenue for strengthening minority rights. This includes affirmative actions to ensure greater representation in the National Assembly, protection of cultural heritage and language, and collection of reliable statistics on ethnic groups. The approach advocated by the Front, which emphasised training civil servants and improving statistics on ethnic minorities, won over an alternative proposal presented by the ILO, which stressed the need to focus on the ratification of its Convention 169, but would have required a much larger, and therefore more costly, technical assistance component.

Package 2 will support the Central Rural Development Office in the task of clarifying the Focal Site Strategy, in particular the mechanisms for prioritising sites so as to make more explicit whether their primary function is economic, social or defence. It is expected that this work will be linked to IRAP, if the latter is continued. Support to the Central Rural Development Office seems to be a wise investment, given its current and likely future role in rural development. There is, nevertheless, an urgent need to clarify its responsibilities vis-à-vis the State Planning Committee. There is also a need to clarify how the Focal Site Strategy will be revised and implemented.

In contrast to other donor agencies, UNDP has generally supported the government's Focal Site approach, adopting a strategy of constructive dialogue with the Laotian authorities. However, it remains to be seen whether this strategy of constructive engagement will enable UNDP to play a more catalytic role in bringing about some changes in the most controversial aspects of the country's rural policy, in particular on the issue of resettlement. To play this role, UNDP needs a strategic vision on rural development and anti-poverty policy to guide its dialogue with the government.

Obstacles to reform

It is improbable that policy reform initiatives can succeed in the absence of strong national ownership. Public debate on rural development and poverty reduction is restricted in Laos and, although a certain pluralism of opinions is allowed within the People's Revolutionary Party, the country has no explicit national discourse on poverty yet. 'Poverty', in fact, does not seem to be a popular concept in the political vocabulary of the Party, as is often the case in one-party states. It prefers to emphasise stimulating growth in the rural economy, rather than dwelling on inequality and on the poor as specific social category. The studies financed by the PSI have not had a discernible impact in this respect.

Ironically, in a country where 80 per cent of the population live in rural areas, only 8 per cent of public investments are earmarked specifically for rural development. Although this figure does not include the projects located in rural areas of various line agencies, most of which have substantial donor funding, it nonetheless reflects a strong urban bias in public investments. Moreover, even if we examine the distribution of the Focal Site investments themselves, we observe that as much as 40 per cent go to transport infrastructure, whereas health and education combined receive 14 per cent. In all sectors, the outlays on buildings are quite high, which points to a syndrome typical of many countries in which too little emphasis is given to human capital development and operational costs.

The ideology that drives the Focal Site approach has led the government to define rural development as a 'sector', resulting in problems of vertical and horizontal coordination of development planning. There is, in fact, a serious problem of dual and overlapping responsibilities in the management of the country's rural development policy. The State Planning Committee and its planning offices at various levels are responsible for development planning and monitoring, but the Party has formed a set of new institutions (the Rural Development Offices) with a mandate to supervise the Focal Site Strategy. To complicate matters further, the respective roles of the planning and rural development offices with regard to the line agencies in the formulation, budgeting and execution of projects remain to be clarified. UNDP is trying to foster a more rational division of responsibilities among all the parties involved, but with no significant results so far. Unless these issues are resolved, the absence of institutional coordination will continue to be a critical bottleneck in the management of rural development programmes in the Lao PDR.

There is, obviously, a need for a more comprehensive approach to rural development than the one currently being pursued by the Laotian government. The contribution of the PSI project to this outcome has been modest. Apart from helping to produce a less controversial version of the Focal Site Strategy, the support from UNDP has done little to enhance the government's will to reform its controversial rural development policies.

The only likely exception is the work on ethnic minorities, where the information and advocacy facilitated by the PSI project could provide new encouragement to reformers in the government and elicit support from donor circles. The support to the Lao Front thus seems a promising initiative. The project has opened up an opportunity to promote the ratification by Laos of ILO Convention 169 on the rights of indigenous and tribal peoples. More and better information on the situation of ethnic minorities could also be a useful tool for those within the Lao Front who would like to strengthen the existing policy environment for ethnic groups. If this is achieved, a major point of contention between the government and the donors will have been removed.

Donor engagement

Laos cannot achieve its development targets without substantial foreign assistance. Today, more than 80 per cent of the rural development budget originates with donors. The government now realises that more active participation of donors in rural development policy is both necessary and a 'price to pay' for attracting more resources. Given its central position amongst donors, UNDP can play a major role in this respect.

With 37 projects under implementation in 1999, UNDP remains, in fact, the biggest single actor on the donor side and a preferred advisor to the government on policy matters. The central role of UNDP as an advisor on rural development policy dates back to 1996, when the Laotian government requested its assistance in formulating a national rural development programme to implement a Party resolution that had been passed two years before. The programme's chief goal was to strengthen methods of local level planning by testing approaches to decentralised planning and implementation of projects in remote areas. Despite UNDP's significance as a donor, it is struggling to form its own strategic views in Laos. In this regard, the PSI programme has played an important role not only in providing information, but also in helping UNDP to clarify its own vision.

Another important goal of the programme was to create a better framework for mobilising donor funding. Support was to be concentrated on 5 of the country's 17 provinces, and implementation started with the preparation of provincial socio-economic profiles, followed by donor round tables in each of the provinces. A package of projects, developed on the basis of local consultations, was presented to these round tables, with a view to soliciting pledges from participating donors.

The results were disappointing. Bilateral donors did not come forward and the projects were funded mostly by UNDP sources. The lack of donor response clearly points to the need to strengthen the government's capacity to 'sell' its policies more effectively. Consequently, when funding from the PSI programme became available, one of the main objectives became to support the government's efforts to produce a more sanitised version of the Focal Site Strategy and to engage the donor community in the discussion.

With the exception of some progress in bringing ethnic minority issues to the forefront of the policy agenda, it is not clear that UNDP has succeeded in persuading donors to support the government's policy thrust. The Asian Development Bank and the Word Bank have stated categorically that they cannot support a rural development policy that involves involuntary or coerced movement of people — which, according to the Laotian government, it does not. And while some NGOs have agreed to follow the government's request to work in designated Focal Sites, most of the bilateral donors continue to shy away from them. In this situation, government representatives clearly appreciate any support from UNDP that can help them sell the Focal Site concept to the donors.

At the same time, the PSI project has furthered the collaboration between UNDP and ILO on local-level planning. This collaboration has facilitated the transfer of perspectives from some of the international programmes sponsored by

ILO, which emphasise the promotion of rights and income-generation activities among indigenous peoples. This, in turn, has opened the door for providing support to the Lao Front for National Construction, which is probably the most significant institutional impact of the PSI project. Meetings with the Front, as well as comments from independent observers, confirmed that there is a genuine commitment to pursue policy reform along the lines of ILO Convention 169 on the rights of indigenous and tribal peoples. Other sections of the polity, however, still advocate assimilation and relocation of minorities as the way forward.

Leaving aside the thorny issues of resettlement and ethnic minorities, there are also other reasons for revisiting the approach and improving the message to donors. The experience with area development and integrated rural development in other countries is mixed. Both models have encountered problems related to the implantation of top-down and expert-led project management units that were poorly integrated with local politics and local capacity. Often headed by expatriate personnel, these units have tended to be too obsessed with technocratic approaches to planning, at the expense of a more organic view of development, where government programmes are responsive to community and private initiatives.

The evaluation of the IRAP model, funded by the PSI project, underscores similar lessons. It points to the fact that, in a country characterised by a weak local government structure, donor-managed rural development projects easily may repeat some of the mistakes made in other countries. UNDP can play a role in bringing this type of knowledge and experience to the attention of government and donors in Laos, and demonstrate how more flexible programmes anchored in community initiatives and local government decision-making can be replicated.

Conclusions

Poverty in Laos is predominantly a rural phenomenon. As the political climate does not favour an explicit focus on poverty issues, UNDP sensibly concluded that they would best be addressed through policies dealing with rural development and ethnic minorities. The PSI funds were thus intended to assist the Laotian government in clarifying its development strategy towards the rural sector, especially its controversial Focal Site approach.

Two general lessons emerge from the project. First, donors and development agencies need to accept that policy work addressing poverty issues may have to take place under different banners, without becoming less relevant for that reason. Second, in many countries, dealing with poverty issues will entail engaging in basic conflicts over rights, entitlements and influence. For donors to become involved in such circumstances requires more than money. It demands careful understanding of the situation and a clear vision of the role they want to play.

Clearly, UNDP remains in a position to play a constructive role in rural development policy-making. In addition to its wide experience accumulated over several years of implementing projects, UNDP is the only agency with an overview of the general direction of development planning and implementation in Laos. Its strategy of constructive engagement in policy dialogue has given it a place at the table in a country where weak national capacity has led to a rather fragmented and uncoordinated donor engagement. Given its unquestionable position within the donor community, new donors will go to UNDP for advice if they seek a role in rural development.

UNDP has been supportive of the government's efforts to clarify its Focal Site concept and sell it to sceptical donors. Nevertheless, there are no indications that the assistance provided has either improved the government's salesmanship or its will to reform the policy by shedding some of its more contentious aspects. The studies sponsored by UNDP addressed a rather narrow audience, which severely limited their impact and potential use. One of the studies was requested by a donor agency that needed an evaluation in order to decide whether or not to continue supporting the IRAP project. Other studies provided a general overview of rural management issues in Laos, but lacked an identifiable audience and were not integrated with a genuine national reform process. As a result, key government agencies feel very little ownership of the results of the studies. The report on ethnic minorities appears to be the only one that has contributed some useful analysis that could be used to influence policy reforms.

There are critical institutional barriers to effective rural development planning and implementation in Laos. The Focal Site Strategy seems to be underpinned by an outmoded approach to rural development, dominated by top-down technocratic planning. The dominant picture has been one of institutional fragmentation and competition within the public sector. Capacity-building has been negligible in the first phase of the PSI project, while the linkages of the studies financed by UNDP to national decision-makers have been too weak to exert any pressure on reforming the management structure. Consequently, despite its deep involvement in rural development, UNDP has not been able to move the Laotian government in the direction of resolving the institutional quagmire that hampers implementation. The support to either the CLCRD and its Rural Development Offices, or the State Planning Committee, raises a number of questions, given their fragile institutional set-up and overlapping mandates.

Three fundamental issues need to be resolved to facilitate an improved working relationship between the government and donors. They are the policy towards ethnic groups, the Focal Site approach, and the management of development planning and execution of public projects at the local level. These issues also are critical components of a strategy to reduce poverty. Yet promoting a national strategy for reducing poverty as an integral part of a rural development policy requires a clarification of UNDP's own vision of rural development, poverty reduction and local government in the country.

UNDP is walking a tightrope, trying to assist the Laotian government in its policy efforts while at the same time upholding international standards and best practices. It is evident that the current official policy of resettling ethnic minorities, even if by incentives rather than force will potentially collide with internationally recognised rights of indigenous peoples, like the right to self-determination. The planned support to the Lao Front is therefore a promising initiative, and probably the best course to follow at the present time.

While it awaits the enactment of a more rational local government system, the donor community can probably make its best contribution by systematising experiences on how different Focal Sites have been managed, collecting lessons on various approaches to participatory community development in donor-funded projects, and accessing international experiences on local government support programmes. ■

Notes

The author wishes to acknowledge Adarsha Tuladhar from UNDP Vientiane for organising the programme of interviews and necessary logistics for his mission to Laos, and Alejandro Grinspun for editorial support.

[1] This shows in the statistics as a low Gini coefficient and a low poverty gap despite a high poverty headcount. A major reason is that almost all of the rural households have land use rights or free access to land. This keeps absolute destitution and famine at bay. Socio-economic data need to be interpreted with great caution. There is, for instance, much uncertainty with respect to how to monetise incomes in non-tradable rural produce. Some estimates claim that only 20 per cent of the economy is visible to macroeconomic planners. The remainder is in black market transactions and trade in illicit commodities (timber, wildlife, forest products and drugs).

[2] More recently, the adverse ecological impacts of shifting cultivation have been added to the list of arguments. While many minorities have been able to lead their traditional way of life, with ample nourishment and a sense of cultural dignity, several groups have been victims of man-made or environmental upheaval.

[3] This policy and its so-called Focal Site Strategy date back to 1994 when the Party adopted a resolution that made rural development a priority issue. The rural development policy was further consolidated in the 1995 with the preparation of the five-year Socio-Economic Development Plan (1996-2000). This plan identified eight priority programmes for Laos to achieve the stated goal of moving out of the rank of low-income country by the year 2020. Although only one of the programmes was labelled 'rural development', in a country where 80 per cent of the people live in rural areas the other seven programmes will also necessarily have to target rural areas.

[4] Laos has a long history of population displacement, dating back to the Indochina and American wars. In the post-war period, there was a considerable movement of people returning to their pre-war home areas. Development-induced resettlement is a more recent phenomenon. It includes involuntary resettlement caused by development projects, in particular hydropower schemes, as well as for purposes of 'stabilising' shifting cultivation and combating deforestation. On the other hand, a traditional adaptive strategy of most ethnic minorities has involved relocation in intervals of 10 to 20 years. They are thus seen as accustomed to resettling, which should ease their adaptation to a Focal Site policy. In spite of this, there are examples of resettlement undertaken without due consideration of its impact on people's livelihood. It has turned out to be particularly difficult for upland people to establish viable paddy farming systems. As a result, many have ended up as agricultural labourers for established lowland farmers.

[5] The project was approved in December 1988, with a budget of US$ 200,000 allocated in two phases. The first phase financed four thematic studies and a national workshop. The second phase, which began in mid-2000, includes follow-up activities that where agreed upon during the national workshop.

13 Guatemala and Uruguay

Mercedes González de la Rocha

Situated respectively at the tip of the Southern Cone and the north end of the Central American isthmus, Uruguay and Guatemala represent two very different faces of Latin America. Their development trajectories could hardly have been more dissimilar. Uruguay is an upper middle-income country with some of the highest human development indicators in the region. During most of its modern history, democratic regimes have presided over a highly integrated and homogeneous society. Guatemala is much poorer, with a record of undemocratic regimes and a highly conflicted and stratified society in which the presence of a strong indigenous component of Mayan origin constitutes a distinctive feature.

Paradoxically, these contrasts illuminate the close linkages between poverty reduction and governance in each country. In Guatemala, the great challenge is binding together a war-torn society whose very fragmentation caused four decades of armed hostilities. Uruguay's task is arresting the disintegration of a society whose cohesion was its defining characteristic. Both countries also manifest the impact of the political cycle, notably elections, on the national dialogue on poverty.

This chapter is based on the experience of two projects implemented by the United Nations Development Programme (UNDP) under its Poverty Strategies Initiative (PSI). It begins with basic socio-economic background on each country, then explores the governance challenges faced by both. It then delineates the objectives of each of the PSI projects and the ways in which activities were carried out. Before it summarises the author's conclusions, the chapter discusses the impact of the political cycle in each nation on poverty reduction policy formulation and its prospects.

Background

During the 1980s, Guatemala embarked upon a programme of economic stabilisation and structural reforms that relied on deregulation, privatisation of state assets and incentives to attract foreign capital (Schneider 1999). The implementation of stabilisation policies continued during the 1990s against a background of pervasive poverty and civil war. According to the most recent statistics (1998), the majority of the country's population live in rural areas and a high proportion (48 per cent) is indigenous. Although agriculture contributes a significant share of the nation's income, its rural areas feature high levels of poverty and heavy migration of land-less peasants who have abandoned their communities in search of decent liveli-hoods. A growing number of these migrants look for jobs in other countries, espe-cially Mexico and the United States. Armed conflict has further displaced an undetermined number of people.[1]

During the late 1980s, 83 per cent of Guatemalan households were poor, and 65 per cent faced conditions of extreme poverty (Bastos 2000). The incidence of poverty is highest among the indigenous population. Only 15 per cent of all indige-nous people lived above the poverty line in 1993, compared with 53 per cent for the rest of the population. Sixty per cent of the indigenous population were extremely poor, a figure that underlines the dearth of their livelihood opportuni-ties in this rigidly stratified society.

This situation contrasts sharply with that of Uruguay, where a generous system of social benefits accompanied the development of a welfare state from the 1950s onwards. Public social spending — education, health, social security and housing — continued to increase during the 1960s, but began to fluctuate and then decline in the 1970s and early 1980s, when it stood at significantly lower levels than before the period that Latin Americans term the 'lost decade' of stabilisation and adjust-ment (Lorenzelli 1998). Data on poverty in Uruguay correspond to the urban areas alone, but given the country's high level of urbanisation, they provide a good approximation of the situation nation-wide. In 1995, 15.7 per cent of urban house-holds were poor, representing almost 23 per cent of the urban population. One per cent of households were considered indigent that same year (Zaffaroni et al. 1998).

Despite their different trajectories and social composition, both Uruguay and Guatemala reached a major crossroads in the late 1990s: each faced the challenge of addressing social inequities and poverty as a major governance concern. As indi-cated above, Guatemala's immediate task was the consolidation of the peace process that had begun a decade earlier. Uruguay grappled with arresting a widen-ing differentiation and atomisation that, since the 1980s, had threatened to seri-ously tear its highly integrated social fabric. Coincidentally, both countries faced imminent presidential elections in 2000, which provided — at least in principle — an opportunity for projecting poverty issues into the public arena. Both these fac-tors weighed heavily in the types of activities sponsored by UNDP in each coun-try, furnishing a useful backdrop for comparative analysis.

The governance challenge

In May 1986 with the Declaration of Esquipulas, Guatemala began engaging in a decade of negotiations that culminated in the signing of the Peace Accords in December 1996. The agreements ended four decades of civil war that had decimated the country. Because they contemplated a cessation of armed insurgency in return for government commitments to address the huge inequalities and contradictions that had characterised Guatemalan society, the Peace Accords explicitly recognised the intimate association between poverty reduction and improved governance. Indeed, they attest to the tremendous effort of Guatemalans to transcend violence and build a framework for peaceful and more equitable coexistence among social actors (IDIES 1997). As this nascent transformation owes so much to the organisations and representatives of the indigenous peoples, one cannot understand the context of PSI activities without examining the struggle of their movement for greater participation in decision-making.

To fulfil its part of the Accords, the government implemented a range of institutional reforms negotiated in the context of the peace process. It also focussed public investments on rural development, as well as health and education, which had been identified as priority areas in a special agreement dealing with socio-economic and agrarian issues. However, the government failed to implement a cross-sectoral strategy for addressing poverty in an integrated manner. The challenge of consolidating peace and democracy proved overwhelming, pushing poverty issues *per se* to the background.

To redress this situation and contribute to the implementation of the Peace Accords, UNDP decided to assist the Mayan people in preparing an assessment of poverty and a development plan of their own (Menmagua 1998, 1999). Both were carried out by the *Mesa Nacional Maya de Guatemala* (Mayan National Council, or Menmagua), an umbrella organisation that represents 26 indigenous associations engaged in development activities at the grassroots level. Both the poverty assessment and the development plan were part of a process of internal reflection within the indigenous movement, a 'coming of age' that presupposed analysing and understanding poverty from a Mayan perspective rather than that of external 'experts'. The process of reflection itself was considered as important as the outcome. It aimed at empowering the Mayans to act as change agents, to identify their priorities according to the needs they themselves perceived.

Along with the work on the Mayan poverty assessment and development plan, UNDP sponsored the elaboration of a social sector expenditure review (Schneider 1999). It aimed at examining the volume of public resources devoted to the provision of basic health and education services, in particular whether the government had met the targets for public sector financing set by the Peace Accords.

Except for occasional urban violence during the late 1960s and early 1970s, Uruguay's history has been much more peaceful than Guatemala's. After a brief authoritarian interlude, the elections of 1985 returned the country to the democratic path it had taken for most of the century. Along with the return of democracy came a remarkable recovery of public social spending, which had suffered serious cutbacks during military rule in the 1970s. Between 1985 and 1989, it rose cumulatively to a rate of 5.6 per cent. This trend continued during the 1990s, when the rate of increase of public social expenditure exceeded that of total government expenditure each year (Lorenzelli 1998). The state's traditionally progressive social policies stem from a system of universal entitlements to social services and benefits, particularly health, education and social security. Yet for this very reason, Uruguay has lacked policies specifically targeted to poverty reduction. Instead of a comprehensive strategy to assist the needy, government policy has encompassed a host of largely fragmented and isolated programmes, each of which deals with a specific aspect of poverty.[2]

In addition to having some of the highest human development indicators in the region, Uruguay is one of Latin America's most equitable societies. During the last few years, however, increasing social differentiation has become manifest in growing residential segregation, as well as widening disparities of access to public spaces and services. A sudden trade liberalisation forced many local industries into bankruptcy and closure, increasing the number of unemployed and under-employed. Nor have there so far been signs of a reversal in this trend. Along with unemployment, the number of street children has risen and general security has declined as violence and theft become more common. While this has surprised local commentators, encouraging economic figures have fostered government complacency, even in the face of increasing vulnerability among the poor. Yet it is this very process of social disintegration, this damage to the social fabric of what was once a highly homogeneous nation, that may eventually plunge the country into grave economic difficulties.

From public discourse to public policy

The first aim of PSI activities in Uruguay was introducing the linkage between economic and social trends into public discourse. In close cooperation with the local office of the Economic Commission for Latin America and the Caribbean (ECLAC), UNDP sponsored a study on the roots of social vulnerability, based on analysis of data from the household income and expenditure survey and information obtained from in-depth interviews in various localities (Kaztman 1999).

In Guatemala, too, PSI activities sought not only to furnish fresh data and analyses to inform policy-making but, most importantly, to raise awareness about issues of poverty among decision-makers and the public at large. The goal of the PSI studies, therefore, was not simply instrumental; they also aimed at changing mind-sets and attitudes by revealing certain aspects of the respective societies that had gone unnoticed.

However, there was a fundamental difference between the objectives pursued in each country. In Uruguay, the main audience for the study on marginality and vulnerability was presumed to be the government. Although the study was certainly intended to influence public discourse and therefore included public information efforts, its ultimate goal was informing policy so that measures could be taken to reverse the country's increasing social fragmentation and the concomitant consolidation of 'pockets' of self-perpetuating poverty.

By contrast, the poverty assessment and development plan produced in Guatemala were aimed first and foremost at the Mayan people themselves, and only then at government officials and the rest of society. Quite apart from influencing policy, Menmagua's studies were driven by goal of building self-awareness in the indigenous movement itself, so that it could speak with its own voice in the affairs of government. The production of information was part of that process. Another, more important one was self-empowerment.

The initiative for the studies came from Menmagua itself. In 1996, Menmagua had taken the first steps towards formulating a national development plan, when it drafted its Logical Framework with support from UNDP. Elaborating this plan required a preliminary assessment of poverty. Data on poverty and living conditions in Guatemala were scarce because no household surveys had taken place between 1989 and 1998. More important, though, the assessment could help mobilise the indigenous community behind common goals, provided it was carried out consultatively.

The design of the poverty study grew out of collective discussions that took place within each of the organisations affiliated to Menmagua. As the study progressed, it was discussed in community assemblies throughout the country, which provided forums for the views of the local people as inputs into the analysis, while at the same time validating its results and disseminating them to the community for further reflection and elaboration. Collective participation and debate were therefore actively encouraged, not merely as a safety valve for long-festering grievances, but as contributions towards correcting a hitherto distorted picture of Guatemala and also towards training individuals and communities to transform their own lives. This participation gave the documents a legitimacy they would have lacked had they been compiled through a less inclusive process.

Because of its own substantive capacity shortfalls, Menmagua engaged the collaboration of a foreign expert. Unfortunately, this technical assistance was not provided systematically enough to permit local absorption of new skills for poverty analysis and planning. This is evident in the quality of the documents produced. They are not systematic surveys — a fact that, in the eyes of some academics and government officials, makes them unfit for decision-making. However, more important is the Mayan organisations' strong sense of ownership of the results, especially the Mayan development plan, which they regard as a true reflection of their own views and priorities. Consequently, the documents are being used by many Mayan organisations as instruments of dialogue with other non-governmental organisations (NGOs), and of advocacy and negotiation with government authorities.

Indeed, Menmagua and its member organisations have succeeded in projecting their message into the public arena — that ethnic discrimination and lack of opportunities for indigenous people are fundamental causes of poverty. They have engaged in vigorous outreach and advocacy to promote a dialogue on poverty and bring into the open their proposals for action, contained in the Mayan Development Plan. To influence the national political and economic agenda, discussions have taken place not only among the 26 organisations that compose the Council but also with government officials, political parties, and a range of non-Mayan organisations. This intense lobbying has borne some fruit, as evidenced by the number of academic articles, press reports and editorials that have taken up the issues raised by Menmagua. Its impact on policy, however, has been more limited — a fact that illuminates the long distance Guatemalan society must still travel to recognise its Mayan population as a force to be reckoned with.

As indicated earlier, UNDP also financed the preparation of a social sector expenditure review to assess the volume of public resources devoted to basic service provision. The study was part of a global project sponsored jointly by UNDP and UNICEF within the framework of the 20/20 Initiative, which promotes universal provision of basic social services as a major component of poverty reduction (chapter 7, this volume). In the Guatemalan context, the 20/20 targets converge with the commitments made in the Peace Accords, which set a timeline for increasing public spending on health and education. This has helped anchor the 20/20 Initiative in the national policy-making setting, bringing a global commitment closer to the attention of politicians and civil society leaders. Concomitantly, local actors could now use the 20/20 Initiative to bolster their case for greater attention to health and education. They could argue that the priorities set in the peace agreements were backed by an international agenda sponsored by the United Nations — proof of the validity of the policy thrust embodied in the Peace Accords.

While the Accords had called for greater emphasis on *basic* service provision, they left open the definition of what constitutes a basic social service and thereby invited controversy. The fact that the 20/20 Initiative contained an internationally agreed definition was brought to bear on this debate, facilitating consensus on a common understanding tailored to the local context.[3] The act of definition thereby became the first step towards tracking government efforts to expand the coverage of basic services. The study found that public social expenditure during the 1990s averaged 4.1 per cent of GDP, reaching its peak in 1998 at 5.8 per cent, which was more than two thirds higher than the amount allocated in 1990. Nonetheless, the study stressed the need for further efforts to fulfil the recommendations of both the 20/20 Initiative and the Peace Accords — especially in the education sector, where much remains to be done in terms not only of coverage, but efficiency and quality (Schneider 1999). Because of severe budget constraints that may preclude further expansion of social spending, the study emphasised the need to raise additional revenues so as to achieve levels of taxation corresponding to 12 per cent of GDP.

Translating a study of this kind into policy is not an overnight process. So far, there is actually no evidence of real impact of the study on government plans. Nonetheless, there are reasons to be optimistic. First, the results of the analysis of public spending on basic services were presented to the Forum of Vice-Ministers, who became aware of the close correspondence between the proposals of the global development agenda in terms of social sector financing and the goals established in the Peace Accords. This lent further support to the recommendations made in the study, including the need for stepping up government efforts in order to fulfil the peace agreements. Further, several key individuals, who had given the study strong support, have since moved to important positions in government, among them, the new Secretary of Public Welfare. Happily, too, the prior government's Under-Secretary of Planning has retained his post after the election of early 2000. Both could therefore serve as links between the work sponsored by UNDP and the elaboration of policy in the new administration — if other developments in a highly fluid political situation prove conducive to furthering the social agenda.

In contrast to Guatemala, where public discourse had generally avoided confronting issues of ethnicity and discrimination, the topic of social vulnerability addressed in Uruguay was already part of the academic debate and had even crept into policy discourse. The discussion centred upon alternative methods of measuring poverty — between those who advocate the adoption of a poverty line representing a minimum basket of food and other necessities, and those who prefer to measure poverty by focussing directly on the level of satisfaction of basic needs. Over time, however, the debate became preoccupied with the virtues or weaknesses of the measurement *indicator* itself at the expense of a broader understanding of the *phenomenon* of poverty — in particular its dynamic aspects that, often, elude measurement. This created the need for fresh analyses that could shed new light on the multi-dimensional nature of poverty and, in so doing, better inform the design of public policy.

Thus, the PSI study adopted the concept of 'vulnerability' to analyse the multiple, intertwined ways in which households deal with adverse changes in labour markets that affect their ability to make ends meet (Kaztman 1999). Changes in the structure of opportunities and the portfolio of household assets occupy a central place in the analysis. So do such temporal dimensions as the family cycle, which expose households to varying levels of vulnerability at particular points in time (chapter 3, this volume). The study further underlines the important role of the *barrio* (neighbourhood) as a space that blurs social distinctions between people of different strata, thereby inducting them into a 'culture' of solidarity and cohesion. The progressive weakening of the *barrio* as a space of social integration and its replacement by socially segregated residential areas is therefore a cause of great concern. It erodes ties of solidarity that bind people together, contributing to atomisation and, potentially, the severing of social relations and the perpetuation of poverty. In fact, most children in Uruguay today live in poor households, which themselves tend to be located in areas of high concentrations of poverty. Being socialised into poverty in a context in which opportunities for social mobility become increasingly scarce, these children are unlikely to join the ranks of Uruguay's much-touted 'middle class' — which itself has been shrinking — and may instead be condemned to a life of deprivation.

Apart from analysing survey data, the vulnerability assessment entailed a qualitative research component based on in-depth interviews with key informants and selected households. Local organisations came together in each of the nine districts in which the ethnographic study took place: community centres, NGOs and neighbourhood associations collaborated with contacts and information, facilitating the access of the researchers to the communities and even to the individual families who would provide the case material for the study. Unlike Guatemala, this involvement of local organisations does not seem to have contributed to either greater awareness or ownership of the results in the communities studied. With only one exception, there was no dissemination of research findings to these communities — neither to their leaders, nor to the families interviewed. Thus, in stark contrast to Guatemala, opportunities for empowering them to become change agents were missed.

The vulnerability study nevertheless had other impacts. Many of its themes are reflected in the national *Human Development Report 1999*, which it influenced deeply. Published only six months after the PSI study was completed (Uruguay 1999), the *Human Development Report* highlights the following challenges for the new administration that resulted from the presidential elections of 1999:

- Inter-generational inequity;
- Differences in fertility rates among social strata, underscoring the fact that biological reproduction seems to occur almost exclusively among the poor;
- Processes of increasing social fragmentation, segregation and atomisation;
- Growing segmentation of public spaces and services, especially in education;
- Critical importance of work in the livelihood mix of the poor, in a context of declining employment opportunities and growing informality.

Insights from the ECLAC/UNDP study also influenced a study by the World Bank that took the central concepts of that work — assets and opportunity structures — as its point of departure. Even more auspicious from the viewpoint of validating the approach to poverty analysis adopted in Uruguay is a comparative research study, underwritten by the Ford Foundation, that will examine the relationship between household assets and vulnerability in Argentina, Chile, Mexico and Uruguay. One of the expected outputs of this project is the development of new indicators — some of them qualitative in nature — to promote a better understanding of the dynamic aspects of poverty.

Findings from the study were reproduced and debated in the country's major newspapers, an effect that was further amplified with the almost simultaneous release of the *Human Development Report*.[4] Arguably, the imminent presidential elections of late 1999 could have served to crystallise these issues for the public. In practice, however, the electoral campaign put the country 'on hold', temporarily halting the embryonic debate on the roots of social vulnerability, at least until the new authorities came to power.

Nonetheless, there were good prospects that academics and commentators would resume this dialogue in earnest after the new government came to power. Uruguayan society has developed the remarkable habit of making certain themes of scholarly enquiry elements of public discourse and, eventually, of public policy. Everyone in Uruguay — those who extol the virtues of the current economic orthodoxy as well as those who condemn its failings — is concerned with the unprecedented fissures that this hitherto cohesive society has begun to reveal. Sooner or later, intellectuals and reformers are likely to place such issues as children's poverty, social exclusion and marginality, or rising social and spatial segregation on the political agenda. When this happens, they will be equipped with a solid piece of analytical and empirical work to support their cause.

The importance of the political cycle

Because the very subject of poverty is politically charged, it is inextricably intermeshed with the political dynamics of a country and, consequently, with the type and timing of elections, as well as the ways in which electoral campaigns are carried out. At one extreme, candidates may frame their entire platform in terms of poverty; at the other, they may choose to ignore it altogether. Similarly, events ranging from a natural disaster within the country's borders to financial crisis in another region may foster or impede the inclusion of poverty issues in approaches to the electorate. Whatever the situation, action to reduce poverty is intrinsically long-term, well beyond the electoral mandate of most countries. For this very reason, few candidates wish to invest their political capital in policies and programmes that show few results over a period of four or five years. This becomes all the more true when the issue itself has not become a normal subject of political discourse.

In Uruguay, this was certainly the case. The study on vulnerability provided a thorough diagnosis of the social situation as well as a set of concrete recommendations for public policy. It helped refute the myth that market mechanisms can in themselves resolve the problems of society, stressing instead the need to conceive economic and social development in holistic terms. This requires public action to correct market failures, transcending the boundaries of specific sectors so as to tackle poverty and vulnerability in an integrated manner. Nonetheless, as indicated above, the change of government in early 2000 interrupted the nascent dialogue on vulnerability and inequality. Understandably, the former administration preferred to celebrate Uruguayan achievements in education, health and life expectancy rather than draw attention to the recent HDR finding that most Uruguayan children live in poor households.

Even more serious, perhaps, is tendency of short-term political calculations to interfere with the production of information for decision-making, either biasing or even discontinuing efforts to compile reliable data that may reveal long-term social trends that call for policy formation. This happened as recently as 1995, when the National Institute of Statistics (INE) stopped measuring poverty — at precisely the time when a decade-long decline in poverty rates changed course. Whether the prevailing situation would change under the new administration was unclear. While the emergence of residential segregation has certainly become a subject of widespread discussion, intellectuals contend that their dialogue with political leaders has weakened in recent years — a situation that does not bode well for an imminent resumption of this dialogue and, consequently, the prospects for devising informed public policy.

In Guatemala, too, an election and a change of government dominated the first two months of 2000. Because PSI activities were more in the nature of building awareness about the plight of indigenous people than influencing policy directly, Menmagua organised a series of high-profile events to project the Mayan agenda into the public arena. This vigorous outreach campaign further emboldened Menmagua to convene a 'Presidential Forum' in Solalá to acquaint all the candidates with the poverty study and the National Development Plan. Seven of the ten candidates did indeed attend — not, however, the one who eventually won the election. Nonetheless, the Forum was broadcast nation-wide over two radio stations and was also covered by television and newspaper correspondents. In addition, presidential candidates, including the current incumbent, raised the issue of poverty in their speeches.

The new government seems more sensitive than its predecessor not only to poverty-related issues, but also those associated with inequality, notably the lack of opportunities for indigenous people and the dismal level of basic social services. Short-term political needs, coupled with the novelty of public awareness of the multiple dimensions of poverty, could seriously obstruct the formulation of poverty reduction strategies in Guatemala. Even the Planning Secretariat, which designs policies, saw little need for a public policy specifically aimed at poverty reduction because it will probably not yield results during the four years of the presidential mandate.

Moreover, planning officials claimed that a poverty strategy targeted explicitly to the indigenous communities would be inappropriate, since it would automatically exclude many poor people who are not of indigenous origin. Further complicating matters, the change from one administration to another brought about a period of uncertainty during which several key Cabinet posts remained unfilled, throwing the country as a whole, including the Mayan Council, into a state of suspended animation. Thus, despite intensive lobbying by Menmagua, the prospects for any immediate change in policy seemed rather dim. Since almost half of Guatemala's population are indigenous and live in extreme poverty, this scenario does not augur well for any effective national strategy for poverty reduction.

Conclusion

PSI activities in Uruguay and Guatemala succeeded in bringing critically important issues to the limelight at a time when election campaigns were beginning in each country, eventually resulting in a change of government in early 2000. These problems were certainly not new — ethnic discrimination as a major cause of poverty in Guatemala or rising vulnerability and social disintegration in Uruguay. But they were articulated so as to catch the attention of academics, the press, and policymakers for projection into the public arena as 'hot', if not, indeed, burning issues.

The quality of the work varied from one country to another. The involvement of ECLAC experts and local academics in Uruguay alongside UNDP contributed to a solid body of work that contains state-of-the-art analysis, well-grounded empirical research, and a good dose of policy recommendations for follow-up by decision-makers. The high quality of the study on the sources of vulnerability has also led to new initiatives that aim to analyse similar processes at work in other Latin American countries, thereby potentially enriching the body of knowledge on the dynamics of poverty across much of an entire continent.

This was not the case in Guatemala, where technical support to Menmagua proved insufficient to compensate for its technical shortcomings — themselves the result of the apparently uncoordinated nature of the assistance Menmagua had received from donor organisations over the years. Government officials, even some academics, dismissed the Mayan poverty study and development plan on account of its weak technical quality. Yet, because both documents stemmed from a vision of society outside the purview of official Guatemalan circles, it is conceivable that the government would have disavowed them even if they had been technically adequate.

In any event, focussing on the *technical* content of Menmagua's reflection misses the point of what PSI activities sought to achieve in Guatemala. Their main goal was not to produce information for direct use in policy, but to support the *polit-ical mobilisation* of a constituency critical to both poverty reduction and the con-solidation of the peace process. That was a strategic choice on the part of UNDP in Guatemala, which reveals certain assumptions about the nature of policy change and effective strategies for influencing it. Opening up the policy arena to a disen-franchised group, it was felt, could ultimately lead to more structural, long-lasting change — even if it precluded a more immediate, tangible translation of PSI inputs into policy outputs. Producing a document of the highest *technical* standards appeared less urgent than developing a common *political* platform for the Mayan people. What matters most is that this platform was not only developed *for* the Mayans, but also *by* them. The process of preparing the poverty assessment and the national plan was critical to developing self-knowledge in the indigenous move-ment — and self-knowledge *is* a precondition of self-empowerment.

This process underlines the variety of forms of knowledge and their uses. For donor organisations, an important lesson emerges from the two cases reviewed in this chapter. Dealing with poverty implies far more than supporting the production of knowledge. Because of the indissoluble bond between poverty reduction and improved governance, donors will need to be cognisant of the intricacies and idio-syncracies of local polities. Political processes are *not* linear. They move fitfully, then surge before halting and even ebbing — then surge once more. Accommodating all these movements requires flexibility, openness and, above all, curbing the desire to capture in some standard grid what is essentially dynamic and irregular.

Notes

Dr. González de la Rocha wishes to thank Reyna de Contreras (UNDP Guatemala), Pablo Martínez (UNDP Uruguay) and Alejandro Grinspun (UNDP New York) for their support during her missions and their comments to an earlier draft of the chapter.

[1] Some estimates put this figure at 150,000 Guatemalan refugees in Mexico and an unknown number of internally displaced persons, who migrated to elude the movements of the army. According to the 1990 United States census, Guatemalans in the US numbered 200,000. Remittances in 1995 amounted to US$ 417 million, ranking as the second source of foreign currency inflows after coffee (Bastos 2000).

[2] Still, some of its policies have been quite effective in addressing poverty. In 1989, for example, a constitutional amendment approved in a plebiscite indexed retirement and pension benefits to the level of inflation. This single change had a remarkable effect. In Montevideo, the num-ber of people over 60 who were living in poverty fell from 27 per cent in 1989 to 18.9 per cent in 1994. Other cities experienced similar drops from 21.9 to 15.5 per cent (Lorenzelli 1998).

[3] The study defines 'basic social services' as comprising pre-primary and primary education, and

preventative health services, including water and sanitation (Schneider 1999). According to the 1999 *Human Development Report* of Guatemala, public resources equivalent to 1.1 per cent of GDP were allocated to the health sector in 1998, thereby achieving the goal of public health expenditures provided for in the Peace Agreements. This, however, was not the case in education (Guatemala 1999).

[4] One of these articles, for example, stated that the situation had improved markedly since1986, when nearly 40 per cent of urban households were poor. It noted, however, that poverty began to rise again in 1997 to reach a new level of approximately 15 per cent following the 'tequila' recession. This tone stood in sharp contrast to other articles that continued to emphasise the comparatively superior performance of Uruguay relative to its neighbours in the region.

Alf Morten Jerve

The Poverty Strategies Initiative (PSI) launched by the United Nations Development Programme (UNDP) in 1996 was intended to be a strategic tool for influencing policy reforms, without prescribing the means to be used. Consequently, there is great variation between countries on how the funding was tailored to ongoing and new initiatives. This chapter describes how UNDP made use of this facility in Lebanon and Palestine, identifies any tangible impacts and reflects on lessons that can be learned for future similar undertakings.

Given the small size of country allocations made available under the programme, it is often difficult to ascribe progress in anti-poverty policy directly to the programme. PSI funds were often combined with other sources to enable UNDP to perform several roles in relation to policy reform initiatives. Of particular interest is the extent to which UNDP acted as catalyst or broker in advancing the poverty discourse and policy reform process in countries in which the programme was offered.

The first section of the chapter presents the poverty situation and policy context of Lebanon and Palestine, and gives an account of the nature and history of PSI activities in each. Then we look at the leveraging effects of the PSI projects, focussing on the extent to which they strengthened ongoing policy reform initiatives and institutional capacity, particularly in host government agencies. Did the PSI projects contribute to enhancing the capacity to reform in key institutions? Did they fit into initiatives already taken by government or other donors, thus enhancing cooperation between multiple stakeholders at the country level? Next we examine what may be called the catalytic effect of the PSI programme. The focus here is on whether these projects were instrumental in raising public awareness, improving critical knowledge, forging new forms of institutional cooperation or enhancing the government's commitment to policy reform in favour of poverty reduction.

The two cases demonstrate the merits of a flexible funding mechanism for strategic policy interventions. In both countries, PSI gave the local UNDP offices the ability to seize opportunities for policy work that eventually had effects far beyond the limited financial contribution of the projects. In Lebanon, the publication of the 1998 *Mapping of Living Conditions* helped place poverty, inequality and regional development issues at the centre of an electoral campaign that culminated with the election of a new government in December of that year. In Palestine, PSI funds were used for the publication of the 1998 *Palestine Poverty Report*, which was instrumental in the creation of the National Commission on Poverty Eradication. The success achieved in both cases was no coincidence. In Lebanon as well as Palestine, UNDP has a special standing within the donor community as a trusted adviser to government, and benefits from the experience and extensive networks of highly qualified local staff. With the recent upheavals in the region, however, the cases also amply demonstrate that progress on the poverty policy front may easily be overturned.

Country context

Lebanon

In 1990, Lebanon emerged from a 15-year long civil war that seriously damaged the country's civil infrastructure, business and human resource base. The war inflicted huge losses in terms of human lives and the social and physical displacement of people. Poverty and social inequality in Lebanon have to be understood as well as addressed in the context of these post-war traumas. The country's leadership was challenged with the need to recreate what had been damaged, while balancing on a tightrope in the religiously charged politics of the country.

The first priorities of the governments that followed the Taef Peace Accord of October 1989 were to rebuild the war-torn infrastructure in Greater Beirut and stabilise the economy. From 1992 to 1998, inflation fell from 100 to 5 per cent, massive civil works projects changed the dilapidated façade of Beirut, and foreign capital and international investors started to return. But these successes seemed not to have had the expected effect on the economy. The initial high growth rates of the post-war period have not been sustained. The reconstruction of Beirut has not stimulated productive investments, while the costs to the state have been formidable.

In the government-sponsored building boom of Beirut, one issue fell by the wayside — the rising incidence of poverty and social inequality. The reasons are mixed, but a significant factor has been the fragile balance of power among the sect-based political factions. Raising the issue of social injustice was seen by many as potentially threatening to the power-sharing mechanisms that had been installed, whereas construction projects offered benefits and spoils to all parties. The sense of deprivation among large sections of the population has been increasing, not least aggravated by the memories of 1960s and early 1970s, when a growing middle class had been enjoying steady improvements in living standards. The past periods of prosperity did not benefit all, pointing to deep-rooted structural problems — not only the damages of war — as causes of poverty.

With the change in government in December 1998, there was a shift in the political perceptions at the cabinet level with respect to poverty. The proclamations of the new regime included addressing regional disparities and social development. Poverty, it was now felt, could trigger social unrest if the government did not act.

Making action possible, however, requires knowing who, how many and where the poor are. This is not so easy in a country in which social statistics have traditionally been seen as politically sensitive and treated with caution.[1] By the start of the 1960s, 4 per cent of the Lebanese controlled 32 per cent of national income, whereas 50 per cent were poor, living mainly in the rural areas. By the end of the decade, a period of global economic growth, coupled with conscious efforts by governments to develop a welfare state, had reduced disparities, but not sufficiently to mitigate the escalation of violent conflict.

It was not until the World Summit for Social Development in 1995 that the issue of poverty was brought back onto the political agenda, thanks to the newly created Ministry of Social Affairs (MoSA), which was established in 1993. Assisted by the United Nations Economic and Social Commission for Western Asia (ESCWA) and UNDP, the Ministry flagged poverty as a major national concern and advocated the formulation of a national strategy for poverty reduction. A preparatory study for the Summit, done by a Lebanese expert, gave the first post-war numerical expression of poverty in Lebanon (Haddad 1996). The study created a huge controversy. The poverty estimates of 28 per cent of total households and 75 per cent among farming households shocked the political establishment. These findings derived from a limited sample survey that collected income data from 1,000 households, and computing the minimum costs of a basket of basic expenditure items related to food, housing, clothing, health care, education and other household needs. The study was therefore criticised for its narrow statistical base and crude methodology.

MoSA decided to improve the situation by carrying out a more comprehensive analysis of living conditions in Lebanon, with technical and financial support from UNDP. The study built upon a Population and Housing Survey conducted in 1994, which had established a statistical frame based on 65,000 households. In 1995-1996, more detailed data on housing, demography and education were collected for a sample of 5,000 households. This formed the statistical base for the report on *Mapping of Living Conditions in Lebanon*, whose preparation was financed by the PSI programme. Published in 1998, this comprehensive report of social and regional disparities in Lebanon could now provide the basis for the development of the country's first national poverty reduction strategy.

Palestine

Any assessment of public policy of the Palestine Authority (PA) has to take cognisance of the extreme volatility of the political situation. This accounts for the external relations with Israel and the international community, as well as domestic politics. The faltering peace process, border closures, security problems, and unresolved territorial disputes have made coherent and long-term national development planning virtually impossible. The political need of the PLO leadership to accommodate various factions and interest groups among the Palestinians within the emerging state has, more often than not, overridden development concerns.

On one particular issue, the external and internal constraints have been converging: the rising unemployment. From a pre-Oslo situation with a single digit unemployment rate (excluding the years of the *Intifada*), it rose to more than 30 per cent in early 1996.[2] The single most important factor causing a sharp deterioration in living conditions was the restrictions imposed by Israel on Palestinians seeking employment in Israel, and on Palestinian businesses dependent on the Israeli economy. On the other hand, the single most important factor in reducing unemployment has been public employment by the Palestine Authority, although many feel that they are deprived of benefits from the emerging state apparatus.

Since the inception of the PA in 1994, following the Oslo Accords, there has been a rapid build-up of a public administration and policy-making apparatus, largely financed by international development assistance. Many observers argue, however, that the growth of the public sector has moved beyond sustainable levels, and led to a proliferation of agencies with unclear and overlapping mandates, coupled with an inexperienced, and frequently overstaffed, civil service. The newness of the Palestinian experience of integrating political authority, civil society and development of a market economy seems to have prevented the PA from formulating a development vision guiding public policy.

Understandably, the political priority of the PA leadership is managing the negotiations with the Israelis, while at the same time balancing and uniting the many factions within the Palestinian community. Considerable financial and human resources, directly and indirectly, are tied up in the management of this volatile political situation. This notwithstanding, it is of great concern that the PA already exhibits symptoms typical of many aid-dependent countries: weak coordination of public finances, centralised decision-making, donor-driven policy-making processes, weak mobilisation of domestic revenue, low and declining rates of aid disbursement, and lack of transparency. There is also growing frustration and disenchantment within large sections of the Palestinian civil society with the lack of societal progress.[3] Raising a debate on poverty in this context is bound to be highly controversial. It brings up a discussion of the extent to which social disparities are the fault of domestic politics, rather than external factors.

For these reasons, 'poverty' is a newcomer in the Palestinian political vocabulary, and poverty measurements are still in their infancy. Central to a discussion of poverty and the design of policies to address it is the definition of who is in need and who has the right to claim assistance from the state as some form of compensation or moral due for shortfalls in living standards. In the emerging Palestinian state, however, the formalisation of citizens' rights is still a lingering issue. Current practice recognises two types of legitimate claims: from de facto household breadwinners who cannot participate in the labour market due to old age, illness or single mother status; and from families of people who served in the liberation struggle and were imprisoned, killed or injured. Clearly, these two categories do not embrace all who are poor.

Despite the high incidence of poverty in Palestine, the first national development plan (PDP) covering the years 1998-2000 lacked an explicit poverty focus, as reflected in the limited public sector expenditures devoted to programmes that attend to the needs of deprived households.[4] It is estimated that about nine per cent of the total population receives social assistance from public or private sources (i.e. the Islamic alms or *Zakat* committees). If we compare this with the latest poverty estimates, a substantial 'hole' emerges in this safety net. The households falling through the net are, to a large extent, those headed by unemployed or underemployed men. At the same time, as little as five per cent of social sector investments (or 1.3 per cent of total PDP) are targeted at the two types of beneficiaries or claimants mentioned above, of which liberated prisoners and returnees receive most. The allocation for social welfare projects, the budget line most clearly targeted for poverty alleviation, is a mere 0.5 per cent of the plan.

None of the ministries and institutions responsible for social affairs seems to have a long-term development vision and strategy into which poverty has been explicitly integrated. There is confusion about symptoms, effects and causes of poverty, and little consciousness about possible linkages between causes of poverty and public policy. Existing social assistance programmes suffer from inadequate attention to gender issues, either by not addressing the problem of female unemployment or by associating women's training needs with the traditional requirements of housewives.[5] As it is, there seem to be many hurdles to pass before 'poverty' as a social condition translates into a set of individual rights and state obligations. And yet a national discourse on poverty eradication is slowly emerging in Palestine. As the National Commission for Poverty Eradication states in the *Palestine Poverty Report*, financed by UNDP through its PSI programme:

> *Now, almost five years after the establishment of the Palestine Authority, and in preparation for the future, it is imperative to develop a realistic and a comprehensive developmental strategy to confront the phenomenon of poverty, which is much more widespread than originally thought (Palestine 1998, p. 17).*

This new level of awareness is a positive sign, and it is fair to say that UNDP has contributed in no small measure through the funding of the *Palestine Poverty Report*.[6]

Supporting poverty analysis and capacity-building

Lebanon

Until very recently, Lebanon was falling short on the commitments it made at the 1995 World Summit for Social Development. The government did not establish a follow-up committee, and there has been no high-level or inter-ministerial coordination to prepare for necessary policy reforms. The year immediately following the Summit started with six per cent economic growth and reduced inflation, which encouraged the government to intensify its focus on monetary stabilisation and rebuilding of infrastructure. There was little attention to social development, despite commitments made in Copenhagen the previous year. The strong reactions by the Prime Minister to the 1996 Haddad report did not improve the climate.

Under the circumstances, in November 1996, MoSA and UNDP acted courageously in deciding to seek the acceptance of government for a more thorough mapping of poverty in the country using funding from the PSI programme.[7] The proposal latched onto ongoing initiatives by the Ministry, including the development of a statistical database of welfare indicators, which had been supported by the UN system (ESCWA and UNFPA). MoSA is the only ministry that has been consistently vocal on the poverty issue, but its mandate is restricted mainly to social assistance and safety nets. With the support of UNDP, however, it has embarked on a programme of capacity-building that not only includes poverty analysis and surveys, but also support to community development through local municipalities, using its network of Social Development Centres. This is important because decentralisation is widely regarded as a prerequisite for balanced regional development in Lebanon, where the regions (*kada*) currently play no developmental role and local governments are extremely weak.

In preparation for the study, MoSA and UNDP had to grapple with the widely shared view that focussing explicitly on poverty through setting of a national poverty line was politically unacceptable in Lebanon. Its image as a wealthy country was at stake. This prompted UNDP to form a mission of international experts with a mandate to develop a methodology, adapted to Lebanese conditions and existing survey data, for measuring 'living conditions'. The mission gave an elaborate justification for measuring poverty through what they called the *direct approach*, based on the direct observation of the level of satisfaction of basic needs, as distinct from the *indirect approach* to the measurement of poverty, which is the basis for the setting of a poverty line. Whereas the poverty line method (PL) is useful for capturing needs that are met through current private consumption, the Unsatisfied Basic Needs (UBN) method recommended by the team of international experts is useful for capturing needs that are met predominantly through public spending.[8] The two methods are complementary, and ways of combining them have been devised. In 1997, however, Lebanon had not yet established adequate survey data on household expenditures, which excluded use of the poverty line method. A Household Standard of Living and Consumption Survey, conducted by the Central Administration of Statistics (CAS) was under way, but cooperation between MoSA and CAS proved difficult. The UBN method, therefore, represented a pragmatic solution to the availability of data, while at the same time the focus on basic needs, as opposed to income poverty, helped to allay official concerns and to secure the government's sanction.

As a result, the 1998 report financed by UNDP avoided usage of the term 'poverty', focusing instead on 'living conditions' and levels of 'satisfaction'. Still, the finding that 35 per cent of the population lived below the 'satisfaction threshold' has been widely interpreted as indicative of the level of poverty in Lebanon.[9] The data reveal that the extent of deprivation among Lebanese households is highest in relation to education and income. This implies that 'improving household incomes and the level of education would probably contribute to improve overall living conditions more than would improvements in housing and in water and sewerage services' (Kanaan 1998). It was found, moreover, that 57 per cent of the deprived population lived in urban areas — and about half of them in Beirut, where the deprived are largely urban residents of rural origin who have moved to the cities and towns in search of employment. At the same time, the extent of 'low satisfaction' is substantially higher in rural areas, especially in the North — the Akkar region, which together with the Bekaa Valley, accounts for the bulk of people in 'abject poverty'.

To supplement the results of the living conditions study and assist in priority setting for public policy, UNDP Beirut requested additional PSI funds for the elaboration of a social sector expenditure review, which was conducted in 1999. The report was done by Lebanese experts and approved by the Ministry of Finance in March 2000. It shows that public spending in health is much lower than 20 per cent of the budget and not quite 20 per cent in education. Moreover, the report categorically states that despite the country's high level of spending on health and education as a share of GDP compared to countries at a similar level, 'available evidence does not indicate that the outcomes are comparatively superior' (Social and Economic Development Group 1998). Both sectors are characterised by heavy private financing that caters mainly to the affluent sections of society and is skewed towards the tertiary level, significant government subsidies to private providers, and minimal government regulation, in part to preserve sectarian balance. Under existing health and education policies, inequity will continue to increase. More rational use of existing resources is needed to allow for improvements in service delivery. Consequently, the report sets clear objectives for better targeting of basic social services in the 2001 budget, and for creating greater public awareness on the need to improve services to disadvantaged groups.

A less tangible, although equally important, outcome of the PSI project in

Lebanon has been the sharing of the experience gained in using the UBN method with other countries in the region. Since the method does not require information on household income or expenditure and can be applied to most population surveys, a meeting of poverty experts that took place in Cairo in November 1997 recommended its use by other Arab countries as well.

A number of steps have been taken to follow up on the PSI project. This includes a 3-5 year National Programme for Improving Living Conditions, the first phase of which began in early 1999 with funding from Norway, MoSA and UNDP.[10] The objectives of the Programme are very ambitious: to develop a national strategy for poverty reduction and strengthen the capacity of government to implement it; to improve social statistics and establish monitoring systems to track progress in poverty reduction; and to mobilise civil society in the battle against poverty. The Programme's first phase has financed three types of activities:

- Capacity-building of MoSA, including the training of staff at some 50 Social Development Centres in community development planning, the preparation of information booklets with relevant statistics for each of Lebanon's 26 *kadas*, and efforts to improve coordination among departments of the Ministry;
- A social survey, aimed at enlarging the existing database of CAS on household income and expenditure to facilitate the calculation of a national poverty line and the preparation of a comprehensive poverty profile;
- Community development projects, 15 of which are being implemented on a pilot basis in the Akkar region of North Lebanon, in cooperation among MoSA and local community groups, NGOs and municipalities.

Palestine

At the Copenhagen Summit for Social Development in 1995, the Minister of Social Affairs of the Palestine Authority stated:

> *Poverty in Palestine interlinks with factors different from those in other countries, where it is often attributed to structural social and economic imbalances. In Palestine, poverty basically interlinks with Israeli occupation (Al Wazir 1995).*

This statement reflects the fact that Israeli border closures, land confiscation and restrictions on trade have severely reduced the economic opportunities of Palestinians. It also mirrors the dominant political perception of the PLO concerning the common suffering and shared injustice of the Palestinian people. According to this perspective, all Palestinian people are deprived and deserving of restitution and new entitlements.

But the concept of 'poverty' used in the Western social policy tradition and recently by international aid agencies represents a different outlook. Its focus is on internal differentiation and inequality rather than externally imposed injustice.

The goal is to establish an economic and socio-culturally defined line between the haves and have-nots of a people. The core political issue is the definition of who is in need and who has the right to claim assistance from the state. It is within this context that UNDP attempted to contribute to raising the political awareness of poverty among Palestinians by encouraging a national dialogue on what constitutes and causes poverty in Palestine. And it is against this backdrop that judgements on the success of this initiative have to be passed.

The first living standard survey among Palestinians, done in 1992, discussed social stratification (Heiberg and Ovesen 1993), while the first attempt to establish a poverty line came as late as 1995, claiming that 14 per cent of the Palestinians are poor (Shaban and Al Botmeh 1995). It was felt, however, not only that these figures under-represented the extent of poverty in Palestine, but also that there was a need to develop a national poverty discourse in the West Bank and Gaza, where explicit strategies for tackling poverty were deemed to be missing. To do this, the UNDP Programme of Assistance to the Palestinian People (PAPP) decided to support the preparation of a comprehensive situation analysis of poverty in Palestine, and the formation of a national task force or steering committee that subsequently was constituted as a National Commission for Poverty Eradication. These tasks were accompanied by sensitisation and information campaigns aimed at embedding the emerging poverty discourse in key PA and non-governmental institutions.

The *Palestine Poverty Report*, published in 1998, estimated that almost a quarter (23 per cent) of the households fell below the poverty line, with 14 per cent in 'deep poverty'.[11] These poverty indices were developed using data from the 1996-1997 Expenditure and Consumption Survey. The Palestinian Central Bureau of Statistics conducted the survey, based on a sample of about 4000 households. More importantly for development policy purposes than the exact percentage of poor people are the geographic, demographic and distributional patterns present in Palestinian society. The most salient findings of the *Poverty Report* are:

- Regional disparities are striking, with South Gaza exhibiting a poverty rate of 51 per cent, compared to a low 3 per cent in Jerusalem.
- The highest incidence of poverty is found among refugees, especially in the Gaza Strip, while in the West Bank poverty is mainly a rural phenomenon.
- The poverty incidence is higher among larger households, among households with less education and formal skills, as well as among those headed by women.
- Poverty among the working population is high, reflecting a problem of low wages and irregular employment, and not only unemployment as such.
- The lowest incidence of poverty is associated with employment in Israel, as well as remittances to the household from abroad.

Unfortunately, the report wavers between two competing perspectives, one based on a notion of poverty as the *lack of* something (of assets, basic services or income to sustain a minimum standard of living), the other as the *relationship* of a person to his or her social and physical environment. The report argues that vulnerability and inequality are major issues in Palestine, but that abject poverty is not. It also notes that the lack of social security systems and the close links with the Israeli economy make many Palestinians vulnerable to economic shocks. Interestingly, the former is not a cause of poverty in itself, whereas the latter is, but it is also largely outside the realms of the Palestine Authority.

The second phase of the PSI project involves an assessment of public spending under all development plans since the Oslo Accords, as well as of the current plans and programmes of sectoral ministries. The objective of both studies is to gauge to what extent investments are targeted at the causes of poverty and the problems faced by poor people. As a parallel initiative not supported by the PSI, UNDP proposed to the Ministry of Social Affairs a project targeting the recipients of monthly social security payments. The main concern was to introduce income-generating activities and shift the focus from relief to development. Another major exercise in the pipeline is the Participatory Poverty Assessment to be carried out with funding from the UK Department for International Development (DfID). This is seen as a major vehicle for bringing poverty concerns and the views of the poor into the process of developing the next PDP. Also pending is a clarification of the role and political mandate of the National Poverty Commission that was set up to support the preparation of the *Palestine Poverty Report*.

These pending challenges notwithstanding, what we see today is a glimpse of an evolving *national* poverty discourse, promoted by Palestinian scholars. The fact that this is a national discourse, and not one dominated by outside observers as in many developing countries, is a significant and positive feature. The way UNDP has played its role as facilitator has contributed in a major way towards this outcome.

Galvanising policy reform

Advancement in a policy reform process does not depend only on mobilising support for ongoing initiatives. It is likely to entail in equal, or even greater measure initiatives that change the course of events. Donors can act as change agents and catalysts, and UNDP did so at several important junctures in the poverty debate in Lebanon and Palestine. These experiences are very relevant in view of the international donor agenda that seeks to promote national poverty reduction strategies, even through the use of conditionality, as in the case of the World Bank and IMF requirements in connection with the Heavily-Indebted Poor Countries (HIPC) Initiative. We examine next the role of UNDP, as well as the contributions made by its PSI programme, in enhancing public awareness and political commitment to reform, and in nurturing new forms of institutional cooperation to meet the challenges of poverty reduction.

Enhancing public awareness

Both in Lebanon and Palestine, the bulk of PSI funding was used to finance analytical outputs to fill critical knowledge gaps relating to poverty. Little in the form of new knowledge was produced, as most of the work sponsored by UNDP essentially confirmed findings from earlier studies. But both Lebanon's mapping of living conditions and the Palestinian report on poverty played an important role in establishing a more authoritative basis for public discourse and policy planning.

In Lebanon, UNDP was able to broker a way of obtaining government approval for a new poverty study after the controversies provoked by the Haddad report. As late as 1996, the Lebanese Prime Minister had declared that the country did not have a poverty problem. Then, at the behest of MoSA, a new study was conducted in 1998 to measure living conditions using information from the housing and population database. By the time the study was ready for public release, the incumbent government was approaching the end of its term, and the poverty issue found its way into the election campaign. It took six months of discussions with advisors to the Prime Minister before the report was submitted to the Cabinet in September 1998. It was publicly launched in October, the same month as the elections to the National Assembly.

Apart from revealing poverty among public employees, the MoSA report did not change a picture that was generally known. But the timing of its release contributed greatly to its remarkable impact on the public debate. In fact, the publication underscored the continuing gravity of the poverty problem in Lebanon. Its findings were widely reported in the press and used by opposition politicians in raising the need for addressing social issues. The media raised the figure of 28 per cent poor, reported by Haddad, to 35 per cent (Kanaan 1998) and interpreted this as a worsening of the situation, omitting any reference to differences in methodology. As a result, the new government that emerged from the elections emphasised the urgency of reducing the vast regional disparities highlighted by the MoSA study, particularly the disadvantaged situation of the northern region of Akkar, Baalbeck and Hermel in the Bekaa valley.

Given the controversy created by the Haddad report a few years earlier, the decision to undertake a new study of living conditions was no small accomplishment. It shows that UNDP in Lebanon is well placed to influence the government on sensitive matters. The technical advice provided by UNDP on the UBN method made it possible to overcome official scepticism, clearing the way for subsequent poverty studies in the future, such as the one that will be carried out by Central Administration of Statistics using household income and expenditure data.

Although to a lesser extent than in Lebanon, the publication of the poverty report in Palestine also stirred public debate and improved the general awareness about social conditions to a degree that was previously absent. Prior to the publication of the report, the prevalent view within the Palestinian ministries associated poverty with unemployment and lack of income. The closure of the borders with Israel was seen as the main determinant of poverty (Fawzi El-Solh 1996).

The report financed by the PSI introduced a more nuanced, and more complex picture of poverty. It indicates certain policy areas where improvements are needed to allow people 'to meet their basic needs as a major component of human and citizen rights'. The most crucial ones are the right to education and health care, employment opportunities for those capable of working, and access to a social security net for those who cannot work or are part of a vulnerable social group. The main policy recommendations of the report call for:

- Reducing the exclusion of women from the labour market. The high percentage of deep poverty among female-headed households points to the need to focus on empowering women through skills training, credit and other measures;
- Enacting mandatory pension schemes for public and private employers, including strong survivors' provisions for widows and dependent children. This reform will have to be introduced gradually, not least taking account of the large informal sector;
- Introducing a mandatory health insurance scheme;
- Establishing a national social security and welfare corporation aimed at creating a diversified assistance programme for poor households. The objective is to move beyond charity and to focus on enhancing income-generating capabilities through a closely coordinated approach encompassing the many institutions, public and private, currently involved in social welfare activities;
- Enacting minimum wage legislation to guarantee employment and living standards above the poverty line;
- Developing regional development programmes targeting the highly poverty-stricken areas (the south and middle of the Gaza Strip, and the districts of Jenin and Hebron in the West Bank).

The role of UNDP has mainly been one of providing managerial support to the work of the National Poverty Commission in the preparation of the poverty report. The involvement of UNDP also lent credibility to the outcomes of the study, cushioning it against unwarranted criticism. Published in 1998, the report is the first comprehensive poverty analysis of this kind in Palestine. Although its definition of poverty and fixing of a poverty line will continue to be debated, it is clear that the report has made important contributions to the political discourse. It broadened the scope of policy and analysis beyond a focus on income poverty and unemployment. It confirmed that poverty is a major social problem and determined its incidence, both geographically and by socio-economic group. It also brought social inequality, an issue that had been shunned by the PLO leadership, to the centre of the policy agenda.

The report was issued in both Arabic and English editions. Its release generated substantial media attention and was widely covered by the Palestinian as well as the Israeli press. More than 500 participants attended the launching conferences that took place in Gaza and Jerusalem, including the President of the PA. This underscores the importance and political sensitivity of the poverty issue in Palestine. The President's Office reacted to the relatively high poverty rates presented in the report, especially the rate of 20 per cent in households with their main source of income from public sector employment. The Commission was under pressure to revise or omit this figure, but the issue was put to rest upon the intervention of the UNDP office. Despite the media attention, the Palestine report is much less explosive politically that the one in Lebanon. While critics of the regime are using it to press for changes in public spending, the high poverty rates documented in the report help the Palestine Authority lobby donors for continued international assistance.

Strengthening political commitment and ownership

The question of government ownership is critical to the success of policy reform initiatives. Without it, policy proposals are bound to founder, no matter how well designed. There is considerable variation in the extent to which UNDP succeeded in galvanising a commitment to reform, as well as in the role governments played in the PSI activities in Lebanon and Palestine. While in both cases, there was a linkage with a government agency, it cannot be inferred that the national authorities unambiguously own the reform process. In fact, these two cases demonstrate that a government cannot be considered a monolithic entity. Reform processes often generate much of their momentum from opposing forces *within* the public sector.

Moreover, positive changes in a country's commitment to reform cannot be gauged over the relatively short time span of the PSI projects. It takes time to alter the mindset and entrenched attitudes of key political and administrative actors. There is a long way to go before Lebanon or the Palestinian Authority has a workable national poverty reduction strategy. Even sectorally, attention to basic needs and social inequality is still not high on their agenda.

Yet, the developments in the PA, where UNDP forged a strategically important partnership with the Ministry of Planning and International Cooperation (MoPIC), allow some room for optimism. Below the level of the supreme Office of the President, this is a powerful ministry, vested with a key role in development planning. By being responsible for the new five-year strategic plan, MoPIC is well-placed to integrate poverty concerns across sectors and policy areas. UNDP played the main architect in making MoPIC the coordinator of the process of preparing the *Palestine Poverty Report*. This was undoubtedly a wise investment, since giving the responsibility for coordination to some other ministry would probably have been a blind alley for the reform process.

Equally important has been the move towards institutionalising the reform process through the establishment of the National Poverty Commission, as well as the decision to reach out to the indigenous academic community and involve it in the debate on poverty and the work of the Commission. Bringing in foreign experts might have improved the quality of the poverty report, but it probably would have diminished its political impact, given the scepticism with which government officers and Palestinian intellectuals view donor reliance on foreign consultants. Therefore, vesting the process in several national academic institutions was important from the point of view of local validation and ownership of the outcomes of the study.

Nevertheless, the sustainability of the policy reform process is still very much in doubt. The role and influence of the Poverty Commission is a lingering issue. Its political mandate is not clear, and questions on whether it should remain as an independent technical committee or receive a direct mandate from the President yet to be addressed. The fact that the members of the Commission have been working on a voluntary basis could jeopardise the continuity of their work. But it also helps preserve their independent status. If the Commission were to come under the aegis of the President's Office, it might have to sacrifice the independent role it has had until now.

The same questions apply to MoPIC. Its aim is to have a poverty reduction strategy within two years, provided Palestinian statehood is achieved. However, the Ministry has been largely dependent on UNDP for financial and managerial support, especially for the initial build-up of capacity. The fact that the recurrent expenses of MoPIC have been donor-funded raises questions for the continuity of the policy reform process. The latter is unlikely to materialise unless sufficient political will is mobilised internally to enable the process the move forward even without donor support. Hence, the future of policy reform and aid dependency are intimately linked.

In Lebanon, too, UNDP has established a close partnership with a ministry dealing with poverty issues. The partnership with the MoSA preceded the PSI initiative, dating back to the preparations for the 1995 World Social Summit. But unlike the planning ministry in the Palestine Authority, MoSA has no overarching role in policy-making and holds a relatively marginal position in relation to the influential social sector ministries. Because of its visibility on poverty issues, UNDP decided nonetheless to strengthen the position of the MoSA within the government and to support its role in social policy development. This is in line with the Ministry's own goal of becoming the government's chief architect of social development policies. There is no doubt that the study on living conditions, and the credibility lent to it by UNDP, has contributed to this end. There also remains the problem of overcoming the obstacles posed by the limited mandate of the

MoSA, which has been and is likely to remain focussed on social welfare.

UNDP is inclined to continue its support to MoSA, primarily by strengthening its capacity for policy formulation. UNDP appears to be more ambivalent with respect to the Ministry's role as a community development agency. There is the prospect of making the network of Social Development Centres a multi-sectoral arm of the central government to support local initiatives addressing poverty problems. However, there is still no consensus in government, and MoSA lacks qualified staff to play this enhanced role. Consequently, the future role of MoSA is ambiguous, even though both the World Bank and the European Union are willing to support it in connection with the establishment of a Social and Economic Fund.

The political discourse of the new Lebanese government has changed in a positive manner, but its capacity to deliver on the poverty front has yet to be demonstrated. Post-war Lebanon still struggles with balancing vested sectarian interests, which renders rational development planning difficult at best. At the moment, it is difficult to pinpoint the most critical decision-makers for moving the poverty and social development agenda forward. In the absence of a strong coordinating body for policy-making, the future direction of policy reform is uncertain. Despite the rhetoric of the new government, there is still no political process that embraces several ministries and civil society actors. Lebanon has established a broad-based consultative forum, the Economic and Social Council, to enhance popular participation in the development process. But the Council meets only rarely, and has merely an advisory function, with no role in the policy-making process. In this context, progress towards an effective national poverty reduction strategy is difficult and may even be futile unless a stronger policy-making body emerges. Whether this body could be the Ministry of Finance, which commissioned the budget expenditure review financed by UNDP with PSI resources, remains to be seen.

Forging new forms of institutional cooperation

Success in policy reform hinges partly on the possibility of identifying an agency within government, or a key actor outside of it, with the capacity and stature to take the lead in pushing for policy change. Alternatively, policy reform may depend on the ability to broker partnerships involving various actors , who together can bring a reform agenda to fruition.

The most interesting case of institutional brokerage is the new Poverty Commission in the PA, which started as a project committee for planning the 1998 *Palestine Poverty Report* but has gradually been given a broader and more official mandate under the auspices of MoPIC. While UNDP was clearly very instrumental in its formation and subsequently in supporting its role, the Commission has been gaining credibility as something more than simply a UNDP project committee. One major reason for this seems to be its composition and professional credibility. The

Commission is composed of members that represent leading academic institutions and non-governmental organisations, under the chairmanship of MoPIC. These institutions and NGOs are considered the main centres of poverty research and practice in Palestine. They include the Central Bureau of Statistics, the Palestinian Economic Policy and Research Centre, the Women Studies Institute and the Development Studies Centre of Birzeit University, the Palestinian NGO Network, and the Palestinian Secretariat for Childhood. If allowed to play the role of an accredited but independent reviewer of public policy, the Commission may evolve into a body with significant influence over policy-making.

One lingering problem is that the political mandate and role of the Commission are still not clear. The Office of the President has agreed to endorse the Commission's mandate, but there are concerns that this may jeopardise its independence. So far, the Commission has played no role in the preparation or review of public investment proposals. Even the powers of MoPIC have been limited in this respect, as most of the budgetary process has been controlled directly by the President's Office. The extent to which the role of the Commission becomes more institutionalised, therefore, remains to be determined.

Some other positive institutional developments have taken place in the PA, although it is still too early to assess their significance. The appointment of an inter-ministerial committee, composed of 11 ministries and affiliated to the National Commission, could greatly improve communication on policy matters. Cases of institutional rivalry such as those that have surfaced in the past are likely to be resolved in a more effective manner through dialogue and negotiation. Another positive development is the decision by the Palestinian Central Bureau of Statistics (PCBS) to develop its own capacity for maintaining statistics on poverty. PCBS recently published an updated poverty analysis on its own initiative, and appears to be willing to take this on as a regular function. Apparently, this decision was spurred by the involvement of the PCBS in the preparation of the *Palestine Poverty Report*, and is therefore an important by-product of the PSI project. More recently, the World Bank decided to produce a poverty profile following Bank procedures. UNDP was instrumental in fostering a dialogue between Bank staff and the Poverty Commission on how to make use of this exercise to improve on weaknesses in the 1998 report.

Similar institutional problems are present in Lebanon, where the public sector is characterised by weak horizontal integration. In the absence of a strong coordinating body, relationships between ministries and other public institutions tend to be highly competitive. This makes the formation of effective social development policies extremely difficult, since it requires overcoming fragmentation and adopting policy measures that cut across sectors.

As we have seen, the strategy of the UNDP office in Beirut has been to support the capacity-building agenda of the social affairs ministry, a small but very vocal actor on poverty issues in Lebanon. This was probably the best avenue for building political awareness of the country's poverty problems. However, it may turn out to be a blind alley in developing effective poverty reduction policies. One issue of concern relates to the role of MoSA vis-à-vis other government agencies, some of which are critical of the initiatives it has taken with the support of outside donors. There has been a long-standing dispute between this ministry and the Central Administration of Statistics (CAS) on the responsibility for the production and dissemination of poverty-related surveys and analyses. It is not surprising, there-fore, that CAS refused to collaborate in MoSA's Population and Housing Survey of 1994. The work of MoSA also overlaps with the responsibilities of the Ministry of Health at the primary level, through the functions of the Social Development Centres. When these Centres take on a broader community development role, as is the case in the pilot projects in the northern region of Akkar, new issues of insti-tutional turf and sustainability will come to the fore.

It is noteworthy that the work of MoSA and UNDP, which sprang out of the 1998 mapping study, has had the indirect effect of focussing attention on institu-tional and governance aspects of social development. This is far more critical than further sophistication of poverty measurements. In fact, the institutional set-up for regional development in Lebanon is still in an embryonic stage. UNDP has contributed to different models and experiences, working in partnership with MoSA in Akkar and with the Council for Development and Reconstruction (CDR) in the Baalbeck-Hermel region. Common to both of these projects is that UNDP is directly involved in the implementation through recruitment of project staff, procurement and financial management. Many raise questions about the strong field-level presence of UNDP in a relatively developed country like Lebanon. Others defend the approach, in particular on the ground that it may help defuse sectarian tensions and ensure better quality staff and non-partisan attention to project objectives.

To the extent that these pilot activities in Akkar and Baalbeck represent efforts to develop models and procedures for local government reform, they raise a num-ber of pertinent institutional questions. What is, for example, the role of the Ministry of Municipalities (now merged with the Ministry of Interior) in promot-ing decentralisation and local government reform? What are the institutional jus-tifications for capacity-building of MoSA and its Social Development Centres in this context? How does MoSA's network of Social Development Centres relate to the functions of the Ministry of Municipalities? And what should be their role vis-à-vis the Council for Development and Reconstruction (CDR), which today is the government's main vehicle for coordinating development projects and interna-tional assistance?

Whatever the answers to these questions, there seems to be an urgent need to assist the government in utilising the experiences from various donor-assisted local development approaches. The latest Development Cooperation Report of the UN system in Lebanon is quite pessimistic with regard to this issue:

> There has not been much progress with respect to concrete measures and programmes to favour the development of rural areas. The institutionalisation of such approach is yet to be achieved. The fact that there was no progress on decentralisation has been a further obstacle (DCR 1999).

Given the recent initiative to establish a Social and Economic Fund with substantial funding from the European Union, the need to advance the decentralisation agenda has been further accentuated. Experiences from other countries have shown that the proliferation of 'aid islands' of community development projects may undermine genuine decentralisation rather than support it. Similarly, aid projects may promote local initiatives and resource mobilisation, but tend to undermine processes of forging improved working relationships between the centre and the local level. Local governments and communities benefiting from international aid may use it as leverage to loosen their ties to the centre. The social and political fabric of post-war Lebanon may be too fragile to accommodate strong local governance. At the same time, there seems to be a critical need to develop the capacity for development management and inter-sectoral coordination at the municipal level.

UNDP's strategy of assistance to MoSA may also prove short-lived if, as experience from other countries suggests, the development of effective poverty reduction policy requires strong involvement of all the 'heavy' ministries, particularly in the areas of finance and planning, agriculture, industry, health and education. We are not aware of any catalytic effects yet of the work of UNDP in forging inter-ministerial collaboration at this level.

There are, however, some positive developments worth mentioning, apart from CDR's involvement in the Akkar project together with MoSA. One is the active participation of the ministries of finance, health, and education in the preparation, validation and follow-up to the social sector expenditure review carried out in 1999. Another is the recent agreement by CAS to take part in a new poverty survey under preparation. The new survey is intended to address some of the questions raised about the scientific quality of the living conditions study published by MoSA. The study has been criticised for the paucity of indicators used in applying the UBN method, as well as the subjectivity involved in setting 'satisfaction' levels for each of the indicators and quantifying them for the purpose of developing a composite index. Hence the need for a new study that will combine basic needs data with household income and expenditure data. UNDP has been instrumental in leveraging Norwegian support for the new survey and placing the professional responsibility with CAS. Both examples, as well as a national conference on link-ing economic growth and social development, which UNDP organised jointly with MoSA and the Ministry of Economy and Trade in January 2000 in Beirut, point to the prospect of improved inter-ministerial cooperation in the future.

Mobilising support from other donors

In both Lebanon and Palestine, UNDP finds itself in a major developmental role. In Lebanon, the World Bank and most bilateral donors are newcomers. The UN, on the other hand, has a long history of engagement in the country, and is seen as a more neutral partner. UNDP therefore enjoys the status of a trusted advisor in government circles, despite its limited financial role. The situation is similar in the PA, where the PLO leadership views UNDP as a close ally in development man-agement. It is worth noting that Lebanon and the PA are both examples of weak capability on the governments' side for the coordination of aid.

UNDP has been definitely more successful in leveraging donor engagement in poverty-related work in Palestine. In order to finance the 1998 *Palestine Poverty Report*, UNDP entered into a co-funding arrangement with Saudi Arabia, and received additional contributions from the governments of Denmark and the Netherlands. Despite its positive reception, the report has not been free from crit-icism. This applies, in particular, to its treatment of the causes of poverty and its relative neglect of the role of domestic forces in contributing to both poverty and inequality. Subsequent studies should therefore pay attention to such topics as:

- Urban bias in development investment and political representation, includ-ing in the National Legislative Council;
- Problems of governance and corruption, and their effects on the poor;
- Links between education and poverty, with a special emphasis on vocational education;
- Relationship between employment and poverty, in light of the fact that as many as 76 per cent of poor households have their breadwinners in the labour market;
- Taxation policies and mobilisation of domestic revenues, a highly politically charged issue given that, for instance, there is no capital gains taxation in the Palestine Authority.

Follow-up activities now under way could not only fill important gaps in policy analysis, but also contribute significantly to policy reform. With UNDP as project manager and DfID (UK) as the main donor, MoPIC is preparing a participatory pover-ty assessment as an input to the National Development Plan under preparation. The goal of the project is to elicit the views of the people 'from below' in order to influ-ence the formulation of local initiatives and improve the capacity of municipalities in participatory planning. The project office will be located within MoPIC, while the Poverty Commission will also play a key role by acting as a steering body and professional advisor for the project. By continuing to involve both of these key government agencies, the planned second phase has the potential for building sufficient institutional and professional capacity to carry forward the policy reform process.

From its focal position in Lebanon and Palestine, UNDP has had a continuous dialogue with other multilateral and the bilateral donors, and assists the host governments in monitoring aid flows. In the absence of a strong government hand in the management of aid, we find there is a certain element of competition between donors. Nevertheless, in the two cases examined here, UNDP retains a leading role among the donors on the poverty agenda. Contrary to the situation in many other countries, the World Bank has not taken up these issues in any significant way. It is evident that the UNDP offices in Lebanon and the Palestinian Authority prefer to keep it that way. In this context, it is fair to say that the PSI has also functioned as a hegemonic instrument for UNDP. The fact that UNDP collaborates with Norway in Lebanon and the UK in Palestine in work financed by or resulting from the PSI indicates improved donor coordination less than the leading position of UNDP in each case.

Conclusions

It is unrealistic to expect that the relatively small amounts of funding provided by UNDP through the PSI programme could lead to a complete reorientation of host governments' or donor agencies' priorities. Nor could the level of funding offered by the programme alone form the basis for a completely new UNDP engagement in these countries. The funds were too small. They had to function as a financial add-on and, insofar as possible, be matched by other sources. But it should be expected, nonetheless, that the PSI funds would be used strategically so as to strengthen ongoing initiatives and leverage further commitments and resources in support of a policy reform agenda.

The most tangible output of the PSI project in Lebanon is the report on *Mapping of Living Conditions*, published in 1998 by UNDP and the Ministry of Social Affairs. The report is still the only comprehensive study of social and regional disparities in the country, and is widely used and cited. While there is nothing new or surprising in its findings, the study created an objective basis for addressing social inequality and definitely has had a catalytic effect on the public debate, including discussions in the Parliament. It is apparent that poverty research has made important strides forward in recent years in Lebanon, not least because of the support of UNDP. Several Arab countries have shown interest in applying the Unsatisfied Basic Needs method of measuring poverty, which is seen as particularly useful when survey data on household income and expenditures are inadequate.

The decision to finance a study of living conditions was definitely a strategic one. It built upon previous engagements by UN agencies, which had assisted the Lebanese government in the preparations for the World Social Summit of 1995 and a household welfare survey completed in 1996. When funding from the PSI programme became available, the opportunity was effectively used by the UNDP office in Beirut to obtain the endorsement of the government for a new analysis of living conditions that could provide the baseline data for a comprehensive social development strategy in Lebanon. It is clear that through its support to the Ministry of Social Affairs, UNDP played an important role in raising a public and political debate on poverty in Lebanon. Given its long-standing presence in the country, it is nonetheless equally possible that UNDP would have taken a major initiative on poverty-related work even if funding from the PSI programme had not been forthcoming.

With assistance from UNDP, a National Programme for Improving Living Conditions has been launched as a follow-up to the PSI project. Under the auspices of MoSA, the new programme has the objective of formulating a national poverty reduction strategy. Nevertheless, no concrete steps have yet been taken and there appears to be little progress in terms of policy change. Lebanon still does not have an official poverty line. The figures cited in the MoSA study on living conditions can and have been contested, and cannot easily be compared across national boundaries. Fiscal management appears to be the overriding priority of the government, consistent with the five-year economic adjustment programme. It is therefore tempting to draw the conclusion that the political will or capacity to formulate and implement a national poverty reduction strategy is still absent. The time, it appears, is not yet ripe for an integrated strategy such as would be required to address the structural factors underpinning social disadvantage in Lebanon.

Under such circumstances, it would be wrong for UNDP or other donors to push further for a document that could be labelled a 'strategy', but most likely would not have the ownership of key decision-makers. Instead, donors would be well advised to follow a more sectoral and pragmatic approach until the time is ripe for a genuine national strategy. This engagement should focus on each sector and ministry independently. It is expected that the multi-purpose survey to be carried out by CAS will provide a better understanding of the determinants of poverty and the type of sectoral interventions that can contribute most effectively to poverty reduction. On this basis, donors should seek to engage several of the relevant ministries in an internal review process to identify short-, medium- and long-term measures to alleviate individual and household poverty and address regional disparities within their respective functional mandates. As part of its focus on poverty reduction, UNDP could help the government to develop an applied local government research programme. The purpose would be to distil lessons learned from ongoing local development projects on how to facilitate the mobilisation of local organisations, improve coordination among line agencies, and establish a good working relationship between the central and local levels of government.

In Palestine, we find a similarly positive contribution by UNDP to the evolving national discourse on poverty. Clearly, the 1998 *Poverty Report* played a catalytic role in revealing new insights on the prevalence of poverty in Palestine and providing an authoritative basis for public action. The PSI project was also instrumental in improving the working relationship between the national statistical office and policy-makers, and strengthening local capacity for poverty analysis in indigenous research institutions and the important planning ministry. There are good prospects for a genuine national political process through the work of the Poverty Commission, itself a direct outcome of the UNDP project. This could be further helped by the planned follow-up phase to the poverty report, which will involve a participatory poverty assessment and a review of the current plans and programmes of the line ministries and of all public spending under the development plans since the Oslo Accords.

Nevertheless, many hurdles remain before a general reorientation of policies to tackle poverty and inequality takes place. Poverty is an elusive and highly political concept. This is especially so in the charged political environment in which the Palestinian authorities and society operate. The harsh political realities in the region provide little hope for a major turnaround in the near future. The constrained local market and limited private domestic and foreign direct investments make job creation in Palestine a slow process. Hence, dependency on employment in Israel will remain high.

One encounters the same ambiguity as that found in the *Palestine Poverty Report* when reviewing the official documents of the Palestinian Authority. The first long-term national development plan contains plenty of development jargon, but falls short of providing a comprehensive development vision concerning what kind of society the Palestinians want for themselves. As an analytical concept or a policy priority, both poverty and inequality are missing from the document. Both the public investment figures included in the national plan and information on existing social assistance programmes reveal a serious lack of poverty focus in public sector expenditures.

Despite these problems, one can see a glimpse of an emerging public conversation on poverty in Palestine. There is a growing recognition that quite apart from the Israeli occupation, domestic factors also are at play in creating poverty and vulnerability, and that addressing these conditions is part of the larger challenge of formalising citizens' rights in the emerging Palestinian state.

■　　■　　■

As a general conclusion of relevance to the donor community, it is worth noting that in both Lebanon and Palestine, UNDP relied heavily on the intimate knowledge and personal networks of national, as opposed to foreign staff in its work to influence the national policy discourse on poverty. The UNDP offices in both Beirut and Jerusalem have qualified national staff dealing with the poverty portfolio. This highlights the importance of using high-quality national programme officers in aid management.

To become an effective change agent, however, requires not only knowledge and networks, but also a vision. In the two cases reviewed in this chapter, we find UNDP often struggling to articulate its own views on some of the critical dilemmas and challenges related to poverty. Merely advocating for the design of national poverty reduction strategies may easily turn into a mantra, which can be frequently repeated but does not communicate what it implies. Tackling poverty is first and foremost a political struggle, not a technical issue. UNDP, therefore, needs to develop its own thinking on some of the thorny political issues it will have to confront when joining governments, donors and civil society on a policy reform path. ■

Notes

Mr. Jerve is grateful to the following individuals: Randa Aboul-Hosn (UNDP Beirut) and Adib Nehmeh (National Programme for Improving Living Conditions, Ministry of Social Affairs) for coordinating his mission to Lebanon; Sufian Mshasha (UNDP/PAPP) for organising interviews in Jerusalem and Ramallah; and Alejandro Grinspun for editorial support.

[1] The balance of power in Lebanon partly depends on popular images of who resides where and leads what kind of life, among the major socio-ethnic groups — Sunni Muslim, Shi'a Muslim and Maronite Christian. Facts and figures that may distort these images are therefore threatening. But as long as ethnic and religious labelling was avoided, some surveys have been conducted over the last decades.

[2] Dakkat et al. 1997 gives a figure of 28.6 per cent for April-May 1996, while the Palestinian Development Plan 1998-2000 states that 'from late February through early April in 1996, the unemployment rate rose to over 50 per cent' (PNA 1998). By 1999, the situation had improved somewhat, with an unemployment rate of about 15 per cent (Said 1999).

[3] According to data from a public opinion poll conducted for the preparation of the 1998 *Human Development Report*, sentiments of growing impoverishment and inequality are widely shared. Forty-four per cent of Palestinians felt that their standards of living have not changed since the establishment of the PNA, while 41 per cent felt their conditions have deteriorated. Fifty-five per cent of those interviewed disagreed with the view that 'all sectors of society benefit from the development projects implemented by the National Authority'. And 73 per cent maintained that the gap between rich and poor has been increasing in recent years (Said 1999).

[4] The Plan contains only cursory references to poverty. It consists mainly of a list of aid projects, and almost 50 per cent of public investments are earmarked for physical infrastructure. A quarter of all project financing falls within the social sectors, which is a high percentage by international standards. Looking at the type of investments listed, however, the bulk of the

projects are again related to infrastructure — hospitals, school buildings and housing programmes. The underlying assumption of the PDP seems to be that it is the nation that is poor, rather than groups within it.

[5] A 1996 report by the Women's Study Centre at Birzeit University found a close association between gender inequality and poverty, but contended that gender-segregated views of poverty have restricted the development of comprehensive and effective policies. This holds for job creation and social security measures that have been targeted to men, as well as special social welfare measures targeting women (Fawzi El-Solh 1996). Likewise, the 1998 *Palestine Poverty Report* commissioned by UNDP documented that de facto female-headed households are major recipients of formal social assistance, but 'this assistance does not permit an exit from poverty or address other rights and needs of poor women' (Abu Nahleh et al. 1999).

[6] As the financial ceiling of the PSI programme was considered insufficient, UNDP entered into a co-funding arrangement with the Arab Gulf Programme for United Nations Development Organisations (AGFUND), financed by Saudi Arabia. The total project budget amounted to US$ 240,000. Funds for the publication were also contributed by Denmark and the Netherlands.

[7] The UNDP contribution to the PSI project was US$ 200,000. In addition, there was a minor contribution from the Norwegian Ministry of Foreign Affairs to pay for advisory services from the FAFO Institute for Applied Social Science, Norway. The project covered the costs of an expert mission to develop a methodological approach to poverty mapping in Lebanon using available statistics, which was carried out in 1997, as well as the preparation, editing, publication and dissemination of the report on *Mapping Living Conditions in Lebanon*. Funds were also used for purposes of professional exchange. Most importantly, the methodological approach utilised in the Report was presented to a meeting of poverty experts held in Cairo in 1997, which recommended its adoption by other Arab countries as well.

[8] The Unsatisfied Basic Needs method has been used for poverty mapping in several Latin American countries, and consists of the following steps: a) definition of basic needs and their satisfiers; b) selection of variables and indicators that, for each need and satisfier, express their degree of satisfaction; c) definition of a minimum level for each indicator, or deprivation threshold, below which the need is considered unsatisfied; d) classification of households as poor, *when one or more basic needs are unsatisfied or when a compound index indicates overall deprivation;* and e) every person that belongs to a poor household is regarded as poor (UNDP 1997b). To identify what satisfiers are indispensable in any given society, there is a need for in-depth sociological and anthropological research. As an example, which is counterintuitive to most poverty researchers, the expert team gave the case of the private car in Beirut. As public transport is almost non-existent, a private car tends to become essential in an economy where most have long commuting distance from home to work.

[9] This finding is based on a living conditions index measuring unfulfilled basic needs in four areas: housing, water and sewerage, education and income. For the latter, the study uses three indicators: ownership of car, number of dependants in the household, and type of employment or occupation. In fact, the authors of the *Mapping of Living Conditions in Lebanon* finally decid-

ed not to follow the UBN methodology recommended by the expert team to its full extent, which would have implied that deficiency in meeting only one of several basic needs was enough to be classified as poor. Instead, the 1998 report adopted an overall index score, averaging the satisfaction levels of the individual needs and related indicators. Otherwise, the level of poverty would likely have been higher.

[10] The project management is actively soliciting funding for the next phase, to continue the capacity-building of MoSA and develop a comprehensive regional development project for Akkar. By February 2000, the prospects for continued funding through the Council for Development and Reconstruction were identified, opening up a project execution modality that creates a partnership between MoSA and CDR. This is an interesting development in view of the need to improve the management of integrated programmes at the local level.

[11] In constructing poverty lines, the *Poverty Report* used actual costs of a basket of necessary goods (food, clothing and housing) plus other basic services (e.g. education and health) and amenities (e.g. personal care, domestic utensils and transport) for a reference household of two adults and four children, which is the most typical household composition in the survey sample. This reflected a deliberate decision to avoid a simplistic and absolute definition of poverty based on food intake (caloric content) or costs of a minimum food basket only. The 'deep poverty line' is an expression of what is needed in terms of food, clothing and housing 'providing the minimum for decent survival'. The 'poverty line', in turn, represents an expanded basket of consumption items 'necessary not merely for survival but for minimally adequate living standards'. It was decided to fix the poverty cut-off point at the third decile of the distribution, which corresponds to 60 per cent of the median expenditure, a common definition of a relative poverty line. This resulted in a 'poverty line' for the reference household of 1,390 Israeli Shekels or US$ 400 per month (1,141 Shekels for 'deep poverty'). A demographic equivalence formula was then developed to adjust for actual household size (NCPA 1998).

CHAPTER 15

Bulgaria, Latvia and Tajikistan

Jaroslaw Górniak

ike other countries of Eastern Europe and the former Soviet Union, Bulgaria, Latvia and Tajikistan have all experienced a severe transformation crisis following the demise of communism. In the limited span of one decade, these countries have gone through a major change of both their economic and political systems. The crisis triggered by the disintegration of the previous system and the need to adjust to the competitive demands of the world economy have resulted in rising unemployment, poverty and inequality. Poverty is most acute in Tajikistan, which was already among the poorest countries in the former Soviet Union. But Bulgaria and Latvia have also witnessed a massive deterioration of living standards for vast segments of their population, and the corresponding emergence of poverty as a public policy issue.

Despite alarming social indicators, there has been a low level of awareness about poverty and inequality in these countries. This is partly a legacy of the Soviet era, during which poverty was attributed largely to individual failure and, therefore, associated with stigma and shame. To the extent that poverty resulted from individual failure, it was not seen as a major social problem requiring decisive action from policy-makers. For this reason, a major challenge has been to raise awareness about the question of poverty, provide reliable estimates about its magnitude, and encourage national governments to address poverty by developing the tools required for monitoring it, while also strengthening their capacity for policy design.

This chapter reviews the experience of three projects sponsored by the United Nations Development Programme (UNDP) in Bulgaria, Latvia and Tajikistan under the auspices of the Poverty Strategies Initiative (PSI). The chapter starts by presenting a brief socio-economic background since the early 1990s to set the framework for the subsequent discussion. Then it analyses the main contributions made in each country to improving the measurement of poverty, enhancing public awareness, and building local capacities for policy research. Next we assess the overall impact of the projects on the development of policy for poverty reduction. The final section of the chapter reviews the different modalities of donor engagement and collaboration that have been present in the respective projects.

Country context

Bulgaria

Following the economic crisis of the early 1990s, Bulgaria introduced only superficial market reforms and put off more urgently needed structural changes in the public sector until hyperinflation brought about another major crisis in 1996. Real GDP fell for two consecutive years in 1996 and 1997 by 10.9 per cent and 7.4 per cent, respectively, while inflation reached 578 per cent in 1997. This has been accompanied by a rising trend in unemployment, which after a short-term fall in 1994-1995, began to climb again in 1996. The effect of these changes has been a steep decline in real wages in the late 1990s to 30 to 40 per cent of their 1989 levels. To complicate matters even more, the Russian crisis of 1998 and the war in neighbouring Yugoslavia have deterred investors and compromised further the economic reform process in Bulgaria.

In addition to the long-term decline in GDP combined with high inflation, poverty has increased as a result of a substantial rise in income differentials among households. According to the World Bank, the Gini coefficient for earnings has increased dramatically, from 0.28 in 1995 to 0.4 in 1997 (World Bank 1999). The 'grey' economy, which is believed to account for 20 to 40 per cent of GDP, has expanded to shelter many of those who have lost their jobs. But this expansion of unregistered economic activity, combined with the fall in real incomes, has narrowed the direct tax base, preventing the government from financing public programmes. Consequently, the government has had to transform the previous social welfare system based on universal subsidies and allowances into one that targets resources and programmes to those who are most in need. This has left many people whose incomes have fallen as a result of the economic crisis without adequate social protection.

The crisis of 1996 resulted in a change of government in April 1997. In cooperation with international organisations, the new administration is trying to carry out essential reforms and lead the country out of the crisis. The currency has been devalued and pegged to the Deutsche Mark, and a currency board has been set up to make decisions on monetary policy. The government has also made a commitment to fight poverty. To do this, it needs to resolve a number of problems. The first and most obvious one derives from the lack of knowledge about poverty. For various reasons, there has been no reliable information on the extent of the problem or the characteristics of those who are most affected. A related problem is the need to establish a poverty threshold that will be accepted politically for use in determining eligibility for targeted social assistance. Finally, the country needs to define a more effective income policy, especially in relation to the public sector, if it is to arrest the ongoing deterioration of incomes in a context of tight budget constraints.

Latvia

The collapse of the Soviet Union had a major negative impact on the Latvian economy, which until then had enjoyed, along with its Baltic neighbours, a relatively privileged position within the Soviet bloc. The economic problems were aggravated by high inflation, with a tenfold increase in prices in 1992, which contributed to a fall in real incomes to 45 per cent of their 1990 levels. A subsequent collapse of state banks in 1995 caused many Latvians to lose their life savings, significantly eroding their living standards.

Since independence, the Latvian government has embarked on a programme of economic reform involving far-reaching structural changes, including the privatisation of most state enterprises with the exception of a number of large firms. At present, the share of the private sector in agriculture, manufacturing, construction, and trade exceeds 90 per cent (Latvia 1999). Western countries account for an ever-growing share of foreign trade, and foreign investment has been rising as well.

The profound economic changes adopted since independence have helped stabilise the economy and generate growth from 1996 onwards. Already by 1997, the situation had improved somewhat, allowing real incomes to recover from the low point of the early 1990s to reach 60 per cent of their pre-transition levels (Latvia 1998a). The country's steady growth rate suffered another reversal in August 1998 following the Russian crisis, but in the second half of 1999 it had once again recorded an economic upturn. Yet, while inflation fell to 4.7 per cent in 1998, a steep rise occurred in rents (33.3 per cent), as well as in the cost of medical services, public transport and electricity. This has severely affected the living standards of many households, particularly those struck by unemployment, which increased to reach 10.2 per cent of the economically active population in April 1999.

Latvian society may be regarded as well-educated. More than 12 per cent of the population above the age of 15 has received higher education, making Latvia the country with the highest enrolment rate in the Baltic region. Households are generally well-supplied with appliances, average dwelling stock per capita amounts to 21.5 m^2, and most apartments have piped water (93 per cent), central heating (82 per cent) or gas (85 per cent). To a certain extent, this helps mitigate the effects of poverty, ensuring a basic level of comfort and providing people with a cushion during hard times. Poverty, in fact, is primarily related to income shortfalls arising from unemployment and low wages or pensions.

This situation of rising income poverty in the midst of relatively adequate standards of living in comparison with other post-socialist countries has prevented policy-makers from coming to grips with the sudden impoverishment that has befallen on many Latvian households. Not only was poverty not a political issue until recently; it was not even part of the political vocabulary in the country. Raising awareness among politicians and opinion makers was therefore a precondition for developing policies to address poverty.

Tajikistan

With a population of 6.2 million and 93 per cent of its territory covered by mountains, Tajikistan is the poorest of the countries that emerged from the breakdown of the former Soviet Union. Almost three fourths of the population live in the countryside, where arable land is approximately 0.2 hectares per capita. In spite of a decline in the population growth rate from the mid-1980s, the birth rate was still relatively high in 1997 at 2.5 per cent. Almost half of the country's population is made up of children aged up to 14 years old.

Tajikistan had the lowest GNP per capita in the Soviet Union. Its economy, which was largely dominated by cotton production, was highly dependent on the Soviet market, as well as on subsidies received from the centre. For this reason, Tajikistan was hit very hard by the crisis in Russia and the other former Soviet republics, and by the breakdown of the single market that followed the disintegration of the Soviet bloc.

Nevertheless, the main contributing factor of Tajikistan's social and economic crisis was the civil war that broke out in 1992, which brought the country to the brink of collapse.[1] In spite of efforts to stabilise the situation, the country is still regarded as unsafe, a reputation that has deterred international donors and investors from playing an active role. In October 1997, with the help of international financial institutions, the government launched a three-year reform programme aimed at stabilising the economy.[2] In 1998, a 5 per cent growth in GDP was recorded, while inflation fell from 164 per cent in 1997 to 2.7 per cent in 1998. The crisis in Russia that year dealt another blow to the Tajik economy, from which it is still recovering.

The problem of poverty has been overshadowed by the need to defuse the country's long-term armed conflict. Only after achieving a minimum level of stability has it been possible to turn the attention of policy makers toward that question. International and non-governmental organisations (NGOs) are currently trying to assist in alleviating the effects of poverty and promoting socio-economic development. However, one of the problems in planning and coordinating action has been the lack of awareness concerning the scale and character of poverty in the country. As in Latvia, filling this gap was thus seen as an essential first step toward solving the country's severe social problems.

Assessing poverty

Faced with the need to tackle simultaneously the challenges of political and economic reform, and to restore peace in the case of Tajikistan, politicians in these countries did not regard poverty as a priority issue during the early years of the transition. Measures taken as part of the PSI programme have played an important role in raising awareness among political elites and public opinion. There is a growing recognition that while the vast majority of society is bearing the costs of the transition process, some groups are particularly susceptible to poverty and are in danger of being marginalised. Driven by this awareness, the governments are now trying to devise policies aimed at counteracting poverty.

Bulgaria

The PSI programme in Bulgaria went through a number of changes during the course of its implementation. Initially, the government asked UNDP for assistance in its efforts to promote the National Programme of Action for Social Development, which was developed shortly after the 1995 World Social Summit held in Copenhagen, Denmark. In accordance with this goal, a national conference was organised in 1996, which approximately two hundred people, representing key ministries, civil society associations, trade unions and academia, attended. The conference is believed to have played an important role in increasing poverty awareness among the political elite and the general public.

The change of government following the economic and political crisis of 1996 brought this work to a halt, and resulted in a reorientation of the PSI programme. It was felt that previous activities had not been adequately integrated with other public sector policies, and that more attention should be devoted to assisting in the development of policy and analytical instruments for the design of policies against poverty.

A new project was therefore launched in 1997. It was a joint undertaking of UNDP and the Ministry of Employment and Social Policy, with the International Labour Organization (ILO) acting as the executing agency. The purpose of the project was to assist the government through the provision of various analytical inputs with direct application to policy, particularly with regard to minimum wage policy and social welfare reform. Subsequently, additional activities were launched to develop a government strategy for the reduction of poverty, on the recommendation of the Ministry of Employment.

During this phase, the UNDP project produced three main outputs. The first one was a report prepared by a large team of national experts representing the scientific community, government departments, civil society, the statistical office and trade unions (Bulgaria 1998a). The report contains an analysis of the nature of poverty, as well as the operations of the social welfare system, and several recommendations for social policy. Its chief aim, however, was to suggest a poverty threshold that could be used as a basis for public policy, particularly for determining eligibility for social assistance. This was in response to the government's commitment to reform social security by abandoning the principle of universal benefits and replacing it with a benefit system targeting the social categories most in need. Together with a reorientation of economic policy, the commitment to reform social security was a centrepiece of the agenda of the government that took over in 1997. Carrying out this reform required agreeing on a certain yard-

Table 1. Poverty in Bulgaria, 1995 and 1997

	1995		1997	
	Higher poverty line	**Lower poverty line**	**Higher poverty line**	**Lower poverty line**
Poverty Rate	5.5	2.9	36.0	20.2
Depth	1.7	0.9	11.4	5.9
Severity	0.8	0.4	5.3	2.7
Average per capita consumption*	117,208		62,604	
Gini coefficient	0.271		0.314	

* In June 1997 prices (Bulgaria Leva)

Source: Bulgarian Integrated Household Survey 1995, 1997 (World Bank 1999)

stick that would not only be accepted politically, but would also be feasible from a fiscal standpoint.

The controversy surrounding the definition of a poverty line was the starting point for the main project launched under the PSI programme. The poverty rate in any country obviously depends on the threshold adopted for determining who is poor. The World Bank has chosen a lower and an upper poverty line for Bulgaria, set respectively at 50 per cent and 66.7 per cent of average per capita consumption in 1997 (World Bank 1999). Based on these two lines, Table 1 shows the scope and depth of poverty in 1995 and 1997.

Other poverty lines were proposed in the report prepared within the framework of the PSI programme (Bulgaria 1998a). The lowest threshold corresponds to the basic minimum income (BMI), which is calculated using a basket comprising 22 food items and energy expenditure. The BMI is an administrative yardstick that has been used since 1992 as a criterion for assigning social allowances. It has never been adopted officially as a poverty line, as it clearly underestimates the scale of poverty in the country (3.9 per cent of households in 1997).[3] The report also considers an upper threshold calculated on the basis of the share of expenditure on food per capita, making allowance for non-food expenditures, which gives a poverty incidence of 65.5 per cent of households in 1996. Various other normative methods for calculating the poverty line produced incidences that range from 53 to 68 per cent. The report is inconclusive as to which yardstick should be adopted for monitoring poverty, but it emphasises the potential conflict between the theoretical legitimacy and fiscal feasibility of a poverty line, if it were to be used as basis for granting social assistance (see chapter 6, this volume).

The second output of the UNDP project was an assessment of the impact of the country's anti-poverty policies and strategies on women (Bulgaria 1998b). Prepared by a team of Bulgarian experts from the Agency for Social Analysis, the report examines the consequences of economic change for the situation of women and identifies female-headed households as being particularly at risk of poverty, especially those headed by single mothers and women from ethnic minorities. The following social groups were also found to be among the most vulnerable to poverty:

- Inhabitants of rural areas;
- National minorities, especially Gypsies, followed by Turks;
- Households composed of at least five people;
- Members of female-headed households, mainly single mothers and elderly single women;
- Children;
- People with low levels of education;
- Pensioners, who make up 60 per cent of the poor.

The third and final output was a study on income policy conducted by two experts, one from Bulgaria and the other one from the ILO. The document recommended the determination of a poverty line or subsistence minimum level, an increase in the minimum wage, a reform of the wage-tariff system, and a de-linking of all social benefits from the minimum wage, using instead the subsistence minimum as a criterion for social assistance (Bulgaria 1998c). The arguments presented in this study were used in negotiating the conditions of an economic aid package from the International Monetary Fund, which agreed to a slight increase in the minimum wage as recommended in the document.

It is apparent that the assistance provided by UNDP helped Bulgarian policy-makers and analysts gain a better understanding of the extent and nature of poverty in their country, as well as the tradeoffs involved in adopting certain policy instruments for designing policies against poverty. As we shall see later, the PSI project also laid the ground for the development of a national anti-poverty strategy.

Latvia

Prior to the transition from socialism, universal access to employment and a guaranteed minimum income resulted in a relatively egalitarian although non-affluent society. Poverty did not appear on the scale it does today, nor was it felt so acutely. A key objective of the PSI programme, therefore, was to raise the awareness of policy-makers and experts and provide them with reliable information about the magnitude and profile of poverty, including the manner in which impoverished people perceive their situation and the mechanisms they use to make ends meet. Five studies were commissioned. Some of them were carried out in collaboration with the World Bank or the ILO.

The first study contains a detailed analysis of the socio-economic and demographic characteristics of poor households using data from standard research on domestic household budgets carried out by the Central Statistical Bureau of Latvia (Gassmann 2000). On the basis of a relative poverty line, the official minimum wage and the crisis subsistence minimum, the report estimated the scope and depth of poverty, identified risk factors and analysed the consumption patterns of poor households.

A qualitative assessment of poverty was also carried out to supplement the results of the first study (Trapenciere et al. 2000). It is based on in-depth interviews with a sample of 400 households chosen to gain insights into the world and living conditions of the poor, how they interpret their situation, and the coping strategies they adopt. The study examines the factors that cause poverty or prevent people from breaking out of the poverty trap. It also assesses the extent to which poor people enjoy adequate access to education, health care and social services.

A third output, which developed the themes raised in the previous two studies, contains a quantitative analysis of the groups who lost out most during the first decade of the transition, their coping strategies, as well as their relationship with social welfare agencies (Gassmann and de Neubourg 2000). The exploration was carried out on the basis of a special questionnaire included as part of the standard research project on household budgets. Data from this research was also used in a fourth study that analysed the relationship between ethnicity and poverty in Latvia, where ethnic minorities make up almost 45 per cent of the population (Aasland 2000).

Finally, the fifth output examines one of the key determinants of poverty: the labour market and unemployment. Using data from the household budget and the labour force surveys of the Central Statistical Bureau, the document confirms that both unemployment and the quality of employment have a great bearing on the risk of being poor (Keune 2000). An adequate level of education is one of the most important determinants of success in the labour market, although it should be noted that the quality of secondary and vocational school education is still inadequate in relation to the needs of the economy (Latvia 2000).

There is no official poverty line in Latvia. The Central Statistical Bureau uses three poverty thresholds, which correspond to the crisis subsistence minimum level (55.7 *Lats*), the full subsistence minimum (82.2 *Lats*), and a relative line set at 50 per cent of average expenditure per adult equivalent (36.6 *Lats*). It is characteristic that the relative threshold is lower than the crisis subsistence minimum level, which indicates the low level of incomes of a considerable number of households located above the official poverty lines. The headcount ratio based on the first and third poverty lines is presented in Table 2.

The information contained in the documents financed by the PSI programme reveals that a wide variety of social groups are at risk of poverty (Gassmann and de Neubourg 2000; Trapenciere et al. 2000; Latvia 2000). The most vulnerable ones are:

- Households with children, particularly those with three or more children;
- Households with an above average number of dependants;
- Single-parent households, especially if headed by a single mother;
- Households with unemployed members, particularly unemployed persons of pre-pension age;

Table 2. Poverty headcount ratio in Latvia, 1996–1998

	Number of persons residing in households whose consumption expenditure is below:					
	Crisis subsistence level (per capita)			50% of adjusted average (per equivalent household member)		
	1996	1997	1998	1996	1997	1998
All households	67.9	68.1	59.6	14.9	16.1	16.8
Urban households	65.4	65.3	53.2	13.9	14.0	13.0
Rural households	73.8	74.8	73.6	17.3	21.2	25.5
Households with 3+ children	90.6	91.6	87.5	27.3	30.7	32.8

Source: Central Statistical Bureau of Latvia

- Households dependent on income from agriculture;
- Households located in rural areas;
- Households where the breadwinner has a low level of general education, lacks professional education or work experience;
- Households in which one or more family members are alcoholics;
- Disabled people.

One important factor increasing the risk of poverty is gender, although it does so in a specific way. Female single-person households are less at risk of poverty than male single-person households. The risk of poverty increases with the number of children, and is distinctively higher when the household head is a woman than where a man is the chief breadwinner. These differences result from the fact that female-headed households are often those abandoned by the father, or where the father does not provide for its sustenance (Gassmann 2000; Neimanis 1999). When a divorced father cannot or will not provide his children with financial assistance, the mother is often unable to combine effective professional employment with her parental functions and the family is at greater risk of falling below the poverty line.[4]

Women, moreover, seem to react differently to poverty than men. Due to their feelings of responsibility towards their children, they tend to actively seek means of subsistence more often than men do. Men are more prone to alcoholism and bouts of depression in such situations (Trapenciere et al. 2000; chapter 3, this volume).

Another interesting finding is that ethnic affiliation has no major bearing on the risk of being poor, other factors being equal. Ethnic minorities are susceptible to higher unemployment, but have a labour market participation rate similar to ethnic Latvians. Nevertheless, ethnic minorities are more dissatisfied and express greater feelings of deprivation than other groups (Aasland 2000).

Still another main source of dissatisfaction derives from the widening inequality that has accompanied the transition from socialism. According to the Central Statistical Bureau, the Gini coefficient reached 0.32 in 1998, up from 0.23 in 1987-

88 (Milanovic 1998). Thus, two factors have bred feelings of deprivation among the lower segments of society: decreasing incomes as a result of unemployment and a drop in real incomes during the 1990s, and the increasing gap between those who have fallen behind and the 'winners' of the transition process.

Tajikistan

According to various sources and criteria, 70 to 96 per cent of the Tajik population currently live in poverty. Nevertheless, precise information about living conditions in the country has been missing, which has not only prevented the design of effective public policies, but also increased the costs of donor interventions. Donors interested in implementing social development programmes have had no choice but to invest their own resources for diagnostic assessments prior to their interventions.

For this reason, PSI resources were mainly used to finance the country's first Living Standards Survey, a joint undertaking of UNDP and the World Bank carried out in 1999 on the basis of a sample of 2,000 households nationwide. Goskomstat, the government statistical agency, was responsible for analysing the data and producing a report based on the results of the survey.

According to data from the survey, almost nine out of ten households have a monthly expenditure of less than US$ 12 at market rates, and 27 per cent spend less than US$ 5. Approximately 3 per cent of the rural population and 6 per cent of the urban population have expenditures greater than 30,000 Tajik roubles per month, which is the equivalent of $1PPP per capita per day (Tajikistan 2000).

Food expenditure accounts on average for 73.7 per cent of total expenditure. Of this, 42.5 per cent goes to cereal products, while 8 per cent is assigned to the con-

Table 3. Monthly expenditures and income grouping urban and rural households, 1999 (in per cent)

Per capita in Tajik roubles	Expenditures			Incomes		
	Urban	Rural	Total	Urban	Rural	Total
Up to 2000	0.2	0.7	0.6	8.5	7.5	7.7
2001–4000	2.9	2.7	2.7	12.2	12.6	12.5
4001–6000	6.5	9.9	9.2	13.1	14.2	14.0
6001–8000	11.6	14.9	14.2	14.9	15.2	15.1
8001–10000	13.7	15.5	15.1	11.8	10.6	10.9
10001–15000	31.3	31.9	31.7	19.5	18.6	18.8
15001–20000	14.2	13.6	13.8	8.1	9.1	8.9
20001–25000	7.0	5.4	5.7	4.4	4.2	4.2
25001–30000	6.7	2.6	3.5	2.3	3.2	3.0
Above 30000	5.9	2.8	3.5	5.2	4.8	4.9

Source: Goskomstat, Living Standards Survey 1999.

sumption of meat. It is estimated that average meat consumption in towns is 20 per cent of the norm, while the corresponding figure in the countryside is 10 per cent. On the other hand, vegetable consumption of town and country dwellers is 41 and 35 per cent of the norm, respectively (Turayev 1999). Households with at least three children face the greatest risk of extreme poverty, which corresponds to the lowest quintile of the income distribution. Single-parent households in this category are the most affected.

Private garden plots and allotments constitute a very important element of the rural economy. Ninety-two per cent of rural households have allotments, as do 38 per cent of urban households. Besides the cultivation of cereal crops and vegetables, cattle husbandry and poultry farming are also developing. This sector of the economy is highly intensive, and every fragment of land is exploited. More than 50 per cent of household revenue comes from the consumption or sale of products from private garden plots.

As a result of the crisis and the war, enrolment rates in primary and secondary schools fell sharply, to 62 per cent in 1996. This may jeopardise Tajikistan's educational achievements, which boasted of a literacy rate estimated to be 99 per cent among men and 97 per cent among women in 1995 (UNDP 1998). Although many private higher educational establishments also appeared at this time, the decline in the school enrolment rate will have a long-term impact on the country's development. Reversing this declining rate is one of the major challenges facing the government and aid organisations.

Enhancing poverty awareness

These countries started with different levels of awareness of poverty in their societies. It is fair to say, however, that their understanding of the problem was generally low. Both politicians and the public were inclined to treat economic distress and deprivation as a transitory effect of the transition to a market economy. The commissioning and publication of surveys and analyses of poverty in both English and the local languages attracted substantial media attention, and played an important role in changing people's perceptions and introducing the issue into the vocabulary of the political elites.

Poverty became an issue in Bulgaria earlier than in the other two countries. In 1993, the government appealed to the World Bank for a loan to conduct research on poverty, which eventually took the form of panel research projects in 1995 and 1997. Concurrently, in June 1995, the government prepared a National Programme for Social Development as a consequence of the commitments it made during the World Social Summit held in Copenhagen. UNDP was asked to assist in promoting the national programme, with support from the PSI programme.

The new government that emerged following the crisis in 1997 was preoccupied with economic stabilisation. Through a revamped PSI programme, UNDP played an important role in increasing poverty awareness among policy-makers. One barrier to developing an anti-poverty policy was that there was neither a clear definition of poverty nor adequate tools for measuring its scope and character. This problem was accordingly tackled within the PSI programme through a comprehensive study of poverty based on all available sources. The study included an analysis of the social safety net and a special research project on the position of women. Work was carried out in parallel with a poverty assessment of the World Bank. Each programme took into account the results of the other's work, mostly to good effect.

By contrast, no initiative had addressed the problem of poverty in Latvia prior to the launch of the PSI programme. It is no exaggeration to say that poverty was simply not an issue before 1997. The situation of sudden impoverishment faced by a growing number of households was certainly well known to local social workers, but neither the government nor society had taken an active interest in the problem. The support provided by UNDP thus encouraged politicians and policy-makers to take note of the fact that not everyone had benefited from the transition from socialism. The publication of five reports accompanied by a press conference by the Ministry of Welfare and UNDP in February 2000 contributed in a critical manner to mobilising societal and political support for addressing social problems in the country. Special care was taken to ensure that the press began to write about the problem with a view to changing the prevailing attitude towards poverty, in which it was perceived as the result of personal failure rather than structurally determined constraints.

Given the dramatic scale of poverty in Tajikistan, nobody needed convincing that there was a problem to be solved. However, the absence of reliable information on its precise nature and extent hampered action by the government as well as international organisations. Shortly after concluding a peace agreement with the opposition, the Tajik government began to cooperate with international donors on the task of economic and social reform. But the methods used by Goskomstat, the state statistical agency, for monitoring living conditions were sorely inadequate and needed updating to be applied effectively to the design of policy. For this reason, UNDP reached an understanding with the World Bank with the aim of jointly financing and conducting a Living Standards Survey, which became the linchpin of the PSI programme. Apart from improving the data collection and processing methods used by Goskomstat, another important goal of the programme was to make international opinion more aware of Tajikistan's problems and attract donors who would contribute to the development and reconstruction of its economy.

Conferences and seminars organised within the framework of the PSI programme were instrumental in for stimulating poverty awareness in the three countries. Efforts were made to ensure that technically complex issues, such as the choice of a poverty line, were treated in a manner that could reach a large audience and become a subject of public debate. A good example of this is Bulgaria. From the outset, it was recognised that defining a threshold that could serve as the foundation of a basic minimum income and an instrument of social policy required more than a solid theoretical justification. It entailed, above all, a political decision that necessitated public approval. In June 1998, at a conference devoted to the problem of poverty, the results of the PSI studies were presented. Both the assessment of poverty trends during the transition and the special report on women attracted great interest among policy circles.

Moreover, since an important objective of the project was to organise a local cadre of social policy experts, a five-day workshop was held in October 1998 on the design, monitoring and evaluation of social security and employment protection programmes. Representatives from the government, municipalities, non-governmental organisations, trade unions and research institutions attended the workshop, which constituted a valuable input into the ongoing examination of Bulgaria's social security system. Because of these dissemination and training activities, the recommendations from the studies supported by UNDP were used during the course of preparing the National Development Plan for the years 2000-2006, as well as in the design of public initiatives targeted at low-income groups.

Similarly, a two-day seminar on the theme of poverty was held in Dushanbe in late 1999. The seminar, chaired by the Deputy Prime Minister, provided an opportunity for presenting the preliminary results of the Tajikistan Living Standards Survey and discussing its policy recommendations with representatives from the ministries, civil society, universities and foreign experts.

Perhaps nowhere has public information played a more salient role than in Latvia. A round table discussion held in May 1998 with participants from various ministries, the Central Statistical Bureau, the Institute of Philosophy and Sociology, and the Latvian Institute of Statistics was the first in a series of events that contributed to placing poverty reduction on the public agenda. This initial event was followed by a seminar on the country's profile of poverty in November 1998, at which the results of the quantitative and qualitative assessments sponsored by UNDP, as well as the report on employment and poverty, were presented to a broad audience of academics, civil society representatives, journalists and policy-makers. This was complemented by five workshops in which poverty issues were discussed in connection with education, social guarantees, health care, and employment.

The culmination of this public relations effort came with the official presentation of the five reports financed by UNDP at a press launch in Riga in February 2000, which opened a regional conference on Poverty Reduction in the Baltic States. Hosted by the Latvian Ministry of Welfare and co-organised by the UNDP missions in the Baltic States, the conference was attended by teams in charge of preparing poverty reduction strategies in Estonia, Latvia and Lithuania, as well as foreign experts and representatives of the state administration, UNDP, the World Bank, ILO, civil society and academics. This participation level produced not only a greater exposure, but also an international dimension to the anti-poverty debate in the region. It also encouraged the formation of a fledgling regional network of poverty researchers across the Baltic countries.

Strengthening technical and institutional capacity

Despite the fact that there is a fairly well developed research infrastructure in the region, foreign experts were involved to a greater or lesser degree in the implementation of the PSI activities in all three countries. What matters for purposes of local ownership and sustainability of the policy reform process is the extent to which capacities and know-how have been transferred and vested locally as a result of the participation of international experts. Here we find different models of interaction and engagement between foreign and local experts and institutions.

The local expertise base was weaker in Tajikistan than in Latvia or Bulgaria. One of the main purposes of UNDP assistance, therefore, was to help create such a base. For this reason, the project was carried out with extensive cooperation between foreign experts and native personnel, and also involved training programmes, workshops and a process of 'learning by doing' under the supervision of experienced consultants.

The experience in Tajikistan offers a model with regard to improving technical skills of local personnel. Carrying out the living standard survey required, as a preliminary task, developing a research infrastructure and improving the operations of the national statistical bureau. Goskomstat was established on the basis of the old Soviet branch, as an agency performing tasks commissioned by the central authorities, but not involved in independent research activities. For their part, government agencies were not fully capable of putting research results to use in their own operations. Thus, the aims of the PSI programme went decidedly beyond the standard tasks involved in carrying out a simple survey.[5]

Intensive training and transfer of know-how were key features of the project. The cooperation between Tajik and foreign experts has been rated very highly by its beneficiaries. Apart from yielding valuable information for use in policy-making, the Living Standards Survey has helped put in place a highly experienced local team prepared to take part in similar exercises in the future. The ability of Goskomstat to carry out statistical research has clearly increased, as evidenced by the report it produced using the results of the survey (Turayev 1999). So has the ability of staff from the ministries to absorb research results, because of the training and the purchase of computer software and equipment made possible by the project.

A different type of relationship between local and foreign experts was present in Bulgaria. The main project outputs were prepared by a large group of domestic experts drawn from various institutions.[6] External assistance was provided mainly through ILO personnel. Although this working model was beset with the usual problems of coordinating the work of a large team, it had other relevant side benefits. Most importantly, a local think-tank was established, charged with the task of carrying out a comprehensive analysis of poverty. The participation of a broad cross-section of local institutions also facilitated the task of disseminating the results of the studies. The experts who were involved in the PSI programme went on to collaborate on new initiatives, including the preparation of several reports commissioned by UNDP as a basis for the formulation of a National Plan of Action against Poverty.

Team members acquired new skills in the course of the work, although more as a result of the exchange of knowledge within the team than through external help. Most valuable from the standpoint of capacity-building, were the workshops on the design, planning and evaluation of social security programmes, which contributed to the transfer of policy-relevant knowledge with direct operational application.

The modality of cooperation between local and foreign experts was found to be more problematic in Latvia. With the exception of the qualitative assessment of poverty (Trapenciere et al. 2000), local experts played only a minor role in producing the studies sponsored by UNDP, which were done mostly by international consultants from the University of Maastricht (the Netherlands) and the FAFO Institute (Norway). The Central Statistical Bureau supplied data for two of the studies. It also carried out research based on a special questionnaire attached to the standard Household Budget Survey, which provided the basis for another two reports. However, staff from the Bureau were not involved substantially in designing the questionnaire. Their role was mostly limited to conducting the fieldwork.

There was also little interaction between the international experts and the members of the Working Group set up in 1999 with the task of preparing an outline for the formulation of a National Strategy for Poverty Reduction. The authors of the PSI reports were not consulted during the course of preparing the strategy until an advanced draft had been completed. At the same time, the Working Group did not receive the necessary advice and information on how to prepare a poverty reduction strategy. Its members had no access to planning workshops or policy papers that might have given them some guidance regarding the final product they were expected to deliver. Although the Ministry of Welfare, which chaired the Working Group, stressed the need for direct cooperation with foreign consultants based on the principle of 'learning by doing', the latter only had a limited working relationship with the Working Group. Neither the Ministry of Welfare nor the other members of the Working Group made full use of the studies commissioned by UNDP, which they perceived to be too generic in their recommendations to be of practical use for policy action.[7]

Consequently, the involvement of international experts in the programme activities failed to develop local research potential. Opportunities for transferring knowledge and skills were missed. To make such transfer possible, the project should have established more extensive contacts with local partners and been more firmly grounded on cooperation with the recipients of the project results. It is therefore not surprising that the Group's work was not entirely satisfactory, although it should also be noted that the participation of the foreign consultants did help increase awareness of the problem of poverty both in the state administration and among those circles represented in the Working Group.

There was an exception to this pattern — the qualitative poverty assessment, which involved a different form of cooperation with foreign experts (Trapenciere et al. 2000). A research team from the Institute of Philosophy and Sociology in Riga carried out the research and prepared the subsequent report, in collaboration with a World Bank expert. The outcome of this cooperation has been highly rated by the local partners, who as a result of the project, have gained an in-depth knowledge of the situation of poor people in Latvia. The exercise has not only produced a useful report, but also sustainable results in the form of a local team of experts with improved skills. The decisive factor, it seems, was that this project component was better able to establish the necessary conditions for a bilateral transfer of knowledge and experience among its various participants, both local and foreign.

Impact on policy

In spite of the newness of the PSI programme and the limited amount of funding involved, there are clear indications that the assistance provided has not only contributed to enhancing knowledge about poverty conditions, but also to creating a momentum for the design of anti-poverty policy in these countries. The analyses and information produced by the programme have been so timely that steps are now being taken to translate the knowledge acquired into concrete policy measures.

All three countries are going beyond the diagnostic stage into the formulation of programmes or strategies for poverty reduction and the creation of institutional mechanisms for coordinating work on poverty. The results of the studies and surveys financed by the PSI programme are being used for this purpose, as well as for the enactment of legislation and the launching of initiatives that deal with particular aspects of the problem highlighted by those studies.

Latvia has made the most progress in this regard. Despite the problems of insufficient cooperation between international and local experts mentioned above, the efforts to place poverty issues on the public domain have been so successful that Latvian authorities have taken up the issue in earnest. The first step in this process was the creation of the Working Group with representatives from the ministries, municipalities, civil society and academic institutions. The Ministry of Welfare was made responsible for chairing the Group, given the leading role that its Social

Policy Department had traditionally played in developing anti-poverty programmes.

The initial task of the Group was rather limited — to review the five reports sponsored by the UNDP project in order to formulate a set of recommendations for a national policy against poverty. During the course of implementing the project, however, the Cabinet of Ministers decided to set a more ambitious task, the development of a full-blown National Strategy for Poverty Reduction, and assigned the responsibility to the Working Group. A draft version of the Strategy was submitted to the Cabinet in late 1999 and presented to the public at the conference on Poverty Reduction in the Baltic States (January 2000), where it was discussed along with the draft strategies prepared in Estonia and Lithuania. In the meantime, the Cabinet passed a law on social assistance, as well as a resolution adopting a guaranteed minimum income. It has also recommended the preparation of a detailed plan of action, which will serve as the basis for government policy in the fight against poverty.

The draft strategy proposed a set of basic policy measures as well as three alternative poverty lines for designing the threshold for social assistance. They are, respectively, a low-income threshold (persons whose income falls below a level set nationally in accordance to regulations issued by the Cabinet); 75 per cent of the average disposable income per person; and 50 per cent of the value of the full subsistence basket of goods and services. Based on these three lines, the incidence of poverty in Latvia ranges from 15 to 39 per cent.

For reasons explained above, the draft strategy cannot be considered a mature policy document. Certain weaknesses in the draft strategy need to be addressed as a matter of priority. This includes agreeing on a working definition of poverty, setting realistic policy goals and quantifying them, linking with sectoral and other government programmes at regional and local levels, and identifying target groups for specific types of intervention. Furthermore, the scope for financing the programme needs to be identified, and mechanisms for monitoring and evaluation established.

Whether actions aimed at alleviating poverty become a central feature of gov-

Table 4. Poverty lines and headcount ratio in Latvia, 1998

	Poverty line (US$ per person per month)	Headcount ratio (%)
Persons with low income	49.0	15.8
50% of full subsistence basket per capita	70.0	31.2
75% of average income per capita	79.0	39.3

Source: Central Statistical Bureau of Latvia

ernment policy will depend on the quality of the action plan being designed by the Working Group. It is important, however, to highlight the strong commitment that appears to be present at the highest political level. This is a major achievement in a country in which the existence of poverty was barely recognised only a few years ago.

Similar moves towards institutionalising anti-poverty policy have been taken in Bulgaria and Tajikistan. Bulgaria undertook a thorough diagnosis of poverty following a reorientation of the PSI programme in 1997. This work provided the basis for subsequent policy initiatives. The social segment of the National Development Plan for the years 2000-2006 was prepared with assistance and advice from UNDP. PSI activities have also been synchronised with wider reform packages in the social sectors, as reflected in the recent Social Welfare Act. In October 1999, the Minister of Labour and Social Policy appealed to UNDP for additional cooperation in preparing a Plan of Action for Poverty Reduction. The aim of the Plan of Action is to supplement the National Development Plan 2000-2006 in the areas of social assistance for the needy, social integration of vulnerable groups, and labour market legislation. This process culminated in January 2000, with the announcement by the Prime Minister that the reduction of poverty is a major priority for the government. This announcement, which took place at a meeting between the Cabinet and international donors that had originally been proposed by UNDP and supported by the World Bank, signals a spectacular success for anti-poverty programmes in Bulgaria.

The joint collaboration between UNDP and the World Bank in support of the Tajikistan Living Standards Survey has not only produced information that can now be used for policy purposes, but has also increased public policy research capacity within the country. A research infrastructure has been established in Goskomstat and in the policy departments of selected ministries, whose staff received intensive training in data gathering, processing and analysis, as well as in the use of statistical software packages. The Survey was supplemented in two regions by a special health care module, which was commissioned by the Ministry of Health for the preparation of an impending World Bank loan for a pilot health care reform programme. The fact that all of these ambitious goals have been achieved is laudable, given the difficult security situation in Tajikistan and the problems involved in carrying out field research.

Experts from the World Bank and UNDP are using the data generated by the Living Standards Survey to analyse poverty profiles and prepare a poverty assessment, which began during 2000. Concurrently, a Working Group for Poverty Alleviation has been established under the auspices of the Prime Minister's Office, and charged with the task of elaborating the country's first anti-poverty strategy. The group has prepared a preliminary version of the strategy, which still requires further work.

Donor engagement: Modalities of cooperation

Most of the work on poverty done so far in these countries, whether analytical or policy-oriented, has depended on the resources committed by international organisations. Governments have made no financial contribution, except of course at the stage of implementing some of the measures that have been identified as necessary.

There have been different models of cooperation among the donor agencies, as well as between them and their national partners. The model developed in Latvia is especially worthy of attention. The PSI project involved close collaboration between the Ministry of Welfare, UNDP, the World Bank and ILO, assisted by foreign experts from two renowned European institutions. The main partners involved in the project set up a Steering Committee that met regularly to update each of the participating institutions about the progress made in implementation. Such collaboration made it possible to coordinate efforts and combine the resources invested by all the partners. It also enabled the project to adapt more easily to changing conditions, as illustrated by the Cabinet's decision in January 2000 to recommend the elaboration of a national strategy for poverty reduction. Working relationships between international organisations have been highly cooperative, as have their relations with the Latvian authorities. This pattern of collaboration has been further reinforced as a result of the PSI activities, and may be recommended as one of the best practices of the programme.

In Bulgaria, UNDP worked closely with ILO and a large team of domestic experts from various academic, trade union and civil society organisations. By contrast, there was little direct collaboration between UNDP and the World Bank. The PSI studies built upon the results of the poverty research conducted by the Bank in 1997, which they supplemented by assessing the strengths and weaknesses of the existing social safety net, the use of alternative poverty lines for social policy, and the institutional conditions for anti-poverty policy (Bulgaria 1998a). But despite the existence of ample scope for collaboration and cross-fertilisation, both sets of activities were mostly carried out in parallel. Moreover, in 1998, the World Bank began a new poverty assessment project, the results of which were published the following year (World Bank 1999). Given the good working relationship that exists between UNDP and the World Bank in Bulgaria, it appears that cooperation between the two organisations could have been tighter.

Such intensive cooperation between UNDP and the World Bank was certainly present in Tajikistan. The implementation modality adopted for the Living Standards Survey favoured close contacts between specialists from the two organisations, government officials, local experts and Goskomstat personnel, even though no coordinating body was officially established like the one set up in Latvia. The World Bank has made its assistance to Tajikistan conditional upon the preparation of a Poverty Reduction Strategy Paper (PRSP).[8] The model of cooperation and mutual trust between government officials and development agencies engendered by the implementation of the Living Standards Living are likely to ease future negotiations on the content of the country's PRSP.

An important by-product of the Survey is that it may facilitate the development of aid programmes and therefore attract donor interest in operating in the country. The international community in Dushanbe is small. So far, few organisations have set up operations, partly for safety reasons and partly due to a lack of knowledge of the country. By supplying the donor community with updated information on the prevailing poverty situation, the Living Standards Survey will reduce the cost of preparing aid programmes, which has hampered donor efforts in the past. From this point of view, the Living Standards Survey was an important milestone, potentially streamlining the actions of not only the Tajik government, but also its international donors.

To support this process, UNDP organised a meeting of donors in 1999, which was attended by representatives of international organisations and ambassadors from countries interested in promoting development in Tajikistan. At the meeting, the results of the research were presented as a basis for attracting further international aid. For the first time, financial support has been offered by the Know How Fund (KHF), Britain's programme of bilateral technical assistance to the former socialist countries of Europe and Central Asia. This financial contribution, which will be channelled through UNDP, constitutes a major achievement, given the relative isolation from which the country has suffered in the past. Other donors have been slow to come forward. But at least they have now gained a better basis for their activities, should they decide to set up operations in the future.

Conclusion

In Bulgaria, Latvia and Tajikistan the PSI programme has been part of an extensive process of transformation unleashed by the breakdown of the Soviet Union. By their very nature, periods of systemic transformation entail openness to and expectations of change. They are periods during which the basic framework of a new political, economic and social system is being developed, which becomes more difficult to change once the transformation process comes to an end. A major challenge for countries in transition has been to make the public aware of the social woes that have accompanied the transition from planned to market economies, and to induce politicians to become involved in reform programmes. From this perspective, the PSI initiative came at the right time.

Considering the modest scale of the programme, its achievements have been particularly noteworthy. In Latvia, poverty has become a central issue in the public discourse, from which it had been absent until very recently. The profile and situation of poor households have been thoroughly diagnosed, a high-level Working Group was set up to coordinate the development of anti-poverty policy, and a draft version of a National Strategy for Poverty Reduction was submitted to the Cabinet for endorsement at the beginning of 2000. In Tajikistan, the first-ever Living Standards Survey was conducted, local capacity for public policy analysis has been strengthened, and a Working Group was created under the auspices of the Prime Minister to draft the country's PRSP. As a result of the Survey, the donor community has also become more aware of the humanitarian dimensions of poverty in a country that is striving to overcome the effects of civil war. In Bulgaria, a large cadre of local experts has been established, work on the formulation of a National Plan of Action against Poverty has commenced, and poverty reduction has become a top priority for the government, as announced by the Prime Minister in January 2000. These and other positive developments certainly cannot be attributed only to the assistance provided by UNDP, but it is equally clear that the PSI programme has been thoroughly involved in these processes and has contributed directly to most of the outcomes.

The projects sponsored by UNDP also had certain drawbacks. The most salient ones were the inadequate coordination between UNDP and the World Bank in Bulgaria, where cooperation could have been tighter, and the limited contacts between national and foreign experts in Latvia, which reduced the potential for skills transfer and lateral learning. In Tajikistan, it remains to be seen whether the results of the Living Standards Survey translate into more effective anti-poverty policy and whether foreign donors feel encouraged to set up operations in the country. Despite these shortcomings, it has now become common knowledge in these countries that poverty is not simply a problem affecting marginal groups in need of charitable support, but rather an outcome of the manner in which the transition process was managed, as well as a structural barrier to development. Governments have stepped up their involvement in the fight against poverty. Models of cooperation between international organisations and national partners have been developed. Finally, countries have taken the first steps towards institutionalising the anti-poverty drive through the establishment of high-level coordinating mechanisms.

The first stage of work on an anti-poverty policy has thus been largely completed in the three countries. Yet the capacity to design good public policy and implement effective social programmes remains weak. The working groups that have been set up still have to evolve into something more permanent in order to have a lasting impact on public policy. Their members, whether from government, academia or civil society, tend to need preliminary training in policy analysis and design. Representatives from civil society have been included in these working groups, but cooperation has not become institutionalised yet.

As countries move from the diagnostic phase into formulating government strategies for poverty reduction, support from foreign experts will be needed. Any follow-up programme should aim to develop local capacity to prepare, implement and monitor policies and programmes to tackle poverty, and to pilot and disseminate model solutions to those responsible for managing those programmes. There is in these countries a great demand and willingness to acquire the necessary technical skills. For this reason, technical assistance geared towards transferring skills and know-how and vesting them locally is, at present, one of the most attractive features of international programmes. ■

Notes

The author wishes to acknowledge the support of Alejandro Grinspun and Rasheda Selim, as well as UNDP officers in Bulgaria, Latvia, and Tajikistan for their cooperation during the field visits.

[1] The conflict lasted until 1997, when the government signed an agreement with the opposition. This agreement, however, failed to prevent further armed clashes in the north in 1998 and various minor disturbances, especially on the border with Afghanistan. As a result of the war, an estimated 50,000 people have been killed, 500,000 have become economic refugees, and 600,000 have changed their place of residence.

[2] The government is working closely with the IMF, the World Bank and other international organisations to solve basic development problems and maintain the country's still unsteady growth rate. Key undertakings in the field of structural policy have included an acceleration of ownership transformations in agriculture, further reforms in the financial sector, and reform of health care, education and the energy sector. Since 1995, approximately 120 state farms have been transformed into joint-stock companies and leaseholds. Since mid-1999, as a result of pressure from the World Bank, a number of measures have been taken to step up organisational and ownership transformations in another 160 farms. Cotton production continues to be dominated by the centralised state economy.

[3] One criticism levelled at the BMI is that it does not necessarily cover minimum calorie needs. For this reason, the Bulgarian Institute for Trade Union and Social Studies proposed its basic needs consumer basket as an alternative to the BMI, after taking into account the consumer spending habits of the second and third deciles of the income distribution series.

[4] The divorce rate in Latvia is one of the highest in Europe. Thirty-four to 36 per cent of marriages end in divorce after 5-9 years of matrimony. Sixty to 70 per cent of divorced couples have children under the age of 18 (Latvia 1998a).

[5] During the course of the Tajikistan Living Standards Survey, a number of standard tasks had to be carried out: develop a questionnaire; identify, recruit and train surveyors; pilot the questionnaire and make necessary revisions; carry out the survey in 2,000 households throughout the country; input the data and generate profiles of poverty; prepare a final report on living standards; and disseminate the information to the international community and government institutions.

[6] Among others, the National Statistics Institute, the Economic Institute of the Bulgarian

Academy of Sciences, the Ministry of Labour and Social Policy, the Confederation of Independent Trade Unions, the National Centre for the Study of Democracy, and the Agency for Social Analysis.

[7] Representatives from the ministries and the Central Statistical Bureau even maintained a certain critical distance from the research activities carried out by the international experts. It was felt, for instance, that resources from the PSI programme could have been used more effectively to improve the basic household budget survey to ensure a more systematic monitoring of poverty. The reports produced by the international consultants were said to be difficult to use in practice because they did not offer the kind of clear policy recommendations needed by decision-makers. Some researchers were even criticised for their apparent lack of knowledge of the operations of the social welfare system in Latvia, which they were supposed to help evaluate.

[8] Due to the fact that poverty affects rural areas with particular intensity, the World Bank has made rural development a basic goal of its aid strategy for Tajikistan. Other areas of assistance to the Dushanbe government include health, education and a social welfare fund.

References

Country Documents

Angola, 1997. *1998-2000 Medium-Term Stabilisation and Economic Recovery Programme*, summary, Luanda.

Angola, 1999. *Human Development Report on Angola*, United Nations Development Programme, Luanda.

Benin, 1998. *Financement des services sociaux essentiels*, Ministère des Finances, Ministère du Plan, de la Restructuration Economique et de la Promotion de l'Emploi, United Nations Development Programme and UNICEF, Cotonou.

Bulgaria, 1998a. *Poverty in Transition: Strengthening the National Policies and Strategies for Poverty Reduction in Bulgaria*, International Labour Organization and United Nations Development Programme, Sofia.

Bulgaria, 1998b. *Women in Poverty: An Assessment of the Bulgarian Anti-Poverty Policies and Strategies*, International Labour Organization and United Nations Development Programme, Sofia.

Bulgaria, 1998c. *Mid-Term Incomes Policy and Strategy*, International Labour Organization and United Nations Development Programme, Sofia.

Burkina Faso, 1998. *Initiative 20/20 au Burkina Faso: L'allocation des ressources budgétaires aux services sociaux de base pour les années 1990 à 1997*, Economy and Finance Ministry, United Nations Development Programme and UNICEF, Ouagadougou.

Chad, 1998. *L'initiative 20/20: Examen des possiblités de mobilisation des ressources additionnelles en faveur des serveices sociaux essentiels au Tchad*. Ministère du Plan et de l'Amenagement du Territoire, United Nations Development Programme and UNICEF, N'Djamena.

Estonia, 1999. *Poverty Reduction in Estonia: Background and Guidelines*, University of Tartu, Ministry of Social Affairs and United Nations Development Programme, Tartu University Press, Tartu.

Ethiopia, 1998. *Human Development Report for Ethiopia*, United National Development Programme, Addis Ababa.

Gambia, 1997. National poverty monitoring system for Gambia, Central Statistics Department, Banjul.

India, 1997. *India: The Road to Human Development*, United Nations Development Programme, New Delhi.

Indonesia, 1998. *Crisis, Poverty and Human Development in Indonesia*, BPS-Statistics and United Nations Development Programme, Jakarta.

Karnataka, 1999. *Human Development in Karnataka 1999*, State Government of Karnataka, Bangalore, India.

Kazakhstan, 1998. A National Programme and Action Plan for a Healthy Lifestyle, Ministry of Education, Culture and Health, Committee of Health, National Centre For Healthy Lifestyle Promotion, Almaty.

Korea, Republic of, 1998. *Combating Poverty: The Korean Experience*, United Nations Development Programme, Seoul.

Kyrgyzstan, 1998. Comprehensive Poverty Alleviation Programme, (Draft) Proposal of the United Nations Development Programme in cooperation with the Council on Sustainable Human Development, Bishkek.

Lao PDR, 1998. *National Human Development Report,* State Planning Committee and United Nations Development Programme, Vientiane.

Lao PDR, 1998a. *National Rural Development Programme 1996 to 2000*, Vientiane.

Lao PDR, 1998b. *The Rural Development Programme 1998-2002. The 'Focal Site' Strategy*, Vientiane.

Lao PDR, 1999. 'Ethnic Minorities and Rural Development in Lao PDR. Findings and Recommendations', United Nations Development Programme, Vientiane.

Latvia, 1998. Annual Report for 1998: Support to the Development of a National Poverty Eradication Strategy, United Nations Development Programme, Riga.

Latvia, 1998a. 'Social Trends in Latvia', Central Statistical Bureau of Latvia, Riga.

Latvia, 1999. *1999 Social Report*, Ministry of Welfare of the Republic of Latvia, Riga.

Latvia, 1999a. *The National Economy of Latvia: Macroeconomic review*, Central Statistical Bureau of Latvia, Ministry of Economy, Latvian Development Agency, Riga.

Latvia, 2000. *Strategy for Reduction of Poverty*, Ministry of Welfare of the Republic of Latvia, (Draft), Riga.

Lebanon 1997. A *Profile of Sustainable Human Development in Lebanon,* United Nations Development Programme, Beirut.

Lebanon, 1998. *Mapping of Living Conditions in Lebanon: An Analysis of the Housing and Population Database*, Ministry of Social Affairs and United Nations Development Programme, Beirut.

Lebanon, 1998a. 'Preparatory Assistance. National Programme for Improving Living Conditions of the Poor in Lebanon', Ministry of Social Affairs, Beirut.

Lebanon, 2000. *The 20/20 Initiative for Lebanon*, Ministry of Finance, UNICEF and United Nations Development Programme, Beirut.

Lesotho, 1997. *Urban Poverty Assessment in Lesotho*, United Nations Development Programme, Maseru.

Lithuania, 1998. *Poverty in Lithuania: Living Conditions of Social Benefits Recipients*, Ministry of Social Security and Labour, Vilnius University, Health Economics Centre and United Nations Development Programme, Vilnius.

Lithuania, 2000. Poverty Reduction and Alleviation Strategy: Lithuania (Draft), Vilnius.

Madhya Pradesh, 1998. *The Madhya Pradesh Human Development Report*, State Government of Madhya Pradesh, Bhopal, India.

Maldives, 1998. *Vulnerability and Poverty Assessment,* Ministry of Planning and National

Development and United Nations Development Programme, Male'.

Mali, 1998. 'Stratégie Nationale de lutte contre la pauvreté, Volume 1', Ministère de l'Economie, du Plan et de l'intégration, Bamako.

Mali, 1998b. 'Rapport de l'atelier régional sur la stratégie nationale de réduction de la pauvreté, Gao-Tombouctou-Kidal, Gao', Ministère de l'Economie, du Plan et de l'intégration and United Nations Development Programme, Gao, Mali.

Mauritania, 1998. 'Rapport National sur le Développement Humain Durable 1997', Nouakchott.

Mauritania, 1998. 'Programme National de Lutte Contre la Pauvreté 1998-2001', Nouakchott.

Moldova, 1997. National Poverty Alleviation Strategy, United Nations Development Programme, Chisinau.

Moldova, 1998. Short Term Poverty Alleviation Programme, United Nations Development Programme, Chisinau.

Mongolia, 1997. *Human Development Report: Mongolia 1997*, United Nations Development Programme, Ulaanbatar.

Mozambique, 1998. National Integrated Programme for Social Action, Employment and Youth, United Nations Development Programme, Maputo.

Nepal, 1998. *Nepal Human Development Report*, Nepal South Asia Centre and United Nations Development Programme, Kathmandu.

Nepal, 1998a. *Restructuring Budget and Aid in Nepal, 1986-1997*, National Planning Commission, UNICEF and United Nations Development Programme and the Institute for Sustainable Development, Kathmandu.

Palestine, 1997. *Palestinian Development Plan 1998-2000*, Palestinian National Authority.

Palestine, 1999. *Human Development Report Palestine*, Summary report, Development Studies Programme, Birzeit University.

Papua New Guinea, 1998. *Papua New Guinea Human Development Report*, Office of National Planning and UNDP, Port Moresby.

São Tomé e Principe, 1998. *Rapport du Développement Humain, Sao Tomé et Principe*, United Nations Development Programme, São Tomé.

São Tomé e Principe, 1999. 'Cadre Stratégique de lutte contre la Pauvreté São Tomé et Principe', United Nations Development Programme, Paloma Anos.

São Tomé e Principe, 1999. 'Exercice de consultation auprès des groupes vulnérables à la pauvreté', United Nations Development Programme, Paloma Anos.

São Tomé e Principe, 2000. 'Mémorandum de politique économique et financière pour 2000', Ministère du Plan, des Finances et de la Coopération, São Tomé.

Sudan, 1998. *Towards Poverty Eradication in the Sudan: An Analysis of Human Capability Failure and a Foundation for a Strategy*, International Labour Organization and United Nations Development Programme, Khartoum.

Sudan, 1997. *Poverty Study of El-Nil State*, International Labour Organization and United Nations Development Programme, Khartoum.

Tajikistan, 2000. *Living Standard of the Population of the Republic of Tajikistan*, State Statistical

Agency, Dushanbe.

Turkmenistan, 1998. *Living Conditions Survey in Turkmenistan*, National Institute of Statistics and Forecasting and United Nations Development Programme, Ashkhabad.

Uganda, 1999. 'Uganda Poverty Status Report, 1999', Ministry of Finance, Planning and Economic Development, Kampala.

Uganda, 1999a. 'Kampala District Report', Uganda Participatory Poverty Assessment Project, Ministry of Finance, Kampala.

Uganda, 1999b. 'Kapchorwa District Report', Uganda Participatory Poverty Assessment Project, Ministry of Finance, Kampala.

Uganda, 1999c. 'Kumi District Report', Uganda Participatory Poverty Assessment Project, Ministry of Finance, Kampala.

Uruguay, 1999. *Human Development Report on Uruguay*, United Nations Development Programme, Uruguay.

Ukraine, 1997a. Poverty Strategies Initiative in Ukraine, United Nations Development Programme, Kiev.

Ukraine, 1998. *Ukraine Human Development Report*, United Nations Development Programme, Kiev.

Ukraine, 1999. *Social Budgeting in Ukraine*, Report of a Joint Task Force in Collaboration with the International Labour Organization, the World Bank and United Nations Development Programme, Kiev.

Vietnam, 1998. *Basic social services in Vietnam: An analysis of state, public and donor expenditures*, United Nations Development Programme, Hanoi.

Yemen, 1988. An Operational Strategy for Community-Based Regional Development in the Republic of Yemen, United Nations Development Programme, Sana'a.

Zambia, 1998. National Poverty Reduction Strategic Framework, Ministry of Community Development and Social Services and United Nations Development Programme, Lusaka.

Zambia, 1998a. *Human Development Report*, United Nations Development Programme, Lusaka.

Zambia, 1999. 'National Poverty Reduction Action Plan: 2000-2004', Ministry of Community Development and Social Services, Lusaka.

Zambia, 1999a. 'The 20/20 Initiative on the Provision of Basic Social Services', Ministry of Community Development and Social Services, Lusaka.

Articles and consultancy reports

Aasland, Aadne, 2000. 'Ethnicity and Poverty in Latvia', Social Policy Research Series, Ministry of Welfare and United Nations Development Programme, Riga.

Abu Nahleh, Lamis, Rema Hammami, Penny Johnson, Fadwa Labadi and Johanna Schalkwyk, 1999. *Gender,Rights and Development in a Time of Transition: A Country Gender Profile of the Palestinian Territories*, Women's Study Centre, Birzeit University.

Adato, M., L. Haddad, D. Horner, N. Ravjee, and R. Haywood, 1999a. 'From Works to Public Works: The Performance of Labour-Intensive Public Works in Western Cape Province, South Africa', Report submitted to the Department for International Development, London.

Adato, M., T. Besley, L. Haddad, and J. Hoddinott, 1999b. 'Participation and Poverty Reduction: Issues, Theory and New Evidence from South Africa', Draft background paper for the World Development Report 2000, World Bank, Washington, D. C.

Adauta de Sousa, Mario, 1998. 'Informal Sector in Luanda. Contribution for a better understanding', Mimeo.

Ajluni, S., H. Zomlot, K. Islaihi, R. Wihaidi and R. Raqeb, 1999. *Report on the Palestinian Economy: Donor Disbursements and Public Investment*, Office of the United Nations Special Coordinator (UNSCO).

Akesbi, Azeddine, Najib Guedira and Mounir Zouiten, 1998. 'Le financement des services sociaux essentiels au Maroc', Rabat.

Al Wazir, Iman, 1995. 'Statement to the World Summit for Social Development', unpublished document.

Al-Bustany, Basil, Mohammed H. Bakir, Shafeeq Al-Ottoum, Raida Al-Qutub, Elias Salameh, Nadia Takriti and Ghazi Abu Zaytoon, 2000. 'Monitoring the 20/20 compact on budget and aid restructuring', United Nations Development Programme and UNICEF, Amman.

Allen, R., 1992. *Enclosures and the Yeomen*, Oxford University Press, Oxford.

Andre, C. and J. P. Platteau, 1997. 'Land Relations under Unbearable Stress: Rwanda Caught in a Malthusian Trap', *Journal of Economic Behaviour and Organization*, vol. 34 no. 3 (1-47).

Aristy, Jaime E., Rita M. Peguero and Arturo M. Gómez, 1999. 'Gasto público en servicios sociales básicos en República Dominicana', in E. Ganuza, A. León and P. Sauma, eds., *Gasto Público en Servicios Sociales Básicos en América Latina y el Caribe*, UNDP, ECLAC and UNICEF, Santiago de Chile.

Ascher, W. and R. Healy, 1990. *Natural Resource Policymaking in Developing Countries*, Duke University Press, Durham N.C.

Atkinson, A.B., 1987. 'On the measurement of poverty', *Econometrica*, vol. 55, no. 4, (749-764).

Baker, J. and P.O. Pedersen , eds., 1992. *The Rural-Urban Interface in Africa*, Scandinavian Institute of African Studies, Uppsala.

Baker, J., ed., 1990. *Small Town Africa: Studies in Rural-Urban Interaction*, Scandinavian Institute of African Studies, Uppsala.

Barrig, Maruja, 1993. *Seis familias en la crisis*, ADEC-ATC, Asociación Laboral para el Desarrollo, Lima.

Barry, B., 1998. 'Social exclusion, social isolation and the distribution of income', Centre for the Analysis of Social Exclusion Paper No 12, London School of Economics, London.

Bastos, Santiago, 2000. '*Cultura, pobreza y diferencia étnica en la ciudad de Guatemala*', Doctoral thesis in social sciences, Guadalajara: Doctoral Programme in Social Sciences, CIESAS and University of Guadalajara.

Becker, C.M., A.M. Hamer and A.R. Morrison, 1994. *Beyond Urban Bias in Africa: Urbanization in an Era of Structural Adjustment*, Heinemann, Portsmouth, New Hampshire.

Benería, Lourdes, 1992. 'The Mexican debt crisis: restructuring the economy and the household', in Lourdes Benería and Shelley Feldman, eds., *Unequal Burden. Economic Crises, Persistent Poverty and Women's Work*, Westview Press, Boulder, Colorado.

Bhalla, A. and F. Lapeyre, 1997. 'Social Exclusion: Towards an Analytical and Operational Framework', *Development and Change*, vol. 28 (413-433).

Blair, H., 1995. 'Assessing Democratic Decentralization', CIDE Concept Paper, USAID, Washington, D.C.

Blair, H., 1998. 'Spreading Power to the Periphery: An Assessment of Democratic Local Governance', USAID, Washington, D. C.

Blair, H., 2000. 'Participation and Accountability in Periphery: Democratic Local Governance in the Periphery', *World Development*, vol. 28 no. 1 (21-39).

Buvinic, Mayra and Geeta Rao Gupta, 1994. *Poor Woman-Headed Households and Woman-Mantained Families in Developing Countries: Views on a Policy Dilemma*, International Center for Research on Women, Washington, D.C.

Buvinic, Mayra and Geeta Rao Gupta, 1997. 'Female-Headed Households and Female-Maintained Families: Are they Worth Targeting to Reduce Poverty in Development Countries?', *Economic Development and Cultural Change*, vol. 42 no. 2, The University of Chicago Press, Chicago.

Buvinic, Mayra, 1995. *Investing in Women*, International Center for Research on Women, Policy Series, Washington, D.C.

Ceita, Camilo, 1999. 'O Papel da Mulher na Sociedade Angolana. Analises Estatisticas sobre o Genero', Luanda.

Černiauskas, Gediminas, 1999. 'Monitoring Poverty', Seminar 'Poverty and Policy', United Nations Development Programme, Vilnius.

Chamberlain, James R., 1999. 'Ethnic Minorities in Rural Development', Working Paper 4 of the *Improving the Management and Implementation of the National Rural Development Programme*, ILO.

Chambers, Robert, 1988. *Managing Canal Irrigation: Practical Analysis from South Asia*, Oxford University Press, Delhi.

Chambers, Robert, 1994a. 'The Origins and Practice of Participatory Rural Appraisal', *World Development*, vol. 22, no. 8.

Chambers, Robert, 1994b. 'Participatory Rural Appraisal (PRA): Analysis of Experience', *World Development*, vol. 22 no. 9.

Chambers, Robert, 1994c. 'Participatory Rural Appraisal (PRA): Challenges, Potentials and Paradigm', *World Development*, vol. 22 no. 10.

Chant, Sylvia, 1991. *Women and Survival in Mexican Cities*, Manchester University Press, Manchester.

Chant, Sylvia, 1997. *Women-Headed Households: Diversity and Dynamics in the Developing World*, Macmillan Press Ltd., U.K.

Chant, Sylvia, 2000. 'Las unidades domésticas encabezadas por mujeres en México y Costa Rica', in M. González de la Rocha, ed., *Divergencias del modelo tradicional: hogares de jefatura femenina en América Latina*, CIESAS/Plaza y Valdés Editores, México City.

Cohen, J. and M.L. Weitzman, 1975. 'A Marxian View of Enclosures', *Journal of Development Economics*, vol. 1 no. 4 (287-336).

Cohen, S. S., J. W. Dyckman, E. Schoenberger, and C. R. Downs, 1981. *Decentralization: A Framework for Policy Analysis*, Institute of International Studies, University of California, Berkeley.

Conyers, D., 1983. 'Decentralization: The Latest Fashion in Development Administration', *Public Administration and Development*, vol. 3 no. 2 (97-109).

Conyers, D., 1984. 'Decentralization and Development: A Review of the Literature', *Public Administration and Development*, vol. 4 no. 2 (187-197).

Curtis, D., 1991. *Beyond Government: Organizations for Common Benefit*, Macmillan, London.

Dakkak, I., 1997. *Palestine: Human Development Profile 1996-1997*, The Human Development Project, Birzeit University, Palestine.

Deaton, A., 1997. *The Analysis of Household Surveys*, The Johns Hopkins University Press, London.

Diallo, Zima Jean, 1997. 'Pauvreté et disparités régionales : le cas de Mopti', Mopti, Mali.

Edwards, M. and D. Hulme, eds., 1992. *Making a Difference. NGOs and Development in a Changing World*, Earthscan, London.

Edwards, M. and D. Hulme, eds., 1995. *Beyond the Magic Bullet. NGO Performance and Accountability in the Post-Cold War World*, Earthscan, London.

Edwards, M., 1999. 'NGO Performance — What Breeds Success? New Evidence from South Asia', *World Development*.

Esman, M. and N. Uphoff, 1984. *Local Organizations: Intermediaries in Rural Development*, Cornell University Press, Ithaca.

Fausto, G., 2001. *Learning Patience*, Balma-Korenblum Press, New York (in print).

Fawzi El-Solh, C., 1996. 'Poverty Eradication and Gender-Sensitive Priority Actions in the West Bank and Gaza Strip', Mission report, United Nations Development Programme.

Foster, J.E. and A.F. Shorrocks, 1988. 'Poverty orderings', *Econometrica*, vol 56, no. 1 (173-177).

Foster, J.E., J. Greer and E. Thorbecke, 1984. 'A Class of Decomposable Poverty Measures', *Econometrica*, vol. 52 (761-6).

Fowler, A., 1997. *Striking a Balance: A Guide to NGO Management*, Earthscan, London.

Gassmann, Franziska and Chris de Neubourg, 2000. 'Coping With Little Means in Latvia', Social Policy Research Series, Ministry of Welfare and United Nations Development Programme, Riga.

Gassmann, Franziska, 2000. 'Who and Where are the Poor in Latvia', Social Policy Research Series, Ministry of Welfare and United Nations Development Programme, Riga.

Glewwe, P. and G. Hall, 1998. 'Are some groups more vulnerable to macroeconomic shocks than others? Hypothesis tests based on panel data from Peru', *Journal of Development Economics*, vol. 56 no. 1 (181-206).

González de la Rocha, M., 1991. 'Family Well-being, Food Consumption and Survival Strategies during Mexico's Economic Crisis', in M. González de la Rocha and Escobar, eds., *Social Responses to Mexico's Economic Crisis of the 1980s,* Center for U.S.-Mexican Studies, UCSD, La Jolla.

González de la Rocha, M., 1993. 'Familia urbana y pobreza en América Latina', document prepared for ECLAC and presented at the Preparatory Meeting for the International Year of the Family, Cartagena de Indias, Colombia.

González de la Rocha, M., 1994. *The Resources of Poverty. Women and Survival in a Mexican City,* Basil Blackwell, Oxford.

González de la Rocha, M., 1999. 'La reciprocidad amenazada: un costo más de la pobreza urbana', in Rocío Enríquez (coord.), *Hogar, pobreza y bienestar en México,* ITESO, Guadalajara.

González de la Rocha, M., 2000. 'Hogares de jefatura femenina en México: patrones y formas de vida', in M. González de la Rocha, ed., *Divergencias del modelo tradicional: hogares de jefatura femenina en América Latina,* CIESAS/Plaza y Valdés Editores, México City.

González de la Rocha, M., 'From the Resources of Poverty to the Poverty of Resources? The Erosion of a Survival Model', in *Latin American Perspectives* (in print).

Goudineau, Yves, 1997. *Resettlement and Social Characteristics of New Villages,* Vols. 1 and 2, ORSTROM Survey, United Nations Development Programme, Vientiane.

Gramsci, A., 1971. *Selections from the Prison Notebooks of Antonio Gramsci,* International Publishers: New York.

Gray, M. L., 1999. 'Creating Civil Society? The Emergence of NGOs in Vietnam', *Development and Change,* vol. 30 no. 4 (693-713).

Greeley, Martin, 1994. 'Measurement of poverty and poverty of measurement', *IDS Bulletin,* vol. 25. no. 2.

Grootaert, Chris and Ravi Kanbur, 1995. 'The lucky few amidst economic decline: Distributional change in Cote d'Ivoire as seen through Panel Data Sets, 1985-88', *Journal of Development Studies,* vol. 31 no. 4 (603-19).

Grosh, Margaret and José Munoz, 1996. 'A Manual for Planning and Implementing the Living Standards Measurement Study Survey, Living Standards Measurement Study' Working Paper No. 126. World Bank, Washington, D.C.

Haddad, Antoine, 1996. 'Poverty in Lebanon, Economic and Social Council for Western Asia (ESCW)', Amman.

Hareven, Tamara, 1974. 'The Family as Process: the Historical Study of the Family Cycle', *Journal of Social History,* vol. 7 no. 3, (322-9).

Hedman B, Perucci F and P. Sundstrom, 1996. *Engendering Statistics: A Tool for Change,* Statistics Sweden, Örebro.

Heiberg, Marianne and Geir Ovesen, 1993. *Palestinian Society in Gaza, West Bank and Arab Jerusalem: A Survey of Living Conditions,* FAFO, Oslo.

Hemming, Isabel, M.W., 1999. Report of Consultancy [Healthcare Reform], Ministry of Health of Tajikistan, Dushanbe.

Hopkins, M., 1991. 'Human development revisited: a new UNDP report', *World Development*, vol 19, no. 10.

Instituto de Investigaciones Economicas y Sociales, 1997. *Acuerdos de Paz*, IDIES/University of Rafael Landivar, Guatemala.

Jager, Eric, 1998. 'Mortality in the Maldives, Male' Town and the 20 Administrative Atolls', United Nations Development Programme, Male'.

Jain, P., 1994. 'Managing for Success: Lessons from Asian Development Programs', *World Development*, vol. 22 no. 9 (1363-1377).

Jain, P., 1996. 'Managing Credit for the Rural Poor: Lessons from the Grameen Bank', *World Development*, vol. 24 no. 1 (79-90).

Jenkins, S.P. and P.J. Lambert, 1997. 'Three 'I's of poverty curves, with an analysis of UK poverty trends', *Oxford Economic Papers*, vol. 49, no. 3 (317-328).

Johnson, Penny, 1999. 'Poverty and the Constitution of Citizenship: Poverty Alleviation, Rights, and the Needs in the Emerging State of Palestine', (Draft), Institute of Women's Studies, Birzeit University, Palestine.

Kabaj, Mieczysław, 1999. Programme Outline for Actively Counteracting Poverty and Social Exclusion, Institute of Labour and Social Studies and United Nations Development Programme, Warsaw.

Kairi Consultants, 1998. *Poverty Assessment Report — Grenada*, Tanapuna, Trinidad and Tobago.

Kanaan, Nimat, 1998. *Mapping of Living Conditions in Lebanon*, Ministry of Social Affairs and United Nations Development Programme, Beirut.

Kayateh, M., 1997a. Operation handbook on poverty participation needs for the Gambia, Banjul.

Kayateh, M., 1997b. Field Finding of Selected Village Communities in the Gambia, Banjul.

Kaztman, Ruben (coord.), 1999. *Activos y Estructuras de Oportunidades. Estudios sobre las raíces de la vulnerabilidad social en Uruguay*, CEPAL/PNUD, Montevideo.

Kelly, A.C., 1991. 'The human development index: handle with care', *Population and Development Review*, vol 17, no. 2.

Keune, Maarten, 1998. 'Poverty and the Labour Market in Latvia. Evidence from the Household Budget Survey and the Labour Force Survey', Latvian Ministry of Welfare and United Nations Development Programme, Riga.

Khan, M., 1987. 'Paradoxes of Decentralisation in Bangladesh', *Development Policy Review*, (407-412).

Khundker, Nasreen, Reza Kibria, A.K.M. Ghulam Hussain, Iqbal Ahmed Syed and Khaleda Nazneen, 1999. *Aid and budget restructuring in Bangladesh*, United Nations Development Programme and UNICEF, Dhaka.

Kikula, I. S., B. Dalal-Clayton, C. Comoro, and H. Kiwasila, 1999. 'A Framework for District Participatory Planning in Tanzania', of the University of Dar-es-Salam and the International Institute for Environment and Development, vol. 1.

Klitgaard, R., 1991. *Controlling Corruption*, University of California Press.

Klooster, D., 2000. 'Institutional Choice, Community, and Struggle: A Case Study of Forest

Co-Management in Mexico', *World Development*, vol. 28 no. 1 (1-20).

Korten, David C., 1980. 'Community Organization and Rural Development: A Learning Process Approach', *Public Administration Review*, vol. 40 no. 5 (480-511).

Korten, David C., 1986. *Community Management: Asian Experiences and Perspectives*, Kumarian Press, West Hartford, Connecticut.

Landau, M. and E. Eagle, 1981. *On the Concept of Decentralization*, Institute of International Studies, University of California, Berkeley.

Lazo, José Francisco, 1999. 'Gasto público en servicios sociales básicos en El Salvador', in E. Ganuza, A. León and P. Sauma, eds., *Gasto Público en Servicios Sociales Básicos en América Latina y el Caribe*, UNDP, ECLAC and UNICEF, Santiago de Chile.

Lazutka, Romas, 1999. 'Assessing Poverty and Preconditions for Reducing It', Seminar 'Poverty And Policy', United Nations Development Programme, Vilnius.

Lipton, Michael, 1977. *Why Poor People Stay Poor: A Study of Urban Bias in World Development*, Temple Smith, London.

Lipton, Michael, 1997. 'Editorial: Poverty — Are there Holes in the Consensus', *World Development*, vol 25, no. 7 (1003-1006).

Lipton, Michael, and Martin Ravallion, 1997. 'Poverty and Policy', in J. Behrman and T.N. Srinivasan, *Handbook of Development Economics*, vol 3 (2553-2554, 2572-2583), Amsterdam.

Lomnitz, Larissa, 1997. *Networks and Marginality: Life in a Mexican Shantytown*, St. Martin's Press, New York.

Lorenzelli, Marcos, 1998. '*El gasto público social en Uruguay. Evolución y aspectos distributivos*', in Zaffaroni, Alonso and Mieres, *Encuentros y Desencuentros. Familias pobres y políticas sociales en el Uruguay*, CLAEH, Catholic University of Uruguay and UNICEF, Montevideo.

Manasan, Rosaria G. and Gilberto M. Llanto, 1994. *Financing social programmes in the Philippines: Public policy and budget restructuring*, Manila.

Manikutty, S., 1998. 'Community Participation: Lessons from Experiences in Five Water and Sanitation Projects in India', *Development Policy Review*, vol. 16 no. 3 (373-404).

Manor, J., 1999. *The Political Economy of Democratic Decentralization*, World Bank, Washington, D.C.

Maro, P., 1990. 'The Impact of Decentralization on Spatial equity and Rural Development in Tanzania', *World Development*, vol. 18 (673-693).

Mawhood, P. and K. Davey, 1980. 'Anglophone Africa', in D. C. Rowat, ed., *International Handbook on Local Government Reorganization*, Greenwood Press, Westport, Connecticut.

Mawhood, P., 1983. 'Decentralization: The Concept and the Practice', in P. Mawhood, ed., *Local Government in the Third World*, John Wiley, New York.

May, Julian, ed., 1998. 'Poverty and Inequality in South Africa', Report prepared for the Office of the Executive Deputy President and the Inter-Ministerial Committee for Poverty and Inequality, Summary Report, Pretoria.

Mehotra, Santosh and Aung Tun Thet, 1994. 'Public Expenditure on Basic Social Services: The scope for Budget Restructuring in Selected Asian and African Economies', UNICEF Staff Working Papers no. 14, New York.

Menmagua, 1996. 'Marco Lógico para la formulación de un Plan Nacional de Desarrollo del Pueblo Maya de Guatemala', Mesa Nacional Maya de Guatemala and United Nations Development Programme, Quetzaltenango.

Menmagua, 1998. Situación de Pobreza del Pueblo Maya de Guatemala, Mesa Nacional Maya de Guatemala, Guatemala.

Menmagua, 1999. 'Plan Nacional de Desarrollo del Pueblo Maya de Guatemala', Mesa Nacional Maya de Guatemala, Guatemala.

Mercat, Laurent, 1999. 'Integrated Rural Accessibility Planning — a technical review', Working Paper 3 of the Improving the Management and Implementation of the National Rural Development Programme, ILO.

Mirzakhanian, Astghik, 1999. Labour Market in Armenia: Analysis and Policy, International Labour Organization and United Nations Coordinator's Fund, Yerevan.

Moore, Henrietta L., 1988. Feminism and Anthropology, University of Minnesota Press, Minneapolis.

Moore, Henrietta L., 1994. A Passion for Difference: Essays in Anthropology and Gender, Polity, Cambridge.

Moser, Caroline, 1996. Confronting Crisis. A Comparative Study of Household Responses to Poverty and Vulnerability in Four Poor Urban Communities, Environmentally Sustainable Development Studies and Monographs Series No. 8, World Bank, Washington, D.C.

Motiekaitienė, V., 1998. Poverty in Lithuania: Poverty and Employment, United Nations Development Programme, Vilnius.

Neimanis, Astrida, 1999. 'Gender and Human Development in Latvia', United Nations Development Programme, Latvia.

Nganda, Benjamin M. and David O. Ong'olo, 1998. Public expenditures on basic social services in Kenya, Nairobi.

Nussbaum, Martha and Amartya Sen, 1993. 'Introduction', in Martha Nussbaum and Amartya Sen, eds., The Quality of Life, Clarendon Press/Oxford University Press, New York.

Opio, Fred, Katebalirwe Kalibwani and Enoth Tumukwasibwe, 1998. Uganda's basic social services achievements: Monitoring the 20/20 compact, Kampala.

Ostrom, E. and R. Gardner, 1993. 'Coping with Asymmetries in the Commons: Self-Governing Irrigation Systems Can Work', Journal of Economic Perspectives, vol. 7 no. 4 (93-112).

Ostrom, E., 1994. Neither Market nor State: Governance of Common-Pool Resources in the Twenty-First Century, Lecture Series No. 2. International Food Policy Research Institute, Washington, D.C.

Ostrom, E., L. Schroeder and S. Wynne, 1993. Institutional Incentives and Sustainable Development, Westview Press, Boulder, Colorado.

Ostrom, E., W. Lam and M. Lee, 1994. 'The Performance of Self-Governing Irrigation Systems in Nepal', Human Systems Management, vol. 13 no. 3 (197-207).

Pahl, R. E., 1984. Divisions of Labour, Blackwell, Oxford.

Peters, P. E., 1994. Dividing the Commons: Politics, Policy and Culture in Botswana, The University Press of Virginia, Charlottesville.

Portes, Alejandro, José Itzigsohn, and Carlos Dore-Cabral, 1994. 'Urbanization in the Caribbean Basin: Social Change during the Years of the Crisis', *Latin American Research Review*, vol. 29 no. 2 (3-37).

Rakodi, C., 1995. 'Poverty Lines or Household Strategies: A Review of Conceptual Issues in the Study of Urban Poverty', *Habitat International*, vol. 19, no. 4 (407-426).

Ravallion, Martin, 1993. 'Poverty Comparisons: A Guide to Concepts and Measures', Living Standards Measurement Study Working Paper no. 88, World Bank, Washington, D.C.

Reddy, Sanjay and Jan Vandemoortele, 1997. 'User Financing of Basic Social Services: A review of theoretical arguments and empirical evidence', UNICEF Evaluation, Policy and Planning Working Paper no. 6, New York.

Regina Deveikyte, 1998. *Poverty in Lithuania: Results of Studies of Household Budgets and Living Conditions*, United Nations Development Programme, Vilnius.

Reynolds, Michael, 2000. Notes on the Development of Anti-Poverty Plans in the Baltic States, Follow-up to the Conference on Poverty Alleviation in the Baltics, (Manuscript).

Reynolds, Michael, 2000. 'A Comparison of the Draft Poverty Alleviation Strategies of Estonia, Latvia and Lithuania', Paper presented at the Conference on Poverty Alleviation in the Baltics, Riga.

Roberts, Bryan, 1995. *The Making of Citizens. Cities of Peasants Revisited*, Arnold, London.

Rondinelli, D. A. and J. R. Nellis, 1986. 'Assessing Decentralization Policies in Developing Countries: The Case for Cautious Optimism', *Development Policy Review*, vol. 4 (3-23).

Rondinelli, D. A., S. McCullough, and R.W. Johnson, 1987. 'Decentralization of Public Services in Developing Countries: A Framework for Policy Analysis and Implementation', Working Paper in Decentralization in Developing Country Series. Research Triangle Institute, Research Triangle Park, N. C.

Rosenhouse, J., 1989. 'Identifying the Poor: Is "Headship" a Useful Concept?', Living Standards Measurement Study Working Paper, no. 58, World Bank, Washington, D.C.

Sachs, Jeffrey D., 1999. *Implementing Debt Relief for the Poorest*, Harvard University, Center for International Development, Policy Paper no. 2, Cambridge, Massachusetts.

Safa, Helen, 1995. *The Myth of the Male Breadwinner. Women and Industrialization in the Caribbean*, Westview Press, Boulder, Colorado.

Samoff, J., 1990. 'Decentralisation: The Politics of Interventionism', *Development and Change*, vol. 21 (513-530).

Sarmiento, Alfredo G., Liliana C. Delgado, and Carlos E. Reyes Gonzalo, 1999. 'Gasto público en servicios sociales básicos en Colombia', in E. Ganuza, A. León and P. Sauma, eds., *Gasto Público en Servicios Sociales Básicos en América Latina y el Caribe*, UNDP, ECLAC and UNICEF, Santiago de Chile.

Schmink, Marianne, 1984. 'Household Economic Strategies: review and research agenda', *Latin American Research Review*, vol. 19 no. 3 (87-101).

Schneider, Pablo R., 1999. 'Gasto público en servicios sociales básicos en Guatemala', in E.

Ganuza, A. León and P. Sauma, eds., *Gasto Público en Servicios Sociales Básicos en América Latina y el Caribe*, UNDP, ECLAC and UNICEF, Santiago de Chile.

Selby, Henry, Arthur Murphy and Stephen Lorenzen, 1990. *The Mexican Urban Household. Organizing for Self-Defense*, Texas University Press, Austin.

Sen, A.K., 1981. *Poverty and Famines: An Essay on Entitlement and Deprivation*, Clarendon Press, Oxford.

Sen, Amartya, 1991. 'Gender and Cooperative Conflicts', in Irene Tinker, ed., *Persistent Inequalities: Women and World Development*, Oxford University Press, New York.

Shaban, Radwan and Samia Al Botmeh, 1995. *Poverty in the West Bank and Gaza Strip*, Palestinian Economic Policy Research Institute (MAS), Jerusalem.

Slater, D., 1989. 'Territorial Power and the Peripheral State: The Issue of Decentralization', *Development and Change*, vol. 20 no. 3 (501-533).

Taylor, Alan, 1999. 'Rural Development Issues', Working Paper 1 of *Improving the Management and Implementation of the National Rural Development Programme*, ILO, Bangkok.

Thompson, G., 1998. 'The Geographic Strategy for the Implementation of the National Integrated Programme for Social Action, Employment and Youth', Sustem Consultores, Maputo.

Thompson, J., 1991. *Decentralization, Governance and Problem-Solving in the Sahel. Sahel Decentralization Policy Report*, vol. 1. Associates in Rural Development, Burlington, Vermont.

Tilly, Louise, 1987. 'Beyond Family Strategies, What?', *Historical Methods, A Journal of Quantitative and Interdisciplinary History*, vol. 20 no. 3 (123-125).

Tocqueville, Alexis de, 1961. *Democracy in America*, Schocken Books, New York.

Tracey-White, John, 1999a. 'Rural Development Management Processes', Working Paper 2 of *Improving the Management and Implementation of the National Rural Development Programme*, ILO, Bangkok.

Tracey-White, John, 1999b. 'Background Paper for Technical Consultative Meeting', *Improving the Management and Implementation of the National Rural Development Programme*, ILO, Bangkok.

Transnational Family Research Institute, 1999. Policies for the control of the transition's mortality crisis in Russia, Moscow.

Trapenciere, Ilze, Ritma Rungule, Maruta Pranka, Tana Lace and Nora Dudwick, 2000. 'Listening to the Poor: A Social Assessment of Poverty in Latvia', Ministry of Welfare and United Nations Development Programme, Riga.

Turayev, Barot, 1999. Biednost': Aktualnost' i neobhodimost' ee ocenki w Respublike Tajikistana, manuscript, Goskomstat, Dushanbe.

Tvedten, Inge and Selma Nangulah, 1999. *Social Relations of Poverty: A Case-Study from Owambo, Namibia*, Christian Michelsen Institute, CMI Report R 1999, 5, Bergen.

Uphoff, N. T., 1993. 'Grassroots Organizations and NGOs in Rural Development: Opportunities with Diminishing States and Expanding Markets', *World Development*, vol. 21 no. 4 (607-622).

Uphoff, N. T., ed., 1982. *Rural Development and Local Organization in Asia*, vols 1 & 2.

Macmillan, Delhi.

Valentine, C.A., 1968. *Culture of Poverty: Critique and Counter-Proposals*, University of Chicago Press, Chicago and London.

Vengroff, R. and Johnston, A., 1987. 'Decentralisation and the Implementation of Rural Development in Senegal: the Role of Rural Councils', *Public Administration and Development*, vol. 7 (273-88).

Wade, R., 1987. *Village Republics: Economic Conditions for Collective Action in South India*, Cambridge University Press, Cambridge.

Wallerstein, Immanuel, William Martin and Torry Dickinson, 1982. 'Household Structures and Production Processes: preliminary theses and findings', *Review: A Journal of the Fernand Braudel Centre for the Study of Economics, Historical Systems and Civilizations*, vol. 3 (winter) (437-458).

Wallis, M., 1990. 'District Planning and Local Government in Kenya', *Public Administration and Development* vol. 10 (437-452).

Watkins, K., 2000. *The Oxfam Education Report*, Oxfam UK, Oxford.

Wisner, B., 1988. *Power and Need in Africa: Basic Needs and Development Policies*, Earthscan, London.

Wold, Bjorn K. and Julia Grave, 1999. *Poverty Alleviation Policy in Angola: Pursuing Equity and Efficiency*, United Nations Development Programme, Luanda.

Wratten, E., 1995. 'Conceptualizing Urban Poverty', *Environment and Urbanization*, vol. 7, no. 1 (36).

General Reference

Development Initiatives, 1998. 'Better reporting on donor support to basic social services: opportunities and constraints', In cooperation with OECD/DCD and UNICEF, New York.

International Monetary Fund, various years. *Government Financial Statistics*, IMF, Washington, D.C.

UNICEF and United Nations Development Programme, 1998. 'Country experiences in assessing the adequacy, equity and efficiency of public spending on basic social services', New York.

UNICEF and World Bank, 1998. 'Universal Access to Basic Social Services: A key ingredient for human development', New York.

UNICEF, various years. *State of the World's Children*, UNICEF, New York.

United Nations Development Programme and World Bank, 1998. 'Working together to promote the 20/20 Initiative: The role of CGs, RTs, PERs, SALs and NHDRs', New York.

United Nations Development Programme, 1999. *Diversity and Disparities in Human Development: Key Challenges for India*, United Nations Development Programme, New Delhi.

United Nations Development Programme, 1996. 'Socio-economic profile of Sayabury Province', Rural Development Programme Formulation and United Nations Development Programme, Vientiane.

United Nations Development Programme, 1998. *Poverty in Transition?*, Regional Bureau for

Europe and the Commonwealth of Independent States, New York.

United Nations Development Programme, 1999. *Human Development Report for Central and Eastern Europe and the CIS*, Regional Bureau for Europe and the CIS, New York.

United Nations Development Programme, 2000. *Overcoming Human Poverty: UNDP Poverty Report*, United Nations Development Programme, New York.

United Nations Development Programme, UNESCO, UNFPA, UNICEF, WHO and World Bank, 1996. 'Implementing the 20/20 Initiative — achieving access to basic social services', New York.

United Nations Development Programme, various years. *Human Development Report*. Oxford University Press, New York.

World Bank, 1990. *World Development Report 1990: Poverty*, Oxford University Press, New York.

World Bank, 1999. *Bulgaria. Poverty during the Transition,* World Bank, Washington, D.C.

World Bank, 2000. *Voices of the Poor: Can anyone hear us?* Oxford University Press, New York.

World Bank, 2001. *World Development Report 1990: Attacking poverty*, Oxford University Press, New York.

About the Authors

Mercedes González de la Rocha is a Mexican social anthropologist who works as a Professor and Researcher at the Centro de Investigaciones y Estudios Superiores en Antropología Social (CIESAS) in Guadalajara, México. She is the author of *The Resources of Poverty: Women and Survival in a Mexican City* (1994), among many other books and publications on the topic of the social organisation of households and household economy.

Alejandro Grinspun is a sociologist from Argentina whose interests include the dynamics of poverty and the political economy of social policy formation. He did his Doctoral work in Political Science at Columbia University and, since 1994, has worked as an Advisor on poverty issues in the Bureau for Development Policy of UNDP, New York.

Jaroslaw Górniak is a sociologist and economist, specialising in methodology of social research and data analysis. Dr. Górniak is an Adjunct Professor at the Institute of Sociology, Jagiellonian University in Krakow, Poland, and researcher and lecturer at Malopolska School of Public Administration, Krakow University of Economics. He is a consultant on research methods and data analysis at SPSS Polska Ltd.

Julia Harrington has social science and law degrees from Harvard University, Massachussetts, USA. She is co-founder and Executive Director of the Institute for Human Rights and Development in Africa, which uses African human rights law to advance human rights and human development through litigation and training.

Alf Morten Jerve is a social anthropologist with more than 20 years experience in development-related research, consultancy and operational work, with a major focus on rural development in poor areas. This includes studies of agro-pastoralism, traditional water transport and integrated rural development and local government. He is presently Assistant Director at the Chr. Michelsen Institute in Bergen, Norway.

Julian May is an Associate Professor in the School of Development Studies at the University of Natal, South Africa. His research interest is in the dynamic analysis of poverty and the relationship between persistent poverty, asset accumulation and sustainable livelihoods. He has published almost 50 articles in both South African and international books and journals.

Siddiq Osmani is Professor of Development Economics at the University of Ulster, United Kingdom. He previously worked at the World Institute for Development Economics Research and the Bangladesh Institute of Development Studies. His research interests include poverty, inequality, hunger, famine and nutrition, and development problems in general. He is currently Special Adviser to the United Nations High Commissioner on Human Rights on matters related to economic rights.

Catherine Porter is a development economist with interests in welfare economics and labour markets in developing countries. She is currently working as a Fellow of the Overseas Development Institute (ODI) in the UK.

Sanjay Reddy is an Assistant Professor of Economics at Barnard College, Columbia University. He holds a Ph.D. in economics from Harvard University. His current work relates to development economics, political economy and international economics. He has authored numerous articles on the role of the state in basic social service provision.

Pierre Hassan Sanon is a sociologist with expertise in social and community-based development. He has 12 years of experience in managing field programmes in developing countries in relation to social development and poverty reduction. To date, he has been employed by the French Cooperation Agency, UNDP, UNICEF, ADB, European Union, and the World Bank.